I0411281

Essential Philosophical Insights For Techno-Scientists

Professor Ashoka Jahnavi Prasad

TABLE OF CONTENTS

Part III. Far-East Tradition

Part IV. Islamic Tradition

INTRODUCTION

EXPANDING THE HORIZONS OF PHILOSOPHY AND SCIENCE

> There is no such thing as one universal truth for all. We must preserve everything which constitutes the riches of people, their world. We must know how to listen to each other, not be contented with what we have already got, always searching, seeking the perfection of ourselves and of the society as a whole.1 - Hilary Putnam

Although philosophy and science had originally been closely related, the relations between the two disciplines have frequently been marred by tension, rivalries, mutual misunderstanding and criticism. One known example of a perfect accord between philosophy and science is the Arab world in the IX-XII century, where the "Eastern Peripatetics," such as alKindi, al-Farabi, Ibn Sina (Avicenna) and other representatives of the falsafa, were always philosophers as well as scientists.

The divergence between philosophy and science emerged and became pronounced during the periods of radical social change and transformation of scientific and philosophical paradigms. There is no doubt that our age of groundbreaking innovation requires a full and profound reflection within a global context, with the existing diversity taken into account. It is for this purpose that the Third Moscow International Conference on comparative philosophy was conceived, its theme formulated as Philosophy and Science in the Cultures of the East and the West (22-25 May, 2012). The conference aimed to maintain the tradition of comparative forums established by the Centre for Oriental Philosophies' Studies at the Institute of Philosophy, Russian Academy of Sciences.

The Conference was attended by philosophers and scientists from Russia, Germany, Great Britain, France, India, Iran, Japan, Lithuania, Syria, Turkey and the United States. Its programme included two plenary and three thematic sessions focusing on the Far Eastern, Indian and Muslim traditions, respectively. However, we prefer to present the texts of the papers grouped by relevance to the contemporary global discourse and not by region.

---

1 From Hilary Putnam's paper presented at the Sixth East-West Philosophers' Conference (1989).

IS THERE A NEED FOR UNITY BETWEEN SCIENCE AND PHILOSOPHY?

This question often gets a negative response - not only from the man in the street, but certain prominent scientists as well. Among them are the Nobel Laureates in physics S. Weinberg and R. Feynman, who claim that philosophy of science is unable to provide modern scholars with any practical advice relevant to their work, and that despite the fact that philosophers tend to discuss matters essential to science, they allegedly tend to spew erroneous inanities for the most part.

Despite their commitment to a variety of cultural traditions, all the authors of this volume are unanimous in answering the above question in the positive. The argumentation is conducted within three temporal strata the past, the present and the future. In the former case, the necessity and the benefits of the union between philosophy and science are demonstrated by numerous historical precedents both in the West (Roger Smith, Freedom of the Will: Western Alternatives to Biological Reductionism; Yelena Mamchur, The Heuristic Role of Metaphysics in Scientific Knowledge; Vitaly Gorokhov, Traditions and Innovations: Russian and German Experience of the Development of the Innovative Systems), and in the East (Natalia Kanayeva, The Relation between śāstra and darśana in Traditional Indian Culture; Gholamreza A'avani, How Can Islamic Philosophy Contribute to a Comparative Study of Philosophy; Mehmet Bayrakdar, Philosophy and Science in Islam. An Outlook).

The enormous pertinence of philosophical reflection to modern scientific discoveries is demonstrated by Michel Hulin in The Neurologic Approach to Consciousness: Scope and Limits and Armin Grunwald in Technology Assessment and its Relations to Philosophy.

As for the future, it has been discussed with both the short- and the long-term development strategies taken into account. The developed countries of today are becoming a part of the so-called Knowledge Society. This very issue is addressed by Vladislav Lektorsky in Philosophy, Sciences and Modern Technologies. The Knowledge Society is a society where the production, dissemination and use of knowledge play the leading part in all economic and social processes. Obviously enough, science is of paramount importance to this type of society. However, science is changing by becoming increasingly interwoven with its technical applications. A novel phenomenon of technoscience is being born. The new information technologies and the converging BNIC (bio-, nano-, information and cognitive) technologies that follow them create a new living environment and call into question many of man's habitual modes of orientation in the world as well as traditional human values.

"Human world" is a historical and cultural concept. It has undergone repeated changes, and may differ from culture to culture. Yet it has always retained a certain set of invariants, which are being encroached upon nowadays as a result of the impact made by science and technology.

Knowledge Society is trying to go "beyond all natural limits." This does not imply "circumventing" the laws of nature - that much is a patent impossibility. No, the real agenda here is the design of new entities that cannot occur spontaneously - based on the laws of nature. It also applies to the construction of a new type of human, both in body and in mind.

V. Lektorsky emphasises the challenge associated with the plans of bringing about a new human corporeality. He refers to such movements as 'trans-humanism" and "immortalism," whose enthusiasts believe that by manipulating the gene and the nervous system, replacing human bodily organs by artificial analogues, and enlisting the assistance of such disciplines as genetic engineering, nanotechnology, computer and information technologies, one can extend the human life expectancy dramatically - perhaps even to the extent of utter immortality, in which case the problem of death, which is so crucial for culture, will lose its meaning.

Events that transpired in Fukushima are but a tragic evidence of how the modern technoscience can spin out of human control. Mitsuru Eguchi (Orientation in the Development of Sciences and Technology after the Tragedy on 11 March, 2011 Suggested by the Contemporary Japanese Philosophers) tells us about the reaction of her fellow countrymen to the Fukushima Daiichi nuclear disaster. The enormous damage inflicted on the Japanese by advanced technology made them ponder such questions as "Why did it happen to us?" and "Do we live our lives righteously?" This would eventually lead to the conclusion that a global revision of human attitude to scientific and technological advances was past due.

Japanese philosophers Shunsuke Tsurumi and Daisaku Ikeda addressed their compatriots with a plea to begin a new life as "refugees of civilisation" and a proposal to find the solution in the Buddhist conception of "mutually dependent emergence," respectively. In his article entitled Peace Proposals 2012 - Security and Sustainability: Sharing Reverence for the Dignity of Life Daisaku Ikeda emphasizes that everything that exists in its present form is a result of the interplay of an infinite multitude of "causes" and "conditions." Since all living beings and all phenomena are permanently connected, no human being can achieve happiness or wellbeing in isolation from the world and the people around. This is what the conception of mutually dependent emergence stands for.

How can we foresee possible negative consequences of new discoveries made by technoscience and remain ready to face its challenges? This issue is addressed by Armin Grunwald, who speaks of nanotechnology for the most part, pointing out that nanoscience integrates such classical disciplines as physics, chemistry, biology and engineering science into a new type of science. Nanotechnologies lead to social problems that give one reason to contemplate the radical changes that the Western civilization has been going through - in particular, the change in human attitude towards science and technology. There are assumptions that a new Baconian approach is arising to herald the "formation of the world atom by atom," as made possible by nanotechnology, and espouse a new wave of optimism where everything seems technically feasible. Others believe that nanotechnology may lead to the kind of uncertainty that is rather hard to imagine, when everything is possible but nothing appears to be controllable. Finally, there is the point of view that nanotechnologies are "the cipher of the future" and will play the part of a catalyst of sociological, philosophical and scientific discussions concerning the relationship between people and technologies in the future.

All of the above are possible, and it appears pertinent to contemplate every possibility. This is important for the understanding of just what happens to be at stake, representing a contribution to the "hermeneutics" of possible change of the elements of human existence. Thus, philosophy might lay down the foundations of applied ethics and technology assessment in anticipation of the moment when they will become better defined.

The relationship between philosophy and science in the context of a long-term strategy of humanity's evolution is discussed by Vyacheslav Stepin, the author of Scientific Knowledge in a Socio-Cultural Dimension. His forecast accounts for the unique nature of philosophy and science as forms of cognition.

Philosophy addresses eternal issues related to the ultimate reasons for human existence and human actions and the universal methods of one's involvement in the outside world. It formulates a certain kind of framework that is then filled up with actual content in particular cultural and historical situations. Complex theoretical and empirical levels of scientific knowledge appeared later than philosophy, which had been instrumental in their emergence. We can point out two core principles of science - the first being its orientation towards the research of objects that can enter the field of human activities, whether actually or potentially. Science looks for regularities that affect such objects. The second core principle is the capacity of science for studying objects outside the range of those included in already existing types of activity. It constantly crosses the boundaries of production and everyday experience of the contemporary historical epoch and studies objects whose practical usage will only become possible in later stages of our civilisation's evolution.

These two fundamental characteristics of scientific knowledge are organically linked to its means, methods and the knowledge it produces as a product of scientific activity, as well as the specifics of science's internal ethos. The latter is based on the principles of searching for true objective knowledge and constant accumulation of such knowledge (novelty value).

Science occupies a position of priority in the axiological system of modern civilization. But Vyacheslav Stepin reminds us that this has not always been the case. In traditionalist cultures the development of science was always held in check by mythological, religious and philosophical ideas about the world. These ideas would form a holistic picture of the world with which the knowledge produced by science had to conform.

Independent Weltanschauung functions and the right for autonomous development were attained by science as a specific type of civilisation emerged. It is often referred to as Western civilisation, since it had originated in the West. Stepin calls this civilisation technogenic, seeing as how scientific and technological process has been playing the part of the defining factor in its historical development.

A technogenic civilisation sees innovation as valuable in and of itself, and prioritises creative activities over the adaptive. Its notion of power is not merely the domination of one person over another, but also the domination of man over natural and social objects.

The system of core values of the technogenic type of culture has been evolving over the course of the three great epochs of European culture - the Renaissance, the Reformation and the Enlightenment. Having entered the contemporary stage of this process, science claims the right to create an autonomous world view of its own, which changes and evolves under the influence of new fundamental scientific discoveries made on a regular basis. The system of technogenic culture has given rise to constant interplay between scientific and technological progress and the domain of economics, which has led to the multiplication of public wealth and raising the level of consumption. Ethical and socio-political ideas that dominate the technogenic culture are based of rationalising its values as human life priorities.

Consumer society values and lifestyle are suggested to take the part of the main values of a globalising world and the model of its way of life. However, a ubiquitous implementation of consumer standards typical for the developed Western countries would spell a global ecological catastrophe. Since following the already adopted strategies of development shall exacerbate all sorts of global crises, we have to reconceptualise our attitude towards nature that involves a forced transformation of our natural and social environment - we need to develop new ideals of human activity and a new understanding on human prospects. In other words, we need to make the transition to a new type of evolution for our civilisation.

No such transition is possible without the formation of a new type of scientific rationality. It is associated with intense scientific and technological development of conceptually new types of objects that represent complex self-evolving system. Changes in scientific rationality open new opportunities for the dialogue of cultures. A lot of what modern European science used to reject as non-scientific superstition of traditionalist cultures suddenly begins to resonate with the new idea of the cutting edge of science. The new type of rationality that is currently getting established in science and technology immanently reflects on its own values and resonates with the ideas of relatedness of truth and ethics characteristic for traditional Eastern cultures. Science becomes a key factor of intercultural dialogue, and the latter is a necessary condition for the establishment of new axiological guidelines and new strategies for the evolution of human civilisation.

DIALOGUE OF CULTURES: PURPOSES AND METHODS

1. Experience shows that different participants of the dialogue of cultures may pursue different goals. For some it is a method of establishing hegemony of their own culture, which they believe to be superior to others. This stance is the most typical for the Westerners - first and foremost, the USA. Americans tend to believe their nation to have been chosen by God from Abraham Lincoln who called the USA "the last best hope of Earth" to George W. Bush, who kept claiming the USA were charged with a special mission by the "Maker of Heaven."2

Adherents of this teleological view of the historical process consider the essential purpose of the dialogue to "convince" all non-Western nations of the futility of resisting the "predetermined" motion of humanity towards the "end of history" and accept it as imminent and inescapable. One recollects the famous statement about the end of history made by Francis Fukuyama in 1989 and reiterated in another article as recently as 2001: "We remain at the end of history because there is only one system that will continue to dominate world politics, that of the liberal-democratic west....Time is on the side of modernity, and I see no lack of US will to prevail."3

Certain representatives of the Eastern world also bid for global leadership. The Islamic world appears to be the most blatant and industrious in its attempt of countering the imperial Western model of globalism with just as hegemonistic a scenario of globalisation. The intent of transforming the entire human society into *Dar al-Islam*, or a Muslim *Ummah*, is not only voiced by fanatics who resort to terror for furthering their goals, but even official government representatives. Suffice to recollect the words of Ayatollah Khomeini, who claimed there was but one way to liberate the Islamic world from the influence of the imperialists, namely, to establish a truly Islamic state and to overthrow any other tyrannical pseudo-Muslim government imposed on the people from abroad, and, once this is accomplish, to bring about a global Islamic reign.

It is all the more astonishing when such views are voiced by the intellectuals - in particular, people who received their education in the West and adhered to secular views. This bizarre metamorphosis happened to Hassan Hanafi, a prominent Egyptian philosopher.

He claims, "One perceives Islam to be the world's only salvation. It is the foundation of the new world order, and it really offers a solution to the crisis in the East and the West. The Islamic *Ummah* stands ready. It is the best *Ummah* that has ever existed upon the face of Earth. It is the keeper of

---

2 See John B. Judis, "The Chosen Nation: The Influence of Religion on U.S. Foreign Policy", *Policy Brief* (Carnegie Endowment for International Peace, 2005, March).

3 Francis Fukuyama, *The West has Won: Radical Islam Can't Beat Democracy and Capitalism* (http://www/guardian/co/uk)

principles and universal values....Islam is the last revelation, the end of the prophecy and the perfect model of life."4 At the same time, Hassan Hanafi claims to be in favour of the dialogue of cultures: "Humanity has suffered enough from the conflict model of interaction. But the time when the dialogue model will prevail is drawing near."5 One gets the impression that the Egyptian philosopher's point of view is ultimately identical to that which considers cultural dialogue as a means of establishing the hegemony of one's own culture, which is viewed as superior to all the others.

2. There are many who consider cultural synthesis to be the purpose of intercultural dialogue. The potential of cultural synthesis (in the realm of philosophy in particular) have been actively discussed since the middle of the XX century. And yet the opinions expressed by John Dewey, Sarvepalli Radhakrishnan and George Santayana about the project of a "substantial cultural synthesis" of East and West as put forth by the founder and first editor-in-chief the Philosophy East and West Journal, Charles Moore, have all been negative. George Santayana was the most vocal critic of the project: "You speak of 'synthesis' between Eastern and Western philosophy: but this could only be reached by blurring or emptying both systems in what was clear and distinct in their results....From a literary or humanistic point of view I think it is the *variety* and *incomparability* of systems, as of kinds of beauty, that make them interesting, not any compromise or fusion that could be made of them."6

The above refers to the conception of a global synthesis - not the synthesis that implies the absorption of ideas useful for the development of one culture from another.

One of the first Chinese philosophers to voice the idea of such a synthesis was Kang Youwei (1858-1927), who dreamed of "Great unity" of the elements of the Chinese and the Western cultures. Another attempt of implementing the idea of cultural synthesis was made later by Feng Youlan (1895-1990), the founding father of contemporary Neo-Confucianism, which, decades later, would come to dominate the Taiwanese philosophical thought (the schools of Comprehensive Synthesis, Contemporary NeoConfucian Synthesis and Chinese Neo-Scholastic Synthesis).7

The new political situation associated with the economic reforms in China that started in the early 1980's, gave the cultural synthesis trend a chance to re-emerge. This is how the theory of "creative synthesis" came into being. Zhang Dainian, being the leading theoretician to develop it, urges to abandon the "rigid axial way of thought" that opposes China to the

---

4 Hassan Hanafi, *Islam in the Modern World.* (Cairo: The Anglo-Egyptian Bookshop, 1995), vol. 2, p. 21.

5 Ibid., p. 499.

6 *Philosophy East and West*, vol. I, No. 1, p. 5.

7 See Shen Vincent, "Creativity as Synthesis of Contrasting Wisdoms: an Interpretation of Chinese Philosophy in Taiwan since 1949." *Philosophy East and West,* vol. 43, No. 2.

West and to set forth towards the convergence of Chinese and Western culture.

The concept of "new synthesis" has been introduced by Professor Yersu Kim, one of the most prominent philosophers of South Korea. He opines that "new synthesis" will eventually replace "the Western cultural synthesis based on the ideas of individualism, rationalism, scientism and belief in progress - a synthesis that had seemed self-evident and persuasive," which "no longer seems to offer a sure guide to human flourishing."8

Dialogue as a means of understanding another culture and borrowing from it to benefit one's own is perfectly acceptable. This is particularly evident in case of Japan. Lyubov Karelova is perfectly right to point out in Some Features of the Development of Science and Technology in the 17th 19th Century Japan in the Context of National Spiritual Tradition, Japanese genius is not their ability to invent, but rather their talent for adaptation of new cultural elements - first from China and Korea, and then from Europe and the USA. The adopted elements develop a life of their own, and quite often transform beyond all recognition. According to L. Karelova, such formulae as *Wakon-Kansai* (Japanese spirit and Chinese scholarship) as coined by Sugawara no Michizane (845-903), or *Tōyō Dōtoku Seiyō Geijutsu* (Eastern Ethics and Western Skills) coined by Sakuma Shōzan (1811-1864), which defined the establishment of the adaptive mechanism of Japanese culture, had been greatly influenced by the Buddhist Two Truths doctrine. This distinguishes between the conditional, or conventional truth, and the unconditional ultimate truth that can only be perceived through enlightenment. Allowing for a multitude of conditional and conventional truths of an instrumental nature opened the way for acceptance of new teachings and knowledge. To the Japanese, "truths were not monolithic but plural, not holistic but partial. Without context, there is no truth."9

The Japanese have focused their scientific and technological potential on perfecting foreign technology and adapting their production facilities for its mass production. This appears to be the formula of Japanese scientific and technological creativity.

Nevertheless, the danger of rendering all dialogue to deliberately inculcated synthesis - in particular, the kind that involves a single ideology - is still very real. Memories of crusades, the age of Christian missions and the tragic consequences of totalitarian ideologies warn us against it. "Intercultural dialogue should not be viewed as a process that leads to the creation of some universal synthesis. Cultural differences and the sheer

8 Yersu Kim, "World Change and the Cultural Synthesis of the West," Ron Bontekoe and Marietta Stepaniants (eds.), *Justice and Democracy. CrossCultural Perspectives* (Honolulu: Hawaii University Press, 1997), p. 431.

9 Thomas P. Kasulis, "Sushi, Science and Spirituality: Modern Japanese Philosophy and Its Views of Western Science," *Philosophy East and West*, vol. 42, No. 2, p. 234.

uniqueness of each culture define its boundary and its limit - they represent necessity and salvation....Cultures are not merely particular and singular. They are unique. They cannot be added to, or subtracted from, one another. Each one of them is ultimately equal to itself."10

3. Unity and diversity. And, finally, ability to recognise the purpose of intercultural dialogue as the means to seek for a way of preserving cultural identity without sinking into isolation, let alone direct confrontation - to reveal and support what unites people of different cultures and to prevent unification for the benefit of a single civilisation. This is the very position supported by Sarvepalli Radhakrishnan, who commented on the proposition of "philosophical synthesis" as mentioned above in the following manner: "What we want is neither a conflict between East and West nor a mergence of the two. Each will retain its integrated structure but acquire from the other whatever is of value. By such a cross-fertilization of the two developments we will develop a world perspective in philosophy, if not a world philosophy."11

But is this dialogue possible if the parties engaged in it fail to understand each other? Furthermore, some voice the opinion that full mutual understanding is impossible. The most in-depth answer to this question has been given by the prominent Iranian philosopher Gholamreza A'avani in How Can Islamic Philosophy Contribute to a Comparative Study of Philosophy.

A'avani recognises the fact that certain philosophers consider various schools of philosophy to be as autonomous as non-interlocking circles or parallel lines, with no common elements whatsoever. Thus even if one might assume different schools to discuss similar issues, each such discussion really needs to be understood and interpreted within the limits of its own particular context and only inasmuch as it relates to the corresponding fundamental principles. In other words, comparative studies of philosophical problems imply tearing them out of context, which will eventually compromise their purpose. However, this line of reasoning implies philosophy and philosophical studies to be ambiguous to such an extent as to make common understanding between philosophers virtually impossible. One might even say that philosophy, whose very nature implies a deeper understanding of reality, loses the basis of its existence. Apart from that, the viewpoint in question eventually leads to relativism, rendering the search of truth, which has traditionally been regarded as the singular purpose of philosophical activities, superfluous and pointless.

Comparative philosophy can, and must, become the moderator of inter-cultural dialogue (philosophical dialogue in particular); in turn, it only becomes a viable pursuit under specific conditions. First and foremost, one

---

10 Abdusalam Guseynov, "How is it Possible to Engage in Intercultural Dialogue?" *Dialogue of Civilisations: The Agenda* (Moscow: Institute of Philosophy RAS, 2005), pp. 51-52.

11 *Philosophy East and West*, vol. I, No. 1, p. 4.

needs in-depth knowledge of two philosophical traditions or, at the very least, two different philosophical schools and knowledge pertaining to a specific philosophical problem. Obviously, a superfluous approach to any such issue will be inadequate. One must also be aware of the historical evolution of a given problem to gain an insight into the changes that occurred to a given idea or philosophical term over the course of history. This will also help to prevent deficient and extraneous comparisons implied by literal or external forms of philosophical problems under study, which impede their comparative analysis instead of facilitating it. Excessive attention to the letter of philosophy kills its spirit. However, one often encounters substantial discrepancies between philosophical problems as addressed by two different schools, or complete dissimilarity between two philosophical terms, which evaporate after a closer study. There is much to substantiate this observation in such papers as Viktoria Lyssenko's Buddhist Atomism in the Light of Modern Concepts such as Emergent Qualities and Qualia (based on Vasubandhu's *Abhidharmakośa-bhāṣya*) and Andrei Terentyev's Everett's Concept as Expanded by M. B. Mensky.

DISTINCTIVE CHARACTERISTICS OF THE EASTERN SCIENTIFIC AND PHILOSOPHICAL TRADITION

Modern dialogue of cultures ostensibly lacks the knowledge of nonWestern cultures. Most authors of the texts that have been brought to the reader's attention strive to clarify the specific nature of Eastern scientific and philosophical tradition and make it more obvious.

Let us cite but a few examples.

In his paper entitled Chinese Culture and Atomism Artyem Kobzev claims to be convinced that the theory of atomism demonstrates the fundamental difference between the Chinese and the Western scientific and philosophical tradition. Chinese physics remained true to the philosophical prototype of the wave theory, rejecting atomism. Chinese thinkers have not come up with any independent version of the atomistic theory. All fundamental states of material as well as spiritual phenomena were conceived of as uninterrupted and continuous (*Pneuma* as *Qi*, seed/spirit as *Jing*), since dominant ideas of matter revolved around waves and continuity. Artyem Kobzev has developed the theory of two opposite, or alternative, types of philosophising - the Occidental (Mediterranean and Indian), with its discrete substantivisation approach to ontology and its idealising/logical methodology, and the Oriental (Chinese) with its ontology and naturalising/numerological methodology based on isolating languages and ideography. By developing it and using Marshall McLuhan's idea that the Chinese with their nonphonetic writing are capable of deeper and more holistic perception voiced in 1968 as well as the research of the asymmetry of the brain and semiotic systems in Vyacheslav Ivanov's book Odd and Even (1978) as a basis, he formulates the following theses: "Unlike hieroglyphic characters, letters as phonetic abstractions atomise the experience recorded in writing on the most basic of levels. The very fact of dismembering words into letters leads one to the idea of dividing the very existence into smaller parts in order to elicit pre-experiential or post-experiential underlying principles. This was the direction chosen by the Ancient Greek philosophy....The desemanticised nature of the linguistic proto-element, or the letter, translated into the lack of 'secondary' or sensual qualities in the ontological proto-element, namely, the atom or the idea. Lacking desemanticised linguistic units, traditional Chinese culture failed to come up with the conceptions of atoms or ideas. Correspondingly, the notion of primary and secondary qualities, or the qualities of letters and words in linguistic projection, was lacking as well. Since the concept of writing became ontological (the character *wang* could stand for both cosmological structure and bird tracks on the ground), the world was perceived similarly to a series of hieroglyphic characters - as the finite sum total of all things perceived by human senses (*wang u* or *wang yu*).

According to Kobzev, the fundamental philosophical position that makes China different from Europe and India is the ontological idealism of the former. The traditional Chinese Weltanschauung was naturalistic and holistic in nature, which precluded the independent evolution of either atomism or a valid idealism, which correlates with the omnipotent hieroglyphics that became a symbol of the whole culture.

Kobzev's reasoning concerns the dominating discourse of Chinese philosophy. But it also had more marginalised representatives; one of them, the Mohist school, is discussed by Stanislav Rykov in Certain Specifics of Perceiving the Object, or Xi, by Late Mohists.

The efflorescence of the late Mohist school dates to the IV-III century B. C., or the Warring States Period that coincides with the "Golden Age" of Chinese philosophy. Many parameters make this school oppositional to the mainstream of the Ancient Chinese philosophy.

Mohists have explicitly been involved in the development of methods of cognition and substantiation of knowledge, which was by no means as popular an activity for an ancient Chinese thinker as, for example, pondering the moral qualities of an ideal ruler and the reasons leading a state towards order or chaos (in other words, ethics and politics). Moreover, this method had influenced the most prominent non-Mohist thinkers of that age such as Chuang Tsu and Sung Tsu. Mohists set the trend in the methodology of traditional Ancient Chinese science and philosophy.

Additionally, late Mohists were probably the only Ancient Chinese thinkers to develop what one might refer to as the Ancient Chinese natural science. One might consider them the Chinese equivalent of Positivists. The three most important characteristics of this school of Western philosophy dating from the XIX - early XX century, namely, its anti-metaphysical bias and its propensity for scientism as well as different kinds of reductionism, echo the late Mohists in a variety of significant ways.

The works of the late Mohists provided Chinese philosophy with an alternative form of rationality. The dominant form of rationality, or "numerological" methodology, was countered by the Mohist "proto-logical" methodology. If we consider actual natural scientific research conducted by the late Mohists, we shall see enough reasons to claim that here, too, they managed to formulate an original conception of a "thing," or, rather, an "object", as well as its genesis and composition, that was at odds with the rest of Ancient Chinese philosophy.

In her paper Relations between Science/*śāstra, vidyā* and Philosophy/*darśana* in Traditional Indian Culture, Natalya Kanayeva points out that in traditional Eastern cultures the relationship between science and philosophy was never as dramatic as in the West. In the West, the roots of conflict were inherent in the very foundations of theoretical thought as the ideal and objective of knowledge, whereas in the East (in India, for example) the relationship between the domain of knowledge that dealt with Weltanschauung conceptions and the more specific disciplines did not involve any conflict.

Firstly, there was no contradiction between *darśanas* and *śāstras/vidyās*, so the question of whether or not there was any need for philosophy was unknown to the Indian culture. Secondly, these relations could not engender a conflict because the values and objectives of Indian *śāstras* (or *vidyās*) and *darśanas* had originally been given a different potential - the ideal of rational truth was not the objective of knowledge and the criteria of rationality were not the criteria of the ultimate truth.

Lack of conflict between science and philosophy resulted from the following factors.

1) The non-existence of any relationship issues between the *śāstras* and the *darśanas* and a wholly different scope of major problems traditionally discussed in philosophical compendia *(saṅgraha)* - specific texts of a polemic nature.

2) The correlation between the semantic fields of the Sanskrit terms "*śāstra,*" "*vidyā*" and "*darśana.*" Their actual uses covered a wide variety of meanings as well as rather substantial semantic fields, which partially overlap in all three cases. Their usage in the more specific contexts of science and philosophy is a later phenomenon dating from the Middle Ages when Indian doxographists started to record the comprehensive Brahmanic codices of scientific, religious and philosophical systems. A comparison of the semantic fields of the Sanskrit equivalents of "science" and "philosophy" reveals that they referred to the same texts and the same mental representations - identical objects, not dissimilar, let alone oppositional. However, there are also semantic differences between the terms in question, which result from their etymology: the term *śāstra* emphasises the didactic, or normative nature of the teachings, and *vidyā* the informative, whereas *darśana* focuses on such issues as superconsciousness and Weltanschauung.

The criteria of truth and rationality inherent in the culture of India differ from the classical Western criteria of rationality in a variety of ways.

The Sanskrit equivalent of the term "truth" is *satya*, which may also stand for veracity and reality. Therefore, it has three dimensions - the logico-epistemological, the ethical and the ontological. This explains the existence of several types of teachings dealing with the truth in India, each of which embodies a single facet of *satya* and facilitates the stratification of these dimensions of truth.

The ontological concept of two truths, or levels of reality, is the most important: higher truth, or *paramārtha* and lower truth, or (*vyavahāra*). Supreme reality is transcendental, beyond regular human senses or cogitation and defying description, whereas the lower reality is knowable and describable. However, transcendental reality is attainable via spiritual practices (*sādhana*), which are integral to all *darśanam*. Since the kind of truth that results from cognition pertains to the lower level of reality, logicoepistemological truths attain a lower status than the truths instrumental in reaching a higher level of reality. This higher level was known as the Absolute (*Ātman* or *Brahman*), and the ascension to this level was known as "liberation" (*mokśa, mukti,* or *nirvāna*). The process of liberation is practical and not theoretical. It follows the acquisition of theoretical knowledge and may thus be regarded as post-theoretical and supertheoretical. Orientation towards the attainment of a higher level of reality thus became tantamount to transcendence of the rational and the theoretical. It could not be regarded as a theoretical stimulus for the cognition of the material world aimed at understanding the essence of things, which is why the kind of science that serves the needs of technology did not attain a high level of development in India. The influence of Aristotle resulted in the ideal of theoretical knowledge as the ultimate kind of truth becoming an integral part of the Western culture, and this knowledge was perceived as the ability to understand the fundamental nature of things. The Indian tradition oriented one towards the super-conscious knowledge as the key for mastering one's own existence. Its purpose was the restoration of the natural spiritual harmony of human life and the return of life on earth to its transcendental source. This knowledge did not leave the sphere of human existence and could not ignore it.

Indian sages did not recognise any "objective" or "absolute" theoretical truth, which was a logical extension of the Indian belief about the multiple faces of dharma and their dependence on the agent of cognition. The logico-epistemological truth is of the lower kind; it is "functional" on the level of the world of phenomena. The criteria of traditional Indian rationality do not even hint at the possibility of any conflict between science and philosophy because the "higher" metaphysical truths are relegated to the super-theoretical level.

In our comparison between the Islamic traditions and their Western counterparts we must bear in mind the following: there is an abundance of radically different views of what characterises the Muslim philosophy or science as such - not only among scholars, but, most importantly, among the representatives of the culture in question as well. Some concur with the majority of specialists in Middle Eastern Studies who maintain that the period of efflorescence of science and philosophy in the Islamic world can be dated to the IX-XIII century A. D. and is directly attributable to the prominent Eastern Peripatetics. Others (contemporary Iranian philosophers first and foremost) claim, like Hamidreza Ayatollahi in Possibility, Purpose and Significance of Comparison in Islamic and Western Philosophy, that the type of philosophy to be viewed as typically Islamic was essentially developed during the epoch beginning with Averroes. Ayatollahi insists that authentic Islamic philosophy came into existence and reached maturity in the period that postdated the invasion of the Mongols, the culmination of its creative energy being the Safavid period in Iran. It is described as a specific type of philosophy that had been brought about by the Iranian Shia Muslims and eventually became known as *hikmah*, or "wisdom." It is based on the combination of rational thought and gnostic intuition, or mystical experience. Historically, this proclivity for "spiritualising" philosophy can be traced back to the metaphysical vision of Great Sheikh Ibn ʿArabī and Sukhrawardi. One must nonetheless remember that *hikmah* also possesses a logical structure and thus reaches beyond the scope of the views of Ibn ʿArabī and Sukhrawardi, going all the way back to Avicenna and the first stage of Islamic philosophy.

The most important figure of the second stage of Islamic philosophy is Mulla Sadrā (1572-1640), whose "transcendental philosophy" was, in a certain sense, relying on the four centuries of the Post-Mongolian period of thought and the classical schools of that epoch, namely, the peripatetics, the illuminationists (*Ishraqiyyun*), the gnostics (*Irfani*) and the theologians (*Mutakallimiin*).

Transcendental philosophy implies an approach to science that is essentially different from that of secular philosophy. Seyed Javad Miri points out in The Meta-Theoretic Issues of Secular Philosophy of Science: a Transcendental Outlook that the meta-theoretic postulates of secular science can be rendered to several fundamental axiomatic principles whose main underlying concepts form the foundation of modern philosophy and deal with the idea of "provability." In the metaphysical sense the idea of provability meets the idea of mathematising the principles of reality in its sensory and rational manifestation. When reality becomes an object of metaphysical consideration, the line between mathematisation and "quantitative methods" as applied to "quality" is very fine indeed, for there is a constant risk of having one criterion pertaining to a single level of empirical reality replace all the other criteria, where the idea of "reduction" would undeservedly be elevated to the position of a unique independent philosophical viewpoint. The Iranian philosopher and his colleagues believe the modern philosophy of science to oppose transcendental philosophy regardless of its realm of application (nature or society), since the latter relies on a "hierarchical perception of reality" and is anti-reductionist in its very metaphysical core. The notion of proof remains an effective criterion in transcendental philosophy, but the application method of this conceptual mechanism differs fundamentally from that suggested by the modern approach, considering the existence of a dedicated verification method for each level of reality. *Borhan* as used in the Islamic tradition of transcendental philosophy is one such; it may be expressed as *Borhan Enni* (proof *a posteriori*), *Borhan Etqan Sonn* (a teleological argument, or proof of God's existence by citing the existence of purpose in nature), *Borhan Aqli* (intellectual proof), *Borhan Lemmi* (causal proof), *Borhan Kholf* (proof by *reductio ad absurdum*) and *Borhan Kaoni* (cosmological proof).

IS IT POSSIBLE TO EXPAND THE HORIZONS OF PHILOSOPHY AND SCIENCE?

One of the tangible and highly significant results of the intense intercultural dialogue that is a sign of our times is the inexorable rise in awareness of the necessity to expand the horizons of philosophy and science.

Great minds have warned us against unsubstantiated arrogance towards the non-Western cultures much earlier: "It would be most precipitate and presumptuous for the likes of us...just barely out of barbarity, to allow ourselves treating a teaching as ancient with contempt merely because we consider it to be at odds with the scholastic concepts that we are accustomed to," wrote Leibniz about Chinese philosophy in his letter to Nicole Remond.12 "By discovering vestiges of the truth in the writings of the ancients, we can obtain gold from sediment, diamond from rock and light from darkness; that would certainly be an eternal philosophy of a certain sort (*perennis quaedam Philosophia*)."13

It is high time to raise the acknowledgement of the fact that philosophy came into existence a multitude of times and not just once, and in different parts of the world. However, this will entail a great deal of revision - first and foremost, we have to revise the very notion of philosophy that we are accustomed to.14

---

12 Gottfried Wilhelm Leibniz, *Letters and Essays on Chinese Philosophy and Binary Arithmetics*, transl. in Russian by V. M. Yakovlev (Moscow: Institute of Philosophy RAS, 2005), p. 274.

13 Ibid., p. 49.

14 The necessity of expanding the horizons of philosophy, or aiming for a new understanding of its very meaning, has been pointed out by philosophers from all across the world. The stance of Enrique Dussel, a prominent Latin American philosopher, which was expounded in depth in his paper entitled "A New Age in the History of Philosophy: The World Dialogue between Philosophical Traditions" that he read at the plenary session of the World Congress of Philosophy in Seoul (2008). Dussel criticised Eurocentric approaches and insisted on the necessity of recognising what is currently known

It is known that the concept of "philosophy" has been ambiguous for the entire duration of the history of Western thought. It carried a variety of meanings depending on the nature of the epoch in question, the specific nature of the areas of knowledge that interested a given thinker the most, and, finally, on the subjective traits of individuals. Nevertheless, it is considered justified to accept the generalised definition of philosophy as the discipline of rational, methodical and systematic reflection on the kinds of problems that people consider to be the most important.15

If this is how we define philosophy, one might think that estimates which deny the Eastern cultures the right for having a philosophy of their own, tracing the origins of this discipline to the Greeks, and claiming it to be non-existent anywhere in the East, are in fact acceptable.

One must, however, bear it in mind that there is no consensus about the definition of philosophy in the West, either. Even though the Greek word is usually translated as "love for wisdom," other versions are possible as well - "pursuit of wisdom," 16 or "attainment of divinity." 17 This system does not rely on intellect exclusively to attain wisdom - or, rather, get closer to it. Unlike the West, the East is more in favour of an expanded notion of philosophy that is closer to the etymology of the word, which implies the existence of other sources of knowledge but rationality, and often their higher authority as well.

This is precisely what many participants of the conference whose materials are collected herein seek to remind the reader, directly or indirectly. The argumentation that strikes one as the most convincing is presented in the papers of Gholamreza A'avani, How Can Islamic

---

as regional philosophies, by which he means not only the main Eastern traditions (the Chinese, the Indian and the Arabic Muslim tradition), but also their Latin American and even African counterparts. He also urged to reject the obsolete religious and mythological concepts as well as their correspondence with philosophy. Dussel claimed that humanity in general and the philosophical community, in particular, are entering a new epoch, which he calls the epoch of trans-modernity. Trans-modernism is primarily characterised by its pluralism and the ability to thrive on sources pertaining to other philosophical traditions besides the Western. In other words, the process has got nothing to do with the establishment of any meta-philosophy and represents the preservation of the multitude and diversity of traditions for mutual benefit. This does not rule out the possibility of coming up with a number of common views on major problems that concern humanity the most and are vital for its survival in

general.

15 *The New Encyclopedia Britannica. Macropedia* (Chicago: Helen Hemingway Benton Publishers, 1973-1974), vol. 14, p. 248.

16 Maria Solopova, "Predislovie," *Antichnaya filosofiya. Enciklopedicheski slovar.* In Russian. (Moscow: Progress-Tradition, 2008), p. 36.

17 Plato, "Theaetetus," *Plato. Collected Works in 4 volumes.* In Russian. (Moscow: Mysl, 1993), vol. 2, pp. 232-233.

Philosophy Contribute to a Comparative Study of Philosophy, and Arindam Chakrabarti, Can there Be a Science of Meditation?

The Iranian philosopher finds it necessary to distinguish between the general and more specific meaning and applications of the term "philosophy." He writes: "When we treat a certain philosophical issue in Avicenna, we are no doubt talking of philosophy in the proper and specific sense; but when we compare, for instance, Ibn ʿArabī with Śaṅkara, Meister Eckhart or Lao-Tzu, here we are taking philosophy in its broader and more general sense….Islamic intellectual history is suffused with many themes in speculative Sufism, rational and dogmatic theology which a modern lover of comparative philosophy would not be inclined to condone." However, A'avani believes that our efforts will be more successful and fruitful once we stop confining ourselves to the questions that pertain to the domain of the more specific interpretation of philosophy. There are many issues of great philosophical significance that lie outside the realm of narrowly interpreted philosophy, which it will be detrimental for everyone to ignore.

Arindam Chakrabarti proves the arbitrariness of excluding the disciplines of the Eastern thought that recognise the authority of holy scriptures from the realm of philosophy - he refers to Sāṃkhya and Yoga in particular. According to the Indian philosopher, "There is a wide-spread misconception...that Yoga must consist in the cultivation of an irrational, hence unscientific temperament because one is not supposed to use concepts at all let alone think logically when one is meditating. But nothing could be further from the truth of the text and practices." Chakrabarti claims that we must always remember that the practice of Yoga relies directly on the cognitive theory of Sāṃkhya, which is perfectly scientific in the modern sense of the word. Sāṃkhya recognises three sources of knowledge perception, the authority of holy scriptures and conjecture. However, it rejects the possibility that either of the former two (sensory perception or verbalised evidence) may show us the way to complete liberation from suffering. What do we end up with? Contrary to common expectation, Sāṃkhya does not appeal to extra-sensory perception. No experience could give us truly liberating knowledge. What kind of knowledge concerning the differences between the manifest multitude of consequences and their unmanifest causes on the one hand, and pure consciousness on the other, could give us absolute and endless freedom from suffering? It must be knowledge through discussion or logical conjecture. This is the official response given by Sāṃkhya. According to Chakrabarti, "Yoga does not depart from this in spirit in so far as samadhi, are first described as 'with rational discrimination', 'with inner argumentation' and then only proceeds to the non-conceptual highest states."

The central part played by logical conjecture in the practice of Yoga has been recognised as such a long time before Patañjali - namely, in the ancient text known as the Maitrāyaṇīya Upanishad, which refers to the six stages [petals] of yoga. They are as follows: breathing exercises (*Prāṇāyāma*), withdrawal of the senses (*Pratyāhāra*), meditation (*Dhyāna*), recollection (*Dhāraṇā*), reflection (*Tarka*) as well as the unification and concentration of the conscious mind (*Samādhi*). This Upanishad clearly states that primary knowledge of the Brahman is only given as a result of cogitation: "Having stopped the streams of conversation, consciousness and vital forces directed outside, we can perceive Brahman by medium of cogitation (*brahma tarkeṇa paśyati*)!"

Arindam Chakrabarti advocates a simultaneous expansion of horizon for such concepts as "philosophy" and "science." He gives a thoroughly substantiated positive answer to the question of whether a science of meditation (meditation science) is a possibility and reminds the reader that "science" in its original meaning, without military or commercial applications, implies wisdom and study of live human experience "especially because modern Western science has had an unholy alliance with war, environmental exploitation and colonialism, it has an obligation now to turn towards an unbiased examination of the methods of characterdevelopment and stress-reduction and self-knowledge, and cultivation of unselfish compassion, suggested by ancient contemplative traditions, Buddhist, Hindu, Christian, Jewish or ancient Greco-Roman. A new conception of science may emerge just out of noticing how much work has already been done in the sciences of meditation by these ancient tradition and how much more needs to be done in the modern spirit of biological and empirical psychological and phenomenological sciences." The Indian philosopher believes that a science of meditation is not only possible, but accessible by means of uniting a philosophy of the neo-Sāṃkhya type with the efforts of cognitive scientists.

The horizons of the modern concept of "science" can be expanded by means of utilising traditional knowledge. The paper of Vrinda Dalmiya entitled Preserving Objectivity and Reclaiming Traditional Knowledges: Philosophy of Science Looks at the Spiritual EcoFeminism of Vandana Shiva reminds us that orientation towards progress, based on the Western science and usually considered to represent a transition to modernity, may result in grave ecological catastrophes. "The 'reclaiming' of *Prakriti*-based traditional knowledge systems as a counter to Western science need not signify either a 'rejection' of science nor a relativistic celebration of 'Indian' ethno-sciences. Rather, making visible such alternative knowledges is important as a strategy for deepening the very objectivity of scientific thought...consideration of indigenous Indian knowledge systems by mainstream science can help redress these injustices and how such rectification is a necessary condition for science to be objective in a postcolonial society...the project of retrieving epistemic alternatives found in non-Western civilizations could deepen the very objectivity of modern science."

"Shiva's insistence on giving indigenous insights a hearing around the table of knowledge-exchange thus becomes a move to end the epistemic marginalization of rural communities associated with these positions and thereby ensure the *trustworthiness* of science in their eyes."

The cognitive range of Eastern traditions is quite broad; nevertheless, due to the persistent prejudice of the Western man, it remains overlooked in the solution of the scientific problems of today. One feels an emerging necessity for paying more attention to astronomical research as conducted in the realm of astrology.

In his paper entitled The Epistemological and Cosmological Foundations of Indian Astrology and Divination Audrius Beinorius points out the following: "In India, from their inception, astronomy and astrology have operated concurrently and in complementary fashion providing a grammar and syntax for a single semantic universe. Formal cosmological structure is coupled with a rich mythological tradition to support a living, meaning-filled cosmos....However, an earlier generation of European scholarship had, with rationalistic bias, assumed that astrology represented...little more than an antiquated and fallacious epistemology....Rather, the Indian astrological system, as system, implies its own epistemological foundations that must be understood within the broader context of an Indian cultural and intellectual agenda. The epistemological underpinnings of Indian astrology emerge through the dialectical transactions of the analogical imagination that inform the entire symbolic system of astrology, transactions that...'guarantee the convertibility of ideas between different levels of social reality.' (Levi-Strauss 1966, 76) The result is a vitally alive, richly complex cultural system, grounded in myth, imagination, and the exigencies of everyday life, that orients the person within a meaningful and multidimensional order of being."

The Lithuanian Indologist further opines as follows: "Opposing the common assumption that astrology is merely an expression of archaic - and degrading - superstition, my paper concludes that the Indian divinational system - as cultural system - is based on a particular cosmic vision and lends human experience value and meaning....All human life is lived symbolically and in conformity to various theories, mythologies and ideologies, so the ready availability of a symbolic statement about one's own life, containing both explicit and implicit structures that denote continuity with other areas of symbolic life such as religion, medicine, and human relationships, seems a credible and worthwhile exercise."

Problems formulated and discussed in the present oeuvre are of a general theoretic nature and have no short-term solutions. They will remain on the agenda for the entire duration of the XXI century at the very least. We would like to hope that the ideas and arguments voiced on the pages of this book will find their audience and prove useful to future research.

We would like to conclude by pointing out that the Third International Conference on Comparative Philosophy in Moscow became a possibility because of the grant of the Russian Scientific Humanities Foundation (project No. 12-03-14023). We would also like to thank the Embassies of India and Iran and the Russo-Turkish Culture Society for different sorts of assistance.

(Translated from Russian by Mikhail Yagupov)

PART I

A GENERAL STATEMENT OF THE PROBLEM OF THE RELATIONSHIP BETWEEN PHILOSOPHY AND SCIENCE

CHAPTER I

SCIENTIFIC KNOWLEDGE IN A SOCIO-CULTURAL DIMENSION

Man's knowledge of the world and of himself as part of the world takes different forms: scientific, philosophical, artistic, everyday knowledge, as well as religious and mythological experience.

The set of cognitive forms may differ at different stages of human history and in different cultures and civilizations. Thus, philosophy emerged after art and myth. Science, in its developed states that include theoretical and empirical levels of knowledge, appeared after philosophy and with its active participation.

Each kind of knowledge possesses its own specifics, its own salient features that distinguish it from other sciences.

Two major system-building traits can be set apart from among the distinctive features of science that correlate with all the others. The first is that a scientific study focuses on objects that are or can potentially become objects of human activity. Science is on the look out for patterns that govern these objects. Like King Midas of ancient legend whose touch turned everything into gold, science turns anything it comes in contact with into an object of its scrutiny: any fragments, aspects and/or phenomena of the world whether natural, social, human or cultural, and states of human consciousness. Yet everything that falls into the scope of its investigation is treated as an object that is governed by certain laws.

This approach does not encompass all the varieties of human existence; therefore, its importance notwithstanding, science can not replace other forms of human knowledge and the entire diversity of culture.

The second system-building feature of science is its ability to study objects that may not yet be included in the range of existing activities. Science constantly transcends the scope of production and the everyday experience of the historical period to which it belongs, and is able to explore objects whose practicable development may only be possible at future stages of civilisational development.

Related with these two fundamental characteristics of scientific knowledge are its means and methods, or knowledge it produces as a product of scientific activity, and some specifics of inherent scientific ethos. Underlying its basis are two main regularities, or objectives - a search for true and objective knowledge and a striving to permanently build up this knowledge. Hence, two basic ethical bans: on a deliberate distortion of truth to suit one or another social motivation and - a ban on plagiarism.

Science is one of the priority areas in the value system of modern civilization. This was not always the case. In traditionalist cultures, science developed under the supervision of mythological, religious, and philosophical ideas about the world. As these ideas formed a complete picture of the world, knowledge produced by science had to match it.

Only with the emergence of a special type of civilization did science acquire independent ideological functions and the right to autonomous development. It is often called the Western type - by the place of its origin. But nowadays, this type of development also has been realized in the East and in other parts of the world as well. I call it a technogenic or man-made civilization, given the determining factor of its historical development as scientific and technological progress.

Science and the technologies (industrial and social) it generates often transform, within the life of one generation, the entire environment of human activity (the so-called second nature), a system of social relations and human communication. Social changes, too, take place here at an accelerating pace.

All this is in stark contrast to the way of life of traditionalist societies, where activities and their means and objectives can go on virtually unchanged for hundreds of years. Though innovations also occur in traditional cultures, they are not regarded as a priority value and are always disguised as tradition. As for technogenic civilization, here innovations acquire a special value while innovation as an activity becomes a tradition. In contrast to a traditionalist society, priority in a technogenic civilization is given to creative, not adaptive activities. Gradually taking root here is a conception of man as a transformer of the world and the conception of nature as some kind of an inexhaustible reservoir of resources for human activities. An ideal is being born of a free and sovereign individual possessing natural rights, and an understanding of authority is formed not only as the domination by one person over another, but as a rule of man over objects (natural and social).

All these values and meanings - alternative as they are to those underlying traditional cultures - form the basis of the cultural and genetic codes of technogenic civilization, a kind of genome ensuring its reproduction and development. Scientific rationality has become an integral part of this system, its dominant value and essential component.

The system of basic values of the man-made type of development has evolved over the three great periods of European cultural evolution - the Renaissance, the Reformation, and the Enlightenment, with the ideal of the self-worth of scientific rationality clearly manifesting itself at the final stage of this process. Science has been winning the right to create its own autonomous worldview, which, in contrast to the religious and mythological conceptions, has been changing and evolving in the new fundamental discoveries.

The system of European education is being gradually rebuilt, with the focus on basic sciences. This process is marked by the scientific worldview producing corresponding images of nature, society, man and his place in the universe in the minds of a growing number of people. Scientific rationality is increasingly involved in the development of human mentality.

Although not always obvious, this involvement is present and manifests itself in the formation of deep structures of the organization of our thinking. In acquiring knowledge in the process of education, we also acquire operational schemes involved in the production of knowledge and methods for its justification. This in turn forms the mental structures that ensure the correctness of logical reasoning and argumentation.

Bearing on this subject are studies by prominent psychologists L. Vygotsky and A. Luria, which were conducted in the USSR in the 1930s when a cultural revolution was in the making in the republics of Central Asia. The study of the mentality of peoples of that region, with its traditionalist cultures, was to serve as a preliminary basis for that undertaking. It was to reveal the extent to which traditionalist consciousness was able to accept science, technology, a new organization of life, and a new system of education. Vygotsky and Luria developed tests that were used in interviews of local *kishlak* inhabitants. It was found that the majority of traditional groups who were not familiar with science, experienced great difficulty in solving problems that require formal reasoning based on syllogism.

For example, they were asked a question such as "Berlin is a city in Germany. There are no camels in Germany. Are there camels in Berlin? "Rules of logic provide for the answer to be negative ("no"). But most of the interviewed villagers replied, "There may be some." They justified their answer by saying that since Berlin is a large city, some Turkmen or Tajiks could make their way there with a camel.

The argumentation logic used here relies on past experience and the reduction of an unusual situation to this experience. A person's consciousness remains in the realm of ordinary experience and does not transcend its borders. It follows the tradition and reduces novelty to tradition. There is nothing defective in this type of thinking, which provides an appropriate orientation in a stable social environment. Science for its part is oriented toward search for the new, an intention imprinted in the very structure of scientific knowledge. Science education, the assimilation of evidence and justification of knowledge forms an ability to not just fantasize about the future, but to think about it, to operate with abstractions without linking every argument with familiar situations encountered in the familiar world.

It is noteworthy that children from the same villages who had had some training in math and sciences, easily solved logical problems that caused difficulties for the wise elders.

A similar important situation arose in 1946, approximately ten years after Vygotsky's and Luria's work in Central Asia when well-known American psychologists M. Cole and S. Scribner duplicated their methods in a study conducted in Liberia and obtained the same results. This was an experimental proof that the structures of thought in people from traditional societies were identical and that these structures change as a result of learning science.

The history of technogenic civilization has known many instances when ideological functions of science became a prologue to a wide application of its achievements in the most diverse practices. Thus, in the era of industrialization, it became obvious that science could function as a productive force. Later, at the turn of the industrial and postindustrial eras, science became a social force that, by introducing new technologies, could restructure means and methods of activities in various spheres of social life and, in fact, create new kinds of activity. Science has dramatically increased the variety and volume of generated knowledge in the system of man-made culture. There has come into being a sustained interaction between scientific and technological progress and the economy, which ensured growth of social wealth and increased consumption. Furthermore, ethical, social, and political ideas dominant in technogenic culture were focused on the justification of these values as a priority of human life.

One of the options for implementing these priorities was a consumer society, which emerged in Western Europe and North America in the last third of the 20th - early 21st centuries in the course of the transition from the industrial to the postindustrial stage of civilization. The same period also witnessed acceleration of globalization processes.

Globalization grew out of the modernization process. Borrowings from Western science, technology, and educational organizations helped modify traditionalist cultures and redirect traditional societies onto the path of technological development. At present, participants in the globalization process can be identified either as technological societies that have emerged on its own (the West) and manmade societies that have arisen in the process of modernization and have preserved some fragments of past traditions in their culture.

There is a fundamental difference, however, between the past modernization processes based on borrowing Western experience, and the processes of contemporary globalization: unlike the former, the latter are occurring in the face of the deteriorating global crises generated by the development of technogenic civilization.

Crises represent the reverse side of the technological and economic achievements of this civilization (improved quality of life, progress in science and technology, growing consumption, etc.).

Presented as the core values of the globalizing world today are values inherent in consumer society and its life patterns. Most of the rapidly developing countries are geared to increase per capita consumption and ideally - to match this indicator in the developed Western countries. Yet the effectiveness of development based on copying Western models is being seriously questioned. It is estimated that if all of humankind were to switch to the level of per capita consumption realized in the U.S., energy resources that have already been explored and developed on earth today would have been exhausted literally within the life of one generation. To this one should add that proportional to increases in consumption are increases of environmental pollution. Presuming that all the mankind would switch to the standards of consumption of the developed Western countries, the ecological catastrophe on earth would occur in just a few years.

This means that a simple extension of the already adopted strategies is most likely to exacerbate the global crisis. Therefore, other strategies are needed, which in turn raises the question of new values and new world-view orientations.

This calls for a rethinking of the former attitude to nature and of the ideals of relying on enforced transformation of the natural and social world; new ideals of human activity and a new understanding of human perspectives have to be developed.

So radical a revision of the basic values of modern civilization postulates a transition to a new type of civilisational development, the third one in relation to the traditionalist and technogenic.

It is important to establish whether the present stage of development is conducive to the emergence of internal conditions for new ideological orientations, whether there are in modern culture any points of growth of new values, which could be perceived by different cultures, including those that have retained some stereotypes of traditionalist mentalities.

It is critical to detect these points of growth in various areas of technological culture - in political and legal consciousness, in art, religion, morality, and, most importantly, in the nature of scientific and technological rationale. Primarily this is because scientific and technological development is the core of technogenic civilization, the basis of its change and of the newly arising states of social life.

In the past few years, I have repeatedly analyzed from this angle changes in the technological evolution of the late 20th - early 21st century. The crucial point in terms of growth of new values is formation of a new type of scientific rationality. It is associated with an intense scientific and technological development of fundamentally new types of objects that represent complex self-developing systems.

They have gradually come to dominate the forefront of reaserch. Examples of such systems are all biological objects that are considered in the light of their evolution, all social objects (society and its subsystems, including culture) taken in their evolution, objects of modern nano-and biotechnology, computer networks using "man - computer" interaction, the global Internet, etc.

The second half of the 20th century saw even physics, which had long excluded the idea of evolution from its cognitive arsenal, coming close to the study of self-developing systems. A different situation shaped up in the second half of the 20th century: on the one hand, the development of modern cosmology (the Big Bang concept and the inflationary theory of the Universe) led to the idea of formation of various types of physical objects and interactions. A new notion hypothetized the appearance in the course of evolution of different types of elementary particles and their interactions as a result of the splitting of some primary interaction and its subsequent differentiation. Contributing to the development of the idea of evolutionary objects, on the other hand, were non-equilibrium thermodynamics (I. Prigogine) and synergetics. It was the mutual influence of all these areas of research that gradually incorporated concepts of self-organization and development into the system of physical knowledge.

Self-developing systems are characterized by openness to the external environment. They are in a constant exchange with the environment of matter, energy and information.

In a stable state, they appear as self-regulating systems. Their development involves phase transitions, when one type of self-regulation (homeostasis) is replaced with another qualitatively new type. At the stage of phase transitions, the system enters a state of dynamic chaos, which modern science describes with the help of nonlinear dynamics and synergetics. At which stage there appears a whole range of possible directions of system development. Some of them may lead to the simplification of the system, its destruction and death. Other possible scenarios provide for an emergence of new levels of organization which can transform the system to a qualitatively newer state of self-development. Thus, a new order emerges from dynamic chaos. (Prigogine).

Each new level of organization impacts the previously established levels of the system and modifies them. The new levels are beginning to operate the system as a totality. Their formation implies the emergence of new parameters of the order.

Serving as an example of the new levels' control functions with regard to the previously established levels can be the impact of culture on the functioning of biogenetic programs of human behavior. Man lives according to two programs: a biological one provided by the genetic codes, and a social (suprabiological) one represented by cultural codes.

Such fundamental biological programs as the food instincts, selfpreservation, and the sexual instinct are realized differently in human behavior depending on the nature of cultural traditions and the regulatory norms and customs peculiar to a given tradition.

Here is another example of restructuring that a developing system undergoes as new levels of organization arise in it.

Modern biological research reveals many manifestations of restrictions that affect the functioning of cells within a multicellular organism. In ontogenesis, the features of phylogeny are concisely reproduced during the embryonic development of multicellular organisms, when a new level of organization of the living matter, which historically occurred in the process of the evolutionary transition from unicellular to multicellular organisms, alters the properties of cells as elements of the whole. It was found that individual genetic programs in a cell's genome are selectively blocked depending on the cellular environment, which leads to the formation of specialized cells and organs of a multicellular organism. In some experiments with frog embryos, a cell that was to develop into the intestines was moved to the head portion of the tadpole, and, in the new environment, that cell evolved into an eye.

With the emergence of new levels of organization, a system is differentiated and new relatively independent subsystems and new types of forward and backward links arise in it.

Activities of complex developing systems have their own characteristics. These activities do not constitute a purely external factor to the system, but become its component, thus actualizing some scenarios and reducing the likelihood of others. In such cases the developing systems acquire a human dimension. There are a myriad of human-dimension systems in which a human person is included as a separate component. In studies and practical exploration of these systems it is important to identify scenarios that could have negative consequences for humans.

Such scenario assessment implies that the internal ethos of science alone is not enough. Thus, each time one needs to relate demands to search for truth with humanistic ideals and adjust the inherent ethos of science with additional ethical regulatives. Today this kind of correction takes the form of a social and ethical review of scientific and technological programs and projects.

This results in substantial modification of the ideal of the self-worth of scientific and technological innovations as one of the basic values of technogenic culture. Science is still science and although its basic objectives of seeking truth and increasing true knowledge remain the same they acquire a new interpretation. A social and ethical review does not alter these settings; on the contrary, it appears as a condition of their realization.

This is a point of growth of new values arising in science in presentday culture. Thus, not the rejection of science, but its new humanistic dimension appears as one of important aspects of looking for new strategies of civilizational development.

These changes of scientific rationality open new opportunities for dialogue between cultures. Much of what modern European science previously discarded as unscientific delusions of traditionalist cultures, suddenly begins to resonate with new ideas of forefront research.

I would single out three main points here. First, the Eastern cultures (like most traditionalist cultures) always proceeded from the assumption that the natural world in which man lives is a living organism, rather than an impersonal nonorganic field that one can re-plow and redo at will. For a long time modern European science treated these ideas as vestiges of myth and mysticism. After the development of modern conceptions of the biosphere as a global ecosystem, it became clear that our immediate environment is indeed a holistic organism which includes humans. In a sense, these ideas are beginning to resonate with organismic images of nature that were integral to ancient cultures.

Second, the process of cognitive and technological development of complex self-systems may reveal that an active use of force in their transformation may not be all that effective. In case of a simple increase of external pressure, a system may start reproducing one and the same set of structures and not generate new structures and levels of organization. Meanwhile, even a little impact - a shot administered in a certain spacetime locus in a state of instability or at bifurcation points - is often capable of producing (due to cooperative effects), new structures and levels of organization.

This method is similar to the impact of non-violence strategies that were developed in the Indian cultural tradition, as well as actions that accorded with the ancient Chinese principle of *wu-wei*, which held minimal impact as ideal if carried out in accordance with the understanding and awareness of the rhythms of the world.

Thirdly, strategies dealing with complex, human-dimension systems bring forth a new type of integration of truth and morality, of goal- and rationality-oriented action and the value- and rationality-oriented one. Western cultural tradition used to consider reliance on rationality as the basis of ethics. When Socrates was asked how to live virtuously, he replied that one must first understand what virtue is. In other words, guidelines for moral behavior are to be set by the true knowledge of virtue.

A fundamentally different approach is typical of Eastern cultural tradition. It will be recalled that in the Orient truth was not separated from morality, and moral improvement was deemed the prerequisite and the ground for comprehending the truth. In ancient Chinese culture, the same character *Tao* meant law, truth and a moral way of life. When the disciples of Confucius asked him how to understand Tao, he gave different answers to each one of them as each of his students had taken a different path of moral improvement.

A new type of rationality which is being currently approved in science and technological activities and which immanently includes a reflection on values is resonant with the ideas about the relationship of truth and morality inherent in traditional Eastern cultures. Thus, science is emerging as an important factor in the dialogue of cultures. Today, this dialogue is one of the conditions for forming new value-based guidelines and new strategies for the development of civilization.

(Translated from Russian by Serge Gitman)

CHAPTER II

PHILOSOPHY, SCIENCE AND MODERN TECHNOLOGY

Some people believe that philosophy began to pay serious attention to science only in the 20th century and that the term "philosophy of science" appeared at that time. Adherents to this view are divided into two groups. Some believe that having entered into contact with science, philosophy of science becomes scientific, acquires a firmer footing and an opportunity to answer questions that it had failed to resolve for centuries. Others are of the opinion that attempts to transform philosophy into science eliminate it as a separate discipline dealing with eternal problems of human existence.

I can not share either point of view. Because philosophy and science have been originally linked with one another, and will be linked for as long as there are people. This does not mean that philosophy is just one of the sciences. Philosophy is not like science in several respects. If only because, unlike science, it keeps solving the same the so-called "eternal" questions all the time, questions which defy a final answer. The reason is that philosophy deals with issues that are special in that they are concerned with the ultimate grounds of life and human activity, and with the universal modes of man's functioning in the world. Moreover, it deals with certain frameworks, which are filled with specific content in specific cultural and historical situations. These situations change because man himself undergoes changes. And man will always change his world and himself. Therefore, new conditions call for decisions of what seem to be the same questions, but which in fact have acquired a new content.

Philosophy arises in a crisis situation when the usual understanding of the world and man ceases to satisfy those who think. It appears as a critique of the everyday world, as a way of transcending the accepted cultural stereotypes. Philosophy attempts to uncover an underlying reality beyond the visible, and to compose a picture of this reality with the help of novel concepts ("eidos," "form," "Entelechy," "truth," "being," etc.) that are alien to the ordinary life-world. Thus, alongside the appearance of philosophy there comes into being a theoretical approach to the world, a kind of double reality. It is important to emphasize that while pretending to know what is, philosophy is a means of creating new types of intellectual and practical activities. The study of existing and the positing new rules are the two sides of philosophizing that presuppose each other.

At the same time, there comes into being science (i.e., mathematics, mechanics, astronomy, etc.), which tries to understand and explain the world by going beyond the limits of what seems clear and obvious to common sense. In the beginning, it will be recalled, science was part of philosophy, sharing with it the task of theoretical study of the world. To illustrate, science introduces concepts that are unfeasible in ordinary experience - such as a straight line with no width, a point devoid of any measurement, or an atom, which can not be perceived in experience, etc.

In building its world view, philosophy has always tried not only to separate it from the world of everyday concepts, but also to find bridges between them - both in the sense of comprehending reality and with regard to what a person should do. Because man has lived initially in a world of everyday life, human cognition and behavior could be oriented only after building, or finding, bridges between his world and the "truly real" one. It was equally important to establish a bridge between these worlds and the world drawn up by science. Especially when the scientific picture of the world became extremely remote from the everyday-life world, as happened during the 17th-century scientific revolution. New experimental science proceeded from notions that were not only different from the ordinary, but in fact were contrary to common sense: a rectilinear uniform motion that takes place without any attached external force, changes in a situation given in experience as a way of finding out what takes place in reality (a scientific experiment), etc. Without the help of philosophy, particularly epistemology, it was impossible to build bridges between different realities, and to comprehend the world in which man lived.

Philosophy, therefore, has always been concerned with comprehension of science - in antiquity, in the Middle Ages, and in modern times. Moreover, it did not do all that as a mere "servant" of science, but so it could solve its own problems: to understand man and his place in the world. Without philosophical interpretations of classic European science, the systems of Descartes and Kant, which largely determined the development of Western philosophy of the last centuries, would be impossible. This is not to say that science did not take a great deal from philosophy to be able to reflect on its own grounds.

One sometimes hears the argument that it was 20th-century analytic philosophy that has placed philosophy on a scientific basis. Many attribute the emergence of philosophy of science to the emergence of analytic philosophy. It is true that logical empiricism, one of the main currents in analytic philosophy, proceeded from the premise that science alone could generate true knowledge, for which reason traditional philosophy had to leave the scene. But everything else that this assertion ascribes to analytic philosophy is incorrect.

First, because analytic philosophy as such is heterogeneous. Whereas logical empiricism focuses on science, linguistic philosophy, as one of the main currents of analytic philosophy, can rightly be regarded as antiscientistic.

Second, because the 20th century saw other influential philosophical concepts - empiriocriticism of E.Mach, neo-Kantianism, the French school of neorationalism, etc. - that investigated the agenda of philosophy of science, but did not share the attitudes of analytic philosophy.

Third, because the concepts of philosophy of science (such as postpositivism and the historical school) that were in the mainstream of the last 40 years, went not only beyond the scope of logical empiricism, but also of analytic philosophy in general, having set themselves the task of philosophical and theoretical understanding of the empirical data produced in the history of science, rather than of a formal analysis of the language of science, as was the claim of the logical positivists.

One can argue that analytic philosophy as a research program proved impossible. Indeed, it purported to use language analysis (the language of science in the case of the logical positivists, ordinary language in the case of the linguistic philosophers) to produce a final solution of philosophical problems either by eliminating them (as pseudo-problems) or by reducing them to those that can be resolved by empirical or mathematical research. This task proved impossible. The elimination of metaphysics did not take place. Nearly all major metaphysical positions (different and contending with each other) have been reproduced in the framework of analytic philosophy. Therefore, the name of analytic philosophy today does not refer to what was intended to function under the name or to what was originally understood as such. The name today refers to a broad and not very definite movement which includes mutually exclusive philosophies that are united only by the accuracy of analysis and arguments favoring provisions they have put forward (i.e., what was inherited from the founders of this movement). Moreover, analytic philosophy today may include - after certain interpretation - concepts it was originally set up to oppose. I mean, in particular, the so-called “analytic Hegelianism” (R. Brandom, J. McDowell); it will be recalled that Hegelianism was one of the main objects of criticism by such founders of analytic philosophy as B. Russel and J. Moore. I do not even refer to the assimilation of Kant's ideas - one of the most influential trends in the evolution of modern analytic philosophy (P. Strawson, H. Putnam and others). There is even “analytical Marxism” (J. Cohen, J. Elster, etc.).

Also noteworthy is the fact that modern science often draws fruitful ideas from philosophical concepts that classical analytic philosophy used to regard as a jumble of meaningless utterances.

The founder of synergetics, I. Prigozhin acknowledged, for example, the influence of A. Whitehead and H. Bergson. Likewise, V. I. Vernadsky recognized the effect of H. Bergson on his concept of time.

An intense evolution of a cognitive science designated as the interdisciplinary study of cognition has been going on almost 40 years. It was analytic philosophy that had considerable influence to the initial program of cognitive science. Subsequent developments in this area brought about a revision of the initial positions, however, with the result that some experts in cognitive science today are searching for new ideas in E. Husserl and M. Heidegger. A special journal, “Phenomenology and Cognitive

Science," is published whose authors include some famous philosophers and scientists (remember that Heidegger's work was an epitome of metaphysical nonsense for such classics of analytic philosophy as R. Carnap, and E.Husserl's understanding of consciousness came in for a scathing criticism by G. Ryle).

Analysis of science in its epistemological, metaphysical, and ethical dimensions remains the most important task of philosophical inquiry, especially today. This does not transform philosophy into one of the sciences, however; it preserves its features, continuing to make sense of metaphysical problems, which are made more concrete today, acquire rather unusual meanings, and, at the same time, exhibit a special practical significance.

Modern science gives rise to numerous problems requiring philosophical reflection. This applies to mathematics, physics, biology, and the social sciences and humanities. I would like to draw special attention to a complex of philosophical issues related to what is referred to as Knowledge Society. I will not analyze the different conceptions of what such a society is, or what makes it similar to and different from what is understood as information society. I do not deem important the differences in concepts and the controversies among their authors (this may be the subject of a special study); what is important to me in this case is the position that is essentially shared by all who write on the topic. The point is that in the Knowledge society, which is being joined by all developed countries these days, the production, distribution, and use of knowledge is beginning to determine all economic and social processes. Science, naturally, plays a crucial role in such a society. But science has been changing lately in the sense that it is increasingly merging with its technical applications. A novel phenomenon of technoscience is being born. It is important to emphasize that the new information technologies and the socalled BNIC (bio-, nano-, information and cognitive) converging technologies create a new living environment and call into question many of man's habitual modes of orientation in the world and traditional human values. Man's life world is a historical and cultural concept. It has undergone repeated changes and was different in different cultures. Yet it has always retained certain invariants. These invariants are being broken-up today by the impact of science and technology.

For centuries, science and philosophy have interested a very narrow circle of people. With an ordinary man facing the problem of selfpreservation today, problems generated by the development of science and technology defy solution without the aid of philosophy.

Today's knowledge society is trying to "go beyond the natural limits." This does not mean to "get around" the laws of nature - no one can do that. It is about designing new entities that can not occur spontaneously based on laws of nature. It also applies to building a new man: mind and body.

The spread of new information technologies, particularly the Internet, creates tremendous opportunities for manipulating human psyche. Impenetrable boundaries disappear between my and not-mine. New restrictions of human freedom appear, and the need to rethink the very notion of freedom is urgent. The old philosophical problem concerning the relationship between the real and the apparent, and between knowledge and opinion is getting more aggravated, because information technology can help fabricate new knowledge about reality, and thus fabricate reality itself to a certain degree. One can create a virtual 'I' and, in a sense, to live in a virtual space in which the differences between the real world and the world of dreams are dissolving.

I would like to focus specifically on a challenge that arises in connection with the plans to construct a new human corporeality.

I refer to movements called "trans-humanism" and "immortalizm." Proponents of these movements, who include experts in various fields of knowledge, believe that by working - with the help of genetic engineering, nano-technology, and computer and information technology - on genes and the human nervous system, and by replacing some human organs with artificial copies, one can first enormously extend the duration of human life and ultimately make a man immortal. In which case the problem of death, so important for all historical culture, will lose meaning.

To be sure, it looks like yet another utopia at this time. One could argue that it is a sheer fantasy if it were not for the fact that a number of participants in this movement include serious researchers, and if they had not yet started practical work to create such a being, a being that would transcend the limitations of human existence as they were known till now. If questions arise even today as regards possible achievement of immortality for this future being, who is sometimes called "superman" or "post-human," the possibility of interference with the biological nature of man apparently does exist. The U.S. Department of Defense, for example, is funding research to create a "perfect soldier" endowed with increased abilities to receive sensory information and process it faster, increased physical abilities, and a reduced need for sleep and rest. All this is only the beginning of such experiments to break through the human limits - which is the goal of the "transhumanist movement." If one is to raise the question of the meaning of life not with regard to an individual, but to the humankind, the "transhumanists" see it in creating conditions for the replacement of man with a "post-human." It is believed that in the long term this will lead to immortality.

It is definitely a challenge to philosophy.

Any intervention in the complex genetic and neural structures of man is very dangerous. Its outcome may be very similar to an ecological disaster resulting from an attempted technological transformation of nature. Instead of a more physically and mentally healthy being, we may end up with a monster. But even if we can understand all the complex genetic and neural structures and accurately predict possible effects on them (from which we are very far today), there is no assurance that the emerging Superman will not completely destroy our culture - with its notions of human opportunities, of what is acceptable and unacceptable, and the rights and responsibilities - a culture that makes us human. In the past, people dreamed of a more humane society, a society of "post-humans" will be antihumane.

If further progress were possible and post-humans became immortal (another dream of the transhumanists), it would have brought about a number of fatal consequences. First, there would be no need to give birth to new people, because solution of problems facing such a society would require only a certain number of immortal post-men. The infinite life of the same beings would minimize the possibility of social and cultural updates (even though the very existence of a culture seems unlikely in such an inhuman society). It would be a life without such principal and meaningful human values as caring for children and the elderly (because there would be neither), or understanding another person and his problems (because there won't be any of them), or love for another person, as it includes caring for and understanding a loved one, or understanding the fragility of human life. Disappearing or loosing the meaning would be such virtues as courage and heroism, for they are linked to the possibility of self-sacrifice and loss of life.

In short, the disappearance of death means the loss of the meaning of human life. A transition to the post-human stands not for the elimination of death, but rather for a collective suicide of humanity - for the post-human is an exterminator of the man.

I think that humanity will not follow this path. Still, we need to speak up about the dangers of such thoughtless experimentation of man with man. Modern science and technology that have given rise to knowledge society, is a challenge for philosophy. The role of philosophy today is not to be simply an "experimental metaphysics" or groundwork for designing and constructing possible worlds and possible humans, or post-men. Indeed, man's future depends in many ways upon the part philosophy would play in comprehending the new world created by science and technology, and in providing value orientation in that world.

Science and the world generated with it help constitute today the main problem field of philosophical research. Philosophy can not shun from analyzing this issue by referring to the fact that science has failed to deliver on its expectations. It is precisely because modern technoscience may get out of human control that we are aware of the essential need for philosophy. Because the destiny of man himself is at stake.

(Translated from Russian by Serge Gitman)

CHAPTER III

THE HEURISTIC ROLE OF METAPHYSICS IN SCIENTIFIC KNOWLEDGE

Does science need philosophy? The question is not trivial. Not all scientists respond to it positively. Among them are Nobel Prize winners in physics S.Weinberg and R.Feynman. "One should not expect that the philosophy of science can hand over to today's scientists a useful guide on how to work..." says Weinberg. 1 The same opinion is expressed by Feynman, who remarks ironically: "Philosophers sometimes talk a lot about things that are absolutely necessary to science and it's always...naive and, apparently, wrong." 2 Given the caliber of these scientists it is worth considering why many of them have developed a negative attitude to philosophy.

While reflecting on this question, one should, first of all, note that what scientists have in mind is not philosophy as such, but philosophy of science as a special professional activity that has been dubbed analytic philosophy in the western English-language literature. As for philosophy per se, it is treated with great respect, as is well known, and some philosophical ideas are often referenced in scientific activities. The same Weinberg writes, "All this does not mean denying the value of philosophy, much of which has no … relation to science."3

Nevertheless, the fact remains: neither Weinberg nor Feynman much praise the philosophy of science. The blame for this goes first and foremost to those philosophers of science who seek to dictate to scientists what they should be concerned with in their specific field of research and what criteria to use in evaluating results of the cognitive process. Generally speaking, the situation is more complex. After all, the time when philosophers dictated to science how it should be developing has long been a thing of the past. Paradoxical as it may sound, science does not need philosophy of science, which more precisely, is necessary not so much to science as to philosophy itself. The activity of a professional philosopher of science is aimed more at philosophy than at science. Science occupies such a significant place in the system of human culture that philosophy simply cannot afford not studying it. Philosophy, after all, is a theoretical world outlook of the epoch. How can

1 Steven Vainberg, *Mechty ob okonchatel'noi teorii.* In Russian. (Moscow: URSS, 2004), p. 132.

2 R. Feiman, P. Leiton, M. Sends, *Feimanovskiye lekzii po fizike.* In Russian. (Moscow: Mir, 1976), vol. 1, p.48.

3 Steven Vainberg, *Mechty ob okonchatel'noi teorii,* p. 132.

a world outlook function without knowing what scientific knowledge is about and how it works? That is why philosophy studies science through one of its disciplines - the philosophy of science.

Naturally enough, philosophers are hoping that scientists will not ignore their criticism of the ongoing cognitive activity, if they find it productive. Philosophy of science has retained its critical feature, which is entitled to the right to exist. It may, in fact, prove useful to scientists since philosophers of science specifically examine characteristics of the cognitive process, for which a busy scientist simply does not have the time. In fact, one often finds that a "thinking" scientist is the best methodologist - it refers not only to the 20th century scientists such as N. Bohr, A. Einstein, and W. Heisenberg, but also to many of our contemporaries - R. Penrose, S. Weinberg, K. Rovelli, L. Smolin.

But this is philosophy of science. What about philosophy as such? Why should science need it? The most common answer to this question is this: philosophy extends horizons of scientific thinking and enhances the scientist's culture and erudition. True as it is, the answer is unlikely to convince skeptics, who would probably say that erudition and the breadth of approach to scientific problems is conditioned not so much by philosophy as by science itself and its past experience, while moral norms are perceived in other fields of culture - literature, film, television, and theater. Einstein is on record as saying that novels by Dostoevsky and the music of Mozart had influenced him more than the works of any scientists or philosophers. An initiation in human culture magnifies the personality of an individual scientist. And it has been noted long ago that the truly revolutionary breakthroughs in scientific knowledge were achieved by scientists renowned for the magnitude of their personality.

Those who are skeptical of the usefulness of the philosophy of science need more specific arguments to justify the heuristic role of philosophy in scientific work. This takes us back to the question formulated at the beginning of the article: do scientists need philosophy.

HISTORICAL ARGUMENTS

Convincing arguments that philosophy plays a heuristic role in science can be found in the history of science.

For example, N. Bohr, one of the men to transform modern science, was greatly influenced by ideas of the Danish philosopher Kierkegaard. It has been suggested that many of Bohr's ideas concerning his interpretation of the quantum theory were inspired by Kierkegaard's philosophy.[4] There has been noted the similarity between Kierkegaard's ideas about jumps in an individual's spiritual evolution by which his transition between different

4 See G. Holton, "The Roots of Complementarity," *Deadalus* (1970), vol. 99, No. 4; L. Feuer, *Einstein and the Generations of Science* (New York: Basic Books, 1974).

spheres of existence (religious, ethical, and aesthetic) is achieved and the notions of the discrete nature of the atom's energy states and abrupt changes occurring in these states, which constitute the essence of Bohr's original atomic theory. Some people perceive an analogy between the limits in the fixed stages of existence of Kierkegaard's "I" and a limited set of orbits in the Bohr atom. Bold and even questionable as these assumptions may appear to many, Professor of Philosophy H. Höffding, who taught philosophy to Bohr, was strongly influenced by Kierkegaard's philosophy and could instill these ideas in his student's mind.

Assertions of the influence on Bohr of Kantian philosophy seem more convincing. A. Petersen, who knew Bohr well and studied his philosophical views thoroughly, stated that when Bohr was asked whether quantum mechanics reflected the microcosm it described, Bohr would say "It was wrong to think that the task of physics is to discover what nature is. Physics is only interested in what we can say about nature."5 In other words, without denying the existence of objects of the micro-world, Bohr, quite in keeping with the philosophy of Kant, believed that by themselves they are unknowable just as the Kantian thing in itself. All that we may know are results of measurements (the phenomena). This was the background against which Bohr built his interpretation of the quantum theory. Moreover, the serious teaching of Kantian philosophy in western universities facilitated the perception and acceptance of the quantum theory among theoretical physicists. Conversely, many Soviet physicists found it difficult to accept the quantum theory, because they had actually not studied Kant. Instead of studying the dialectical materialism of F. Engels (an interesting and largely correct philosophical concept), they were taught its dogmatized and extremely simplified version.

Likewise worthy of note is one particular feature of the influence of philosophy on scientific work. Mention is usually made not of any one philosophical doctrine, but of different philosophical ideas. This point drew the attention of Albert Einstein who would argue that in the eyes of a consistently thinking philosopher, a scientist "appears as an opportunist who rushes from one extreme to another."6 Many scientists are shocked by these words, even though there is nothing offensive to them here. In the context of our agenda, this means only that in their work, scientists use a system of philosophy which they perceive as a basis for their specific conceptual constructions. Therefore, they may apply different philosophical systems at various stages of their work and even in the development of different

5 Aage Petersen, "The Philosophy of Niels Bohr", *Niels Bohr: A Centenary Volume*. (Cambridge, Mass.: Harvard University Press, 1985), p. 305.

6 Albert Einstein, *Sobraniye nayuchnykh trudov*. In Russian (Moscow: Nauka, 1967), Vol. 4, p. 11.

aspects of one and the same theoretical system that is being built.7 This is demonstrated amply enough by the history of scientific knowledge.

Thus, Einstein himself was greatly influenced by the philosophy of E. Mach. Serving as the philosophical foundation of his theory of relativity, which was related with the abandonment of the concepts of absolute space and time, and of the ether as an absolute frame of reference, was Mach's idea that only those concepts and values that are somehow attested in the experiment should be included in a theoretical system. Concepts unrelated to the empirical level of knowledge, at least indirectly, must be removed from the theory.

The same philosophical idea was used by W. Heisenberg when he excluded from the quantum theory he was constructing the notion of the electron trajectory in the atom, since it was not verifiable in principle.

The concept of verifiability of theoretical terms belongs to positivism, of which Mach was one of the founders. Does that mean that Einstein and Heisenberg were positivists too? Not in any case. They simply took from positivism a philosophical notion that seemed to be true and that accorded with their scientific instinct. Neither one nor the other shared other ideas of positivism. It would be difficult to suspect them of denying the importance of philosophy to science. Yet the slogan "Science is philosophy in itself!" was central to positivism.

In developing his scientific ideas, Einstein relied on other philosophical ideas as well. Thus, he was an adherent of rationalism (influenced by the philosophy of Spinoza) when, convinced of the strength of theoretical reason, he argued that no logical path leads from observational data to theoretical principles, and he built his theory not by means of inductive generalization of experimental data, but by putting forward hypotheses based on his scientific intuition. It was assumed that hypotheses would not be tested directly, but through comparing their effects with experimental data.

He also acted as a Spinozist when he spoke about the incompleteness of the quantum theory in its Copenhagen interpretation. Einstein believed that a theory is complete if it provides an unambiguous answer to the question about the behavior of a microscopic object at any point in space and at any moment of time. He believed that the probabilistic interpretation of quantum mechanics was unsatisfactory and temporary, and that for it to become full, it should reinstate pervasive (Spinoza) determinism. Therefore, Einstein's philosophy was a conglomerate of philosophical ideas congenial to him.

---

7 This idea has been developed by V.P. Vizgin. See, for example, V.P. Vizgin, "Einstein i problema postroyeniya nauchnoi teorii," In Russian. *Voprosy filosofii,* 1979, No.10, pp.54 - 64; V.P. Vizgin, "Chem opredeliaetsia duga Einsteina?" *Einstein i perspectivy razvitiya nauki.* In Russian (Moscow: Repronix Ltd., 2007), pp. 20-25.

Equally versatile was the philosophical position of W. Heizenberg. Having applied the above-mentioned positivist idea, which seemed fruitful in the construction of the quantum theory, he did not become a positivist. He was a Platonist in interpreting the nature of micro-objects, although Platonic ideas radically contradict those of positivism. He is known to have rejected the atomism of Democritus and believed that elementary particles are geometric Platonic bodies. While reflecting on the ontological problems of the quantum theory, on the other hand, Heisenberg was considering the Aristotelian idea of the potential and actual levels of the being of natural objects. This is how this idea was formulated in his interpretation of the micro-world objects: before the act of measurement, micro-objects have only a potential existence, and only the act of measurement renders their existence actual.

EPISTEMOLOGICAL ARGUMENTS

Historical arguments alone do not solve the problem of the relationship of science and philosophy. It is important not only to fix instances of positive philosophical influence on specific sciences, but also to explain this phenomenon epistemologically. Noteworthy in this regard is the following: no matter how scientists treat the matter or how they shy away from philosophy, it is already contained in their theories - in the form of metaphysical and epistemological assumptions determining the direction of scientific research. "There is no philosophy-free science, there is only a science whose philosophical baggage had been taken on board without examination," - rightly notes Daniel Dennett, a famous biologist.8

Occupying the most prominent place in philosophy is metaphysics. The notion of metaphysics is rather complicated by nature. With no consensus about its content available, let us take as a basis the definition given by Heidegger, who pondered over the nature of metaphysics more than any other philosopher in the 20th century. Defining this concept, he wrote that whereas science is the knowledge of what exists, "metaphysics is a questioning super existing, beyond it, so that after this questioning we get the existing to understand it as such and as a whole."9

As Kant would say in his time, metaphysics is concerned with questions whether the world is simple or complex, whether there are ultimate "building blocks" of matter; whether there is freedom in nature or everything is governed by necessity, whether the world is finite or infinite. Some or other preliminary answers to these questions appear in research programs as the basic principles of studies of nature.

---

8 D. Dennet, *Opasnaya ideia Darvina.* In Russian (Moscow: IF RAN, 1995)

9 M. Haidegger, "Chto takoye metafizika," M. Haidegger, *Vremia i bytiye.* In Russian (Moscow: Respublica, 1993), p. 24.

One can see this in the premises of any fundamental scientific theory. The basic claim of all fundamental theories in physics, including the most modern ones, is that an explanation of the world implies a search for the common beginning of all things. This principle was put forward for the first time by Thales, a philosopher of the Antiquity. This idea can be embodied in the principles of reductionism or antireductionism. Espousing reductionism are physicists who hope to build a final theory, claims for which are currently being made by the superstring theory. These include, for example, S. Weinberg, whom we already mentioned.

Also metaphysical in nature is the thesis of the universality of causation. Science is looking for causal relationships - always and everywhere. One may argue that the present period of scientific development has seen this idea shaken, because quantum mechanics, as the theory of the micro-world, is indeterministic by nature. True as it is, it is important to emphasize that the idea of causality had already been presented in discussions about the destiny of determinism in quantum mechanics by the very questioning of its existence. When the notion of probabilistic causality was introduced into the quantum theory, it restored to some extent the rights of determinism.

Metaphysical premises of fundamental scientific theories are not directly verifiable because they are beyond any possible experience. A priori as they are, they can not serve as criteria in evaluation of any specific scientific material. According to Kant, they only play the role of the regulatory principles of cognition. Indirectly, however, metaphysical principles can be tested by experience. One criterion of their fertility is success of the fundamental theory whose basis they are forming.

Hence, the question whether science needs metaphysics (and philosophy in general) is an idle one. Metaphysics is at the basis of scientific theories, without asking permission from representatives of specific sciences. Newton once said, "Physics, beware of metaphysics!" yet he could never avoid metaphysics himself. It became part of his mechanics in the form of his action at a distance principle, of his ideas about atomic structure of matter and the concept of absolute and related space and time.

Nevertheless, the mere presence of metaphysical presuppositions in theories is not an argument in favor of heuristic role of metaphysics in science. Skeptics may say that the metaphysical premises can not reliably guide scientists in their search for the true theories because they themselves are subject to constant revision. Suffice it to recall that the metaphysical assumptions of Newtonian physics were replaced with metaphysics of the electromagnetic theory and Einstein's relativistic physics.

This is a valid observation. Let us try to answer it. It seems that the heuristic role in scientific knowledge is performed not by specific metaphysical principles or their content, but by the very existence of the realm of super existing. Operating in this sphere allows the scientist to raise the question about the world as a whole, which he cannot ask staying within the realm of existing only. The heuristics of metaphysics consists in that it stimulates the scientist to put such questions. The answers vary, and many of them have to be given up as scientific knowledge advances to a new level of research into being. Science continues to evolve and move forward in so far as the desire to pose metaphysical problems and seek answers to them is retained and constantly reproduces itself. It seems that scientific knowledge is a sphere where something akin to the Nietzschean "eternal return" is taking place. In our case, it is a return to metaphysics.

Oblivion of metaphysics takes "revenge" on science, dooming it to stagnation. The evidence is to be found in the current state of affairs in physical knowledge. Renowned theoretical physicist Lee Smolin argues that the "explosive growth" of physics, which lasted more than two hundred years, has stalled in recent decades, and he sees the reason for this in the present style of managing science. Modern physics is dominated by the ideology and strategy of instrumentalism. It has dominated particle physics from the 1940s. Instrumentalist thinking is pragmatic and encourages virtuoso calculations, Smolin says, but it is very different from the way science was executed by Albert Einstein, Niels Bohr, W. Heisenberg, E. Schroedinger, and other revolutionaries of the early 20th century. Their work arose out of a deep reflection on the most basic questions of being.10

Notwithstanding the genius of R. Feynman, F. Dyson, and S. Weinberg, who developed the standard model of particle physics, these scholars did not give much thought to metaphysical issues. On the one hand, this allowed them for almost thirty years to develop successfully various applications of the standard model, without distracting themselves with discussions of fundamental problems of science. On the other hand, this has eventually led to slowing down the development of physics.

Smolin describes the transition to a pragmatic style of thinking and instrumentalist methodology as "a triumph of craftsmen over prophets."11 Unflattering words to many scientists working in particle physics. But in this case Smolin simply uses Einstein's terminology, who distinguished between two types of scientists - "ordinary workmen" and "genuine seekers of truth." The first, Einstein said, "see many trees, but never see the forest." By focusing on details, they do not see the whole. This ability is granted to those willing and able to come out into the sphere of metaphysics.

We do not hold a very common belief that modern science is in a crisis. In our view, Heidegger was right when, in arguing against Husserl, he said that, science as such is not in a crisis, and that there are only difficulties encountered in the interpretation of the basic concepts of some disciplines. Nevertheless, slower growth is observed.12 To overcome it we have to give up the ideology of instrumentalism and the penchant for applied

---

10 Lee Smolin, *Nepriyatnosti s fizikoi: vzliot teorii strun, upadok nauki i chto za etim sleduyet* // http:// vidimfigu.ru /?06631284317867618346

11 Ibid.

12 M. Haidegger, "Nauka i osmysleniye," In Russian. M. Haidegger, *Vremia i bytiye* (Moscow: Respublica, 1993), p. 250.

applications and to return to the strategies targeted at the formulation of fundamental metaphysical problems. Smolin is right when he says that physics today is more than ever in need of "prophets."

By turning to philosophy, scientist gains a broader perspective of the current situation in scientific knowledge. It enables him to rise above the routine of his particular field of study and more critically consider and (if necessary) overcome stereotypes shared by scientific community.

(Translated from Russian by Serge Gitman)

CHAPTER IV

FREEDOM OF THE WILL: WESTERN ALTERNATIVES TO BIOLOGICAL REDUCTIONISM

Two kinds of statements, which look at first glance as if they contradict each other, are common in contemporary western speech. There are expressions of total freedom, taken to their extreme in the advertising slogan, 'Just do it', but also present in 'the American dream' that the path to wealth and the White House is open to every American citizen. At the same time, we hear expressions of total determinism, for example in popular science writing which states that individual freedom of action does not exist because of 'the selfish gene', because 'you are your brain' or because the conscious will is 'an illusion'.

I offer a historical observation. The co-existence of such opposed statements is not new: for three centuries it has been a marked feature of the Enlightenment project to seek knowledge of the laws of nature, including human nature, in order to benefit humankind. This is a project to learn the *necessary laws* of nature in order to exercise wise *choice about what to do*. When Bacon and Descartes formulated early versions of this programme, they presupposed a God-given freedom of will. Descartes wrote: 'I see only one thing in us which could give us good reason for esteeming ourselves, namely, the exercise of our free will ... It renders us in a certain way like God by making us masters of ourselves.' 1 In modern versions of the programme, however, the pursuit of science appears to have shown belief in the will to be false. This raises many questions.

The purpose in this paper is to use debate about free will in order to illustrate relations between philosophy and science. Neither philosophy nor science is a unified entity; they are multiple activities, and there could be no one to one relationship. It is therefore necessary to discuss relations through particular engagements between them. The example of debate about free will is of interest because currently there is a popular science literature which claims that 'science is now proving' belief in free will to be false. The objections to such claims are philosophical (as well as scientific), and so the relations of science and philosophy are part of the dispute. The free will debate, in the past and in the present, reveals much about the relations of science and philosophy. I will first say something about the background to the free will debate and the common arguments for and against belief in

1 "The Passions of the Soul", *The Philosophical Writings of Descartes*, ed. Cottingham, (Cambridge: Cambridge University press, 1985), vol. 1, p. 384.

free will. Then in the second part of the paper I will illustrate late nineteenth-century attempts to rethink the philosophical basis and authority of science in the light of conceptions of the will. For illustration, because the writing will at least in part be familiar to many people, I cite Dostoevsky, Nietzsche and Bergson.

Western contributors to the debate about whether free will 'really' exists tend to assume that they are discussing a timeless and universal question. Yet, as people at this conference will hardly need reminding, there are many cultures not only where there is no such notion as free will but not even the categories of nature, human and person which appear to be intrinsic to the western articulation of the notion. In everyday English language, reference to free will is an expression of belief in individual agency, and people who belong to certain social groups do, as a matter of social fact, often say that she chose what to do, that she could have chosen otherwise and that she is responsible. Such language in the West, as the scholar of classical philosophy, Michael Frede, has argued, originated at a particular historical juncture, in the thought of the late Stoic philosophers and the early Christian Church Fathers like Origen and Augustine. These writers sought to show why in a benevolently ordered world, in which everything is as it is and not otherwise, individual people must still take action in order to live well. (They also struggled against the fatalism they found in popular belief in astrology.)

My task is not to trace this, and I jump to the nineteenth century. This was when scholars and their public audience became preoccupied with claims that the advance of scientific knowledge clearly threatens belief in free will and hence, also, threatens the social and legal culture of individual responsibility. Examining this will provide my case study of relations between philosophy and science. In my own research, forthcoming as a book, *Free Will and the Human Sciences in Britain, 1870-1910*, I have studied this debate in one national context in some detail. But throughout Europe and North America at this time there was a literature expressing a fear of determinism, a fear aroused by advances in physiology, evolutionary theory, statistics and history. A century later, from the 1980s to the present, there has been a debate about free will and determinism in similar terms, but this time influenced by large advances in empirical knowledge of the brain and the workings of natural selection.

One reason for the great influence of Locke's *Essay Concerning Human Understanding* was that he claimed to argue about what it is possible to know according to the 'the experimental method'. Throughout the eighteenth century, this meant to argue on the basis of experience, which included the use of experiment in the modern sense but more often meant trying to perceive how the mind operates by reflection or introspection. Thus reflecting or examining his experience, Locke analysed the concept of power, which he traced to the awareness each person has (he claimed) of a capacity to move his or her body. When we engage in 'reflection on what passes in our selves, … we find by Experience, that barely by willing it, barely by a thought of the Mind, we can move the parts of our Bodies'. (*Essay*, II.xxi.4) He said that each person has the experience of 'willing' occurring in the mind and resulting in a change in physical movement. This has been repeated ever since as an argument for free will. A century after Locke, Dr Johnson, in one of his famous declarations of common sense, said: 'Sir … we *know* our will is free, and there's an end on't.'2 And a century after that the Victorian moral philosopher, Henry Sidgwick noted that whatever the arguments for scientific determinism, the bottom line for those who believe in freedom is the experience of that freedom. 'Against the formidable array of cumulative evidence offered for Determinism there is to be set the immediate affirmation of consciousness in the moment of deliberate action.' Another Victorian, the jurist James Fitzjames Stephen, asserted: 'Every human creature attaches to the words "to will" […] as vivid a meaning as every man with eyes attaches to the words "to see"'.

Thus there was a tradition in British philosophical culture of asserting that each person has knowledge of free will by experience. At the same time, there was a tradition of writing asserting that this experience gives false knowledge, because we know by *reasoning*, that our actions must in fact follow 'by necessity' from previously existing conditions. (In English, the word 'determinism' was not in common use until the 1870s, and earlier debate was in the language of 'liberty and necessity'; see Harris, *Of Liberty and Necessity*.) There were different kinds of religious, philosophical and scientific reasoning in support of belief in necessity. The theological argument had its strongest expression in Calvinism: God is omnipotent, and His ways are inscrutable let alone questionable, and all events, and most especially human actions, result from His Will, and if that Will saves, it is a matter of transcendent Grace, not of human will. If a prideful person thinks he has a will, prayerful humility reveals his actions as in fact dependent on God's Will. The philosophical argument was that all of nature is subject to uniform natural law, and hence, once it is demonstrated, as it was in the nineteenth century, that human beings are part of nature, we must accept that all human actions too are uniform and law-like. The argument of natural philosophy, or natural science, was that experience shows our actions regularly and without exception to follow motives, and shows that the action which actually occurs is the outcome of one motive prevailing over the others. Actions result from the competition of motives and not from free choice. With the rise to prominence of evolutionary neuroscience in recent decades this last argument has again become the focus of debate. Some scientific writers declare: the state of relations among neurones in the brain determines what we do. This argument, however, has many contemporary critics, of which the central criticism relevant to us is that it involves a misunderstanding of the relations between scientific knowledge and other forms of forms of knowledge, including the kind or reasoning called philosophy. The criticism is that denials of free will are a

2 *Boswell's Life of Johnson* (Everyman's Library: 1993), p. 82.

species of scientism, belief that there is only one form of knowledge, the kind of knowledge actually found in the natural sciences. For the critics, there is other knowledge, like everyday moral knowledge, in which, they say, we can legitimately and properly refer to free will.

I may briefly remind you of the main ways in which the advance of science in the nineteenth century appeared to demonstrate necessity, or in later language, determinism, in human affairs. In physical science, the first law of thermodynamics, the law of the conservation of energy, formulated around 1850, left no room for a force, such as will (of either God or Man) to intervene in the energy system of nature. Then, Darwin's theory of evolution described humankind as the outcome of the operation of natural laws and, as such, fully subject to necessity. At the same time, conviction spread that the brain is the organ of mind and that there can be no mental event independent of nervous processes, leading, in T. H. Huxley's words, to the belief that we are 'conscious automata'. ('The hypothesis that animals are automata and its history') As part of the development of historical science, scholars turned to examine the roots of Christianity and the historical evidence for the life of Christ, and this resulted in a literature which treated religious faith as itself the outcome of historical and social conditions. Lastly, the systematic collection of data about human affairs, like age of mortality and rates of suicides, demonstrated that there is a regular order even in phenomena which appear to be due to chance, like the chance of being murdered. H. T. Buckle, in the 1860s, caused a scandal across Europe with his book on *The History of Civilization in England* because he described the rise of civilisation as subject to natural law and not the will of great men or outcome of a moral law or spiritual purpose. The playwright George Bernard Shaw wryly captured the black mood of his contemporaries at the beginning of the twentieth century: 'We are part of a cosmic system. Free will is an illusion. We are the children of Cause and Effect. We are the Unalterable, the Irresistible, the Irresponsible, the Inevitable.' ('Back to Methuselah', in *Collected Plays*, p. 952)

Some modern authors have reached the same kind of conclusion. The US psychologist Daniel M. Wegner writes that 'the real causal mechanisms underlying behavior are never present in consciousness'. Hence, he argues, the subjective experience of free will which earlier philosophers and ordinary people alike made so much of is a deception: 'each of our actions is really the culmination of an intricate set of physical and mental processes'. (*The Illusion of Conscious Will*, pp. 97, 27) I want to use Wegner's words to illustrate a capital point for this talk. In arguments for and against the freedom of the will, from the time of Locke to the present, and in spite of the frequency of claims that something about the mind is a fact, there is commonly a lack of clear analytic distinction between philosophical statements and scientific or empirical statements. I don't assert this simply to say that this is wrong, that there should always be a clear distinction, though many analytic philosophers have held this view. In as far as I understand it, there is little agreement in contemporary philosophy on this complex matter. I do observe, however, that scientists bring in philosophical assumptions in the process of making what they say are scientific points. In the middle of the sentences I have just quoted from Wegner, he uses the word 'real' (or 'really'). In doing so he makes an ontological claim, a claim about what is in the universe. Wegner would perhaps say that he's just using ordinary language - and he is - but ordinary language too is full of ontological presumptions. Both scientific and everyday speech stake out philosophical stances. Wegner's position is the belief that neuronal processes in the brain are real in the way other things, like the exercise of free will are not, and hence if we are to have knowledge of mind it must be knowledge of the real physical basis of mind. There is, Wegner implies, one kind of knowledge in terms of which everything else must finally be known. This is what I have called scientism. This philosophical presumption influences the scientific argument about free will because it builds into Wegner's thought from the beginning the assumption that all 'real' events are determined. His claim that free will is an illusion is a *logical* consequence of his way of thought not an *empirical* fact. Here we have a good example of the muddling of philosophical and scientific statements in contemporary culture.

I can state three large objections to the denial of free will which we find in Wegner and in other writers in neuropsychology. First, there is no realist theory of knowledge which commands universal or even widespread agreement, and not a few philosophers and ordinary people are sceptical of the possibility of there being such a theory. So, scientists cannot refer to what is 'real' as if there was agreement about what this means. Outside of the community of people who write about 'the neuronal self', there is a social world in which people use language to describe free will, phenomenological description of a person's sense of agency and responsibility as real. When Wegner uses the word 'real', he denotes what a large community of people, the neursoscientists and their fellow-travellers, call real.

The second objection states that it is simply a category mistake to attribute free will to, or deny free will to, a brain or to neuronal processes. Wittgenstein had a large influence on this kind of argument. Language about free will is language using an everyday legal, moral and social category, and in this language it is proper to talk about a *person*, and only about a person, exercising free will. In this language, people are real, and hence capacities or processes attributed to people, like free will, are real - in terms of this language. It is a misuse of language to discuss free will as a topic in neuropsychology. (See Bennett and Hacker, *The Philosophical Foundations of Neuroscience*) Let me amplify this objection a little. The way of thought of the physiological sciences exists in order to seek, and it has its proper object in seeking, causal explanations; this thought plays by the rules of the natural science game in which it is *logically necessary* for every event to have a physical cause. In this discourse there can be no talk about freedom. Period. No empirical evidence of the kind which physiology provides can help us decide whether there is free will or not. Empirical evidence, for example of clinical symptoms, may help a decision about whether a person belongs in a social category of people to whom we do not attribute free will (e.g., a mentally disturbed person); but this is another matter. In the social worlds where we talk meaningfully about free will, as we do in many areas of everyday western moral and social life, we do so by talking about people not brains. When we talk about people and ask why they do what they do, we want answers in terms of categories appropriate to people, like reasons and volitions, desires and fears, pleasures and pains, and not brain events. The language of free will belongs to a way of thought (to return to a point already made) in which there is an ontology of persons.

The third objection is that neuroscientists have experimented on and discussed free will as if it concerned a simple, limited action, like choosing slightly to move one wrist (the task in much discussed experiments by Benjamin Libet which Wegner cites). But acts of free will are not like this; they are much more like choosing to contribute a talk to this conference rather than taking a holiday in the Seychelles. Each and every human action has a history and a context, and any decision about whether or not free will is involved must occur in the setting of a narrative about this history and context. Even people who take part in scientific experiments which require them to choose to move their wrist do what they do in the experiment in the light of a long history of how they actually got themselves into the experimental situation. (See Tallis, *Aping Mankind*) Free will pertains to the real social life of taking part in neuropsychological experiments not to the wrist movement which the scientists actually record.

In the very act of making these objections, I reassert the independence of certain kinds of philosophical or conceptual argument from science. My paper *performs* a relationship between philosophy and science. The kind of relationship I think it to be is implicit in the kind of activity I engage in. I leave to philosophers the business of sorting out the formalities of relations. They argue. There are contemporary philosophers, like Patricia Churchland and Daniel Dennett, who announce that the philosophy of mind can make progress only by building on what empirical science learns. Arguing this, they clearly see that they turn against the dominant twentiethcentury tradition in analytic philosophy which had sharply distinguished logical and empirical statements. They build on the famous paper by W. O. Quine, 'Two dogmas of empiricism', supporting a naturalistic epistemology. They are opposed by other philosophers, for example the Wittgenstein scholar P. M. S. Hacker. (If I were informally to put my own position, I would say that there are no more grounds for asserting that empirical knowledge of the brain is the foundation for all other knowledge than for saying that empirical knowledge of the history of science, that is the story of how we came to know about things like brains, is the foundation for all other knowledge. Most natural scientists would find this very strange, since they live in a world, as they experience it and as their ability to manipulate and predict the world appears to confirm, in which they deal with 'really' real physical nature. I would say, however, that there is a history to what is thought 'real' and a historian lays the basis for a historian's knowledge in that reality not in nature. What 'reality' in itself is, or even whether it is meaningful to enquire, I do not claim to say as a philosophical contribution.)

When a scientist like Wegner makes an assertion about what is 'real', he does not appear to be aware of the implications of his own language. It is clearly the business of philosophy to be aware of such implications. When we become aware, there are, I think, two intellectually significant directions in which we may go. The first is sociological, and the second philosophical. Though on this occasion, our business is with the second, I want briefly to note the sociological possibilities for discussing free will.

As I have said, the language of free will is found within some cultures and not others, and even in the contemporary West reference to free will is not on everyone's lips. This variation in the availability of the category cries out for social or ethnological explanation. (See Lloyd, *Cognitive Variations*, chapter 6, on the variety of causal theories.) Many writers in the social sciences do not talk about free will but rather about 'agency', and they use this term to characterise the different power and degree of freedom to act which a person in any particular social group may have. A large body of research in social psychology, for instance, has studied the *attribution* of agency to individuals. In this intellectual context, free will is not something which a person has but is something which, in certain social settings (commonly involving responsibility), people attribute to a person. This is not a philosophical matter but a matter of understanding where, when and for what social purpose people use a certain way of describing people which attributes causes and power to people rather than things. It is a matter which is often of the greatest importance for the sense of dignity and worth people have. Social relations and the legal system alike, in a liberal and individualistic society, depend on the possibility of making this kind of attribution. Western legal jurisprudence indeed defines a person as an *actor*, an agent to whom it is legitimate to assign free will and legal responsibility. Among social philosophers (like Barry Barnes, whose book on *Understanding Agency* exemplifies the position I am describing), there are those who would say that once we have understood the social operation of the rules of language about will and responsibility, we have understood all there is. This is, in effect, to treat sociological categories and rules (not neurones!) as real.

There is much more to be said about this, but I return to what philosophers do. I can report that there is a huge body of analytic work on freedom of the will, much of it refining the argument (called 'compatibilism') that it is reasonable to believe in both the uniformity of events in nature and human freedom of choice. This is the not my field. What I do instead is look again at the late-nineteenth-century literature on free will, a literature written in response to science. There was a significant opposition to deducing determinism in human life from science, and on many occasions this involved assertions about the relations of philosophy and science. I shall mention three famous but very different instances Dostoevsky, Nietzsche and Bergson.

Speaking in Russia, I do not need to say much about Dostoevsky's now 'classic' rejection of science in order to uphold individual freedom, as articulated in his *Записки из подполья* (*Notes from Underground,* in English, 1913). Though published in 1865, this work had influence only later, as the Russian public of the 1860s, longing for social reform, regarded the *Notes* as perverted rantings at odds with the humane use of knowledge. Dostoevsky portrayed the tormented world of a man (unnamed) whose commitment to free will is such that he sacrifices everything, both the desperately poor and innocent Lisa and what might be thought his own interest, in order to sustain it. Nature or society or love may seek to bind him, but, he thinks, his soul does not have to submit. 'What have *I* to do with the laws of Nature, or with arithmetic, when all the time these laws and the formula that twice two make four do not meet with my acceptance?' (*Letters from the Underworld,* pp. 16-17) The outcome is a tragically degraded life, an 'I' enclosed by 'stone walls' - but *it is nevertheless* an 'I'. The 'I' sacrifices all in order to exercise its freedom. Dostoevsky knew of what he wrote: through the years of his convict ordeal in Omsk in Siberia, he was staggered by the means which prisoners found to maintain individual identity, to show to themselves that they had a will even under brutally coercive conditions.

As Joseph Frank, Dostoevsky's English-language biographer has argued, the *Notes from Underground* were a furious parody written in reaction to the Russian publishing sensation of the early 1860s, Nikolai Chernyshevskii's novel, *Что делат?* (*What Is to Be Done*?) That novel portrayed a trio of students who achieve personal and political harmony in their lives through taking to heart the material truths of the human condition which physiology was then making known. In the same year as Chernyshevskii's novel appeared, I.M. Sechenov published the first version of his essay, '*Рефлексы головново мозга*' ('Reflexes of the brain'), later to acquire canonical status in Soviet ideology as the world breakthrough to a materialist and realist science of human nature. (Frank, *Dostoevsky*, chapter 21; Joravksy, *Russian Psychology*, pp. 53-63, 92-104) Sechenov's main aim in his essay was to demonstrate that knowledge of the brain could, at least in principle, account for what people would ordinarily call a voluntary action. Thus Dostoevsky's portrait of the individual will, acting come what may, was a direct response to the view that following nature and viewing agency as the function of nerves can satisfy the independent spirit, the dignity, of men and women. Dostoevsky believed that brain science has nothing to say about the will; he mocked the failure of science to confront good and evil.

Dostoevsky's grim tale also helps to clarify a confusion of language found in talk about free will. Scientific critics of belief in free will (e.g., T.H. Huxley) have sometimes said that if there were free will, it would amount to a chance or random event in the order of nature. Belief in that, they say, is irrational. We should consider, however, that the antonym of free will is constraint - in the moral order; the antonym of randomness is determinism - in the physical order. Free will, in cultures where there is such a notion, is a state attributable to a person, and, in these cultures, a *person's* actions are neither determined nor random, but either free or compelled (or in some degree both). Dostoevsky's anti-hero, though rejecting both arithmetic and love in order to preserve his sense of being a free self, does not act randomly, and what he does has physical causes and consequences. He does not believe, irrationally, that because he is free to choose, he is thereby free to fly. The writer of Dostoevsky's *Notes* acted freely within the constraints of the human condition, constraints which include the laws of nature from which he suffered.

If I turn now to comment on Nietzsche's work, it is with awareness that interpretation of his writings is an intellectual project in its own right. My excuse is that he touched on a number of issues central to debate about causation and freedom of the will. He witnessed in his own age how scientific explanations in terms of history, heredity and social conditions were replacing moral purposes as the drive of human actions, substituting a language of determinism for a language of the will. As a consequence, Nietzsche thought, it had become impossible, if one is honest, to maintain, as liberal intellectuals then still did, belief in the advance of the spiritual life of humanity in old terms. The scientists' claim to objectivity - to what Nietzsche called a '"will-less" contemplation' of the world, supposedly eliminating the 'choosing, judging, interpreting subject' - has left the pursuit of values without any rational or spiritual foundation. There must be new foundations - for science included. Pursuing this, he noted that the advance of deterministic science, by criticising the notion of free will, has freed the word 'will' of it moral and Christian inheritance. For Nietzsche, this meant that the word 'will' was available for new use, a 'rechristening'. (*The Will to Power*, ed. Kaufmann, § 95. See Nehemas, *Nietzsche*, pp. 7679) He sought philosophical foundations in a new notion of 'will', which he called 'the will to power'. Thus, in Nietzsche's writing, belief in the impossibility of free will in a world understood in scientific terms, led to argument for 'will', understood in a new way, as the reason for the pursuit of science and philosophy alike.

Nietzsche was highly sceptical, when not downright scornful, of the old, Victorian notion of the will as a personal virtue, a virtue of character. Bourgeois people, he contemptuously wrote, have a fine capacity for motives which they do not know or deny having. They repeatedly attribute to will what really originates with hidden desire. 'Do I have to add that the wise Oedipus was right, that we really are not responsible for our dreams but just as little for our waking life, and that the doctrine of freedom of the will has human pride and feeling of power for its father and mother?' (*Daybreak*, § 128; also § 124) However, he rejected embracing scientific determinism as the alternative to hypocrisy - the route which Freud took. Rather, Nietzsche looked to transcend the polarity of free will and determinism through knowledge of the human being as the wilful 'interpreting subject', in his phrase.

Nietzsche was far from being alone in believing that the scientific reduction of knowledge to sequences of events, to physical causes not linked by any purposive connection, had left values bereft of meaning. Fear that this was true, but that a return to Christian belief was impossible, created 'the crisis' of European thought which so preoccupied Germanlanguage scholars at the end of the nineteenth century. That there was a 'crisis' was implicit in the work of scientists themselves, who zealously promoted science as if it needed justification, as if the value of truth in general and the value of obedience to the laws of nature in particular were self-evident. Nietzsche exposed (as he saw it) the incapacity of science to provide itself with reasons for the pursuit of truth or any other value. Values, instead, he set out to trace to 'the *innocence of becoming*', which he was apt to describe as 'will'. (*The Will to Power*, § 552)

Nietzsche also touched, in this like Dostoevsky, on the notion of free will as central to human dignity and responsibility. If there is value in being human, Nietzsche argued, this value must be at the origin of things - an ultimate cause not a contingent effect. In this context of argument, he asserted the freedom of the will: 'The value of man is posited as a *moral* value: consequently his morality must be a *causa prima*; consequently there must be a principle in man, a "free will" as *causa prima*.' (*The Will to Power*, § 288). This is, I think, a decisive statement: *if* there is to be a culture built on the free actions of persons, free action must be posited as a first cause. The argument, however, is moral, existential and cultural indeed, philosophical: free will is not and could not be an empirical matter, the kind of empirical matter about which a natural science might give us knowledge.

My last example of opposition to scientific reduction and the elimination of reference to free will as unscientific is Bergson. As with my comments on Dostoevsky and Nietzsche, my purpose is not to promote a philosophy but only to show that there were, and are, philosophical alternatives to deterministic forms of science. Bergson's first book, *Essai sur les données immédiates de la conscience* (1889), which appeared under the title *Time and Free Will* in English (1913), was a direct response to debate about free will. Bergson's argument began with the popular claim that we have a direct experience of being freely active: 'We picture to our minds a psychic force imprisoned in the soul like the winds of Aeolus, and only waiting for an opportunity to burst forth: our will is supposed to watch over this force and from time to time to open a passage for it.' In his book he attempted to replace the metaphysics behind this ludicrous picture of the will as a psychic force.

Bergson's innovation was to reject the physical scientists' quantitative conception of time as if it were a fourth dimension of space. Space, he argued, is the source of quantitative representation of the world. But time, he declared, is not succession, cannot be represented spatially.

Time is *duration*, an 'organic whole'; and 'inner duration, perceived by consciousness, is nothing else but the melting of states of consciousness into one another, and the gradual growth of the ego'. For Bergson, there is a self or soul, if these words are understood to denote a process not a thing, a coming into being with duration, an activity of self-determination not the causal outcome of mechanical events. Freedom is a process, in action. Of course, we can give an account of our actions and refer to determining causes, but when we do this determinism is a feature of the retrospective construction of narrative about a process understood as if it were like a dimension of space. By contrast, when we represent our actions as free we describe a process occurring: 'Now the free act takes place in time which is flowing and not in time which has already flown.' He therefore concluded with the statement, strikingly at odds with the view point of conventional natural science, that among the facts 'which we observe there is none clearer' than individual freedom. This really turned the generally accepted position in natural science on its head: the secure foundation of knowledge is the phenomenology of active becoming; the causal events which scientists describe are abstractions.

Scientists, Bergson claimed, have followed Hume in analysing causation into sequential relations, with no 'efficient' connection (or active power) between things. He rejected this analysis. The relation which we subjectively experience as will is not a relation between two things, as if they were in space, but the expression of the being of self in duration. If, then, we take this awareness as the basis of knowledge, we have a model for understanding events in nature which 'ascribes to things a duration absolutely like our own', that is, treats the physical world as constituted as an organic being in time. In his later lectures on *Creative Evolution*, Bergson therefore drew upon subjective awareness of action as the source of the most basic intuitions: 'Let us try to see, no longer with the eyes of the intellect alone, which grasps only the ready made and which looks from the outside, but with the spirit, I mean with that faculty of seeing which is immanent in the faculty of acting and which springs up, somehow, by the twisting of the will on itself, when action is turned into knowledge, like heat, so to say, into light.' He restated belief in the subjective experience of free action as the prototype for knowledge of the creative becoming of the world. He fully embraced the anthropocentric implications of his argument, rejecting objectivity as understood in the natural sciences and turning instead to intuition. For some years, he reached a large and enthusiastic public audience with a philosophy which (to adapt Weber's famous expression) 're-enchanted' the world. 'There are no things, there are only actions', he wrote in *Creative Evolution.* Such ideas were widespread in speculative philosophy and in innovative areas of the arts, in free dance for example, in the opening decades of the twentieth century.

I come to the end. In order to discuss relations between science and philosophy in particular terms, I have examined writings contrasting the self-experience of agency, which in common English people call free will, with the conclusion of deterministic science that the will is an illusion. At the end of the nineteenth century, this contrast stimulated profound attempts to rethink the philosophical foundations on which scientific knowledge had been built, rejecting scientism and re-asserting the contribution of philosophy. Western intellectual life at its best, I would say, has been built on such arguments rather than on the dominance of any one world view. The Enlightenment project was never one simple programme but always contained both science concerned with the laws of nature and philosophy concerned with the place that science has in relation to other forms of thought. The late nineteenth-century contrast between a deterministic scientism and a philosophical culture open to, if not founded on, some conception of free action reappears in debate now about the implications of the neurosciences. There is, I have maintained, a large role for historical and philosophical argument in questioning assertions by scientists that descriptions of neuronal events describe the 'real' world.

CHAPTER V

THE NEUROLOGIC APPROACH TO CONSCIOUSNESS: SCOPE AND LIMITS

The traditional field of psychology has been invested during the last 30 years by cognitive neuroscience. This is the case, for example, of functions such as perception, memory, imagination, voluntary decision, the brain mechanism of which was more or less cracked. Last conquer dated: abstract reasoning, now interpreted (by the use of Boolean algebra) as "computation" and decomposed into elementary operations whose sequence can be assigned to a "Turing machine" or, precisely, a computer. Not that everything in these functions has been fully understood and has become potentially reproducible by Artificial Intelligence, but we fail to see what obstacles oppose now a full conquest, although the extreme complexity of mental operations involved requests us to place this event in a rather distant future. However, at the strictly philosophical level, the accelerated development of neuroscience seems somehow impose the full option of materialism or "physicalism". This, actually, comes in several versions. They range from behaviourism or from the so-called "eliminative" materialism - which relegates the notions of fear, desire, pleasure and pain, desire etc. in the field of "folk-psychology" and claims to get them replaced by the description of the corresponding neurological mechanisms - to functionalism, which considers, too, the psyche as the overall expression of the functioning of the nervous system but respects some autonomy of mental states insofar as it refuses to associate them, term to term, with determined states of the nervous systems. Between these two extremes there are still all sorts of intermediate versions, but the assumption common to all of them is that the "secret of the mind" will be found in the structure and functioning of the brain, and nowhere else.

A few voices, however, have been raised to expose the falsity of this paradigm, or at least, its supposed all-encompassing character. Their common thesis consists in assuming that the phenomenon of consciousness *principially* - and not only temporarily - escapes any reduction to the neurological level. Their position, however, can be understood only on taking care of distinguishing two distinct meanings of "consciousness." In one sense, "being conscious" means something like "being aware", "informed", "attentive to", etc.. In this sense, the presence or absence of awareness will help distinguish the informed subject from the uninformed, the person who is awake from the one who is asleep or anesthetized, the careful person from the distracted one, etc. This first range of meanings of the term "consciousness" does not represent any particular difficulty for physicalism because the presence of consciousness and its absence can always be interpreted in terms of functional integrity or disruption of the relevant neural circuits. Like a light bulb connected to a circuit with a rheostat, the "light of consciousness" will shine or not shine, or glow with varying intensity in dependence on the state of the neural circuit that feeds it, i.e. its degree of integrity and functionality.

In another sense, however, what is meant through the term "consciousness" is the purely subjective sense of experiencing or of "being" something, the "what it is like" 1 of living any particular experience or "being in the shoes" of a particular individual. This new dimension of consciousness is what the Anglo-Saxon philosophers are accustomed to designate by the term "qualia" (Latin *quale*, "(being) such"). The field of *qualia* includes all that is experienced subjectively, "from the first person perspective": colors, sounds, smells, pleasures and pains, moods, etc.: of course, not the representative content of these experiences, which is always communicable to others, but their emotional impact, in itself indescribable, on the subject. So saying, they do not deny in any way that these experiences have also - just as pure information contents - their own neural substrate. They maintain only that there remains an irreducible "explanatory gap" between these experiences and the corresponding states of the brain. And it is in this sense that *qualia* are considered by some authors as the impregnable stronghold of consciousness, the ultimate frontier that materialism is doomed never to cross. Is this claim justified or not? I would like to bring here some thoughts on this point, with reference to a text almost as famous as Th. Nagel's article on bats, namely the fable invented by F. Jackson about "Mary the color scientist":2

> Mary is a brillant scientist who is, for whatever reason, forced to investigate the world from a black-and-white room *via* a black-and-white television monitor. She specializes in the neuro-physiology of vision and acquires, let us suppose, all the physical information there is to obtain about what goes on when we see ripe tomatoes, or the sky, and use terms like *red*, *blue*, and so on.

> She discovers, for example, just which wavelength combinations from the sky stimulate the retina, and exactly how this produces *via* the central nervous system the contraction of the vocal chords and expulsion of air from the lungs that results in the uttering of the sentence "The sky is

---

1 To borrow the title of a famous paper of Th. Nagel, originally published in 1974 in the *Philosophical Review* (83) and reprinted in *Mortal Questions* (Cambridge University Press, 1979), pp. 165-180.

2 "Epiphenomenal Qualia," *Philosophical Quaterly*, 32, (1982), pp. 127
136.

> blue". [...] What will happen when Mary is released from her black-and-white room or is given a color television monitor? Will she *learn* anything or not? It seems just obvious that she will learn something about the world and our visual experience of it. But then it is inescapable that her previous knowledge was incomplete. But she had *all* the physical information. *Ergo* there is more to have than that, and Physicalism is false..."3

This ingenious "thought experiment" has generated an incredible amount of feedback. In the decade following the publication of that article in the Philosophical Quarterly, there were over forty reviews, not counting the chapters devoted to the consideration of this fable inside books of more general scope. Obviously, there can be no question to examine in detail each of these positions. However, we can roughly divide them into two groups. The first ones come to consider as a mere prejudice - not at all as something obvious - the idea that Mary necessarily learns something on leaving her black-and-white room. The second ones actually admit that she will acquire something. But not any genuine real knowledge, rather a kind of practical ability to discriminate colors and match their names to the various colorful things she now has a direct perception of. This second objection includes a variant according to which Mary does not learn a new set of facts but rather to know in another way a set of facts she already was acquainted with. The common conclusion of the first and second objectors is that the case of Mary does not actually call into question the truth and completeness of Physicalism. Let us briefly examine these two types of objections as well as the replicas of F. Jackson himself, or those that could be formulated from a perspective similar to his.

The first type of objection is at best illustrated by Daniel C. Dennett's case. It consists essentially in refusing Jackson's initial postulate that Mary could be somehow omniscient, as far as neurophysiology of color is concerned. In fact, according to him, our knowledge of the brain is currently much too far from the situation we are asked to imagine that we cannot exclude that Mary's spontaneous reaction on seeing for the first time - say ripe tomatoes - would be something like: "Oh yes! That's exactly the way I had anticipated the red color would look like!"

---

3 "Epiphenomenal Qualia," *Philosophical Quaterly,* 32, (1982), p. 128. Curiously enough, this argument was anticipated as early as 1690 by John Locke in his *Essay Concerning Human Understanding* II, 1, 6 "...I think it will be granted easily, that if a child were kept in a place where he never saw any other than black and white till he were a man, he would have no more ideas of scarlet or green, than he that from his childhood never tasted an oyster, or a pine-apple, has of those particular relishes", ed. A.C. Fraser (Reprint Dover Publications, New York, 1959), p. 126.

In other words, while evoking the idea of a neurophysiological kowledge that would be absolutely encyclopedic, we haphazardly extrapolate from our current knowledge. First, we do not know if such a thing is really possible. On the other hand, we imagine this hypothetical knowledge on the model of ours, but somehow "better", "more complete". In doing so, we arbitrarily exclude the possibility of a qualitative leap that would be linked to the advent of such a total knowledge, that is to say, the possibility for it to give us *in addition* direct access, perceptual or quasiperceptual, to sensible qualities. In Dennett's words, "The image is wrong; if that is the way you imagine the case, you are simply not following directions!" The reason no one follows directions is because what they ask you to imagine is so preposterously immense, you can't even try; the crucial premise is that "She has all the physical information." That is not readily imaginable, so no one bothers. They just imagine that she knows lots and lots - perhaps they imagine that she knows everything that anyone knows *today* about the neurophysiology of color vision. But that's just a drop in the bucket, and it's not surprising that Mary would learn something if *that* were all she knew."4

Other authors, however, first and foremost L. Nemirow and D. Lewis,5 concede that Mary really learns something but they note that terms like "to know", "to be aware of" or "to learn" as contained in the premises of Jackson's reasoning, are ambiguous: do they refer to *knowing-that* (propositional knowledge) or to *knowing-how* (skills, capacity)? According to them, when Mary finally comes to have sensations of color, she does not acquire any kind of propositional knowledge but only different capabilities which were previously lacking, for example, that to imagine what it is like to see a ripe tomato. This does not mean that her factual knowledge was defective or incomplete. She knew everything that we can learn about the experiences of others, but failed, among other things, to make a number of visual discriminations that only people living in a world of color are capable of.

A reflection of the same type was recently presented by a French author, Joelle Proust.6 Nothing prevents, she observes, to go quite far in the scientific characterization, certainly not of the *content* of any color or taste quale, but of its *position* in a diagram of relations between qualia, as, for example, the famous "color triangle". Now, does the lack of reference to the subjective quality of each position within the diagram - namely to *what it is like* of currently enjoying a sensible quality - mean that some type of reality positively escapes every scientific approach? No at all! The only thing that escapes it is the ability to identify objects on a diagram of relationships, to

4 See *Consciousness Explained* (Little, Brown and Company, 1991), p. 399.

5 *Loc cit.*

6 See *Comment l'esprit vient aux bêtes* ("How do animals get a mind," Paris, 1997), pp. 336-341.

memorize them in their outward appearance, to imagine or recognize them from their position in such a diagram.

Still another variant of that type of answer is to be found in authors like T.Horgan, M. Tye and P.M. Chuchland.7 The proponents of this variant also believe that Mary really does not acquire a new object of knowledge but only a new understanding of a subject she had been acquainted with for a long time. Jackson says that Mary already had "all the physical information" needed on color perception. T. Horgan notes in this context that it is necessary to distinguish between an explicitly physical information about a certain process - for instance color vision - and an ontologically physical information about the same process. The first one has meaning only within the framework of a particular scientific theory (here neurological), while the second one simply refers to entities of the outside world such as are recognized by common sense. In this perspective, the only thing that Jackson's reasoning shows is the impossibility of considering every information as of *explicitly* physical order. In other words, when Mary discovers the *what it is like* to see ripe tomatoes and exclaims "So, ripe tomatoes look *this* way!" her sentence certainly does not express any information of *explicitly physical* ("scientific"), but only of *ontologically physical* order. The novelty of information consists in the fact that Mary acquires a new perspective on phenomenal redness, in Horgan's language an "ostensive perspective in the first person." In sum, the particular circumstances of her life led her to travel in reverse order the very route of experience that is - or could be - that of the vast majority of men: that is starting with an everyday familiarization (but already "ontologically physical") with sense data and later on, only in the case of a few people, elaborating this firsthand information into something explicitly physical.

A slightly more sophisticated version of the same argument has been developed by J. Perry, a well-known linguist. 8 According to him, the weakness of physicalism consists in clinging to a somehow "incomplete" version of the research program of physical sciences. Actually, the latter, on behalf of a narrow and rigid conception of objectivity, have a tendency to exclude any consideration of the variety of contexts and existential situations. Even if one accepts that conscious experience is nothing but a cerebral phenomenon - which is the very definition of physicalism - there is no reason to believe that *having* an experience (perceptual, emotional, intellectual, whatever) is similar in some way to *observe* its appearance and unfolding in one' own brain. These are, in fact, two modes of access, essentially different, to one and the same brain process. Therefore, what

---

7 See T. Horgan, "Jackson on Physical Information and Qualia," *Philosophical Quaterly,* 34, (1984); M. Tye, "The Subjective Qualities of Experience", *Mind,* 95, (1986); P.M. Churchland, "Reduction, Qualia, and the Direct Introspection of Brain States", *The Journal of Philosophy,* 82, (1985)

8 See J. Perry, *The Problem of the Essential Indexical* (Oxford University Press, 1993)

Mary got, according to him, while escaping her black-and-white environment, is not a knowledge of something totally new, but a representation *referred to her own situation* of something, namely the world of colors, of which she had hitherto only an abstract representation, in so far as it was obtained "from the third person perspective". Perry, in short, reasons thus: "Suppose I know a certain person accurately: his name - say" Z " - as well as his address, occupation, political or religious opinions, etc. - But all that only indirectly, that is without ever having met him, or having got the opportunity to see a photograph of him or hear a sound recording of his voice. One day, for example during a reception, I see another person approach "someone", saying: "Hello, Z!" Immediately, my mind brings together that "Z", who till now was known to me only by hearsay, and some figure or face present *hic et nunc* before my eyes. The case of Mary would be of the same type. The only benefit she obtains on leaving her black-andwhite room, is the opportunity to apply to concrete situations the allencompassing perceptive knowledge she already possessed. For this exemplary student in "chromo-neurophysiology", to confront herself with the redness of ripe tomatoes, the "greenness" of grass or the "blueness" of the sky will amount to resolve, as if in play, as many "practical exercises".

So much for the main lines of argumentation followed by the upholders of physicalism. The rejoinders from the neo-dualistic camp have been various and, seemingly, not always compatible with one another. Presently, I am going to limit myself to the exposition of their most cogent and relevant arguments.

The majority of the authors quoted above consider the scientific study of the phenomenon of color, on the one hand, and subjective experience, on the other hand, as so many distinct "modes of access" to one and the same reality. As such, none of these modes should *a priori* be favored over its counterpart. In practice, however, the status conferred on the objective or "scientific" mode of access is superior to the one conferred on the "only subjective" one, to the point that this first mode of access is quite currently identified with the very reality it provides access to. It is indeed difficult to interpret otherwise the assertion that the qualitativesubjective type of experience is a mode of access to a *physical* process, in this case neurophysiological, or even can be reduced to an element of that very process. Here emerges the recurrent temptation of sciences to secrete their own ontology: the objective, or rather the objectified, tends to be equated with the "real", which in turn is implicitly understood in strictly physical terms. Correspondingly, the adjective "physical" comes to carry two seemingly indissociable meanings: it refers both to what is the concern of physical science (the objective mode of access) and to the inner constitution of things (what there is access to). This tendency to blindly identify objectivity to Reality as such can be considered as the congenital defect of physicalism. In sum, the theory of dual access, as argued by proponents of physicalism in philosophy in defence of their position, comes to support a form of psychophysical parallelism in which the physical element has an absolute ontological priority on the psychical, the latter appearing as the mere auto-reflexivity of the former.

But this type of approach entails another, perhaps still bigger, difficulty. Let us come back to Mary's experience when walking out of her black-and-white room. She is supposed to be able to immediately match the color *qualia*, with which she is suddenly confronted, to their neurophysiological counterparts. These authors implicitely assimilated her situation with that of some ideal student of physics who would be capable to fulfil on the spot any "application exercises." Doing so, however, they lost sight of a striking difference between the two situations. For that student, the general laws of physics (or of neurophysiology, for that matter) on the one hand, and the particular numerical data of the exercises proposed to him on the other hand, are somehow homogeneous. In his case, studying the theory and solving the application exercises do not call for basically different intellectual exertions. Not so for Mary! Getting perceptual access to those colors she was hitherto a mere theorician of is not at all the same thing as applying her general knowledge to particular cases.The fundamental difference is that she now gets a sense of being *personally involved* in the situation. The concrete colors she is now directly confronted with are not just interchangeable samples of those ideal, intelligible, or "platonician" colors that have for a long time no secrets for her. They are now seen from a certain distance, under a definite angle, a certain lightning and so on. These "situational" elements - if only due to the infinite potential variety of them - could not be anticipated, along with their own *how it is like*, in Mary's encyclopedic but abstract knowledge. The "view from nowhere" (Nagel), which is a tacit but fundamental assumption, common to all varieties of physicalism, is structurally unable to make place for the unlimited variety of "views from somewhere", the intersection of which composes actual human perception.

Does this mean that we have no other alternative but to return to some form of dualism, interpreting experience in terms of the interaction of body and soul? Not necessarily, because, as noted by Th. Nagel: "The feeling that physicalism fails to account for the essential subjectivity of psychological states is the feeling that nowhere in the description of the state of a human body can be housed a physical equivalent of the fact that "I", and not just this body, am the subject of these states." 9 While emphasizing the radically "egological" - and not just "spiritual" - character of mental states, Th Nagel implicitly suggests that the invocation of the inalienability of these states in relation to their subject goes against not only physicalism but also every theory of mind that would identify the subject of experience to any substance whatsoever, corporeal or immaterial. Therefore, any description of the world that could be considered as complete in terms of interactionist dualism (i.e. that would include a specification of the states

9 See "Physicalism". C.V. Borst (ed.), *The Mind-Brain Identity Theory*, (London: Macmillan, 1970), pp. 221-234.

of the soul as well of its relationship to a body) necessarily leaves aside the fundamental fact that this soul is *mine*, that *I* am the one who dwells in that body. In Th. Nagel's words: "the particular kind of possession that characterizes my relationship to my psychological states cannot be represented as the possession of certain attributes by a subject." 10 That means that the true psychological subject cannot be identified with anything present in the world. Following up this line of reflection would bring us in the vicinity of Wittgenstein's famous definition of the *I* as "the limit of the world".11 Let us conclude, quite provisionally, that physicalism, even if it represents a philosophical impasse, at least had the merit of forcing dualistic or "spiritual" currents of thought to move into the direction of the transcendental.

10 *Ibid.*, p. 228.

11 See in particular *Tractatus logico-philosophicus*, 5.632-5.641.

CHAPTER VI

META-THEORETICAL ISSUES WITHIN SECULAR PHILOSPHY OF SCIENCE: A TRANSCENDENTAL PERSPECTIVE

The current debate is mostly on relativism versus rationalism, and most relativists are oriented towards antirealism[1] because currently, many of the most influential arguments against realism derive from a variety of forms of relativism. And it is via this influence which one can see the merging of arguments resulting from the debates within philosophy, history and sociology of science. Relativists argue that which scientific claims are put forward and the grounds we develop for accepting those claims are, in some deep sense, dependent on historical or cultural circumstances. This debate has come to be called in the current literature as the GalileoBellarmine Controversy, in which relativists take the issue just as a matter of "...who had the better argument on rhetorical, social, or political grounds."[2] This controversy is aimed to make the relativists' case stronger by providing grounds for denying that science can achieve the transcultural, trans-historical knowledge that realists, in its various forms (Prospective, Weak, Scientific, Critical, Theoretical), seek. The current arguments put forward by relativists and accepted by most realists derive from the historical facts regarding the emergence of science and the context related content of its existence and sustenance. The relativists argue that science came into being in specific cultures at specific points in their history and that some cultures are better able than others to sustain specific social structures. The realists do not deny the original theory but try to provide specific reasons for holding that scientific procedures allow us to establish results in a way that transcends the culture in which those results were put forward and accepted. The other versions of this argument are often to be found in the current literature on history and sociology of science. The relation between proponents of ontological relativity and those who advocate the strong program in sociology is the conviction that truth is just a term honorifically attached to those items of belief that have managed to prevail-by whatever strategic or rhetorical means-in the contest for the high ground of scientific 'knowledge' and 'progress'. There are others within the current debate who have extended the scope of these arguments, people like

---

1 Of course, there are those who seek to establish antirealism without recourse to relativism as a viable theory of knowledge.

2 Feyerabend quoted in C. Norris, "Truth, Science, and the Growth of Knowledge," *New Left Review*, 210, (1995), p. 109.

Michel Foucault and Jean-Francois Lyotard in France or Barry Barnes and David Bloor in Britain. The latter propose a social construction of reality in philosophy and sociology of science and the latter should be related to the incommensurability thesis in history of science.3

My comment on the Original Theory is twofold: there is a vast literature on the connection between the emergence of modern science in Europe and the other cultures which had some kind of exact science. The second point is the argument by realists against relativists which should not be a priori. They should refer the problem to the historical research and assess the credibility of the Original Theory. The current mode of research seems to be dogmatic about the origin of modern science and this dogmatism is endangering the realism of science. Realists uncritically yield to the historical accounts presented by relativists regarding the culturerelatedness of science and concoct two different aspects in this debate. The one is the original theory and the other is the sustenance theory. The argument that core countries are better able than the countries in the periphery to sustain scientific institutions are part and parcel of political economy and unrelated to the central question of originality in science. In other words, the sustenance of scientific institutions is a matter of policy and should not be mixed up with the problematique of origin of science. The reason for the popularity of this myth is its ideological value for certain groups in some Western Core countries which would like to keep alive the myth of occidental uniqueness. But this myth undermines the vital point in how different civilizations borrow from each other and how the process of interaction is between human civilizations and the form of knowledge resultant from these civilizational interactions.

One final remark: empiricism, in its antirealist version is based on a theory of knowledge according to which one can only establish relations among perceptions, and such relations do not allow us to make definite claims about the world: outside these relations there is no reality knowable.4 Such an epistemology implies holding that the relation between explanandum and the explanans that science establishes need not to be objective, and in fact represents an internal, functional link of logical, conceptual, or conventional character.5 But there is a fundamental flaw in this argument which cannot be solved by reference to the linguistic formation of human knowledge. Because if one assumes that these are internal affairs which do not relate to the external formation or structures of

---

3 Barry Barnes, *About Science* (1985); David Bloor, *Knowledge and Social Imagery* (1976); Christofer Norris, "Truth, Science..," *New Letft Review,* 210, (1995); Gray Gutting, Michel Foucaults, *Archeology of Scientific Reason* (1989); Jean-Francois Lyotard, *The postmodern Condition* (1984).

4 H. Poincare, *Science and Hypothesis* (1952), p. xxiv.

5 V. Mosini, "Fundamentalism, Antifundamentalism, and Gibbs' Paradox," *Studies in History and Philosophy of Modern Physics,* vol. 26, No. 2, (1995), p. 152.

world, how did these ideas get, in the first place, into these closed, internal and non-objective realms?

Certainly, what is of importance in this debate is the very notion of truth and its applicability (realists), and inapplicability (antirealists) to scientific theories. Here, I think we are talking about science as a weltanschauung and science as a technological means which empower us to overcome our needs. But even science in the second sense, historically, is implicitly related to some kind of worldview. To reduce the credibility of the former and insist on the importance of the latter are a part of general philosophy which take us to the realm of ontology and the Manniskosyn as Swedes say, i.e. our view about the human being. How do we chart the possible limits of human knowledge? Where is the boundary of possible versus impossible? Antirealists, without getting into these debates have declared the discussion over due to the assumed epistemic risk.6

Elsewhere on Historiography or Philosophy of History I argued that the major contemporary academic debates are between modernist versus postmodernist philosophers of history. Here that line of argument will be

---

6 C. Hooker, "Surface Dazzle, Ghostly Depths", *Images of Science,* P. Churchland and C. Hooker, eds., (Chicago: Chicago University press, 1985), pp. 153-196. However, more on this debate *Empiricism vs Realism* in an historical perspective see Craig Dilwonh (1990). "Empiricism Vs. Realism: High Points in the Debate during the Past 150 Years," *Studies in History and Philosophy of Science,* vol. 21, No. 3, pp. 431-462. The only shortcoming of this historical survey is the total negligence of debates by Bhaskar and Critical Realists. About this last point see Christopher Norris, "Truth, Science, and the Growth of Knowledge," *New Left Review,* 210, (1995), pp. 105-124. To complete Norris or to amend his view on the relation between epistemology and ontology and their impact on the debate regarding Worldview, see *Physics and Our View of the World,* ed. Jan Hilgevoord, (Cambridge: Cambridge University press, 1994). More on realism and the terminological confusion within this debate see *The Philosophy of Science,* ed. David Papineau, (Oxford: Oxford University press, 1996), esp. the introduction. About the antirealism which has appeared under a variety of names, most notably, pragmatism, instrumentalism, conventionalism, phenomenalism, and idealism see Peter Skagestad, *Hypotetical Realism,* in *Scientific Inquiry and the Social Sciences,* eds. Marilyn B. Brewer and Barry E. Collins, (New York: Jossey-Bass, 1981,), pp. 77-97. Further on realism and its recent developments within philosophy which covers issues in philosophy, history and sociology of science and the impact of Bhaskar's position and the difference between his realism and American philosophers such as Hilary Putnam-whose discussion of realism has been cast more in terms of epistemology and semantic notions such as truth and reference and how the Kuhnian turn shifted the balance in the current debate in favor of those approaches which take Philosophy of science in relation to history and sociology; and the impact of these discussions on the history of human sciences see: W. Outhwaite, "New Developments in Realist Philosophy, " *History of The Human Sciences,* vol. 1 No. I, pp. 105-112.

followed in other context than historiography and it will be clear that no area of intellectual value is free from this broader issue between modernity versus postmodernity. The problem of modernity as a philosophical issue has been an essential part of Western intellectual discourse for quite some time-and in recent time, i.e. since the post-world war it has defined the dissatisfactions of European High Culture. The term and concept of modernity in itself poses problems for those who wish to designate its start, scope, and process. There is a current controversy within the Western academy about the status and fate of modernity, particularly the dispute about such issues as the end or completion or the very legitimacy of modernity. Although the problem of the nature or even the existence of a modern epoch is a very old one, this elusive topic, as Robert B. Pippin notes, has recently attracted renewed attention in a wide variety of academic disciplines and has come to involve very different issues in philosophy of science, history, sociology, art, political theory, theology, music, criticism, and literary theory. This challenge of postmodernity has an equivalent within the field of philosophy of science. Here in this study, I am concerned with this aspect of debate.7

Modernism in the philosophy of science demands a unified story about what makes an inquiry scientific, and the general idea in the postmodernist philosophy of science seems to be to interpret the history of science in terms of a modernist story of progress or rational development. Postmodern philosophy of science challenges the ubiquitous notion of progress by its combination of respect for the local context of inquiry with resistance to any global interpretation of science that could constrain local inquiry. As such it refuses any overall pictures or grand narratives that would aspire to explain science as a unified endeavor with an underlying essence, and makes sense of everyday science by seeing it as a set of narrative enterprises. 8 At the same time, the postmodernists argue, this postmodern philosophy of science would raise serious political issues by sharply focusing on the autonomy and cultural authority of the sciences. The concern to uphold the political autonomy and cultural authority of successful scientific practice is part of the modernist legacy of logical positivism, which had always claimed the epistemic and cultural primacy of mathematical physics by asserting that mathematics exemplifies the very structure of rational thought, and that our sense experience can be the only basis for knowledge of the world.9

---

7 For a more detailed discussion on the problem of modernity see: Robert B. Pippin, *Modernism as a Philosophical Problem or the Dissatisfactions of European High Culture,* (Oxford: Blackwell, 1991) esp. the Introduction.

8 H.P.P. Lotter, "A Postmodern Philosophy of Science," *South African journal of Philosophy,* 13, No. 3, (1994), p. 160.

9 Wentzel van Huyssteen, *Theology and the justification of Faith: Constructing Theories in Systematic Theology*, (Wm. B. Eerdmans Publishing,

Those who advocate postmodern philosophy of science versus this modernist version argue that, postmodern philosophy of science, on the other hand, realizes that science must be understood as a historically dynamic process in which there are conflicting and competing paradigm theories, research programs, and research traditions.10 This important fact reveals that the reasons, arguments, and value-judgments employed by the community of scientists are fundamentally related to, or grounded in, social practices. In this account, the very criteria and norms that guide scientific activity thus become open and vulnerable to criticism, as does in fact the idea of philosophy of science itself. Postmodern philosophy of science in this mode rejects any attempts at legitimating science by means of grand narratives,11 and urges scientists to resolve philosophical issues pertinent to their work themselves, or to follow the NOA's third way.12

The emergence of postmodernism in the domains of science and philosophy of science may of course be said simply to reflect intellectual currents in the Western High Culture, 13 but even so it presents a sharp refusal of the uncritical reliance on modern science, and in particular the prime pillars of modern ideas of objectivity and progress. However, the postmodern camp is not as unified as is sometimes claimed, especially in relation to politics. Zuzana Parusnikova, a la Calvin O. Schrag, who talk about antireason postmodernists, 14 distinguishes between deconstructive

---

1989), pp. 3-10; also Joseph Rouse, "The Politics of Postmodern Philosophy of Science," *Philosophy of Science,* 58, (1991), pp. 607-627.

10 Richard J. Bernstein, *Beyond Objectivism and Relativism* (Philadelphia: University of Pennsylvania Press, 1983), p. 171 and onward.

11 Arthur Fine, "Unnatural Attitudes: Realist and Instrumentalist Attachments to Science," *Mind,* vol. 95, (1986), pp. 147-179.

12 This way, as Fine defines it, (and in so doing deprives us from any comprehensive picture and eschews any further discussions on the relations between science and worldview and the impact of scientific ethos on issues like Ultimate Reality and Existential Concerns-and [he reversal impact of these concerns on science as an attitude towards life, not just in biological terms but *sociological* realms.) is a *radical* deflationism that eschews additions and attachments to science (*See ibid.,* p. 177).

13 See: Robert B. Pippin, *Modernism as a Philosophical Problem: on the Dissatisfactions of European High Culture*. The most intriguing part of his discussion, in my view, is the relation between this dissatisfaction and what he calls *German Homesickness.* What distinguish the German tradition which he calls *Kant-Heidegger Cycle* from its British or French counterpart are the very preoccupations of German thinkers with the idea of *Modern; t*he very relation of a modern epoch to the human ideals of freedom and its realization.

14 Calvin O. Schrag, "Rationality between Modernity and Postmodernity," Stephen K. White, ed., *Lifeworld and Politics: Between Modernity and Postmodernity* (Notre Dame, Indiana: University of Notre Dame Press, 1989), p. 86.

postmodernists and other branches of postmodernists, 15 an idea that is developed by Pauline Marie Rosenau where she distinguishes between two broad strands within the current debate on postmodernism: affirmative and skeptical postmodernism. 16 In either strand, one can see that the abandonment of the Grand Narrative has brought down commitment to any coherent idea, such as Socialism, Freedom, Justice, or for that matter, the very idea of Reality. In this camp, regardless of its affirmation or skepticism, what is of importance and counts is Discourse, which undermines the very idea of scientific truth, rationality, and objectivity. 17

Among those who reject the idea of modernist philosophy of science and at the same time do not yield to postmodernism as a new philosophy for the scientific enterprise, one should mention Joseph Rouse. He rejects the very idea of the philosophical project of globally legitimating scientific knowledge, not just its current versions, but much of recent discussions within sociology of science-which stands as a counterpoint to philosophical and popular images of science as a model of rational, truth-approximated inquiry.18 Like Arthur Fine, Rouse and his agenda belongs to that group of philosophers, historians and sociologists of science who view that the methods of science themselves are not unitary. This can be seen in Dudley Shapere's argument that science has developed into independent domains, in the new philosophy of experiment advocated by Ian Hacking and Peter Galison, in which experiment has a life of its own independent of theory, in Arthur Fine's advocating of an antiessentialist view of science as a way of getting beyond debates over realism, in John Dupre's pluralistic metaphysics, and in Thomas Nickles's claim that scientists concern themselves only with domain-specific methods. These discussions proposed by these authors constitute part of the wider debate which takes the issues within rationalism versus relativism and attempts to take the debate beyond both rationalist and relativist views of science. 19 They agree with

---

15 Zuzana Parusnikova, "Is a Postmodern Philosophy of Science Possible?" *Studies in History and Philosophy of Science,* vol. 23, No. I, (1992), pp. 21-37. In her view a postmodern philosophy of science is an oxymoron, and to fuse philosophy and science in a postmodern frame of reference is a modern idea which contradicts the purpose of postmodernism. See her tentative answer in p. 36.

16 P. M. Rosenau, *Postmodernism and Social Science* (1992) 17 Christopher Norris, "Truth, Science, and the Growth of Knowledge,"
New Left Review, 210, (1995), p. 118.

18 Joseph Rouse, "The Narrative Reconstruction of Science," *Inquiry,* 33, (1991), pp. 179-196.

19 See: *The Disunity of Science: Boundaries, Contexts, and Power,* eds. Peter Galison and David J. Stump, (1996), esp. the Afterword by David J. Stump; regarding Peter Galison see History, "Philosophy, and the Central Metaphor," *Science in Context,* 2, 1, (1988), pp. 197-212; regarding Thomas Nickles see: *Philosophy of Science and History of Science,* (OSIRIS, 1995), 10, pp.139-163; last but not least is Ian Hacking, *Representing and Intervening:*

sociologists of science who demonstrate the inadequacy of philosophical interpretations of science by introducing empirical sociological studies of scientific practice, but condemn their conclusion that science is in need of a global philosophical legitimation.20 In Rouse words, the sociologists who adopt an ironic stance seem too thoroughly indebted to the philosophical views which they are apparently so anxious to reject. The irony, he argues, is that this tacitly presupposes the modernist dichotomy: either a grand narrative of rational legitimation or else irrationality, relativism, or the multiplication of world-views. 21 My critique on Rouse et. al. is twofold. What he takes for the strength of the California School22 is actually the base of the shortcoming of an excellent critique which could prove decisive in the debate between realists versus empiricists. However, the flaw in Rouse's account is related to his denial of the need to connect the local to the global, or the individual to the whole. This connective attempt is a sine qua non not just for science, but for the purduit of all human knowledge. Rouse et al take this general feature of human approach to the knowledge for a modernist construction and by denying one, deprive us from the other too. Besides, if one accepts, as Rouse does, that the scientific activity is situated within differing social domains and constitutes a collective which is related to the politics of nation state-system, then one cannot go any further via their accounts in relation to issues such as Socialism, Freedom, or Dialogue. The second point is related to Rouse' critique of sociologists. He takes the multiplication of world views as equivalent to irrationalism or relativism. In my view, what these sociologists of science argue could be termed a critique of those who take the scientific rationalism as the only translation of Human Reason. This debate is parallel to the language debate which takes language as the only frame of reason. As far as the linguistic debate is concern, the proponents of 'discourse is all' are wrong because language is just one attribution of Human Reason. When it comes to Rouse and the multiplication of worldviews, I should argue that this is an empirical issue, and the 'rationality' could and should be assessed on an empirical basis. In other words, the problem of Rationality and Scientific Rationality are part of the current debate among those who take Rationality as a matter of emergence versus the proponents of invention.23

Introductory Topics in the Philosophy of Natural Science (Cambridge University Press, 1983).

20 Joseph Rouse, "The Politics of Postmodern Philosophy of Science," *Philosophy of Science,* 58, (1991), p. 93.

21 Ibid., p. 194.

22 The stance presented and vehemently defended by Arthur Fine who sees the philosophical explication of science as an attachment to scientific *local* activity. See his article: "Unnatural Attitudes: Realist and Instrumentalist Attachments to Science," *Mind,* vol. 95, (1986), pp. 147-179.

23 See Ronald Curtis, "Institutional Individualism and The Emergence Of Scientific Rationality, " *Studies in History and Philosophy of Science,* vol. 20,

The postmodern critique, if taken in its ethical aspect and as an internal affair within modernity could prove useful. But if this critique is taken as an epistemological commitment which defies any logic or coherence, then the very notion of human knowledge, regardless of its locality or globality, would be in grave danger. I agree with postmodernist when they take the ethical and political aspects of science as problematic dimensions of knowledge enterprise, but disagree with what they propose in the realm of epistemology and ontology. Besides, it would be uninteresting to have a science which would take us to Mars but would not allow us to ask about its reality, due to Giere's, Suppe's or van Fraassen's philosophy of science which downplays the role of universal laws and focuses instead on models that may be applied to individual systems.24

However, whatever, the shortcoming of Logical Empiricism, one should agree that the very notion of Logic existed prior to their cultural appearance and their demise should not be equaled to the demise of logic as such. Besides, what makes the knowledge pursuit such an important pursuit is the very ability to connect the parts and make a whole and total view. Of course, our views and total pictures run the risk to be incomplete and sometimes wrong, but this should not be interpreted as the demise of the pursuit as such. Whether, one likes or dislike, the total pictures are part and parcel of human social life and an inevitable category which we as humans cannot escape from. In other words, if those who are engaged with science, meaning a systematic approach to reality regardless of its realm, take the issue of total picture seriously in a rigorous scientific manner, then the

---

No. 1, (1989), pp. 77-113. However, I should mention that I do not agree with Curtis in all aspects. Is 'Rationality' a matter of emergence or invention, cannot be solved ala Popper. Why? Because, even one assumes that 'rationality' is a matter of invention and then re-discovery, one cannot solve this on a philosophical way - but it is an empirical issue and should be investigated historically. However, this mistake on the side of Popperians does not give any credit to Curtis revisionist Polanyitism. Why? Because he rules out the external and sociological impact on the emergence of 'Rationality' due to his naïve conception of'externalism' which is equivalent, a la Lakatos, to 'irrational'. This problem, as in the case of Rouse, should be connected to the research on Scientific Revolution and investigated in a historical manner. Further on The Scientific revolution see Wilbur Applebaum's article: "Epistemological and Political Implications of the Scientific Revolution," *Science, Pseudo-Science and Utopianism in Early Modern Thought,* ed. Stephen A. McKnight, (Columbia: University of Missouri Press, 1992).

24 R.N. Giere, *Explaining Science: A Cognitive Approach* (Chicago, London: University of Chicago Press, 1988); F. Suppe, *The Semantic Conception of Theories and Scientific Realism* (University of Illinois Press, 1989); B.C. van Fraassen, *Laws and Symmetry* (Oxford: Clarendon Press, 1989); R.N. Giere, Essay Review, "Interpreting The Philosophy of Science," *Studies in History and Philosophy of Science,* vol. 22, No. 3, (1991), pp. 515523.

international community could avoid talking about the shortcomings of nationalism, and scientists could instead focus on internationalism and its would-be implications. In the recent history of social ideas, one can discern the emergence of some universal ideas which were discredited due to their impracticality or alleged inconsistency: ideas like Socialism, Internationalism, Cosmopolitanism, and so on. However, the alleged shortcomings of these ideas were not assessed on their own basis, but related to the practice of nation-state-system, even as the full workability of this system were not permitted to function globally. The phenomena of Colonialism and Imperialism hampered the very international function of that incomplete nation-state system. What I mean is simple: if those who are scientifically engaged with the reality and its various realms and appearances, do not take the parts in relation to the whole and disregard the importance of vision, that does not bring about the end of ideology - but only brings this as a new ideology. In other words, if we do not discuss the significance of cosmopolitanism as a viable and coherent unit-idea, that does not necessarily prove the impracticality of this idea. It proves the dominance of unreason and the distortion of parochialism which wrongly is related to the impossibility of having any logical stance to assess the consistency of a thought-system. However, the idea of logic, meaning the very way of finding a coherent frame to reach outside and assess the credibility of this search, should not be compromised in the name of the demise of Logical Empiricism.

CONCLUSION

If one reduces the gigantic complex of modern philosophy and metatheoretical assumptions of secular science to a few fundamental axiomatic principles one can discern that the Ultimate background assumptions of these fundamental principles, which constitute the very pillars of modern philosophy, is the idea of 'Demonstrability'. In its metaphysical sense the idea of 'Demonstrability' is aligned with notion of mathematicalization of principles of Reality within the sensible and rational domains.

When the order of Reality is taken into metaphysical consideration the fine line between 'mathematicalization' and 'quantification' in relation to 'Quality' is drawn with great metaphysical care for fear of violation of First Principles. However once these considerations and concerns lose their metaphysical endorsement within the intellectual tradition, then the criterion of one level of empirical reality wrongly turns to replace all essential criteria and the notion of 'Reduction' wrongly takes the position of an independent philosophical perspective sui generis. All aspects of modern philosophy of sciences, regardless of the realm of its application (natural or social), display a unanimous front vis-à-vis Transcendental Philosophy, which is based on a 'Hierarchical View of Reality' and is profoundly antiReductionist in its very metaphysical grounds. The notion of demonstration is a valid criterion within the Transcendental Philosophy too but the very way of application of this conceptual tool fundamentally differs from the modern approach by keeping in mind that each level of Reality has its particular mode of demonstration. 'Borhan' (Proof), that one employs within Transcendental Philosophy (in Islamic Tradition), could be: 'Borhan Enni' (posteriori demonstration): 'Borhan Etqan Sonn' (argument from design), 'Borhan Aqli' (intellectual proof), 'Borhan Lemmi' (causal proof), 'Borhan Kholf' (proof by reductio ad absurdum) and 'Borhan Kaoni' (cosmological proof). How these all could be different from the secular philosophy of science are issues which are going to be addressed in my forthcoming essay on Metaphysics and anti-Metaphysics in Modern Philosophy and Transcendental Philosophy.

CHAPTER VII

TECHNOLOGY ASSESSMENT AND ITS RELATIONS TO PHILOSOPHY: INTRODUCTION AND OVERVIEW

Technology Assessment (TA) constitutes a scientific and societal response to problems at the interface between technology and society (Bechmann et al. 2007; Grunwald 2009). It has emerged against the background of various experiences pertaining to the unintended and often undesirable side effects of science, technology, and technicisation which, in modern times, can sometimes assume extreme proportions (Grunwald 2010).

What characterises TA as specific type of research is its combination of knowledge production (concerning the development, consequences, and conditions for implementing technology), the evaluation of this knowledge from a societal perspective, and the recommendations made to politics and society. TA is thus both interdisciplinary and transdisciplinary and in accordance with its research methods, it can be classified as a "post-normal science" (Funtowicz/Ravetz, 1993), showing the following specific properties (following Grunwald 2009):

Knowledge for Action and Decision-Making: TA supports public opinion and public participation in decisions on science and technology. In this endeavour, it aims at embedding TA knowledge and orientations into the perspective of decision makers: TA knowledge is knowledge for those who are to be advised. Because decisions always affect the future, a reference to the future is always included. TA always functions ex ante with regard to decisions.

Side Effects: In TA, it is a matter of combining "comprehensive" decision support with the widest possible contemplation of the spectrum of foreseeable or presumable effects. Beyond classical decision theory, which establishes the relationship between goals and means according to the viewpoint of efficiency, TA turns its attention to unintentional side effects as a constitutive characteristic (Bechmann et al., 2007).

Uncertainty and Risk: Orientation to the future and the problems posed by side effects often lead to considerable uncertainty regarding TA knowledge. TA therefore always has to do with providing decision-making support in conjunction with complex innovations under conditions of uncertainty. The impact of such decisions is difficult to predict.

Value-Relatedness: The rationality of decisions not only depends on knowledge about the systems involved and of the available action-guiding knowledge, but also on the basic normative principles. The disclosure and analysis of the normative positions involved is therefore also an aspect of the TA advisory service (e.g. depending on ethical reflection or sustainability evaluations (Grunwald, 2009)).

TA contributes to problem-solving, but does not pretend to provide actual solutions. TA provides knowledge, orientation, or procedures on how to cope with certain problems at the interface between technology and society but it is neither able nor legitimized to solve these problems. Only society can do this, through its institutions and its decision-making processes, e.g. in parliaments and governmental bodies. The main objectives of this paper are

• to introduce the main motivations of TA and its development (Sec. 2),

• to give a brief overview about different roles of TA in different fields of actors influencing technology development (Sec. 3)

• and - this is the main part of the paper - to analyse the relations between TA and philosophy. There are strong relations with applied ethics but also with epistemology, political theory and anthropology (Sec. 4)

At the end of the paper some brief remarks are made on the status of TA reached so far in Europe.

MOTIVATIONS OF TECHNOLOGY ASSESSMENT

In the twentieth century, the importance of science and technology in almost all areas of society (touching on economic growth, health, the army, etc.) has grown dramatically. Concomitant with this increased significance, the consequences of science and technology for society and the environment have become increasingly serious. Technological progress alters social traditions, fixed cultural habits, relations of humans and nature, collective and individual identities and concepts of the self while calling into question traditional ethical norms. Decisions concerning the pursual or abandonment of various technological paths, regulations and innovation programs, new development plans, or the phasing-out of lines of technology often have farreaching consequences for development. They can influence competition in relation to economies or careers, trigger or change the direction of flows of raw materials and waste, influence power supplies and long-term security, create acceptance problems, fuel technological conflict, challenge value systems and even affect human nature (Habermas 2001).

Since the 1960s also adverse effects of scientific and technical innovations became obvious some of them were of dramatic proportions: accidents in technical facilities (Chernobyl, Bhopal, Fukushima), threats to the natural environment (air and water pollution, ozone holes, climate change), negative health effects as in the asbestos case, social and cultural side effects (e.g., labour market problems caused by pro-ductivity gains) and the intentional abuse of technology (the attacks on the World Trade

Centre). The experience with such unexpected and serious impacts of technology is central to TA's motivation. Indeed, in many cases, it would have been desirable to have been warned about the disasters in advance, either to prevent them, or to be in a position to undertake compensatory measures. This explains why the methodologically quite problematic term "early warning" with regard to technological impacts (Bechmann 1994) has always had a prominent place in TA discussions from the very beginning (Paschen/Petermann, 1991, p. 26).

Early warning is a necessary precondition to make societal and political precautionary action possible: how can a society which places its hopes and trust in innovation and progress, and must continue to do so in the future, protect itself from undesirable, possibly disastrous side effects, and how can it preventatively act to cope with possible future adverse effects? Classic problems of this type are, for example, the use and release of new chemicals - the catastrophic history of asbestos use being a good example (Gee/Greenberg, 2002) - and dealing with artificial or technically modified organisms (for further examples, cf. Harremoes et al. 2002). In order to be able to cope rationally with these situations of little or no certain knowledge of the effects of the use of technology, prospective precautionary research and corresponding procedures for societal risk management are required, for instance by implementing the precautionary principle (von Schomberg, 2005).

Parallel to these developments, broad segments of Western society were deeply unsettled by the "Limits of Growth" (Club of Rome) in the 1970s which, for the first time, addressed the grave environmental problems perceived as a side effect of technology and technicisation. The optimistic pro-progress assumption that whatever was scientifically and technically new would definitely benefit the individual and society was questioned. As of the 1960s deepened insight into technological ambivalence led to a crisis of orientation in the way society dealt with science and technology. Without this (persistent!) crisis TA would presumably never have developed.

New and additional motivations entered the field of TA over the past decades from which the most relevant seem to be:

- issues of democracy and technocracy, or of democratizing technology (von Schomberg 1999): from the 1960s on there are concerns that the scientific and technological advance could threaten the functioning of democracy because only few experts were capable of really understanding the complex technologies. The technocracy hypothesis was born painting a picture of a future society where experts would make the decisions with respect to their own value systems. One of the many origins of TA is to counteract and to enable and empower society to take active roles in democratic deliberation (Joss/Belucci 2002, Grunwald 2003).
- the experience of technology conflicts and of legitimacy deficits and little acceptance of some decisions on technology motivated TA to think about a more socially compatible technology. The very idea was to design

technology ac-cording to social values - and if this would succeed, so the hope, problems of rejection or non-acceptance would no longer occur at all.

- in the past decade the innovation problems of Western societies influenced also motivations and driving forces of TA. TA was considered part of regional and national innovation systems (Smits/ten Hertog 2007) which could contribute to "responsible innovation" and "responsible development" (Siune et al. 2009) by taking into account not only technical and economical but also social and ethical aspects.

- shift in the societal communication on new and emerging science and technology (NEST): techno-visionary sciences such as nanotechnology, converging technologies and synthetic biology entered the arena. Visions and metaphors mark the expected revolutionary advance of science in general and became an important factor in societal debates. To provide for more rationality, reflexivity and transparency in these debates, vision assessment was proposed (Grunwald 209b) as a new TA tool addressing not directly the assessment of technologies but rather the assessment of visions (Grin/Grunwald 2000).

- finally, recent debates around ethics in the field of biomedicine (e.g. stem cell research, xeno-transplantation, reproduction medicine) led to a convergence of applied ethics and TA in some regard and complemented the agenda of TA by issues of bioethics and medical ethics.

Compared to the initial phase of TA a considerable increase of its diversity and complexity can be observed. In modern TA, it is often not only a question of the consequences of individual technologies, products, or plants, but frequently of complex conflict situations between enabling technologies, innovation potentials, fears and concerns, patterns of production and consumption, lifestyle and culture, and political and strategic decisions.

TECHNOLOGY ASSESSMENT IN DIFFERENT SOCIETAL FIELDS OF ACTION

Different TA approaches have been proposed and practised responding to the societal context and to elements of technology governance, e.g. participative TA (Joss/Belucci 2002), constructive TA (CTA, Rip et al. 1995), interactive TA (Grin et al. 1997), TA relying on innovation systems research (Smits/ten Hertog 2007), and others. Many of them are related to a systems analytical point of view and methodology (Gorokhov 2004). On the one hand the differentiation is due to different questions each of them is suited to address, on the other it is due to different basic distinctions and assumptions about technology governance which relate directly to images and models of the technological evolution, the role of the state or the market in modern societies, how shaping of technology should work in democracies etc. In this Section I would like to present a separation of TA according to different fields of action and different groups of actors involved at different places in the overall technology governance: (1) TA as policy advice, (2) TA in public debate and (3) TA in engineering contexts.

TA for Policy Advice

The undoubted fact that technology and innovation development is definitely mainly taking place in the industry under market conditions does not exclude or diminish the relevance of political influence on technology. In a thought experiment we could distinguish between different aspects of technological products or systems: aspects bound to political reasoning (environmental norms, safety regulations, technical standardizations, general statutory provisions, etc.) and aspects which could be delegated to market developments. The relation between both may differ in the individual cases: the difference will be much bigger in ethically and politically relevant questions than in the optimization of the marginal benefit of established technologies. Policy-advising TA only covers technology aspects which are subject to policy, like safety and environmental standards, the protection of citizens against encroachment on their civil rights, the setting of priorities in research policy, the definition of framework conditions for innovations, etc. This is exactly where the largest part of policy-advising TA is taking place.

Parliamentary TA is part of TA with a tradition of decades and with diverse forms of institutionalisation (Cruz-Castro/Sanz-Menendez 2004). It is about advising parliamentary actors within the frameworks based on the respective structures of the nation state. Parliamentary TA as a subcategory of policy-advising TA presupposes that parliaments play a crucial or at least an important and relevant role in technology governance: necessary assumption is that parliamentary action is relevant for technology governance. It is obvious that this assumption is facing problems since the role of parliaments in democratic decision processes is often categorized as declining, sometimes as hardly noticeable any more. The possibilities of parliamentary TA are not only limited by the restricted role of the state in technology governance, but also by the restricted role of parliaments in the distribution of power in democratic systems. If TA is institutionalized in parliaments, its influence also depends on the respective institutional setting. In an analysis of the roles of parliamentary TA in technology governance based on a theory of institutions, a variety of possible combinations of different institutional configurations occurs (CruzCastro/Sanz-Menendez 2004), which is also enriched by the characteristics of the democratic institutions of a nation state and various political traditions (Vig/Paschen 1999).

TA In Public Debate - Conflicts and Participation

Conflicts are characteristic of decisions in the field of technology, while consensus tends to constitute the exception. Making decisions in such conflict situations often results in problems of legitimation because there will be winners (who profit from specific decisions) and losers. This is frequently the case when decisions must be made about the site of a technical facility such as a nuclear power plant, a waste disposal plant or a large chemical production plant. Depending on the selected location, people in the direct neighbourhood will have to accept more disadvantages than others. Problems of legitimation always surface when the distribution of advantages and disadvantages is unequal.

In view of the decades of experience with a number of very serious acceptance problems and certain grave conflicts over technology it has become clear that the question of legitimation is obviously important. Many examples can be given such as: opposition to nuclear power, the problem of expanding airports, establishing new infrastructure elements such as highways or railway connections, the problem of how to dispose of radioactive waste, the release of genetically modified plants, the Strategic Defence Initiative ("Star Wars", SDI), and regional and local conflicts on waste disposal sites, waste incineration plants, and the location of chemical processing facilities. In these areas, political decisions are sometimes not accepted by those affected or by the general public, even though they are the result of democratic decision-making procedures. Conflict regulation and prevention are of highest importance and a subject for TA in its history.

Since the very beginnings of TA, there has been repeated demand for participative orientation, frequently following normative ideas from the fields of deliberative democracy or discourse ethics (Barber 1984). According to these normative ideas assessment and evaluation of technology should be left neither to the scientific experts (ex-pertocracy) nor to the political deciders (decisionism) (see Habermas 1970 on this distinction). It is the task of participative TA to include societal groups stake-holders, affected citizens, non-experts, and the public in general - in assessing technology and its consequences. In this manner, participative TA procedures are deemed to improve the practical and political legitimacy of decisions on technology. Such TA is informed and advised by science and experts and, in addition, by people and groups external to science and politics (Renn/Webler 1998, Joss/Bellucci 2002).

The participation of citizens and of those affected is believed to improve the knowledge basis as well as the values fundament on which judgements are based and decisions are made. "Local" knowledge, with which experts and decision-makers are often not familiar, is to be used in order to achieve the broadest possible knowledge base and to substantiate decisions. This discernibly applies especially to local and regional technological problems, in particular, to questions of location. Furthermore, in a deliberative democracy, it is necessary to take the interests and values of ideally all those participating and affected into consideration in the decision-making process. Participation should make it possible for decisions on technology to be accepted by a larger spectrum of society despite divergent normative convictions. In the end, this will also improve the robustness of such decisions and enhance their legitimacy. Several approaches and methods have been developed and applied in the recent years, such as consensus conferences, citizens' juries, and focus groups (Joss/Belucci 2002; Decker/Ladikas 2004).

TA for Shaping Technology

In the engineering sciences, the challenges with which TA is confronted have been discussed as demands on the profession of engineers. The value dimension of technology has been shown in many case studies, especially in engineering design processes (van de Poel 2009). Decisions on technology design involve value judgements. In this respect there is, in other words, a close relationship between TA on the one side and professional engineering ethics and the ethics of technology on the other.

TA is one of a number of activities that provide orientation and support societal opinion-forming and political decision-making. Within the various approaches which can be subsumed under the social constructivist paradigm, the impact of those activities is primarily seen in the field of technology itself: ethical reflection aims to contribute to the technology paths, products and systems to be developed (Yoshinaka et al. 2003). Theory-based approaches of shaping technology have been proposed, for example by means of constructive technology assessment (CTA, Rip et al. 1995) or variations of social construction of technology (Bijker/Law 1994). They have introduced strong claims for influencing technology by reflecting its social role and its consequences in the debate. The central message is that a 'better' technology could be designed and constructed by using SST and CTA or other social constructivist approaches. The overall aim "to achieve better technology in a better society" (Schot/Rip 1997) shall be realised by looking at the very shape of technologies itself.

The basic assumption with CTA (which was developed in the Netherlands) is that TA meets with difficult problems of implementation and effectiveness whenever it concerns itself with the impacts of a technology after the latter has been developed or is even already in use (Rip et al. 1995). According to the Control Dilemma (Collingridge 1980), once the impacts are relatively well-known, the chances of influencing them will significantly decrease because that knowledge will only be available in the later stages of development. It would therefore be more effective to accompany the process of the development of a technology constructively. The origin of technological impact is traced back to the development phase of a technology and the many decisions to be taken there so that dealing with the consequences of technology becomes a responsibility that already starts in the technology design phase. CTA argues for the early and broad participation of societal actors, including key economic players, users and people affected in these early stages. In the normative respect, CTA builds on a basis of deliberative democracy with a liberal picture of the state putting emphasis on self-organising processes in the marketplace.

TECHNOLOGY ASSESSMENT AND PHILOSOPHY

All the various questions regarding TA concepts, methodology and content are linked to philosophy (Grunwald 2009, Gorokhov 2007). In terms of all the normative questions that have a bearing on technological evaluation and technological design, there are close ethics of technology ties (Grunwald 1999), as well as links with the respective branches of applied ethics (e.g., bioethics, medical ethics, information ethics). Questions on the validity of the available knowledge are relevant to the philosophy of science, especially in conjunction with scientific controversy, the ratio of knowledge to non-knowledge, and the divergent interpretations of the societal implications of scientific knowledge (as currently, for instance, exemplified in neuroscience). Normative and epistemic questions (knowledge and values) are often interwoven, like for instance, when it comes to the application and consequences of the precautionary principle (Harremoes et al., 2002). Many TA topics are, furthermore, pertinent to the philosophy of technology or are anthropologically relevant, such as questions regarding the man-machine interface, the substitutability of human beings by robots, the increasing degree to which living beings are being penetrated by technology, or the "technical enhancement" of human beings (Roco/Bainbridge 2002, Grunwald 2007). TA even has been regarded as applied philosophy of technology (Gorokhov 2007, p. 270ff.).

Issues for the philosophy and ethics of technology relevant to TA manifest themselves in normative uncertainties as they result from the development, use, and disposal of new science and technology. These general issues include, for example, human rights, the ban on human instrumentalization, the principle of self-determination regarding personal information, and informed consent. Normative uncertainties regarding technology appear above all in several cross-cutting issues (discussed in the following sections) that appear in probably all debates on technology. These topics are (1) the safeguarding of human autonomy, (2) the problem of dis tributive justice, (3) the relationship between technology and the environment, (4) the relation between technology and life and (5) the necessity of dealing with the uncertainties of our knowledge of the consequences.

Human Autonomy Versus Technization

Advances in science and technology lead, according to many interpretations, to an expansion of man's opportunities for acting. This increases human autonomy by creating the possibility to select among several different options. The flip side is that technological progress can also remove previous options or make them less accessible. For example, in a technologically perfected world the life of a handicapped person might get less appreciation. It is also possible that technological systems might force adjustments, limiting our freedom of choice and thus an individual's autonomy. Self-determination regarding information, a part of an individual's autonomy, can be limited by technology, just as technological means can be used to achieve external controls over humans. In particular, the word "technicalization" is frequently associated with a subordination of man under technology, a loss of control, a discontent caused by man's dependence on technology, and a loss of individuality, emotionality, and spontaneity. Finally, the relationship between technology and human autonomy also concerns the question of how far technology can be formed or whether it follows its own dynamics, forcing society to adapt (Dolata/Werle 2007). The relationship between human autonomy and technical progress is ambivalent.

Distributive Justice

The distribution of new opportunities provided by technology, such as regarding affluence and health, as well as of the possible but unintended consequences for persons and groups, does not correspond per se to the accepted standards of fairness. This leads to debates and normative uncertainties. The persons who benefit from a technology are for example often different from those potentially affected by the possible risks. This leads to asymmetry in the distribution of opportunities and risks. The de facto distribution of risks and benefits in society that stem from technology - in a spatial and temporal sense and with regard to the groups affected frequently displays deficits in fairness caused above all by differences in affluence or power but also by decisions about locating something such as an atomic power plant, a garbage incineration plant, the route of a highway, or factories. Some of these problems of distribution arise locally as with the issues just mentioned, some regionally or nationally, and others globally with regard to problems of development (such as when hazardous waste is exported to third-world countries). One particular aspect is that of fair access to new technology, such as in relation to the supply of energy or of infor-mation, which is also a relevant issue for nanotechnology (Sec. 5.3).

One aspect that is particularly important in this context is the problem of assuming responsibility for future generations. The consequences of technology often reach unforeseeably far in the future, as with the problem of establishing a final repository for radioactive waste or in the relevance to tomorrow's climate of the technology used today. The degree to which we today can compel future generations to tolerate the consequences of technological activity is a matter of controversial discussion in the ethics of technology (Jonas 1979; Brown-Weiss 1989).

Technology and the Environment

Our natural environment is being changed to a large degree by technical innovations. Technology needs natural resources, which are thus taken away from the environment. Technology's use of these resources leads to emissions and waste, which in turn has consequences for ecosystems. Technology and innovation are among the factors that substantially determine the degree of sustainable development on the part of the way the human economy functions. The relationship between technology and sustainable development is ambivalent as a matter of principle. On the one hand, technology is viewed as a problem for sustainable development and as the cause of many environmental problems; on the other hand, it is seen as the solution for problems of sustainability or at least as one component of the solution. In view of the further growing global population and the legitimate need for development in the poorer and emerging countries to help them catch up, it is impossible to imagine steps in the direction of sustainable development without innovative and more sustainable technology. The question is not whether technical progress works for or against sustainability, but rather how the scientific-technical progress would have to be organized for its consequences to be positive contributions to sustainable development. Issues from the ethics of technology in this context are closely linked with questions of environmental ethics (Rolston 1988) and sustainable development (WCED 1987).

Technology and Life

Classically, the ethics of technology has been concerned with artifacts of engineering technology (e.g., Ropohl 1996). The scientifictechnical development of the past decades has however begun to make the traditional border between inanimate technology and the realm of the living more permeable. One aspect of this is that technical interventions in the sphere of molecular biology have led to genetic engineering, which cannot be understood as a classical (natural) science but as technology or a technoscience (Latour 1995). The recent debate referred to this under the keyword biofacts (Karafyllis 2006). Another aspect is that in nanotechnology, or more precisely in nanobiotechnology, the approaches to transcend the classical borders go substantially further, extending even to the visions of a synthetic biology (Chap. 8). The eli-mination of these borders is a challenge to established ideas of morality, which for example speak of living beings as being "God's creatures," since artificially produced living beings would be man's creatures. It raises new questions as to the paths of development and possible risks since artificially produced or technologically modified life would develop further according to the principles of self-organization and could possibly reproduce and get out of control.

Uncertainty of Our Knowledge of the Consequences

Large technical systems such as energy plants or infrastructure systems, new cross-cutting technologies such as nanotechnology but also control measures or support for research are marked by high complexity, poor prognosticability of the intended consequences, and the frequent presence of unintended consequences. The development and introduction of new technology and also attempts to influence them thus pose an act in a state of uncertainty and risk. With regard to the risks caused by decisions on technology policy or the direct use of technology, the ethics of technology is concerned with the normative basis of the questions as to how, to what degree, for which reasons, and under which conditions society can be expected to tolerate them. This is all the more true since precisely conflicts over technology and normative uncertainties are triggered by the question as to which risk is acceptable under which conditions (cf. nuclear energy, genetic technology, radiation, the hole in the ozone layer etc.). The epistemological uncertainty regarding the consequences contains a moral dimension, which Hans Jonas formulated very pointedly in forming the question of whether the entirety can be made "a bet as part of a wager" (Jonas 1979, pp. 78f.).

All these issues gave raise to propose the concept of an "explorative philosophy" (Grunwald 2010b, 2011) which addresses features, properties and impacts of new and emerging science and technology (NEST) possibly relevant to philosophy. Explorative philosophy is concerned with very early and in part unavoidably speculative evaluations of new developments in science and technology and of their consequences for man and society. As such, it is in no way supposed to provide orientation for action in areas of concrete development. Its task is to prepare for possible coming debates in a conceptual, theoretical, and methodological sense as well as with a view to basic distinctions and relationships from the philosophy of technology and anthropology such as man-technology, life-technology, or naturetechnology. Such an explorative philosophy would comprise (without claiming full coverage of the field) the following sub-disciplines which were discussed at the occasion of nanotechnology and the related challenges to philosophy (taken from Grunwald 2011):

Epistemology. The emergence of nanotechnology has raised expectations of a new unity in science (Roco/Bainbridge 2002). Following these expectations, nanoscience - as the science of "shaping the world atom by atom" - should integrate the former classical disciplines of physics, chemistry, biology, and the engineering sciences into a new type of science. Obviously, these projections challenged the philosophy of science and philosophical epistemology in order to uncover the underlying assumptions of those expectations and to question the conditions of their validity. The assumptions can be traced back to a naturalistic understanding of atoms as something similar to bricks or stones in the macroscopic world. "Shaping the world atom by atom" would then mean building new structures from atoms in complete analogy to building systems from macroscopic elements such as bricks. Epistemological reasoning has questioned the validity of this simple analogy and the "atomic reductionism" behind it.

Nano Anthropology: The Relationship Between Humans and Technology. Nanobiotechnology is emerging at the interface between biotechnology and nanotechnology. It bridges the gap between inanimate and animate nature, and aims at combining biological modules at the molecular level as well as producing functional building blocks on a nanoscale that might include technical materials, interfaces, and bounding surfaces (Schmid et al. 2006). The point of departure is the fundamental belief that life processes take place on the nanoscale because the essential building blocks of life are just this size (for example, proteins and DNA). The processes in a cell can be analyzed with nanotechnological methods and possibly rendered technologically utilizable. In nanobiotechnology, the language of mechanical engineering is employed to describe the mechanisms and parts of cells: cells and their organelles are interpreted as micro- or nanomachines. Literally speaking, we see nanotechnology infiltrate molecular biology, genetics, and neurophysiology, all of which are integrated under technical points of view. The nanotechnical (and possibly feasible) duplication of fundamental life processes is the essential prerequisite for crossing the borderline between technical and living systems.

In transferring this process to the relationship between humans and technology, speculation emerged about the convergence of humanity and technology. The concept of "cyborgs" as technically enhanced humans or as humanly enhanced technology can be raised. An aspect that frequently turns up in visions of nanotechnology is related to the borders between humans and technology and to the question of whether information or material can be passed from the one to the other. This aspect deeply affects our selfunderstanding and, consequently, our distinction between what a human being is and what he/she creates with the aid of technical achievements and applications. These developments - currently no more than a concept in spite of their widespread presence in the ethical discussion - obviously pose questions as to whether and to which extent this would increasingly place human beings in the realm of technology (Grunwald/Julliard 2007). The presence of such questions also indicates, however, the necessity of renewed reflection on our self-understanding as human beings and our relationship to technology.

Nanotechnology Hermeneutics: Philosophical Interpretations of Nanotechnology. The fascinating new opportunities of manipulating matter provided by nanotechnology but also the many visions about nanotechnology that are related to social issues have motivated thinking about the deeper changes in human civilization and its relationships to nature and technology. Roughly, three different positions have been expressed so far. First, there are assumptions that a new Baconian approach is arising. Nanotechnology - as "shaping the world atom by atom," to use a phrase from the National Nanotechnology Initiative - could be interpreted as a new manifestation of optimism by making everything appear to be technically possible. Second, the opposite story starts from the "enabling" character of nanotechnology and assumes creation of the greatest uncertainty imaginable: everything could be possible, and probably nothing could be controlled. The third story regards nanotechnology as a "cipher of the future" that serves as a catalyst for societal, philosophical, and scientific debates on issues such as the future relationship between humans and technology and the future of human nature in avoiding strong substantial claims about controllability or other issues.

* All of these fields - and there might be others, too - are speculative in a sense. Thinking about these issues nonetheless seems worthwhile even though no direct policy actions depend on their results. It is more for understanding what is at stake and at issue, a contribution to a "hermeneutics" of possibly changing elements of the human condition. In this way, explorative philosophy can prepare the groundwork for applied ethics and for the technology assessment of the developments when they become more concrete. Ultimately this promotes a democratic debate on scientific-technical progress by investigating alternative approaches to the future of humans and human society with or without different nanotechnology developments.

TECHNOLOGY ASSESSMENT IN A EUROPEAN PERSPECTIVE

The basic idea behind technology assessment (see Sec. 2) originated in the U.S. Congress in the 1960s. The Office of Technology (OTA) in Washington was an influential institution for decades in the United States (Bimber 1996). After several years that have seen TA decline in importance and visibility following the abolishment of the OTA in 1995, we are currently witnessing its renaissance. There is now renewed awareness at the political level, a new demand for TA on the part of companies and engineers, and increasing interest in the growing Asian economies. In addition, TA is increasingly involved in the development of a deliberative democracy and a civil society, mainly in the debates on technology-based futures and visions, and there is renewed interest in the social sciences and humanities. New concepts such as ethical, legal and social implications of technology (ELSI) or environment - health - safety (EHS) studies can be regarded as specifications of the basic idea of TA to particular ends and purposes. The growing field of ethical parallel research is a further indicator that can be interpreted as an outcome of earlier TA debates.

Without exaggeration it can be said that TA has well developed in the past decades in Europe. The largest part of TA worldwide is located in Europe which was one indicator to think about a "European model" of shaping the interface between science and technology on the one hand, and society on the other (Siune et al. 2009).

Already soon after the creation of the OTA several European countries started to discuss if similar institutions were needed in Europe as well and how they should be organized. However, it took considerable time until TA institutions were founded. Only in the second half of the 1980s did several European countries establish (mostly small) institutions for parliamentary technology assessment. Since then, the number of these institutions has been growing slowly but steadily.

The individual European countries established conceptually and organizationally different models of parliamentary technology assessment (Petermann/Scherz 2005; Cruz-Castro/Sanz-Menendez 2004; Vig/Paschen 1999). These institutions vary in their degrees of freedom and independence from parliament, e.g. regarding their right to choose their topics, different degrees of scientificity, different levels of importance of participation and effects on the public; some of them also vary considerably in their size and infrastructure, their access to processes of parliamentary advice, and their organizational embeddedness.

In 1990, parliamentary TA institutions teamed up to form the European Parliamentary Technology Assessment Network (EPTA, www.eptanetwork.org). EPTA is guided by the EPTA Council which consists of the directors of the TA institutions and the responsible Members of Parliament. The most prominent activity is an annual conference which is organized and hosted by the TA institute of the country that holds presidency at that time. Its aim is to exchange information, agree on new subjects, strengthen the cooperation, and recognize new transnational developments. During the last years, the European cooperation has been intensified. Parliamentary TA is traditionally oriented on national policy traditions and cultures; this includes the use of the respective national language and makes cross-border cooperation difficult. However, in the meantime a number of joint projects were carried out by EPTA members to identify a European perspective beyond national viewpoints on topics like genetically modified plants or the protection of privacy, a database has been set up which can quickly provide information on the research results of other EPTA members on a certain subject, and first externally funded projects were realized in the European Framework Programme (Joss/Belucci 2002; Decker/Ladikas 2004).

Descriptively, one can identify certain characteristics of a European Model, especially in contrast with the US. One clear difference derives from political cultures: the European commitment to the welfare state, and, linked to this, the acceptance of centralised governance. For science (and technology) this has implied that science (and later technology) policy was seen as an explicit and legitimate domain for national governments which is not the case in the US. The precautionary principle is a case of contention between the EU and the US. The EU decided to introduce the principle in 1999 and it is now part of regulation. Participation by citizens, while linked to democracy - which is the main thing in the US - is also seen as a way to improve policy. That also explains why TA in Europe was able to develop varieties of participatory TA.

To illustrate further complexity, consider Parliamentary Technology Assessment (PTA) offices. They were 'invented' in the United States, with the establishment of the Office of Technology Assessment by Congress in 1972, but they developed (later) mostly, and in interesting ways, in Europe. Their goals and tasks include the provision of many different types of science policy advice and to support informed deliberation, informing parliaments on questions of scientific and technological progress as well as on innovation aspects; preparing decision makers for future developments by foresight exercises; exploring political, especially parliamentary occasions for action or need for action; developing options for political action; and fostering public debate. Parliamentary TA has been implemented in most of the western and northern European countries for many years (in some, for more than 20 years), also in the European Parliament, in several Mediterranean countries and in some regional parliaments. The institutions form the EPTA network (www.eptanetwork.org) which has been growing (slowly) over the last years. Seen from an EU perspective there should be interest in supporting New Member States by systematically exploring the possibilities for PTA in those countries, with their specific needs, political and cultural traditions relevant to TA, available science and research potentials, etc. The PACITA project funded by the EU Commission was launched in 2011 to meet exactly this objective.

The European-model aspect has to do with how TA in Europe survived (while the US Office of Technology Assessment was abolished in 1995) and was able to develop varieties of participatory TA. By taking part in that movement, some Parliamentary TA Offices were able, eventually, to bridge parliamentary democracy and citizen participation in practice, at least to some extent, and thus contribute to 'deliberative democracy' (Joss/Belucci 2002, Decker/Ladikas 2004). For Europe, the move to transnational activities is important, like the EPTA Network itself, and the Meeting of Minds project which applied the approach of a consensus conference in parallel in nine European countries.

All of these SiS activities can be seen as articulating a European political and cultural identity. Thus, the European model is not just instrumentally important, as a good way to approach science-in-society issues, but also normatively important, as something that indicates what Europe desires to be, and might become.

REFERENCES

G. Banse; A.Grunwald; I. Hronszki; G. Nelson (eds.), 2011. *On Prospective Technology Studies*. Karlsruhe: KIT Scientific Publishing. B.R. Barber, 1984. *Strong Democracy. Participatory Politics for a New Age.* Berkeley: CA.

G. Bechmann, 1994. *Frühwarnung - die Achillesferse der TA?* Grunwald/Sax (eds.), pp. 88-100.

G. Bechmann, M. Decker, U. Fiedeler, B.-J. Krings. 2007. "Technology Assessment in a Complex World." *International Journal on Foresight and Innovation Policy 3*, pp. 6-27.

U. Beck,1986. *Risikogesellschaft. Auf dem Weg in eine andere Moderne.* Frankfurt.

W.E. Bijker, T.P. Hughes, T.J. Pinch (eds.), 1987. *The Social Construction of Technological Systems. New Directions in the Sociology and History of Technological Systems*. Cambridge: Mass.

W.E. Bijker, J. Law (eds.) 1994. *Shaping Technology/Building Society.* Cambridge: Mass.

B.A. Bimber, 1996. *The politics of expertise in Congress: the rise and fall of the Office of Technology Assessment.* New York.

N. Brown, B.Rappert, A.Webster (eds.), 2000. *Contested Futures. A sociology of prospective techno-science*. Burlington.

E. Brown-Weiss, 1989. *In Fairness to Future Generations. International Law, Common Patrimony and Intergenerational Equity.* New York D. Collingridge. 1980. *The Social Control of Technology*. New York L. Cruz-Castro, L. Sanz-Menendez, L. 2004. *Politics and institutions: European parliamentary technology assessment. Technological Forecasting and Social Change* 27, pp. 79-96.

M. Decker, M. Ladikas (Hg.) 2004. *Bridges between Science, Society and Policy. Technology As-sessment - Methods and Impacts.* Berlin. U. Dolata, R. Werle, (Hg.) 2007. *Gesellschaft und die Macht der Technik. Sozioökonomischer und institutioneller Wandel durch Technisierung.* Frankfurt/New York.

S. Funtowicz, J. Ravetz, 1993 "*The Emergence of Post-Normal Science.*" In von Schomberg, R. (Hg.) *Science, Politics and Morality.* London. 2002.

"Asbestos: from 'magic' to malevolent mineral." Harremoes et al, pp. 49-63.

V. Gorokhov, 2004. "Technikfolgenabschätzung als Systemanalyse." Kornwachs (Hg.) *Technik - System - Verantwortung.* Münster, p. 419. V. Gorokhov, 2007. *Foundations of the Philosophy of Technology And Engineering Sciences.* Moscow: Gardariki (in Russian).

J. Grin, A.Grunwald, (eds.) 2000. *Vision Assessment: Shaping Technology in 21st Century Society.* Heidelberg: Springer (mit J. Grin, Hg.). A. Grunwald, 2003. "Technology assessment at the German Bundestag: 'expertising' democracy for 'democratising' expertise". *Science and Public Policy.* 30 (2003) 3, 193-198.

A. Grunwald, 2006. "Scientific independence as a constitutive part of parliamentary technology as-sessment". *Science and Public Policy* 33 (2006) 2, 103-113.

A. Grunwald, 2009a "Technology Assessment: Concepts and Methods." In A. Meijers (ed.): *Philosophy of Technology and Engineering Sciences.* Vol. 9, Amsterdam, 1103-1146.

A. Grunwald, 2009b. "Vision Assessment Supporting the Governance of Knowledge - the Case of Futuristic Nanotechnology." Bechmann et al. 2009, 147-170.

A. Grunwald, 2010. *Technikfolgenabschätzung - eine Einführung*. Berlin A. Grunwald, 2011. "Parliamentary technology assessment as part of technology governance." G. Banse; A. Grunwald; I. Hronszki; G. Nelson (Hrsg.): *On Prospective Technology Studies*. Karlsruhe: KIT Scientific Publishing, 2011, 29-37.

A. Grunwald, 2011. *Technology and Society. Western European Experiences of Technology Assessment*. Moskau (RUS): Logos LTD Publishing Group (in russischer Sprache).

A. Grunwald, Y. Julliard, 2007. "Nanotechnology - Steps Towards Understanding Human Beings as Technology?" *NanoEthics* 1, 77-87.

D.H. Guston, D. Sarewitz, 2002. "Real-Time Technology Assessment." *Technology in Culture* 24, 93-109.

J. Habermas, 1970. *Toward a Rational Society*. Beacon Press. First publication: J. Habermas. 1968 (ed.). *Technik und Wissenschaft als Ideologie*. Frankfurt.

J. Habermas. 2001. *Die Zukunft der menschlichen Natur*. Frankfurt P.D. Harremoes, M. Gee, A. MacGarvin, J. Stirling, B. Keys, B.Wynne, S.Vaz Guedes, (eds.), 2002. *The Precautionary Principle in the 20th century. Late Lessons from early warnings*. Sage.

P.D Harremoes, M. Gee, A, MacGarvin, J. Stirling, B, Keys, Wynne, S. Guedes Vaz (Hg.), 2002. *The Precautionary Principle in the 20th century. Late Lessons from early warnings*. London.

H. Jonas, 1979/1984. The Imperative of Responsibility, 1984. H. Jonas, 1979. *Das Prinzip Verant-wortung. Versuch einer Ethik für die technologische Zivilisation*. Frankfurt

S. Joss, S.Belucci (eds.), 2002. *Participatory Technology Assessment European Perspectives*. Westminster University Press.

N.C. Karafyllis, 2006. *Biofakte. Grundlagen, Probleme und Perspektiven. Erwägen Wissen Ethik* (EWE) 17 (4), 547-558; N.C. Karafyllis, 2008. *Ethical and epistemological problems of hybridizing living beings: Biofacts and Body Shopping*. In: Wenchao Li and Hans Poser (Ed.). *Ethical Considerations on Today's Science and Technology. A GermanChinese Approach*. Münster: LIT, 185-198.

B. Latour, 1995. *Wir sind nie modern gewesen*. Berlin: B. Latour, 1987. *Science in Action: How to Follow Scientists and Engineers Through Society*. Hardward University Press.

H. Paschen, Th. Petermann, "Technikfolgenabschätzung - ein strategisches Rahmenkonzept für die Analyse und Bewertung von Technikfolgen." In: Petermann 1992, 19-42.

T. Petermann, C.Scherz, "Parlamentarische TA-Einrichtungen in Europa als reflexive Institutionen." In: T. Petermann, A. Grunwald (Hg.) 2005. *Technikfolgen-Abschätzung am Deutschen Bundestag*. Berlin, 213-239.

Kastenholz, P. Schild, U. Wilhelm kooperativen Diskurs. Zürich, 3-103.

A. Rip, T. Misa, J. Schot (eds.) 1995. *Managing Technology in Society*. London.

M.C. Roco, W.C.Bainbridge, (Hg.) 2002. *Converging Technologies for Improving Human Performance*. Arlington, Virginia.

H. Rolston, 1988. *Environmental Ethics*. Philadelphia. G. Ropohl, 1996. *Ethik und Technikbewertung*. Frankfurt. G. Schmid, H.Ernst, W.Grünwald, A.Grunwald, et al. 2006. *Nanotechnology - Perspectives and Assessment*. Berlin et al.

J. Schot, A.Rip, 1997 "The Past and Future of Constructive Technology Assessment." *Technological Forecasting and Social Change* 54, 251268.

K. Siune, E.Markus, M.Calloni, U.Felt, A.Gorski, A.Grunwald, A.Rip, V. de Semir, S.Wyatt, 2009. *Challenging Futures of Science in Society*. Report of the MASIS Expert Group. Brussels: European Commission. R. Smits, P. den Hertog, 2007. "TA and the management of innovation in economy and society." *International Journal on Foresight and Innovation Policy* 3, 28-52.

I. van de Poel, 2009. "Values in Engineering Design." In: A. Meijers (ed.): *Philosophy of Technology and Engineering Sciences*. Volume 9. Amsterdam, 973-1006.

N. Vig, H.Paschen, (Hg.) 1999. *Parliaments and Technology Assessment. The Development of Technology Assessment in Europe*. Albany, USA. R.von Schomberg, 2005. "The Precautionary Principle and Its Normative Challenges." In: Fisher, E., Jones, J., von Schomberg, R. (eds.). *The Precautionary Principle and Public Policy Decision Making.*, UK: Cheltenham, Northampton, MA 2005, 141-165.

R. von Schomberg, 2011. "Prospects for Technology Assessment in the 21st century: the quest for the „right" impacts of science and technology. An outlook towards a framework for responsible research and innovation." To appear in: M. Dusseldorp et al. (eds.): *Technikfolgen abschätzen lehren*, Opladen.

R. von Schomberg (ed.) 1999. *Democratizing Technology. Theory and Practice of a Deliberative Technology Policy*. Hengelo.

J.-P. Voss, D. Bauknecht, R.Kemp (Hg.) 2006. *Reflexive Governance for Sustainable Development*. UK: Cheltenham.

WCED - World Commission on Environment and Development. 1987. *Our common future*, Oxford.

Y. Yoshinaka, C. Clausen and A. Hansen. 2003. "The Social Shaping of Technology: A New Space for Politics?" In A. Grunwald (ed.), *Technikgestaltung: zwischen Wunsch oder Wirklichkeit*, Berlin: Springer, 117-131.

CHAPTER VIII

TRADITION AND INNOVATION:

RUSSIAN AND GERMAN EXPERIENCE IN THE DEVELOPMENT OF INNOVATIVE SYSTEMS

SUSTAINABLE INNOVATIVE DEVELOPMENT

The concept of innovation policy can be developed only as a reflective activity. According to N. Luhmann, it is an active process with a strong emphasis on self-responsibility and permanent self-reflection. This means that rational solutions and corresponding rational actions should orient themselves not to their acceptance by the public, but to potential acceptability by society of these decisions and actions. This acceptance is gaining topicality as a result of the rational education of the public, the public debate, and persuasion of the public that the chosen path (or scenario) is correct and may involve certain positive and negative effects and risks.1

Sustainable innovative development is, above all, a political and empirical rather than a theoretical concept. Hence, it is interpreted differently in different countries. In the U.S. and Western Europe it means maintenance of the level and pace of economic growth and a high level of the country's own revenues, often at the expense of resources of other nations. For Central European countries, it stands for the hope to achieve the same high level of income and social protection as is available in the "old members" of the European Union. These hopes are mixed with disappointment, however, due to the increasing cost of this membership and because equality of opportunity is accompanied with increased competition within the EU. For Russia, the concept of sustainable innovative development is linked with the hope for rising living standards, absence of social, technological and natural disasters, the preservation of the achieved democratic freedoms, the non-return to the totalitarian regime, the absence of new revolutionary situations, and a yearning for evolutionary development. No one truly believes that this is possible, but everyone hopes for it - despite historical evidence that, especially in Russia, stability is often replaced with a cataclysm destroying everything that has been achieved.

---

1 A. Grunwald, "Die rationale Gestaltung der technischen Zukunft," *Rationale Technikfolgenbeurteilung. Konzepte und methodische Grundlagen,* A. Grunwald (Hg.) (Berlin: Springer, 1999), pp. 29-54.

The modern concept of sustainable innovative development can be analyzed on two levels. On the one level, it is the development of innovative systems themselves in present-day society and in the historical and cultural context, on the other, a review of basic concepts of innovative development. Although a broad layer of foreign concepts may be selected as empirical material the transfer of international experience to Russian soil requires a prior methodological analysis. This two-level analysis complicates exposition of the importance of innovation systems in addressing crisisrelated problems facing society, yet it also contains important benefits by introducing Western concepts.

Much is being said today about the need for modernization and accelerated advance towards innovative societal development as the principal means of survival in the context of global competition. The principal accent in this discourse focuses on the positive aspects of this development, while its possible negative effects are relegated to the wayside; this is especially true as regards the Russian literature; conversely, the negative aspect appears a key element in the Western concepts of innovation systems, particularly in recent years, given the more advanced status of Western countries as regards the implementation of scientific and technological achievements in the social sphere. Nevertheless, the positive experience of developing an innovative environment is also important for us.

An interesting example in this sense is Technologiefabrik Karlsruhe the "factory of technology (know-how)" - in the technological region Karlsruhe (Germany), 2 founded a few decades ago by the Chamber of Commerce of the Technologieregion Karlsruhe and by the National Credit Bank of Baden-Wuerttemberg (Landesbank Baden-Württemberg [LBBW]).3 Firms supported under this program typically consist of five to six employees and are set up by professors, graduate and undergraduate students at the University of Karlsruhe on the basis of fundamental and applied research and development projects. Russia today is developing the concept of techno and science cities in a similar manner.

---

2 "The goal of the Technologiefabrik Karlsruhe to ease the path of young, technology-oriented companies towards independence is achieved through cooperation with a series of other important establishments in the region" (http://www.technologiefabrik-ka.de/?kat=&lang=en)

3 "LBBW is a universal bank and an international commercial bank. Together with its regional retail banks Baden-Württembergische Bank (BWBank), Rheinland-Pfalz Bank and Sachsen Bank, it offers the whole range of products and services typical of a modern large bank. LBBW is the central bank of the savings banks in Baden-Württemberg, Rhineland Palatinate and Saxony. BW-Bank functions as a savings bank for LBBW in the territory of the state capital, Stuttgart" (http://www.lbbw.de/lbbwde/1000000342-en.html)

SCIENCE CITIES

Let us retrace the evolution of Russian science cities and see what part they may play in the emerging innovation system. At the moment, there are sixty-five science cities in this country.4

Economic factors were nowhere near the top of the agenda when these cities were created in the first place. Throughout the postwar period, the USSR military-industrial complex was the chief consumer and customer as far as science was concerned. Secrecy that dominated that period predetermined the location and organizational structure of science cities: they were academic and military settlements closed to outsiders. After Stalin's death, prominent scientists and engineers enjoyed unlimited support of the Communist Party's Central Committee and had direct access to the first persons of the state.5 Under Khrushchev, political factors, such as the catchword "to catch up with and overtake the United States," came to the fore. Under Brezhnev, party and ideological interests gained supremacy, often to the detriment of the economy. And only recently economic interests have been emerging as dominant, even though the national science and technology policy is just beginning to take shape. No great power can do without a great science, and science cannot do without a strategic innovation policy.

The main factors constituting science cities are political, economic, legal, and social. To date, the evolution of these factors has resulted in the institutionalization of science and technology in the form of urban settlements as a necessary condition for the existence and development of science. Initially, domestic science cities were created as artificial settlements; in the Soviet era, they began to develop as a natural system urban agglomerations with a uniquely democratic social environment; everyone remembered their non-free past in which they were all equal. In addition, these entities were, by definition, interdisciplinary, and, consequently, also became multinational. Instead of Christianity as a consolidating factor in a West European city,6 here the part was performed

4 http://www.souznaukogradov.ru/naukograds/naukograds_inf/179 5 V. G. Gorokhov, "Scientific investigation, technological development and economical governmental support: the historical development of RADAR science and technology I" (http://zhurnal.ape.relarn.ru/articles/2009/105e.pdf)

6 "The medieval city, after all, was still a cultic association....The often very significant role played by the parish community in the administrative organization of medieval cities is only one of many symptoms pointing to this quality of the Christian religion which, in dissolving clan ties, importantly shaped the medieval city" (Max Weber, "The city (non-legitimate domination)," Max Weber, *Economy and Society: An Outline of Interpretive Sociology*, transl. E. Fischoff, H. Gerth, A.M. Henderson, F. Kolegar, C. W. Mills, T. Parsons, M. Rheinstein, G. Roth, E. Shils and C. Wittich, eds.

by communist ideology and the party apparatus; in these cases, the communist ideology and the economic management agenda were subordinate to the need of solving scientific tasks, especially those dealing with the military-industrial complex. Thus, the involvement of the scientific community in military-industrial projects ensures its relative independence from ideological and financial pressure.

The core of a science city is an interdisciplinary research team exploring with the help of sophisticated equipment specific problem areas. The city, as Max Weber said, is a worldwide joint settlement of people who were previously aliens as regards their residence the notion of "community" was forced out by the concept of society as a completely artificial space of communication, regardless of the "natural" definitions of the participants. Every individual is entitled to entry into the space by purely administrative ties specific to the "urban community" as a special institution. "... the burgher joined the citizenry as an individual, and as an individual he swore the oath of citizenship. His personal membership in the local association of the city guaranteed his legal status as a burgher, not his tribe or sib".7

Similarly, gathered in a science city were scientists from different regions of the USSR and from different areas of science, where they created a new interdisciplinary research community under the auspices of the city. Generation of favorable and creative conditions for dealing with scientific and engineering problems is a salient feature and, in fact, the foundation of a science city. As an autonomous self-governing entity, a science city assumes control of the political, social, financial, and, to some extent, legal functions, particularly if the territory allotted to such city is afforded a special tax status. Therefore, a science city becomes an instrument of support, on the local level, of competitiveness of science and an element of the innovation system.8 To increase efficiency of scientific research and its worth to the national economy was roughly the aim to achieve which Germany's Schleswig-Holstein decided to join the ministry of science and the ministry of the economy, calling it the ministry of innovations. The dominant aspect of the new office was control of science, however; otherwise, according to experts, such a union could lead to a decrease in the level of research due to the concentration of efforts to solve narrow corporate economic problems, because a ministry of the economy is more likely to block promising research than to support it.9

A science city organized as a foundation makes it possible to quickly take decisions and manage different tasks, combining the functions of a

---

Guenther Roth and Claus Wittich. (Berkeley: University of California Press, 1978). Vol. 2. Pp. 1244-1247.

7 *Ibid,* p. 1246.

8 "So also the city produced science in the modern sense" (*Ibid.*, p. 234).

9 U. Schneidewind, *Nachhaltige Wissenschaft* (Marburg: Metropolis Verlag, 2009)

municipality and a business entity. Furthermore, large[10] research organizations in Germany take different legal forms. The nuclear research center in Karlsruhe, for example, was organized as a limited liability company, which gives it flexibility in financial matters; 11 but there are major research centers organized as foundations. In January 2004, the rector's office of Karlsruhe University in cooperation with the board of the Research Center of the city of Karlsruhe proposed their gradual merger in the frameworks of the Karlsruhe Institute of Technology, which was established in late 2007. In 2008, the Center merged with the University, which was legalized in August 2009, and also in March 2008, to support this venture, there was established the Hector Science Foundation with a registered capital of 200 million euros. There are plans to institute an exemplary merger of a university with a research organization, which would stimulate the setting up of several such unions.

The main factor in creating projects of this kind in today's Russia is not economics (competitiveness, commercialization, etc.), but creation of organizational and legal conditions that would preclude abuse and produce a protection system against the bureaucracy.

Needless to say the newly established institution should be competitive on a global scale and be able to attract leading scientists, including foreign ones, for which it has to rely on a simplified scheme of financing purchases of new equipment, as is the case in the U.S. or Western Europe. Simplified migration procedures should also be established. For science cities in Russia, including the newly created ones, to attract scientists from abroad we need to reduce administrative barriers and simplify the funding schemes and the creation of special tax conditions.

Moreover, no R&D results will be scored unless conditions for free creative work are provided. The atmosphere of free creativity involves a global mobility of scientists, free exchanges of knowledge, publications in foreign languages, a system of preparing publications, obtaining foreign books and magazines, etc. At the time of Beria, the lack of free exchanges of knowledge was made up for by intelligence data provided through scientific and industrial espionage. That consumed considerable resources, whose use in the open and unclassified conditions could have yielded more significant results.

The current innovation systems should be analyzed in the spirit of Max Weber as a kind of "ideal types" whose development can be traced throughout the history of civilized humankind, though in different forms, which would allow identifying their common features. A conflict between tradition and innovation can be found at all stages of societal development, and even today one comes across elements of the old and traditional and of the emerging new. Ivan S. Turgenev, in his last novel The New, brilliantly showed the coexistence in the late 19th century of the provincial landowners

10 http://www.kommersant.ru/doc.aspx?DocsID=1363409

11 http://www.kit.edu/english/

Fimochka and Fomochka, on the one hand, who continued to live in the tradition of the 18th century, not even noticing - together with their servants - the abolition of serfdom, and the merchant Galushkin, who in fact lived already in the 20th century. Similarly, in our present society, there appear islands of innovation systems in the form of "incubators of new ideas," industrial parks, science cities, etc., which are cultivating the shoots of the new in what for the most part is still a traditional Soviet-era society, despite the fact that it had lost its principal social guidelines. This is the way the evolution of science cities proceeds today from reservations for scientists of the military-industrial complex to free cities of science or technology parks, which, in addition to raising scientific technologies, are assuming certain defensive functions in our increasingly bureaucratized society. It will be recalled that according to Max Weber, it is the bureaucracy that is capable of stifling the free initiative and bring about stagnation of capitalist society based on competition.

The main problem of modern bureaucracies around the world and especially in Russia is where and how to invest available limited funds in order to provide for a more or less stable development of society; this requires some idea about the future as a basis for decision making. This also applies to the field of science and technology policy. The most important problem facing our national science and technology policy is how to ensure proper use of these funds. In this sense, the scientific and technological parks and science cities can become, under certain conditions, forerunners of a kind of democratic management of the innovation process. Indeed, these "innovation units" may not only develop new progressive and competitive knowledge-based technologies, but also ensure their social and humanitarian expertise, if we are not only after the benefits associated with these endeavors, but also strive to avoid consequences that are often unexpected in terms of the natural sciences. Modern societies and states require early commercial and technological results from modern science. While stressing the need for technological applications of science, people usually forget that these applications will only benefit society when they become embodied in specific social structures. Hence the need for the development of new areas of social science, such as the risk studies, the study of the effects of management and economic decisions, social evaluation of technologies, and applied ethics.

THE NEED FOR SOCIAL AND HUMANITARIAN EXPERTISE

The French sociologist of science Bruno Latour12 speaks about the importance of a "laboratory" that is to become an abode of science where

---

12 B. Latour, "Give Me a Laboratory and I Will Raise the World," KnorrCertina, D. Karin, Michael Mulkay (ed.), *Science Observed. Perspectives on the Social Study of Science* (London/Beverly Hills/New Delhi: Sage Publication, 1983), pp. 141-170.

new technologies are created and improved and serve as the starting point of scientific and technological progress. The knowledge gained by scientists in collaboration with engineers, who are often ignorant of the social sciences, may be irrelevant to social conditions and problems. The "things" - i.e., objects of research and technical effects in Bruno Latour's figurative expression - are not passive and "may strike back." Moreover, society as such may then be regarded as a huge laboratory. But social experiments are not identical to experiments in the sciences. Embodied in new technologies and economic structures experimental facilities and processes become part of social reality and as such - objects of study of the social sciences and humanities and not only of the natural sciences and engineering.

Today, one hears more and more that science must serve as the primary engine of social development. In stressing the need for science to deliver technological applications, people typically forget that these applications are appropriated by society only when they become embodied in specific social structures. Hence, it is impossible to do without the social and humanitarian expert evaluation if we want not only to get related benefits, but also to avoid implications that may appear unexpected from the standpoint of the natural sciences and engineering. It follows that today we should speak about the growing role of the social sciences and humanities, which, unfortunately, is not the case. This trend is not unique to Russia either. Support for innovation is interpreted essentially as support for technological innovation, while social innovations have hardly been investigated at all. "In Germany, for example, huge sums are invested in the improvement of automobile engines, but only a few hundred thousand euros in solutions that promise potentially multiple savings. This issue is given much more attention in other parts of the world. Its value is underlined by the fact that Bremen was one of the few German cities that received an invitation to take part in the 2010 Shanghai Exhibition, after its urban logistics concept, namely, an idea to share cars, evoked the interest of the Chinese. Similar situations are observed in other areas. For example, an enormous potential involved in energy savings construction projects is not so much a technological as a socio-cultural challenge.13

Experimental facilities and processes embodied in new technologies and economic structures become part of social reality and as such - the objects of study for the social rather than natural sciences. "From the beginning the social sciences aimed to reform or change society. In recent decades, many social scientists were involved in the discussion of such social and political issues as the debate over nuclear power, genetic, or climatic changes. They acted as experts, consultants, and analysts familiar with the relevant scientific problems, and sometimes even as interpreters of the time or the prophets. But sociologists should be involved in quite different areas - organizers and managers of the process of citizen

---

13 U. Schneidewind, *Nachhaltige Wissenschaft* (Marburg: Metropolis Verlag, 2009).

participation in decision-making, in the course of which experts and amateurs - as well as the experts in the field of social sciences - discuss such controversial issues as the release of genetically modified organisms or the development of scenarios of future technologies, as is the case with nanotechnology."14

We believe that of particular interest to Russia in this regard is the German experience of developing research into problems of social assessment of scientific and technological development.

The most striking example is the study of the contribution that convergent technologies make to efforts to improve human capabilities. On the one hand, this process aims at producing very optimistic "technical" enhancement of human performance, but on the other hand, this kind of convergence is fraught with danger for mankind.15 Therefore, a scientific study of this problem requires consideration of both the "pros" and "cons" not only in terms of science and engineering, but also from the standpoint of the social sciences and humanities. Biotechnological manipulation at the nanoscale place humanity in a borderline situation where results of such treatment are essentially unpredictable and can lead to irreversible negative consequences for humanity as a whole and for its further development on the biological, physiological, social, and psychological levels. Besides the fact that the bodily nature of man is made of atoms, molecules and genes, man is a product of social environment and education. Modified or implanted in the human body, new artificial organs can no longer be considered as mediating tools between nature and man as they become almost an integral part of his individual corporeality. "Almost" is used here because no one knows how consistent with his natural corporeality they will grow over time.

No one has so far explored, however, or even raised the question about what may happen to the human psyche after a nanotechnological adjustment of the subtle neural structures or the addition of new senses both procedures are already described as implementable in the near future. Although man is able, within certain limits, to adapt to changing environmental conditions, including some bodily changes external as regards his mind (for example, in the organs of perception), but they remain external factors nevertheless. Interference in the internal neuropsychic processes can lead to some unpredictable consequences not only for some individual human psyches, but also for society as a whole. Associates at the

---

14 "The Role of Social Sciences in Science Policy Making," *Science, Technology & Innovation Studies,* vol. 5, No. 1, (September, 2009), www.stistudies.de.

15 A. Grunwald, "Converging Technologies for Human Enhancement. A New Wave Increasing the Contingency of the *conditio humana,*" *Assessing Societal Implications of Converging Technological Development.* (Berlin: edition sigma, 2007), pp. 271-288.

Federal research center in Iuelcih, Germany (Forschungszentrum Jülich16) have actually agreed that brain structures responsible for religious feelings could be located in the human brain and deliberately adjusted. This is not just a psychological, but a social and moral issue as well. The definition of this kind of external effect is very similar to the social experiments that were conducted in our country in the 1920s-30s and came to be known as "re-forging." Berdyaev warns that technology can give man or a small group of people a great destructive force. This allows those possessing technical secrets to concentrate power in their hands. Therefore, modern technology cannot be neutral vis-à-vis questions of the spirit. The destiny of all humankind depends on this.

It is very important to take into consideration one's own experience in the development of innovative systems and not to focus only on the transfer of other countries' experience, which one must consider but not be limited by. Voices one hears recently, especially from politicians who have no idea of the specifics of research work and traditions, call for the need to reduce public funding of fundamental research and to concentrate the efforts of national research organizations on solving pressing practical problems facing present-day society. Most of these speakers point to the U.S. experience.

Conversely, the German science researcher Richard Münch claims that unintended negative consequences may arise from attempts to transfer "reform elements from one cultural and institutional context to another, or the application of an abstract theoretical model to practice." This is a reference to the "hegemony" of a concrete paradigm used in the study, in other words, "close links between science and economics at universityindustrial centers," which is being imposed by "the richest American universities."17

Research and teaching is no longer an end in itself. The much larger goal is multiplication of the symbolic and monetary capital of the university enterprises involved. Thus, we witness the disappearance of differences between, say, the BMW automotive concern and Ludwig-Maximilians University in Munich. Hence it is quite understandable that in the context of "academic capitalism" "science managers" are becoming more prominent in higher schools. Today's universities find it much more important to attract financial sponsorship than capable scientists and educators.

As a result, even a qualified specialist in Germany knows only what is within his frames of reference - not an iota more, while Russian programmers - both generalists and those without special professional training - are in great demand there. Richard Münch summarizes his analysis with a statement that, though not optimistic, appears highly

16 http://www.fz-juelich.de/portal/EN/Home/home_node.html 17 R. Münch, *Globale Eliten, lokale Autoritäten. Bildung und Wissenschaft unter dem Regime von PISA* (McKinsey & Co. Frankfurt/M.: Suhrkamp, 2009), pp. 125-131.

relevant for Russia: "These structural changes are due not to functional benefits but to the pressure exercised without any democratic legitimacy by powerful experts linked through transnational networks. Thus the changes become an end in themselves, promoting the self-affirmation of the new elite....Whether the American model will ultimately bring about better results is by no means proven, especially if one considers that the United States is forced to make up for its shortages of trained engineers and scientists by recruiting young professionals from abroad... This shift of symbolic power is accelerated by the development, stabilization, and close interweaving of transnational actors in the network...of social institutions...and paradigms. This has set in motion the self-rising process of transforming to a new paradigm the structure of legitimating and waiting... An essential part of this transformation is the emergence of hybrids, which no longer satisfy the old requirements and not yet meet the new. The development one observes in reality shows that hybrid education will continue."

(Translated from Russian by Serge Gitman)

PART II

INDIAN TRADITION

CHAPTER IX

CAN THERE BE A SCIENCE OF MEDITATION?

What is supported by evidence must be accepted even if it is said by a child, what is unreasonable must be rejected even if it is uttered by the lotus-born Creator. Who will not discipline such a bias-blind person who rejects the pure water of the river in front, and goes back to drink from a dirty well with the justification: "this well belongs to our father"? Just as the ocean is the source of all water, immediate perception (pratyakṣa) is the ultimate source of validity for all other means of knowledge…-Yogavāsiṣṭha Rāmāyaṇa (Mokṣopāya) II, 18/19

I will analyze the actions and appetites of men as if it were a question of lines, of planes, and of solids. -Benedict Spinoza

I speak of phenomenology as a mathematician speaks of mathematics. -Edmund Husserl

When science is universal, can there be in the world of science a place which will remain vacant without an Indian devotee? There certainly is. -Sir Jagadish Chandra Bose

WHAT IS THE QUESTION?

When we use the locution-schema "Science of X" we use it in one of two distinct ways. Analogous with the use of "of" in "the city of London", we sometimes use it in an appositional sense, as in "Science of Logic" or "Science of Botany" when X ***is*** the science we are talking about. But sometimes X is just the topic or subject-matter, in the sense in which cancer is the subject-matter of Oncology and cancer is not itself the Science of Cancer. Botany is the Science of Plants, and plants themselves are not the science. In which of these two senses am I asking whether there can be a science of meditation? The question is easily answerable in the affirmative if we take it in the second sense. Can there be a science which studies meditation as a subject-matter? Of course there can be; there already is, as James Austin, Allan Wallace, and V.S. Ramachandran would tell you from radically different standpoints. Let me try a slightly perverse analogy here. If there can be a science of cancer, why not one of meditation? Meditation and I am not talking about the art or discipline of stilling the mind but the different grades of concentration and relaxation of the mind - may be an irrational process or a supra-normal or an abnormal state of the body and mind but it is not more irrational or abnormal than cancer. If scientists can legitimately investigate why some adolescents suffer from extreme stress or attention deficit disorder, they should be able to legitimately investigate why some people enjoy stress-less or very focused states of mind. At worst some sciences of meditation will tell us that states very similar to meditative states are generated by, say, some form of temporal lobe epilepsy or that they have not yet found any permanent cure for spiritual experiences, but are working on it. Given that spiritual experiences resulting from meditative practices are at least as wide-spread as cancer (and seem to be spreading as uncontrollably) one should be doing very bad science if all one concludes is that strictly speaking meditative states do not occur at all. It would be similar to an Oncologist denying the phenomenon of cancer.

Yet, before we can ask the question of the very possibility of a science of meditation in the strict sense of the terms "science" and "meditation", we have to address two very real anxieties. Can or should anything spiritual be dealt with scientifically? This could be asked by people who respect science but are dismissive or suspicious of spirituality, as well as by those who are respectful of both but take them to be at least as far apart as romantic love and motorcycle maintenance. Secondly, we have to address the anxiety, which is rarely expressed openly any more, but which is always at the back of standard-upholders of Western science: Can any theory of Asian origin ever count as Science in the strict sense, since Science in the strict sense, is a quintessentially European enterprise?

One of the reasons why it is hard to address the first worry directly is that it is nearly impossible to pin down what one means by the adjective "spiritual". Some people use that word as just a "progressive" substitute of the word "religious". And even if most meditative techniques are associated with theistic, atheistic or pantheistic religious beliefs, the process, for example, of noticing and controlling one's breathing and thereby to achieve certain tranquility and thereby clarity and peace of mind has nothing religious about it. What is minimally required for a process to count as "spiritual", I think, is unselfishness or a striving towards effacement of the ego. There may be deep down some egotism essential to the enterprise of science (I could not imagine, for example a scientist inspired by Ayn Rand meditating for spiritual purposes) but on the face of it, science's commitment to objectivity and impersonality seems quite consonant with the non-egotism of most meditational moralities. Indeed the most familiar "spiritual" greeting or prayer word is "namaḥ" which is derived from "na mama" - not mine. Thus, I would simply explain spirituality as the cultivation of unselfishness. If this sort of spirituality is what meditation is supposed to promote, then I would like to argue that in both the senses, a science of meditation is very much possible because it is already actual, alive, and beginning to kick. There is a loose sense of the term "*samādhi*" for example, where it simply means "concentration" or an undistracted one tipped cognitive state focused on a single topic of thought, imagination or perception. After all, yoga is defined by Patañjali very straightforwardly as "arresting or stilling of the fluctuations of mind (both cognitive and affective states)".

But here, one may object that we still have not clearly stated what we mean by meditation. And which definition of "science" are we proceeding with? We should try to clarify these conceptual confusions before seeking answers to the question whether a science of meditation is possible.

WHAT IS MEDITATION?

"I will now close my eyes, plug my ears, and withdraw all my senses. I will rid my thoughts of physical objects - or, since that is beyond me, I shall write those images off as empty illusions. Talking with myself and looking more deeply into myself, I'll try gradually to know myself better."

Don't these lines sound as if they are from some sort of an autobiography of a Yogi? Actually, as some of us recognize, they are the opening lines of Descartes' Third *Meditation (on First Philosophy)*. The coincidence becomes even more intriguing when one reads the rest of Descartes' chapter. One of the alternative objects of meditation recommended by Patañjali in his *Yoga-Sūtras* is the idea of God ("*īśvarapraṇidhānād vā*") - a unique center of consciousness, free from the bondage of *karma* and desires and afflictions, where the seed of omniscience reaches its highest conceivable perfection. This third Meditation of Descartes also happens to focus on the concept of God, though he had a radically different concept of God than the one recommended by Patanjali. Yet, it would be shocking to both Western rationalist-modernists as well as to Eastern lovers of mystical wisdom to call Descartes an unwitting practitioner of Yoga! Descartes was a mathematician, a scientist, posing as a skeptic in his search for perfect certainty through purely logical reasoning, and thereby laying the foundations of European Scientific Epistemology. What does that have to do with Eastern spirituality which is unscientific from the get-go, supposed to help us transcend all logical thinking and plunge us in an oceanic intuitive experience of God, self or nothingness?

Nevertheless, that autobiographical account of Descartes' withdrawal from all the external senses seems to echo Bhagavadgita VIII, 12:

" *sarvadvārāṇi saṃyamya mano hṛdi nirudhya ca, murdhnyādhāyātmanaḥ prāṇam āsthito yoga-dhāraṇam*" "Having restrained all the doors of one's body, and arresting the mind in one's heart, one practices the Yoga of steadfast concentration by gathering the entire vital force on the top of the cranium".

The word "Meditations' was, of course, famously used by the Roman emperor Marcus Aurelius, who was one of the last Stoic philosophers and wrote, in 167 C.E. an autobiographical ethico-psychological didactic book with that title. As a random extract shows, his *Meditations* are but records of an inner dialogue that he was having with different parts of his own mind:

"The ruling faculty does not disturb itself; I mean, does not frighten itself or cause itself pain. But if any one else can frighten or pain it, let him do so. For the faculty itself will not by its own opinion turn itself into such ways. Let the body itself take care, if it can, that is suffer nothing, and let it speak, if it suffers. But the soul itself, that which is subject to fear, to pain, which has completely the power of forming an opinion about these things, will suffer nothing, for it will never deviate into such a judgment. The leading principle in itself wants nothing, unless it makes a want for itself; and therefore it is both free from perturbation and unimpeded, if it does not disturb and impede itself. Eudaemonia (happiness) is a good daemon, or a good thing. What then art thou doing here, O imagination? Go away, I entreat thee by the gods, as thou didst come, for I want thee not. But thou art come according to thy old fashion. I am not angry with thee: only go away."

This would be called contemplative moral reasoning "*vitarka*" or inner discourse "*antaḥ-sañjalpa*" in Buddhist Abhidharma, or Yoga-sūtra or Kashmir Shaiva language. Most often, when we use that word "meditation" these days, we mean "Dhyāna" defined by Patañjali as "single unwavering flow of ideation" *(pratyāya-eka-tānatā)*. It is the penultimate, seventh step, just before "*samādhi*" and succeeds the previous step, "*dhāraṇā*" which is pinning down one's imaginative attention to a particular spot usually in the meditator's navel, heart, top of the scalp, tip of the nose or tip of the tongue, root of the throat etc. Voluntarily induced but settled down into a spontaneous state due to repeated practice, it is a certain proprioceptive awareness of a specific area of one's felt body leading to a peaceful relaxed state of dispassion and not needing to think anything. *Bhagavadgītā* defines Yoga as the dispositional and episodic state of "equality" (*samatva*) or "same attitude towards hedonic and moral opposites". Although the word "yoga" literally means yoking or union, it is technically taken to mean a disunion or "detachment from that involvement or contact with pain which the self gets embroiled into" (*duḥkha-saṃyoga-viyoga)*. As Richard Sorabji remarks in his magisterial survey of Stoic and early Christian recipes of auto-therapy of perturbing emotions and cultivation of peace of mind, many of these ancient exercises, both in ancient Greece, Rome or India, had to do with noticing the self through passage of time. The mind is understood with the moral metaphor of a river which flows in two directions, towards evil and towards good. Even a single wave of a memory, a thought or a desire could be followed through in its three stages of arising, growing, and disappearing. (Yoga-sūtra III.12-16 deals intricately with past, present and future property-alterations or "transformation" (*pariṇāma*) of the same property-possessor [*dharmin]*). Clearly, we have in the metaphysics and epistemology of Sāṃkhya already a science of such meditative practices. Here "science of meditation" does not mean either that meditation itself is a science, or that under controlled laboratory situation practice of meditation is externally observed and experimented with in order to test explanatory hypotheses. Just as the physics of electromagnetism underlies the functioning of an electronic gadget or the neurophysiology of synaptic propagation of a sensory input via the hippocampus underlies the triggering of an episodic memory, the rational-empirical theory of the triple factors of delight-intelligence-essence (*sattva*), dynamicity-energy-pain *(rajas)* and delusion-intertia-matter (*tamas*) underlies or renders possible the mindwatching which thickens into meditation resulting in calming down of the wavy mind, until, as the ancient Maitrāyaṇi Upaniṣad asserts, the very binding fetters of a distracted fluctuating mind turn into the liberating detachment-enabling still waters of a tranquil mind.

This process of meditation could be alternatively theorized as a form of attending to breath, attending to self-awareness, a certain kind of focused and repeated analysis of some moral feelings such as universal friendship, compassion, joyous celebration, and indifference, or as a negative method of isolation of the self from gross to subtler and subtler bodies. Both memory and imagination, which are initially distracting enemies of such staying focused in the current reality could be befriended into aids so much so that one kind of high contemplative state has been described as constant unwavering remembrance of who one is.

While self-observation and introspectiveness are regarded highly, not only by the Upanishadic-Yogic-Buddhist-Tantric traditions, but also by the ancient Stoic philosophers, who influenced Immanuel Kant, Kant is openly averse to meditation in the form of deliberate mind-watching. In his Anthropology (which is his own descriptive and moral psychology), which contains the beginnings of a sophisticated phenomenological science of imagination, Kant shows almost an alarmism against "self-observation." While he recommends self-criticism and (carefully concealed attention to one's own conduct, without appearing embarrassed) watchfulness in social life, he seems to be almost afraid of witnessing the flow of our own involuntary mental states. Since one kind of meditation consists simply in that activity, Kant could be taken as warning us against meditation-practices as running the risk of fanaticism and insanity:

> In observing ourselves we make a methodical inventory of the perceptions formed in us, which supplies materials for a diary of introspection and easily leads to fanaticism and madness....But the real purpose of this section (On Observing Oneself) is to give the strict *warning* (emphasis Kant's) mentioned above, against occupying ourselves with spying out the *involuntary* course of our thoughts and feelings and, so to speak, carefully recording its interior history. This is the most direct route to Illuminism and Terrorism, by way of the confusion caused by alleged inspirations from on high and powers flowing into us, by none of our doing, from some unknown source.

Now, it is a puzzle indeed as to how, the real father of phenomenology, who discovered the threefold synthesis with his brilliant transcendental reasoning about "conditions under which alone knowledge of objects is possible" including the transcendental unity of apperception and other subtle grades of subjectivity, could be so vehemently opposed to selfobservation! Of course, some of it is explained by his life-long love-hate relationship with Swedenborg's claims of extra-sensory perception of disembodied spirits. But Kant himself offers some explanation in the next paragraph, by way of distinguishing the looking-within that he recommends as part of the transcendental method, from the "unstable" anchorless spying after private inner experiences which he asks us to shun.

WHAT IS A SCIENCE?

Although going back to Latin words still adds respectability in Medical sciences, the Latin root of the word "science" does not seem to help us any more in figuring out the necessary conditions for something counting as a science. Scientia meant simply knowledge. Hence one who knows all is omniscient and ignorance or not knowing is nescience. Spinoza called the ecstatic mystical unitive knowledge of all that is there as identical with One Substance, Scientia Intuitiva, which the scientific community will now laugh away as some kind of mystical madness. If "science" meant "method-conscious knowledge-system", we could ask if there can be a *knowledge-system* about meditation. And the answer, as shown above, is too obviously affirmative. Along with most practically essential knowledgesystems such as agricultural botany, mathematics, medicine including pharmacology, parallel knowledge-systems of contemplative mindmanagement emerged in ancient time both in the West and the East. The Sanskrit word for a knowledge-system is "*śāstra*" and Yoga-*śāstra* is what the most well-known Bhagavadgita is called at the end of each chapter. For a knowledge-system of Yoga to exist, it is not necessary that most of those who use the word "Wissenshaft" or "Science" should understand or feel comfortable with the word "*śāstra*." I would like to claim that it should be logically and politically possible for people to be doing science without having heard the word "science" just as it is possible for people to be doing extremely complicated metallurgy without ever having heard the word "metallurgy".

In contemporary philosophy of science, demarcation of science from non- or pseudo-science has been called "boundary work" and is a highly contentious topic. Public lectures and popular writings of John Tyndall (1820-1893) are a good example of how this boundary work was done in Victorian England, while Darwin's *Origin of Species* has announced an open war between Christianity and empirical science which Richard Dawkins is still continuing in the 21st century. Tyndall comes up with four criteria to distinguish a scientific discipline from a religious or spiritual discipline or theology - notice that even "theology" had in it the "logos," which makes "biology" the science of life. And these are:

(a) Science is empirical in that its avenue to truth is through publicly checkable observation and experiment, whereas religious disciplines are based on unquestionable scripture.

(b) Science is practically useful in fueling technological progress which improves material conditions of the nation, while religious discipline (such as prayer or meditation) could be useful at best in improving emotional psychological lives.

(c) Science respects no authority except individual reason and facts of nature, whereas religious (even Buddhist atheist) disciplines require bowing down to a Pope or a Guru or a Rimpoche or Sensei.

(d) Science is objective knowledge free from emotional bias, devotion, or prejudice, whereas religious or contemplative disciplines come with a baggage of faith, loyalty, and communally shared but subjective feelings of sacredness.

In the next 150 years after Tyndall, many of these claims have been falsified about science, and especially Tibetan Buddhist meditation traditions have claimed many of these features of scientificity. It is true that historically we have no record of what experiments were conducted in order to come to generalizations like "from concentrating on the Sun, one comes to have knowledge of all the worlds" (bhuvana-jñānaṃ sūrye saṃyamāt" Yoga-sūtra III.23) and the detail geography and cosmology given in the commentary of all the "worlds" (*bhuvana*) has been falsified by current geography and astronomy. But that does not show that the matter cannot be brought under empirical scrutiny. Also, the concept of science itself harbors an inner tension between dependence on apodictic *reason* versus dependence on continuously falsfiable and upgradable *experience*. Boundary work gets far more complicated when we consider the claims of Freudian Psychoanalysis to be scientific. From what publicly checkable observations and experiments could Freud have concluded that dreams are wish-fulfillments? Can there be an objective science of mind in the same sense as chemistry or anatomy is a science. On the one hand the element of logic, deductive reasoning and mathematization, and on the other hand, the element of personal experience (controlled observation and experiment) and reliance on newer technologies of microscopy and enlargement have problematized the simple concept of "objective observation". When we look at EEGs, it is not clear whether we are seeing brain-waves or drawing inferences from effects to causes. Although meditation, and definitely a Samkhya type theory of meditation, I believe, combines both reasoning and experience, deductive and inductive logic as well as personal experience, prima facie, it may seem that meditative experience eludes both reason and sense-experience. As the devotees of science would put it, it is based on neither reason nor ordinary experience but on unquestionable holy books and private cranky para-normal claims of esoteric experience. And as devotees of meditation often put it, spiritual experience is supra-logical and supra-sensory. Both parties wish to preserve the incompatibility of the scientific approach and the contemplative spiritual approach. Besides, the history and power politics of knowledge makes it extremely hard for Europeans to see science in the strict sense of the term in Asian knowledgesystems.

Science needs to be based on pure rationality, and not on faith or trust in any authority. The theory and practice of meditation that we are talking about here are based on certain Indian traditions which flourished under an allegiance to the unquestioned authority of the Vedas or the Buddha, or some other root-text the truth of which was taken for granted. Meditation curbs the autonomous reasoning of the meditator. Where the forces of tradition and verbal testimony are so dominant, how could *reason* in the Western sense of the term flourish? And without reason how could there be a science?

Three lines of response, of varying degrees of power, and by no means mutually exclusive, can be adopted in the face of this objection. First, while it is correct that mere or "dry" reasoning (*śuṣka-tarka*) has been belittled by great Indian thinkers like Śaṅkara because it is groundless, unstable and conflict-generating (*Brahmasūtra-bhāṣya*, II.1.11), or because, as Bhartṛhari* noted before him, "what expert reasoners have concluded with great logical acumen and effort is disproved by yet other more expert logicians," not *all* Indian thought is blindly supportive of scriptural authority. Having abused the authors of the three Vedas as impostors and cheats, the materialist-skeptical Cārvāka philosophers from very ancient times rejected all trust in religious texts as irrational. Of course, in their case, even inferences, and especially inductive generalizations, are epistemically unjustified, and insofar as testimony is reduced to a form of inference, our reliance on testimony too loses all rational respectability. Right from the Buddha's own sermons up to the sophistication of Buddhist epistemology in the Yogācāra-Sautrāntika school, the Buddhist mind shows opposition to unexamined "say so" as evidence. The Buddha urges his disciples not to believe his own words upon the basis of his personal authority, but to test them by reasoning and individual experience. Accordingly, only perception and inference are admitted as sources of knowledge in Buddhist epistemology, and testimony is either rejected or reduced away. Similarly, in what has been called the "Tradition of Rationalist Medicine,"1 appealing to religious or scriptural authorities in the context of clinical practice has been regarded by Caraka (from the very early Christian era) as committing the fallacy of irrelevance. We shall see, in

1 Debiprasad Chattopadhyaya, "Tradition of Rationalist Medicine in Ancient India", *Philosophy: Theory and Action.* Surendra Sheodas Barlingay, Kalidas Bhattacharya & K. J. Shah (eds.) (Poona: Continental Prakashan for Prof. S.S. Barlingay Felicitation Committee, 1980), pp. 85-115.

a subsequent section on ancient Indian medical reasoning, how "medical integrity" was supposed to consist in reliance on empirical data, inductive probability, practical efficacy, and *not* on religious authority.

Within the mainstream orthodox schools, Sāṃkhya in spite of its lipservice to the Vedas and the "word of the expert" as sources of knowledge very clearly relied on its own variety of reflective reasoning as the sole means of attaining such knowledge as would lead to the pure and permanent cessation of suffering. In the two opening couplets of Sāṃkhya-Kārikā*, observed worldly means of removing pain and scripture-prescribed ritualistic means of removing pain are both rejected as unsatisfactory, because even the heavenly pleasures (after death) promised as rewards for the performance of Vedic rituals are exhaustible, mixed with pain and surpassable in degree. The only method of attaining an inexhaustible, unmixed and unsurpassable state of freedom from pain is rational reflection on the distinction between the manifest (effects), unmanifest (cause) and consciousness (which is neither effect nor cause). Sāṃkhya, therefore, is at heart an out-and-out reason-based system of thought with its own basic presuppositions, such as the three fundamental *guṇa*-strands (mentioned above as delight-dynamicity-delusive intertia) and the doctrine of the preexistence of effect in the material cause, defended by a series of internally coherent arguments.

Second, even Vedānta and Mīmāṃsā the two pillars of Vedic orthodoxy assign a crucial role to reasoning and critical argumentation in extracting the correct meaning from sacred sentences of the "heard" revelation (*śruti*). Far from being antagonistic, reason and scripture coexist peacefully together in coupling compounds strewn all over Vedānta literature (for example, *śruti-yukti, tarkagam, śāstra-nyāya*). What is this assisting role that reason plays in Vedic hermeneutics? In the Upaniṣads, the philosophical cream of the Vedas, one finds statements like "you are that (*Brahman*)". In order to make sense of such identity claims, the reader must first "distill" the meaning of "you," which is coreferential with the reader's (ideally, listener's) use of "I." Causal links are established by what in Vedanta is called the method of presence in presence and absence in absence (*anvaya-vyatireka*). Now, signification or designation is taken as a special case of a causal link, because there is a lawlike connection between the utterance of a word and the consequent grasp, by the hearer, of a meaning. The Upaniṣads start from a proto-materialistic conception of the self (the referent of "I") as the food-constituted body. Śaṅkara* the commentator uses this method of presence and absence to reject, one after another, these "object"-natured candidates for selfhood, the body, the lifebreath, the inner sense, the intellect, because the self seems to be present even in the absence or non-functioning of these elements (in death, dreams, deep sleep, and so on). This method of elimination leaves only a pure nonindividuated subjective consciousness as the possible meaning of "I." A similar isolation of relevant signification is performed on the word "that" (which directly stands for God and the totality of physical and mental entities of the universe). When the direct or primary referents of these two terms are seen to be in partial conflict, because the individual embodied "I" is not *prima facie* identical with "that" world or all that there is, the method of rational exegesis is employed. Secondary significance of words is generally derived from the literal sense by extension (for example, "crying over spilt milk" comes to include a whole lot of spilt other things) and elimination (for example, in "the opinion of the house," "house" does not signify house at all). Thus through "retaining a part and rejecting a part" of their literal sense, the words "I" and "that" are taken in their secondary significance. That part of their distinct literal meaning where they intersect: namely, pure subjective consciousness, is taken as the emerging oblique meaning of the scriptural identity statement. What can never be spoken of, the *Ātman-Brahman,* could thus be got at indirectly by its only testimony, the sentences of an authorless revelation. This is an oversimplified summary of the intricate interpretive technique through which reasoning is used to distill the indirect meaning of the "great sentences" of the Veda. Thus the text is trusted as the sole proof of the *Ātman-Brahman* (the Self which is All) but it is subjected first to a tradition-tested method of critical scrutiny. It is only relentless reasoning which can help us hold on to the distinction between the self (reality) and the not-self (appearance), and without such reasoned discrimination, no blind parroting of the scriptures would get us anywhere. As far as the role of testimony is concerned, even scripture is a ladder to be kicked away after the saving knowledge of non-duality dawns. Thus Śaṅkara's faith in the "truth" of Vedic text is also ontologically *provisional. Tarka* (reasoning) may be baseless by itself (*apratiṣṭha**), but even *śruti** (scripture) is, in the final analysis, ignorance that helps cure ignorance. While discussing the "instability" of autonomous reasoning, Śaṅkara, interestingly, considers and dismisses an objection which it is worthwhile to mention. "This alleged refutability and non-decisiveness of reason," the objection goes, "should be recognized as a good feature rather than a weakness, insofar as it keeps room for correction and improvement." After all, if you have conflicting Vedic texts, reasoning is your only basis for adjudication! Third, we could question the very assumption that relying primarily on an impersonal unquestionable tradition is necessarily irrational. There are two ways in which not only the compatibility between reason and testimony but the essentiality of commitment to the tradition as a necessary condition for rationality can be brought out. The first way can be called the Nyāya-Dummett way and the second the Mīmāṃsā-Gadamer way.

By emphasizing the irreducible role of testimonial knowledge in the acquisition and use of language even in a "scientific community," Nyāya epistemology exposes a fundamental error of Lockean individualistic epistemology. As Michael Dummett remarks,

> It is not a rule of etiquette, or a device for saving time, that we should accept what others

tell us: It is fundamental to the entire institution of language.[2]

There is no rationality without social interaction, because as Wittgenstein showed us, no one can be a private rule-follower. But there is no social interaction without understanding of others' speech. And, Dummett and Davidson, in spite of other major differences, both insist that there is no understanding of others' speech without a basic presumptive trust in their testimony. It follows, therefore, that there is no rationality without a basic trust in the veracity of competent speakers, "be that a sage, a lay Aryan or a *mleccha* foreigner" (to quote Vātsyāyana, the fifth-century Nyāya commentator), unless there is reason to suspect ignorance or deceit or lack of commitment. While this way of putting testimony back into the heart of rationality proceeds through the inescapable *trustworthiness* of fellow-speakers of a language, the other way, adopted by Kumārila Bhaṭṭa and recently articulated by John Taber using insights from Gadamer, turns on an underlying *distrust* of individual speakers and treats a speaker-less body of received tradition to be the only possible source of moral knowledge. Perception or empirically grounded inference never gives us any knowledge of what ought to be done. The verdict of our conscience or moral emotions is highly unreliable. The only ineluctable source of knowledge of right and wrong action, under the Mīmāṃsā view, which is firmly rooted in the epistemological doctrine of the intrinsic validity of all knowledge, is the impersonal objective (beginningless) prescriptive sentences handed down by one's own cultural tradition. The only way meaningful speech could be unreliable is by being spoken by fallible individuals. If it is not spoken by anyone, as Mīmāṃsā takes the Vedas to be, then it is intrinsically knowledge-yielding. The knowledge it yields is also unique, because from no other source of knowledge can you have any rational insight into morality. To quote Gadamer, "The real force of morals...is based on tradition. They are freely taken over but by no means created by a free insight grounded on reasons."[3] Of course, neither Gadamer nor any modern person can swallow the orthodoxy of Kumārila that the Vedic tradition *alone* is the source of *all* moral knowledge (perhaps Kumārila too meant this exclusively for the Vedic people). But it may be necessary to rectify the Enlightenment idea that a fully autonomous external critique of tradition is possible or desirable purely on the basis of individual rationality based on ordinary sense-experience and feelings. A creative but sympathetic understanding of the traditionalist ethics of Mīmāṃsā may enable us to appreciate why it is perfectly rational for a Veda-rooted Indian to assert "I ought to feed the guest first because the Veda says so" and then

---

2 B. K.Matilal and Arindam Chakrabarti, eds., *Knowing from Words*, (Dordrecht: Kluwer, 1994), p. 266.

3 Hans-Georg Gadamer, *Truth and Method* (London: Sheed and Ward, 1989), p. 281

claim, like Wittgenstein, that he has hit the rock-bottom of reason-giving and that is where his spade turns.

Finally, if we look at the favorable accounts of intuitive knowledge in Patañjali's Yoga or Bhartṛhari's word-non-dualism (*śabdādvaita*), we come to realize that it is a deepened or sophisticated form of a reflective rationality which in Yoga takes the form of discrimination (*viveka-khyāti**), and in the hands of the Grammarian takes the form of innate or instinctive capacity for synoptic grasp, for example, of the sentence-meaning as a whole. Both of these contexts are, interestingly, deeply linguistic. A yogapractitioner's *prajñā** (insight) becomes clearer and clearer, according to the *Yoga-sūtra** (I.42 43), first by reflecting upon the distinctness of a word, the concept, and the object, all three of which are confused inextricably in our ordinary consciousness. As one recognizes the conventional character of the word object relation and the memory-mediated character of the concept associated with the word, the pure object in its individuality is supposed to shine more and more distinctly in isolation from its linguistic and cognitive cloaks. The last step of this stripping the pure object of words and imaginations, through which the non-discursive "dropping out of the mind" is achieved is indeed hard to explain.

LOGIC AND YOGA

There is a wide-spread misconception, perhaps triggered by certain Buddhist meditation practices which discourage any thinking at all, that Yoga must consist in the cultivation of an irrational, hence unscientific temperament because one is not supposed to use concepts at all let alone think logically when one is meditating. But nothing could be further from the truth of the text and practices. Even if logical thinking were discouraged, Yogic experiences could still be studied scientifically like studying electro-magnetic interactions, because both are equally "invisible" and "inner". Does Science not study experiences of any kind? What if we could simulate yogic meditation-like behavior in robots? Would questions like "Can computers meditate?" be at least as relevant to the ScienceMeditation problem as the question "Can computers think" was to the Mind-Body problem?

Yoga practice, we must not forget, is squarely based on Sāṃkhya theory of knowledge. My point is that Sāṃkhya theory of knowledge is scientific in the modern sense. Any meditative practice based on such a scientific theory has got to be such that a modern science of that practice must be possible.

Sāṃkhya recognizes three sources of knowledge: Perception, Scriptural authority, and Inference. But it rejects, in so many words, the possibility that the first or the second, sensory perception or testimony would show us the way to complete cessation of suffering. What is left then? Contrary to popular expectation, Sāṃkhya does **not** bring in extrasensory perception at all. No experience can give us liberatory knowledge. What kind of knowledge of the difference between the manifest (*vyakta*) manifold of the effects and their unmanifest (*avyakta*) cause on the one hand and pure consciousness (*jña)* on the other can liberate us, permanently and exhaustively from all kinds of suffering? It has to be knowledge by reasoning or inference. That is Sāṃkhya's official answer. And Yoga does not depart from this in spirit, in so far as samadhi or concentration-states are first described as "with rational discrimination", "with inner argumentation" and then only proceeds to the non-conceptual highest states.

The centrality of logical reasoning in Yoga practice is clearly enunciated in the pre-Patanjali (most likely Pre-Buddhist) ancient text *Maitrāyaṇi Upaniṣad.* It speaks of **six** instead of eight limbs of Yoga. These are:

Breathing exercises (*prāṇāyāma*) Withdrawal of
the senses (*pratyāhāra)* Meditation (*dhyāna*)

One-tipped holding of the mind on an object (*dhāraṇa*) *Inward
reasoning (*tarka*)*
Stilling the flow of the mind (*samādhi*)

Indeed, this Upanishad says that the ultimate experience of Brahman is attained through reasoning alone: "...Having fully arrested the outward flow of speech-mind-and vital energy, one **sees** Brahman **with reasoning**" (*brahma tarkeṇa paśyati)*!"

What does Tarka mean here? Does it mean Reasoning or does it mean meditation? I think it means reasoning of a special kind which amounts to meditation

It is this six-limbed yoga, rather than the eight-limbed yoga of Patañjali, that Abhinavagupta alludes to in his early 11th century magnum opus: *Tantrāloka,* when he asserts, that the most important limb of Yoga is "good reasoning". In the 4th and 13th chapter of this definitive work on Kashmir Shaiva Tantra, Abhinavagupta says that much more essential and effective than breath-control or withdrawal of the senses, is the Yogic method of arguing with oneself and deepening the lessons learnt from one's teacher or scripture by self-critical rational reflection. Adhinava calls this method for the "powerful mind" (*śaktopāya),* which is one of the four alterantive paths to the recognition of the unity of Universal consciousness and the individual knowing self. In some rare cases, such good reasoning dawns on a practitioner without any extraneous instruction from any teacher. For such people, their own intellect or conscience act as their teacher. And in the Tantras, they are said to be "taught by the goddesses- the self-aware sensory powers"

Such a self-taught good reasoner manifests the divine flash of cognitive "genius" (*pratibhā*), an intuitive synoptic insight into all things, and especially into the essence of all languages and authentic spiritual traditions (*āgama*).

But even if one is not graced with such innate talent, with practice of clear thinking, logical reasoning, study of scriptures, instruction by a capable teacher, debate and discussion, the shaky flame of universal cognitive fire becomes gradually steadier and brighter. With a rationally cleansed and brightened light of insight "everything can be known", says Abhinava quoting Patañjali's Yogasūtra. (Tantrāloka: IV and XIII)

Similar importance is given to reasoning in the Mahāyāna Buddhist tradition of meditation as well. Refuting common misconceptions about meditation, Tsong Khapa responds to two anti-intellectualist qualms with characteristic vigor.

The first misconception: "When meditating on the path to Buddhahood, one should not do repeated analysis with discerning wisdom. Such analysis is only useful at the level of preparatory studies". Tsong Khapa responds: "This is nonsensical chatter of someone who is utterly ignorant of the crucial points of practice….First study with someone what you intend to practice and come to know it secondhand. Next use scripture and reasoning to properly reflect on the meaning of what you studied, coming to know it first hand....Thus you need both repeated analytical meditation and nonanalytical stabilizing meditation (*śamatha* and *vipaśyanā*)."

Again Tsong Khapa warns us: "Not knowing this system, some even propound, "If you are a scholar, you only do analytical meditation. If you are a spiritual seeker or adept you only do stabilizing meditation." This is not the case, because each must do both,...you must use discernment for both of these methods of meditation. If you lack or are deficient in such analytical meditation, then you will not develop stainless wisdom, the precious life of the path."[4]

MEDICAL MATERIALISM, UNOBSERVABILITY, UNREPEATABILITY AND OTHER POWERFUL OBJECTIONS AGAINST THE VERY IDEA OF A SCIENCE OF MEDITATION

William James coined a very elegant phrase to describe the tendency to explain away religious experience by giving a clinical causal account of why and how people come to have those "weird" experiences like hearing the music of the spheres or seeing lights or hearing voices of gods and goddesses - which have been reported with recurring patterns from Socrates to Ramakrishna, from Plotinus to Sri Aurobindo. James calls this dismissive explanatory drive "Medical Materialism":

---

4 *The Great Treatise on the Stages of the Path to Enlightenment, or LamRim by Tsong Khapa*. Transl. by Cutler and Newland (Ithaca: Snow Lion Publications, 2000).

> Medical materialism seems indeed a fit appellation for the too simple-minded system of thought that we are considering. Medical materialism finishes up Saint Paul by calling his vision on the road to Damscus a discharging lesion of the occipital cortex, he being an epileptic. It snuffs out Saint Teresa as an hysteric, Saint Francis of Assisi as an hereditary degenerate. Carlyle's organ-tones of misery it accounts for by a gastro-duodenal catarrh....And medical materialism then thinks that the spiritual authority of all such personages is successfully undermined."5

But then William James bites the bullet and claims that not only does tracing out the clinical history of persons with religious experiences have no relevance to the truth-claims of those experiences, the best scientific theories are often produced thanks to an exercise of genius and creativity the neurology of which would invariably brand those states as abnormal, unusual and verging on insane.

> Let us play fair in this whole matter, and be quite candid with ourselves and with the facts. When we think certain states of mind superior to others, is it ever because of what we know concerning their organic antecedents? No! It is always for two entirely different reasons. It is either because we take an immediate delight in them; or else because we believe them to bring us good consequential fruit for life. When we speak disparagingly of (like Kant does in his very interesting but little known book on Swedenborg Dreams of A Spirit Seer) "feverish fancies" surely the fever-process as such is not the ground of our diseseteem - for aught we know to the contrary, 103 or 104 degrees Fahrenheit might be a much more favorable temperature for truths to germinate and sprout in than the more ordinary blood-heat of 97 or 98 degrees.6

The much celebrated work of V.S. Ramachandran 7 has not only shown that people can have pains in phantom limbs. From this, according to

---

5 William James, *Varieties of Religious Experience: A Study in Human Nature* (Amazon, 2002), p 13

6 *Ibid.*, p. 15.

7 With the development of new brain imaging technology, scientists began to be interested in the neurobiological underpinnings of mystical experiences. V.S. Ramachandran, a neuropsychologist at the University of California San Diego, focuses on temporal lobe epilepsy (TLE) patients, who are prone to excessive activity in their temporal lobes. TLE patients experience microseizures, which result in powerful and deeply emotional religious experiences. What is more, the effect of these seizures is not fleeting: most TLE patients are

one reviewer, it follows that all pains are illusory. It is fashionable in the field, both for eliminativist physicalists like Dennett as well as for more Buddhist-sympathetic cognitive scientists like Metzinger to call our sense of self an illusion. We should have known, that if self is an illusion then pain would be an illusion too - an easy way to deny the reality of felt pain is to chant the being - No One mantra - whose pain could it be? If the hand has been amputated then my feeling of pain in the hand is an illusion. But if the pain is stimulated by a cut in my own un-amputated hand then what could it mean to call it an illusion? Phenomenologically, the water-vision in a mirage is indistinguishable from a water-vision in a real puddle. Therefore, is all water illusory?

While Science is based on hard facts personally observable to any ordinary person, Indian contemplative sciences - according to the stereotype - are based on unquestioning faith in the words of the teacher (Testimony versus Personal Observation) - no one can see the the Anāhata Chakra - a four-petaled lotus in the heart by vivisection.8

But, Brajendra Nath Seal began his pivotal work "Positive Sciences of the Ancient Hindus' with a detailed examination of the Sāṃkhya-Yoga system of knowledge treating it as a physics and chemistry. A hundred years after that, one of the leading theoretical particle physicists of United states, George Sudarshan writes "Meditative states are communicable and

---

religious during the periods between the seizures, sometimes to the point of fanaticism. Dr. Ramachandran and his colleagues proposed that heightened electrical activity during these seizures strengthens connections between the subject's temporal lobe sensory areas and the amygdala (a brain region usually associated with emotion), resulting in the patients' intensely personal and emotional reaction to their experiences. With the help of skin conductance response (measuring small rapid changes in perspiration), Ramachandran investigated whether TLE patients would have a stronger emotional response to sexual/violent stimuli or to the stimuli with religious nature. His subjects, indeed, showed heightened arousal when presented with religious words and symbols. In contrast, control subjects displayed the strongest responses to sexual stimuli. Dr. Ramachandran's findings, however, were inconclusive, due to the limited number of test subjects and to the fact that TLE patients often have changes in sexuality. Nevertheless, his studies suggest that the temporal lobe is involved in religious experiences and, according to Ramachandran's 1997 presentation at the conference of the Society for Neuroscience, that individual neural differences in that area may influence the degree of personal religiosity in healthy people. (Mariya Simakova. *Neurobiology and Theology: Friends or Foes?* http://serendip.brynmawr/edu/bb/neuro/neuro06/web1/msima akov.html).

8 Stephen Phillips argues in detail that repeatable publicly available yogic experience, until it is definitely falsified, be given the same epistemic prestige as a laboratory report by a group of scientists as "mystical empiricism". See: Stephen Phillips. *Yoga, Karma and Rebirth: A Brief History and Philosophy* (New York: Columbia University Press, 2009), pp. 132-135

reproducible, and this procedure thus conforms to the standard definition of science."9

In James Austin's 2006 book *Zen-Brain Reflections*, detailed reports of Positron Emission Tomography (PET scanning) of the brains seasoned meditators while they are thinking of themselves and observing their own thoughts while performing specific shared mental tasks, have been statistically compared and correlated with their first person reports. Austin tends to take increased blood-flow within the precuneus and angular gyru when the subjects reflected on their own personality traits as evidence for a heightened sense of self, and yet other Functional Magnetic Resonance Imaging of the brain during the corpse posture relaxation meditation was supposed to have shown near effacement of the sense of ego. Yet even the surfaces of the neurophysiology of even the crudest *prāṇāyāma* practices have not yet been scratched. But it is established beyond doubt that a neuroscience of *dhyāna* is not just possible but is well under way.

CONCLUSION: WHAT IS THE POINT OF ALL THIS?

The point of all this was not to show that science and spirituality can somehow be compatible. The point was to remind ourselves that "science", even in its central use, if freed up from its alliance with military or mercantile "use," still has something to do with wisdom and study of human lived experience. If science has to be knowledge that can be harnessed for human good, then it must turn to such a study of consciousness and its nonpathologically focused, tranquil, contentless, and rejuvenatingly blissful states. Especially because modern Western science has had an unholy alliance with war, environmental exploitation and colonialism, it has an obligation now to turn towards an unbiased examination of the methods of character-development and stress-reduction and self-knowledge, and cultivation of unselfish compassion, suggested by ancient contemplative traditions, Buddhist, Hindu, Christian, Jewish or ancient Greco-Roman. A new conception of science may emerge just out of noticing how much work has already been done in the sciences of meditation by these ancient tradition and how much more needs to be done in the modern spirit of biological and empirical psychological and phenomenological sciences. But more importantly, we might end up finding out, contra Wittgenstein, that not only is Science of Meditation possible, a philosophy like Sāṃkhya is precisely that: the science of meditation. Perhaps like Neo-Nyāya, which revolutionized all theoretical disciplines in India in the 14th-15th centuries after Gaṅgeśa, we now need a Neo-Sāṃkhya working hand in hand with the cognitive scientists to give us a science of meditation.

---

9 Tony Rothman and George Sudarshan, *Doubt and Certainty* (Helix Books, 1998), pp 18-19.

CHAPTER X

THE RELATIONSHIP OF SCIENCE (ŚĀSTRA, VIDYĀ) AND PHILOSOPHY (DARŚANA) IN THE TRADITIONAL INDIAN CULTURE

It is possible to discuss the relationship of science and philosophy only in the context of their clear distinction. Today the importance of such discussion is caused by the dramatic nature of this relationship: by the fact that to start from the turn of the 19th/20th centuries, science and philosophy have not only been differed but opposed as well, that there has been a conflict between them. Taking into consideration unclear contents of the notions of "science" 1 and "philosophy," 2 let's mention that here science refers to all forms of theoretical knowledge on selected aspects of reality, but a philosophy is a theoretically articulated world view (Weltaushaung). These specifications enable us to precise also the character of the conflict as confrontation between the knowledge pertaining to a world view and to a particular science. The indication of their conflict are the heated debates between the philosophers and scientists on the status of philosophy in culture, necessity of philosophy in general or its necessity for science, on the one hand, and on the problem of humanizing of natural science - on the other. Over the last decade increasingly revealing of itself is yet another, the third direction of discussions which is due to the fact that some scientists having groundless expectations towards certain specific Eastern traditions of philosophy are trying to find therein the methods to solve contemporary scientific problems and to enrich their heuristics at the expense of such traditions (the Buddhism is especially popular in this sense). The main historical causes of the conflict are seen as, first, **non-coincidence** of a cognitive ideal in the form of objective and absolute rational truth (the ideal formed yet in the cradle of the Western European culture, in Ancient

---

1 Frits Staal examined in the greatest detail the differences historically formed in the European cultures and in the USA to express the notion of "science" which entails unclear content of the notion - F. Staal, *Concepts of Science in Europe and Asia* (Leiden: International Institute for Asian Studies, 1993), pp. 6-12.

2 The collection of his definitions in the article "Philosophie" may serve as one of the arguments grounding unclear contents of the notion of "philosophy": *Philosophie,* Historisches Wörterbuch der Philosophie / Hrsg. Von J. Ritter, K. Gründer, G.Gabriel. Bd. 7 (Basel/Stuttgart: Schwabe Verlag, 1989), pp. 571923.

Greece) and its real embodiment in scientific and philosophic conceptions suggesting unlike epistemic portraits of the same "objective" reality and, second, **unacceptability** of this non-coincidence within the framework of the Western rationality (meaning "understanding of intelligibility"), 3 which has led the Western theoretical thought to the "oblivion of being"4 and still has not lost its influence in science.

Nowadays the discussions on the relationship between science and philosophy became a reality not only of the Western culture but of the Eastern cultures as well, since the Western European science with its ideals and norms became a part of world culture. However, in the traditional Eastern cultures (which had been developing before the commencement of the globalization processes, i.e. before the XVIIth century), nevertheless, the same as in the traditional Western culture, the relationship between science and philosophy wasn't as dramatic as it became in the West during the Modernity era. If in the West the seeds of conflict were laid into the very foundations of theoretical thinking in the form of ideal and purpose of knowledge and had to sprout by all means, in the East - particularly, in India - (1) **the relationship between the specific science and world view (Weltaushaung) knowledge[s] was conflict-free in the traditional Indian culture**: the *darśanas, śāstras/vidyās* weren't opposed to each other, and as a result Indian culture succeeded in escaping the question about the necessity of philosophy; (2) this relationship **could not have evolved into conflict because the objectives and values of the Indian *śāstras* (or *vidyās*) and *darśanas* were initially charged with another potential: the ideal of rational truth was not a purpose of knowledge there and the rationality criteria weren't regarded as those of absolute truth**. In my paper, I will try to prove these two statements.

The absence of conflict between science and philosophy is deducible from the following facts.

1) From the lack of relationship problem between the *śāstras* and *darśanas* among the most important discussion problems usually presented in the philosophic compendia (*saṃgraha*) — special texts of polemical nature. In particular, the said problem is not raised in the well-known "*Tattvasaṃgraha*" of the Buddhist Śāntarakṣita (VIII cent.) and in Kamalaśīla's commentary "*Pañjikā*", nor does it appear in the well-known compendium of the vedantist Madhva (1198-1278) "*Sarva-darśanasaṃgraha*" with the author's commentary.

2) From the correlation of semantic fields of the Sanskrit terms "*śāstra*", "*vidyā*" and "*darśana*" from which originated the relevant words in the modern Indian languages (particularly, in Hindi and Bengali), and

3 V.N. Porus, "Ratsionalnost," *Encyclopedia epistemologii i filosofii nauki.* In Russian. (Moscow: "Canon+" ROOI "Reabilitatsia", 2009), p. 807.

4M. Heidegger. Was heisst Denken? Tübingen: Max Niemeyer Verlag, 1954. S. 136.

these words are used therein as synonyms of "science" and "philosophy". Unfortunately, with this identification, connotations of the modern Western terminology and, correspondingly, an idea of relationship between science and philosophy are transferred to the Indian terms. Actually, as indologists repeatedly wrote, the relations between those realities of the traditional Indian culture that we call "Indian philosophy" and "Indian science" were of different type than those between science and philosophy in the West. They are clearly discernible if a simple philological scrutiny is made to the meanings of terms in Sanskrit texts of authority, particularly, in an scrutiny given in the well-known dictionary of M. Monier-Williams. The vast majority of primary sources appearing therein shows intuitive use of terms, without explicit definitions, while for us their meaning and sense are determined contextually. Here are some of the meanings.

The meanings of the "*śāstra*" term were: order, command, precept, rule of conduct (in "*Ṛgveda*", *kāvyas, purāṇas*); teaching, precept, instruction, advice, good advice (in "*Mahābhārata*" and *kāvyas*); means of teaching, manual or code of rules, book or treatise, especially religious or scientific, scripture or writing of a divine authority (the name "*śāstras*" was also given to the four *vedas* and classical *brāhmanic* disciplines, the list of which comprises 14-18 sciences). The word "*śāstra*" is often placed after a word designating a book's subject (*dharma-śāstra, kāvya-śāstra, kāmaśāstra*). In this case we understand it as a designation of a specific theoretical discipline. It is also used to designate an individual theory but not by the criterion of its special subject-matter, but by its normative character (for example, the traditional culture gives the name "*śāstras*" to "*Nirukta*" of *Yāska*, "*Mānavadharmaśāstra*", "*Mahābhārata*", *kāvyas* and *purāṇas*). "*Śāstras*" is also a name for systematic teachings of religiousphilosophical character (*vedānta-śāstra, yoga-śāstra*5).6

The term "*vidyā*" was used with the following meanings: knowledge, science, education, erudition, philosophy as well as to designate the three *vedas*, theory, dialectics or philosophy (*ānvīkṣikī*), 7 theory of statecraft (*daṇḍa-nīti*), practical arts (*vārttā*) such as agriculture, commerce, medicine. In the "*Mānavadharmaśāstra*" (VII, 43) "*vidyā*" is used in the expression

5 The name "*śāstra*" is usually given to a systematic teaching contained in a basic text with several commentaries.

6 M. Monier-Williams, *Sanskṛt-English Dictionary*, New ed. with collabor of E. Leumann, C. Cappeller and others (New Delhi: Munshiram Manoharlal Publishers Prvt.Ltd., 1976; 1st ed. 1899), p. 1069.

7 See discussion on the meaning of the "*ānvīkṣikī*" term in: V. K. Shokhin, *Brahmanic filosofia. Nachalni I klasicheski periodis.* In Russian. (Moscow: Vostochnaya literatura RAN, 1994) P. 162-170; idem, "Ānvīkṣikī," *Indiiskaya filosofiya: Encyclopaedia.* In Russian. (Moscow: Vostochnaya Literatura Publishers, 2009), p. 80; W.Halbfass, *India and Europe* (Delhi: Motilal Banarsidass, 1990), pp. 263-264, 273-286.

"knowledge of Absolute" (*Ātma-vidyā*), in other Hindu texts of authority it is associated with the knowledge contained in the texts of the *vedic* complex such as *vedāṅgas, purāṇas,* exegetical texts (*mīmāṃsā*), logicalepistemological texts (*nyāya*) and normative texts - those expounding the law (*dharma*).8

The term "*darśana*" denotes: demonstration, display (in *Pāṇini's "Aṣṭādhyāī"* V.2.6); vision (in *Kālidāsa*'a poem "*Raghuvaṃśa*", XI. 93); cognition, expression, teaching (in "*Mahābhārata*", I.583, and "*Bhaviṣyapurāṇa*", V.4.11); message, observation, visual perception (in "*Ṛgveda*", I.116.23, in "*Śatapatha brāhmaṇa.*", 14, "*Śāṅkhāyana-gṛhya-sūtra*", V.5, in "*Mahābhārata*", in the medical treatise "*Suśruta-saṃhitā*", IV.27); eyesight (in the same medical text, VI.17); point of view, teaching, philosophical systems (namely, six orthodox ones - "*Mahābhārata*" XII.11045 and so on).9

Comparison of the given meanings shows that in their usage the terms "*śāstra*", "*vidyā*" and "*darśana*" were circulating with a multitude of meanings, having rather extended semantic fields which partly coincide for all three of them. These terms begin to be used in the special meanings of "science" and "philosophy" that are of interest to us later than in their everyday meanings: during the Middle Ages among the authors who reflected the shaped sets of *brāhmaṇic* sciences and religious-philosophical systems already consolidated in the culture. It follows from comparison between the semantic fields of the Sanskrit analogues of "science" and "philosophy" that they were used to designate the very same mental contents, i.e. identical but not different and, moreover, not opposed objects. At the same time, the mentioned terms also have semantic differences proceeding from their etymology: the term "*śāstra*" lays emphasis on instructive, normative character of the teachings, the term "*vidyā*" - on their informative character and the term "*darśana*" - on suprarational and world view character.

Overlap in the meanings of the three terms is also registered in the medieval compendia where one can find their explicit definitions. Thus, the already mentioned compendium of Madhva "*Sarva-darśana-saṃgraha*" quotes a definition of *śāstras* given by the *bhaṭṭācāryas* (honorable teachers) wherein the normative character of the orthodox world view is underlined.

pravṛttir vā nivṛttir vā nityena kṛtakena vā | puṃsām yenopadiṣyeta tacchāstram abhidhīyate||

8 M. Monier-Williams, *Sanskṛt-English Dictionary*, New ed. with collabor. of E. Leumann, C. Cappeller and other. (New Delhi: Munshiram Manoharlal Publishers Prvt. Ltd., 1976; 1st ed. 1899), pp. 963-964.

9 *Ibid.*, P. 470-471.

The one by means of which the people, emergence, annihilation or eternal creation are explained, should be understood as *śāstra.*10

3) The *brāhmaṇic* erudition is regarded here as having decisive role in such "symphonic" (concordant) term usage. Although all the schools of religious-philosophic thought contributed to the development of the concepts "*śāstra*", "*vidyā*" and "*darśana*", 11 it was in the *brāhmaṇic* schools where matured the theoretical norms of cognitive activity with initial character of specific science. Later on, they were borrowed by non *brāhmaṇic* sages and transferred to the sphere of world view theorizing because such (philosophy) appeared in India later than individual sciences. Due to inclusivistic attitude of *brāhmaṇic* ideology, the *brāhmaṇas* accumulated a huge array of quite diverse knowledge, expressed it in a complex of sacred *vedic* literature and carried out its stratification using the universal of *dharma* created by them. As is known, the said universal has exceedingly manifold meanings: universal law, universal order, religion, status prescripts, juridical laws, any systematized teachings, good, etc. everything that directs the human life and causes viability of the social organism. The *vedic* complex is built around the four *vedas* (*veda-saṃhitā*), includes both orthodox texts and literary, normative, individual scholastic and philosophical works. The knowledge of individual science is proclaimed to be "auxiliary", "adjacent" to the sacred knowledge *śruti* and is accumulated in two blocks of texts on theoretical disciplines.

block is comprised of the four *upa-vedas* (literally "around vedas"): *āyurveda* (traditional medicine), *dhanurveda* (military theory), *gandharvaveda* (theory of music) and *arthaśāstra* (science of politics). Included in the second block are the six *aṅgas* (parts): *śikṣā* (phonetics) and *vyākaraṇa* (grammar) of *Pāṇini*, *chhandas* (etimology) of *Yāska*, *nirukta* (prosody) of *Piṅgalācārya*, *jyotiṣa* (astronomy with astrology and

10 *Sarva-darśana-saṃgraha* of Sāyaṇa-Mādhva with an original commentary in Sanskrit, ed. V. Sh. Abhyankar. 3d ed. (Poona: Bhandarkar Oriental Research Institute, 1978), p. 417.

11 There is an opinion that *jaina* philosopher *Haribhadra Sūrī* (VIII cent.) was the first who used the term "*darśana*" in order to designate the systematic world view teachings in his compendium "*ṣaḍdarśana-samuccaya*" — see N. A. Zheleznova, "Haribhadra Sūrī," *Indiiskaya filosofiya: Encyclopaedia*. In Russian. (Moscow: Vostochnaya Literatura Publishers, 2009), p. 827. For more on history of the term "*darśana*" see also W. Halbfass, *India and Europe* (Delhi: Motilal Banarsidass, 1990), pp. 264-273.

[redacted]

As far as all the categories of *vedic* literature are recognized in the *brāhmaṇic* ideology (of which Hunduism is a contemporary form) as an exposition of the same "eternal dharma" (*sanātana dharma*), - although with different degrees of particularity and various means oriented at perception levels of different social groups 12 - here is no contradiction between them. It is quite important that all these forms, communicating the knowledge of individual sciences and of world views, are necessary and mutually complementary, all of them as well as their relationship are canonized, i.e. they are not subject to revision and change.

The non-orthodox schools of philosophy did not accept the authority of *vedas* but they apperceived the universal of *dharma* and the necessity for various forms of its exposition, the same as stratification of knowledge types with non-conflict nature of science and philosophy resulting from this stratification.

The correlation of *śāstras* and *darśanas* established and canonized in the *vedic* complex is the third fact to confirm the absence of conflict between science and philosophy in the traditional Indian culture.

4) The last fact well-known to indologists applies to grounding of the second thesis that has been adduced. It regards the criteria of rationality and truth formed in the Indian culture which have a whole number of distinctions from the Western criteria of classical rationality.13

The term "truth" is equivalent to the Sanskrit term *satya* originating from the word *sant* - existing, real, good, being, sanctity. In accordance with etymology, *satya* is verity, truth and reality, i.e. it has three dimensions: logical-epistemological, ethical and ontological. This explains that in India there are several types of truth teachings discovering one of *satya*'s sides and stratifying these dimensions of truth. The most important of them is the ontological conception of the two truths or two levels of reality: supreme *paramārtha* and inferior -*vyavahāra*. The supreme reality is transcendent, unknowable by ordinary human capacities (feelings and thinking) and inexpressible, the inferior is knowable and expressible. But the transcendent reality may be reached by means of spiritual practices (*sādhana*) which

---

12 Sri Swami Sivananda, *All about Hinduism*. The book was first published in 1947, its virtual edition is placed at the address: http://www.sivanandadlshq.org/download/hinduismbk.htm.

13 Here are just some studies on this subject: W. Halbfass, *India and Europe* (Delhi: Motilal Banarsidass, 1990); F. Staal, *Concepts of Science in Europe and Asia* (Leiden: International Institute for Asian Studies, 1993); *The Pandit traditional Scholarship in India*, ed. A. Michaels (New Delhi: Manohar, 2001)

constitute an integral part of all the *darśanas*' teaching. Since truth, as a result of cognition, belongs to the inferior level of reality, the logicalepistemological truths obtain lower status than the truths permitting to reach the highest level of reality. The highest level was named as Absolute (*Ātman, Brahman*) and reaching this level as "liberation" (*mokṣa, mukti, nirvāṇa*). The process of liberation is not theoretical, but practical. It comes after mastering the theoretical knowledge, and in this sense it is posttheoretical and supra-theoretical. In India the orientation towards the highest level of reality became thusly the orientation to transcend the limits of the rational and theoretical. It could not have been a stimulus for theoretical cognition of the material world with the aim of mastering the essence of things, and therefore, within traditional Indian culture science serving the needs of technology has not reached a high level of its development. In Western culture, thanks to Aristotle, an ideal of theoretical knowledge as a supreme form of truth was firmly established and this knowledge was understood as mastering the essence of things. The Indian tradition directed to supra-rational knowledge as mastering one's own being. This knowledge was supposed to restore a natural spiritual harmony of life and to return an earthly life to its transcendental origins. It remained within the circle of human existence and could not have become its "oblivion".

The logical-epistemological concepts of truth were developed in the teachings about the sources of valid knowledge, *pramāṇa-vāda.* 14 *Pramāṇavāda* embodied a rationalistic tendency of Indian philosophy. It was believed to be an important part of systematic teachings of all *darśanas* and therefore their basic texts began with the discussions on the problems of epistemology and logic. In essence, a proof of reliability of their instruments to obtain the truth is a method, independently discovered by the Indians, to verify the metaphysical concepts provided that their empirical verification is impossible (as they teach about the transcendent reality). That's what Th. Stcherbatsky paid attention to when writing: "Any philosophy of them [of the Indians - *N.K.*] begins from psychology, i.e. from the analysis of perception and consciousness phenomena; then it comes to a teaching of syllogism..., and only after establishing such theory of knowledge it comes to the philosophy proper."15

In the logical-epistemological texts, the truth appears in the guise of knowledge (*pramā*) and the truth problem is solved as a problem of the validity criteria of knowledge. For Indians an ideal of truth is related, first, to an ideal of correctness (*avisaṃvāda*) came from grammar which in India took on aspect of a systematized theory earlier than the *darśanas* appeared (in the IV cent. B.C., thanks to *Pāṇini*). Such understanding of truth is

14 The term was first used by the XVth century logician Gaṅgeśa. 15 Th. Stcherbatsky, "Logica v drevney indii," *Notes of the Eastern Department of the Russian Archaeological Society*. In Russian. (St. Petersburg: ZVOPAO, 1902), vol. XIV, p. 155.

correlated with the Western non-classical conceptions of coherent and congruent truths.

From dialectics to epistemology moved the notion of conventional truth developed for common use in debate: regarded as true was the proven under the rules here and now in respect of which the disputing parties came to an agreement. What is regarded as truth today might be refuted in another time and under other circumstances, if someone succeeds to prove the opposite. There was no "objective" and "absolute" truth recognized by the Indian thinkers which followed from the generally accepted Indian notion of a multitude of *dharma*'s aspects and their dependence on a subject of cognition.

The logical-epistemological truth is inferior, it "works" at the level of phenomenal world. Although the empirical-inductive method with which the emergence of Western empiricism is normally linked, was not developing in Indian epistemology, the way in which both orthodox (*āstika*) and non-orthodox (*nāstika*) representatives understood the essence of "inferior" truth, was formed by ordinary common sense and turned out to be empiricist in essence. The *āstika-naiyāyikas* believed the true knowledge to be a representation of reality (*yathārthya*), i.e., in modern terms, kept to the correspondence theory of truth. They affirmed that in a judgment expressing true knowledge, an object (*viśeṣya*) was correlated with that quality (*viśeṣaṇa*) which it had in reality. If a judgment conveys false knowledge, its object is related with a quality that it doesn't have in reality. Knowledge "is that what gives rise to purposeful activity," - *nyāya* representative *Annaṃbhaṭṭa* said in his commentary "*Tarka-dīpikā*" to his own treatise "*Tarka-saṃgraha.*"16

Recognizing the inferior true knowledge as illusionary and revealing nothing about the true reality behind it, even extremely idealistic *nāstikas*, buddhists-*yogācāras*, defined this knowledge as efficient, practically useful (*artha-kriyā-kāritva*), and enabling one to obtain the desired or to avoid the undesirable17. Such understanding of truth is correlated with the pragmatic theory of truth in the Western non-classical epistemology.

Even so briefly mentioned here criteria of the traditional Indian rationality allow to affirm that that they are lacking any single allusion to a possible conflict of science and philosophy because the "supreme" metaphysical truths are upheld on the supra-theoretical level.

(Translated from Russian by Galina Lisenco)

---

16 *Annaṃbhaṭṭa. Tarka-saṃgraha (Code of reasoning), Tarka-dīpikā (Explication for the Code of reasoning),* Sanskrit translation, commentaries and historical-philosophical studies by E. P. Ostrovskaya. In Russian. (Moscow: "Nauka", 1989), p. 206.

17 Th. Stcherbatsky, *The Theory of Cognition and Logic as per Teaching of the Latest Buddhists*: In 2 parts (St. Petersburg: Tipografiya Imperatorskoi Akademii Nauk, 1903-1909), part 1, p. 4.

CHAPTER XI

BUDDHIST ATOMISM IN THE LIGHT OF MODERN CONCEPTS OF "EMERGENT PROPERTY" AND "QUALIA"

There are many definitions of "emergent property". Here, I would propose the most general and abstract of them: "An emergent property of a system is one that is not a property of any component of that system, but is of the system as a whole" (http://en.wikipedia.org/wiki/Emergence). The terms "emergency" and "emergent properties" won wide popularity in many fields of modern research, from physics, chemistry, etc., up to psychology, philosophy and epistemology. In contemporary philosophy of mind and cognitive sciences it is with this concept of emergence that the majority of "solutions" concerning the mind-body problem are related - that is the mind, "I" and psychic phenomena are regarded as emergent properties of the neuronal structures of the brain.

As for the "qualia", this term that has grown popular in our days refers to the properties of sensory experience which being subjective, unique and untransmissible by its very nature, as this is a way of experiencing the world proper to every human being, while at the same time representing continually reproduced universals of human experience. If the concept of emergence is associated with many of the most promising contemporary scientific theories of consciousness, the notion of qualia is perceived instead as an insurmountable obstacle to their final triumph. Qualia remain the sole bastion of subjectivity, which cannot be taken by assault with the help of purely "objective" scientific methods.

My report aims at demonstrating how these important notions of the modern philosophical and scientific discourse could be used for understanding some aspects of Buddhist atomism. As a basic source, I intend to use the famous work of the Buddhist philosopher of the 4th-5th cent. Vasubandhu "Commentary on the Treasury of the Abhidharma" ("Abhidharmakośa-bhāṣya", hereinafter AKB).

One would ask how justified it is to talk about "emergence" or "qualia" in relation to non-Western thought, i.e. to use modern scientific terms not only anachronistically but extra-contextually? Isn't that an impermissible modernization?

In fact, it is a question of general methodological character which could be asked also with reference to many other much more fundamental terms and notions, such as "philosophy", "science", etc. A total skepticism as to the very possibility of using Western notions in the analysis of non

Western traditions seems to be a hermeneutical blind alley. Among our historians of philosophy, such skepticism is based as a rule on a belief in the uniqueness of the Western civilization and its achievements such as philosophy and science. My position is that every case should be investigated separately but in so doing, one should look for analogous problematizations and thematizations in another tradition rather than for analogous terms. Even in the absence of the latter the phenomenon itself designated by it may be well attested. In this case, there is nothing wrong in using the term as an element of our own hermeneutic meta-language.

Within modern Western philosophy developing in a close collaboration with cognitive sciences (neurosciences), Buddhism is no longer taken for an exotic religious doctrine beyond the scientific field. After the epoch-making book of Francisco J. Varela, Evan Thompson and Eleanor Rosch "The Embodied Mind", the Buddhist theories of mind have become a part of the modern discourses.1 In this book the term 'emergence' is applied to some Buddhist realities, first of all, within the framework of the Buddhist teaching of causality (*pratītya-samutpāda*) and its doctrines of consciousness and mental phenomena (*citta-caitta*). My paper refers to "emergence" in the Buddhist theory of atoms. What is meant here?

In AKB one may find a claim that though the individual atoms are neither material, nor able to come into contact with other atoms, nor perceptible, nevertheless they could be material, come into contact and obtain perceptibility in clusters, agglomerates, i.e. gross things. Herein "material" is a general translation of the terms *rūpa, rūpaṇa* (according to an etymological explication from AKB 1.13 - to strike and to be struck, oppress/oppressed). Apart from that, the notion of "material" normally includes impenetrability as well as the property of resisting or of counteracting - meanings of the term *pratighā*; things having this property are called *pratighāta* - impacted upon (referring to physical impact).

AKB suggests two ways of explaining the relationship between the atoms and the gross things formed by them:

According to the first one, the properties of materiality, ability to contact (entering into combinations) and perceptibility are contained not only in gross things, but in atoms (*paramāṇu*) as well; however, they are perceptible only in things, not in atoms. This is the model of the Vaibhāṣika School. I call it **accumulativist**. In accordance with this model, due to the increased number of atoms, i.e. their accumulation up to some critical mass, the properties of atoms become manifested to the point of becoming perceptible. The smallest atomic aggregate is a dust particle in a ray of light. As per some late Buddhist calculations, it contains 1.379 atoms.

According to the second explanation, the atoms have the mentioned properties only in agglomerations (*saṃghāta*), not individually. In this way,

1 Francisco J. Varela, Evan Thompson, Eleanor Rosch, *The Embodied Mind: Cognitive Science and Human Experience* (Cambridge: Massachusetts Institute of Technology, 1991)

these properties are a kind of systemic impact, i.e. they are emergent, therefore I call this model the **emergent one**. Apparently, it belongs to the Abhidharmic School of Sautrāntika.

This is not such an obvious case of emergence as in the Vaiśeṣika Atomism wherein atoms are absolutely lacking those properties ("grossness", "perceived size", etc.) which are characteristic of the things they compose. Nevertheless, what matters for me is the fact that Abhidharmikas raised a problem of certain system properties in relation to atoms although they did not designate those properties by special terms. Now, let's address the text of AKB directly.

It is from the viewpoint of the Sautrāntika model - which I tentatively call "emergent" - that in a commentary to the 13th *kārikā* of the first book of AKB there is an objection brought against understanding of the material/corporeal/color/form (all these are possible translations of the term *rūpa*) as *pratighāta* - the property of resistance:

"In such case (in case of *rūpa* being understood as *pratighāta*), a *rūpa* constituting an atom (*paramāṇu-rūpa*) does not come as *rūpa* [in the proper sense of the word] whereas it is *arūpaṇa*."2

Implied here is an etymological explanation of the term rūpa on the basis of its root *rūp* - to strike, *rūpyate* - "is struck", experiences physical pressure. In other words, a *rūpa* of an atom does not appear to be material in the sense of resisting, being impenetrable. This is the very viewpoint of Sautrāntika according to which atoms obtain "materiality" meaning the properties of impenetrability/resistibility only in the mass-like conglomerations. A Vaibhāṣika answers to this objection: " *Paramāṇu-rūpa* does not exist as something single and separate.3 It (*paramāṇu-rūpa*) suffers a strike/is resistant/is impenetrable only within a conglomerate."4

It turns out that both opponents agree that the atoms (*paramāṇu*) the smallest and subtlest of all the *rūpas* (under the definition of Vasubandhu) - do not exist as separate unitary objects but only in clusters, masses. Besides, from the point of view of both, the clusters of atoms do not form a whole that would be something more than the sum of its components. The AKB commentary to the 43rd *kārikā* claims that "the conglomeration (*saṃghāta*) of atoms does not differ from the [single] atoms." 5 Then what is the difference between the Vaibhāṣikas and Sautrāntikas according to AKB?

The difference is as follows: according to the Vaibhāṣikas, every atom of this conglomeration detains those properties of impenetrability etc. *independently of the other atoms*, while according to the Sautrāntikas - *in dependence of the other units of conlomeration* exactly because it is a part of mass, i.e. its dependence on staying within the system is assumed; an

2 paramāṇurūpaṃ tarhi rūpaṃ na prāpnoty arūpaṇāt//

3 navaiparamāṇurūpam ekaṃ pṛthagbhūtam asti/ 4 saṃghātasthaṃ tu tad rūpyata eva// 5 Na caparamāṇubhyo 'nyesaṃghātā iti/

atom is a kind of "system object". In this case, is there any difference between the Sautrāntikas and their Brahmanic opponents, the Vaiśeṣikas, with whom the whole differs both from its parts and from the sum of parts? I see this difference in the following: if the Vaiśeṣikas regard as emergent the properties of the whole in comparison with the properties of the mechanical sum of parts, in the view of the Sautrāntikas, it is the parts of conglomeration which have emergent properties because they are *in the conglomeration*, in relation to the hypothetic parts *out of the conglomeration*.

Both Vaibhāṣikas and Sautrāntikas in their debates with the Vaiśeṣikas unanimously rejected the concept of whole of the latter (AKB 3.100). They used to claim that a whole as an entity different from its parts, does not exist.6 For the Buddhists, the whole is just a mental construction conventionally uniting various elements. Therefore, from their point of view, collective nouns are just nominal (*prajñapti-sat*) but not real entities (*dravya-sat*) - an argument against the Vaiśeṣika theory of universals.

Talking about the status of the most important classificatory terms in Buddhism - skandha groups (meaning groups of dharmas - elements constituting an individual), *āyatana* (bases) and *dhātu* (elements), the Abhidharma put forward the following important question: provided that each of these terms designates the group of dharmas and in this way comes to be the name of class, does it mean that classes are merely nominal (*prajñapti-sat*) or they are real (*dravya-sat*). The Vaibhaṣikas believed that the three terms designated realities; according to the Sautrāntikas only *dhātu* were real, while Vasubandhu considered the *āyatanas* and the *dhātu* to be real, while the *skandhas* to be unreal.

In the eyes of Buddhist philosophers the reality of *skandhas, āyatanas* and *dhātu* may entail the reality of mental constructions whereto they were referring, or the reality of universals as well as the notion of Ātman or Self. The notion of skandha was particularly dangerous in this respect as there was a group of Buddhists (they were called Pudgalavādins) who regarded skandhas as something more than the simple sum of *rūpa, vedanā* etc. Seen as this "more" was a *pudgala* - an individual, and there was Ātman - a permanent soul not recognized by Buddhists - looming behind this *pudgala*.

The relevant discussion could be found in the commentary to the 20th *kārikā* of the first book of AKB. One of the participants in the discussion (a Sautāntrika) claims: "If *skandha* means a pile or heap, the *skandhas* have

---

6 Whole is a synonym of Ātman; one of the most remarkable examples is the famous refutation of Ātman via its comparison to a chariot in "Questions of King Milinda". What is a chariot if not a simple set of elements? Therefore, the word "chariot" is just a conventional designation of an assemblage of wheels, pole, etc., other well-known examples: a chain of ants is just ants in a certain sequence, etc.

only a nominal existence as a collection of multiple things, like a pile of grain or *pudgala*."7

Thereby he wants to say that *pudgala* is just a name, a conventional designation of the five skandhas and not a separate entity.

However, a Vaibhāṣika objects to that: "No, [*skandha* is not nominal], because a single atom also has the property to be a *skandha*."8

We see how important it was for the Vaibhāṣikas to follow their explanatory model which I called accumulativist as contrasted with the emergent one. In the whole, there is nothing which would be missing in its parts. In what way is skandha real and not nominal? If the Buddhists consider only parts to be real and not the whole composed of them, then every part is a *skandha*: *rūpa-skandha*, *vedanā-skandha*, etc. Their component parts up to the atoms themselves are also skandhas!

Further on, the Sauntrāntika remarks that if so, then the material (*rūpin*) spheres (*āyatana*) must also exist as designations, because atoms of the organ of seeing etc. are those access-doors [etymological meaning of the term *āyatana* - V.L.].9

The Vaibhāṣikas: "Not so. Because every atom (of the agglomeration) is individually the cause [of cognition], or because it has the external sense-field (*viṣaya*) as its cooperative cause (*sahakāri*)."10

On their own, the atoms of sensory organs (internal *āyatanas)*, for instance the atoms of the eye, cannot cause a cognitive event; needed is a joint action by the atoms of the object field which is related to seeing, its external *āyatana*. It means that in the process of cognition permanently involved are both the atoms of sensory organs (*indriyas*) and the atoms of the appropriate object fields (*viṣaya*), i.e. the two *āyatanas*.

A commentary to the 44th *kārikā* says that "taken in isolation, an atom of the sensory organ and that of the object do not engender sensory perception (*vijñāna*). Five types of sensory perception (seeing, hearing, taste, [sense of] smell and touch - V.L.) dispose only of atomic agglomerations as the substrata of sensory organs (*āśraya*) and object (*ālambana*). Thus, the atom is invisible because it is imperceptible."11

In other words, the atoms as system objects exist only in agglomerations but at the same time, as a cause of cognition it is not the whole composed of atoms which fulfills its function but each atom

---

7 Yadi rāśyarthaḥ skandhārthaḥ prajñaptisantaḥ skandhāḥ prāpnuvanti| anekadravyasamūhatvāt rāśipudgalavat||

8 Ekasyāpi dravyaparamāṇoḥ skandhatvāt||

9 rūpīṇyapi tarhyāyatanāni prajñapti santiprāpnuvanti | bahūnāṃ cakṣurādiparamāṇūnām āyadvārabhāvāt||

10 na | ekaśaḥsamagrāṇāṃkāraṇabhāvāt viṣayasahakāritvād vānendriyaṃ

11 nacaikendriyaparamāṇur viṣayaparamāṇur vāvijñānaṃ janayati | sañcitāśrayālambanatvāt pañcānāṃ vijñānakāyānām | ata evānidarśanaḥ paramāṇur adṛśyatvāt ||

individually. However, if an individual atom is imperceptible, then, following the Vaibhāṣika logic, according to which the properties of a part extend to the whole, the things themselves should also be imperceptible. Where does perceptibility come from then?

Apart from the above analyzed "materiality", it is perceptibility which could be seen as one more important "applicant" to the status of emergent property. We read in the 3rd *kārikā* of AKB: "The atoms, although suprasensible, are perceivable in clusters, just like [in the Vaiśeṣika system] the atoms are endowed with the ability to create a substance-effect perceivable by the vision and the other [senses], or just as people suffering from eye diseases perceive masses of hair and a single hair, like the [individual], atom [believed] to be suprasensible."12

However, it was also in respect to this issue, that the successors of Vaibhāṣikas and Sautrāntikas confined themselves to different positions. The Vaibhāṣikas followed a principle formulated in the Mahāvibhāṣā, the "Great Commentary" of which AKB is a synopsis, (hereafter MV): "If a single atom does not have the characteristic (*lakṣaṇa*) of the material aggregate (*rūpa-skandha*), then even an agglomeration of numerous [atoms] also should not be an aggregate" (384a).13

In other words, the atom as an extremely small constituent of macroobjects should have all the properties of these objects; otherwise it is impossible to explain wherefrom these properties come. In the strictly causal system of Buddhism, everything appears due to some causes and conditions (*hetu-pratyaya*). Thereby, the Vaibhāṣikas seem to deny emergent properties, first of all, as some new properties not having preceding homogeneous generative causes. However big atomic masses may be, if each atom of them lacks the property of perceptibility, then the mass itself is to remain imperceptible. Therefore, perceptibility, although to a minimum extent, should be characteristic of the atoms themselves.

According to the Vaibhāṣikas, every atom of sensory objects has a causal potency in relation to cognition, i.e. an ability to cause its cognition which is manifested only when the number of atoms reaches a "critical mass". The same refers to *indriyas* (sensory abilities) also shaped as atomic clusters: they are unable to fulfill their perceptive function if every atom does not have this ability (see AKB 1, 43). If a group is composed of blind people, it won't be capable of seeing. If an atom, having the property of perceiving, performs its function together with the other homogeneous atoms, then a sensory organ is enabled to implement its function as one of the pillars (the second pillar being an object perceived) of a cognitive act (*vijñāna*). Yaśomitra compares that with the combined efforts of carriers

12 Paramānvat indriyatve'pi samastānāṃ pratyakṣatvaṃ yathā teṣāṃ kāryārambhakatvaṃ cakṣurādīnāṃ ca taimirikānāṃ ca vikīrṇakeśopalabdhiḥ / teṣāṃ paramāṇuvad ekaḥ keśo 'tīndriyaḥ.

13 Cit. from K. L. Dhammajoti, *Sarvastivada Abhidharma* (SriLanka: Centre for Buddhist Studies, 2002), p. 244 (hereinafter Dhammajoti, 2002)

making it possible for them to carry big weights too heavy for a single person.

This idea is even more clearly expressed by an opponent of Vasubandhu, the Vaibhāṣika Saṃghabhadra in his discussion with Śrīlāta, a follower of Sautrāntika, who used to claim that perceptibility was what only conglomerates of atoms possess. Saṃghabhadra argues that even an individual atom is actually visible, even though its visibility is almost nil on account of its being very subtle for visual consciousness, which can grasp only a gross object.14 Developing the logic of Saṃghabhadra, it would be possible to assume the observability of the atoms via devices reinforcing visual faculty (i.e. microscopes), while, as per Śrīlāta and Vaiśeṣika logic, individual atoms are imperceptible in principle, as they are suprasensible (*atīndriya*) by their very nature. Therefore - according to Sautrāntika and Vaiśeṣika - the perceptibility of atoms could be called an emergent property.

The Vaibhāṣikas were flatly denying any close contact between the atoms, as they strongly aspired to avoid paradoxes which could follow from the acceptance of this thesis: if the atoms are connected by their sides it has to be recognized that they have parts and are no more indivisible; if they enter in connection entirely, they would just fuse together into something unitary (these paradoxes are mentioned already in MVB). Therefore, in my opinion, the Vaibhāṣikas suggest an extremely anti-intuitive explanation: the atoms just occupy adjacent points in space, without touching one another. Things do not go to pieces only because the atoms keep together owing to the impact of a great element - the wind - which acts as a uniting force (*saṃdhāraṇa*) within the period of the world creation, but at the end of the world period as a dispersing power (*vikīraṇa*) (АКБ 1.43).

Nevertheless, the ability to enter into a compound that is inherent to "gross things" finds its counterpart at the "atomic level". Once again the same logic: there is nothing in the aggregate, which would not be in the atoms. If we recognize that aggregates are connected to each other in the sense that they occupy adjacent points in space, then atoms do the same. We can read in the AKB 1.43:

Since those [atoms] possess resistance (*pratighāta*), and since compounds (*saṃghāta*) are not different from the atoms, those same atoms, that in those compounds are touched (*spṛśyante*) are struck (*rūpyante)* in the same way.15

But let's have a closer look at the Buddhist atom itself. What is this? In compliance with its definition, an atom (*paramāṇu*) is the smallest *rūpa*

---

14 As MB reached us only in Chinese, I am quoting here professor Dhammajoti. He also notes: "Although an individual atom is too feeble to function as a visual faculty, an agglomeration of atoms of the same kind will, in their collective and accumulative capacity, function as such" (Dhammajoti, 2002, p. 201)

15 yataḥ sapratighā iṣyante | na ca paramāṇubhyo 'nye saṃghātā iti | ta eva te saṃghātāḥ spṛśyante, yathā rūpyante |

(for example, AKB 2. 22).16 It cannot be broken, destroyed, penetrated, etc., mentally or practically divided - that is a leitmotif of various definitions. So, the word "atom" ("indivisible") in respect of *paramāṇu* is quite appropriate.

Atomism emerges within Buddhism at a certain stage in the development of the abhidharmic analysis (analysis of reality in terms of *dharmas*) in the early centuries of the CE. This expressly borrowed teaching (wherefrom borrowed - that is a question) was introduced into the doctrine of rūpa and it immediately set off a lot of discussions which could be traced in MV - a text of Sarvāstivāda dating back to the first centuries of the C.E. Within the framework of the Buddhist doctrine - with its cardinal principle of the absence of any permanent substance (*anātman*), instantaneity of every process, (*kṣaṇikatva*) etc. - atomism acquires a rather original character even as compared with Indian atomism (Jaina and Brahmanic), not to mention the Greek one. The atoms do not last but are constantly "reproduced" in the form of instantly emerging and disappearing micro phenomena making up homogeneous series. That's the way Buddhist atomism tries to explain universal impermanence (*anityatā*).

Apart from that, a Buddhist *paramāṇu* as distinct from a *paramāṇu* of the Vaiśeṣika which can have the nature of only one element (either earth, or water, etc.), comprises the fundamental properties of all the four great elements (*mahābhūta*): firmness (of earth), viscosity (of water), temperature (of fire) and mobility (of wind). This is a so called substantial atom (*dravyaparamāṇu*) recognized by the Vaibhāṣikas rather theoretically than practically. According to AKB (2. 22), a minimal atom (*saṃghātaparamāṇu*), existing in the sensory world (*kāma-dhātu*), consists of eight components: four primary elements and their four derivate (*bhautika*) types of *rūpas*: atoms of color-form, smell, taste and tangible [things]. Thus, each atom of the kind, actually a molecule, acts as an ultimate unit not of a certain substance of a qualitative diversity. When the atoms of sensory faculties (*indriya*) are added to a molecule, a number of atoms is increased proportionally. 17 The Sautrāntikas used to recognize only atoms of "secondary properties": color, taste, etc.

---

16 There is the following definition in the MB: "An atom (paramanu) is the smallest rupa. It cannot be cut, broken, penetrated; it cannot be taken up, abandoned, ridden on, stepped on, struck or dragged. It is neither long nor short, square nor round, regular nor irregular, convex nor concave. It has no smaller parts; it cannot be decomposed, cannot be seen, heard, smelled, and touched. It is thus that the paramanu is said to be the finest (sarva-sūkshma) of all rupas" (Translation from Chinese by Dhammajoti, see Dhammajoti, 2002, p. 199)

17 For example, an atom/molecule of sound produced by a hand contains ten components: four atoms of the great elements, four derivates from them, an atom of sound and an atom of (indriya) touch. If a sound is produced by the tongue, the atoms of taste located on the tongue will have to be added to this set (an example from the commentary of SuanTsang).

But, at the same time, the Buddhists recognize a division of atoms into classes of earth, water, etc. Vasubandhu writes in his commentary to the 22nd *kārikā* of the 2nd book: "If the four primary elements, earth element, etc., are never disassociated, but coexist in every aggregate or molecule, how is it that, in any given aggregate, one perceives either solidity, or viscosity, or heat, or movement, and not these four substances or characteristics at one given time?18

- One perceives in any given aggregate those substances *(dravya,* earth element, etc.) that are most active in it, and not the others. In the same way, when one touches a pile of pieces of plants and needles, one perceives the needles; when one eats some salted soup, one perceives the taste of salt.19

- How does one know that a given aggregate consists of the primary elements when their presence in it is not perceived?20
- All of the primary elements manifest their presence through their own actions, namely support *(dhṛti),* cohesion *(saṃgraha),* maturing *(pakti),* and expansion *(vyūhana).*21

Other opinions are also given further on but they do not change a general impression which is that the great elements are not the objects of external world independently of us. They are neither substances nor properties of substances (the Buddhists did not separate a bearer from its property or a property from its bearer) but a sort of functions or forces that enable us to perceive one or another combination of atoms in a certain capacity. Although an extremely small atom is called *dravya-paramāṇu,* strictly speaking, it is not a substantial atom in the sense of the Vaiśeṣika where the term dravya designates a substance, or in the sense of the Greek atomism. The Buddhist reductionism does not bear any resemblance to the other atom theories where qualitative diversity is reduced to a number of classes of homogeneous atoms. A Buddhist atom comprises fundamental qualities of all the great elements with only one dominating by which its class is determined. The Vaibhāṣikas believe that only conglomerates composed of homogeneous atoms are real. Accumulation of homogeneous atoms provides an increase in a certain function, for instance, the things composed of earth atoms are to be heavy due to multiplication of the "mini weights" of the individual atoms.

When the atoms of sensory faculties-*indriyas* join a "molecule" of fundamental properties and sensory qualities making up the objects of

---

18 Katham ihāvinirbhāge bhūtānāṃ kaścideva saṃghātaḥ kaṭhina utpadyate kaścideva dravauṣṇovāsamudīraṇo vā//

19 Yadyatra paṭutamaṃ prabhāvata udbhūtaṃ tasya tatropalabdhiḥ. Sūcītūlīkalāpasparśavat saktulavaṇacūrṇarasavacca //

20 athaṃ punas teṣu śeṣāstitvaṃ gamyate.

21 karmataḥ samgrahadhṛtipaktivyūhanāt, (transl. by Leo M. Pruden).

sensory organs, what is formed then represents a mental-body continuum of discrete properties-energies which determine, as we would say now, the anthropic character of our universe already at the micro level.

In modern terms, the Buddhist atoms could be given the name of infinitesimal qualia. Although, strictly speaking, pure qualia are only the atoms of Sautrāntika, nevertheless, the atoms/molecules of Vaibhāṣika contain qualia, i.e. here the qualia refer to the micro level. This is an ultimate sensory-qualitative component of the world, not the world in itself, as independent of us, but the world from the viewpoint of our experience, from the viewpoint of an observer. We cannot cognize these atomic properties other than by means of experiencing them, "from the first person perspective".

This idea fits quite well to the Buddhist attitude towards the world. The Buddha considered questions about the world as such to be irrelevant to liberation from *saṃsāra*, i.e. irrelevant to the Buddhist soteriological perspective. From the Buddha's point of view, the world represents what is being cognized by one's experience: viewed, partaken, smelled, touched, heard and understood by one's mind (*manas)* (SN 3.169-171). The world is created by an individual as a part of himself: "Sir, with the help of which someone in the world recognizes the world and imagines the world, is given the name of the world in the discipline of the Noble" (SN 3.105). In other words, the world is what we perceive and cognize, i.e. what is determined by our cognitive tools (compare with the Umwelt of Jakob von Uexküll) and not something pregiven and unchangeable, not a kind of objective state of things.

At the same time, the term qualia cannot be applied to Buddhism in the entire range of its modern meanings, because the fundamental opposition of subjectivity and objectivity is just lacking in the Buddhist attitude towards the world and therefore, the qualia do not play the role of counterbalancing the dominating objectivist scientific strategy. The Abhidharmic approach, if we apply modern terminology, could be rather determined as phenomenological or meta-psychological (the term of Alexander Pyatigorsky). However, in spite of that, the term qualia helps us to underline the importance of the first person perspective in the Buddhist explanation of the world.

In the Abhidharma, the division between the external (*bāhya*) and internal (*adhyātmaka*) is a purely conventional one. However, in the Abhidharmic nomenclature the term *sabhāga* "co-sharing", "homogeneous" - emphasizes the identity of all the cognitive events as constitutive only of one's own individual psychosomatic series (AKB 1.39).

So, both terms, emergence and qualia, may legally make elements of our meta-language in respect to Buddhism. Of course, they would be filled with slightly different meanings but that would only serve for their enrichment. Their application enables us to make a place for the Buddhist tradition in the perspective of our contemporary pursuits.

REFERENCES

Abhidharmakośabhāṣya of Vasubandhu. Ed. Pradhan P. Tibetan Sanskrit Works Series, vol. VIII, Patna: K.P. Jayaswal Research Institute. 2nd edition, revised with introduction and indices, by Dr. Aruna Haldar, 1975.

Vasubandhu.Abhidharmakośabhāṣyam. Translated by Louis de La Vallée Poussin; English translation by Leo M. Pruden. Berkeley, Calif., 19881990.

Васубандху. *Энциклопедия Абхидхармы (Абхидхармакоша)*. - Т. 1: Раздел I: Учение о классах элементов; Раздел II: Учение о факторах доминирования в психике / Изд. подгот. Е.П. Островская, В.И. Рудой. In Russian. М.: Ладомир, 1998

[Vasubandhu, *Encyclopaedia of Abhidharma (Abhidharmakośa)*, vol. 1, Section 1, Teaching of the Classes of Elements; Section II, Teaching of Dominating Factors in the Psyche [Teaching of Dominance Factors in the Psyche] / Ed. prepared by E.P. Ostrovskaya, V.I. Rudoy (M.: Ladomir, 1998)]

Васубандху. *Энциклопедия Абхидхармы (Абхидхармакоша)*. Т. 2: Раздел III: Учение о мире; Раздел IV: Учение о карме / Изд. подгот. Е.П. Островская, В.И. Рудой. In Russian. М.: Ладомир, 2001

[Vasubandhu, *Encyclopaedia of Abhidharma (Abhidharmakośa)*, vol. 2, Section 3, Teaching of the World; Section IV, Teaching of Karma / Edition prepared by E.P. Ostrovskaya, V.I. Rudoy (M.: Ladomir, 2001)]

Васубандху. *Энциклопедия буддийской канонической философии (Абхидхармакоша)*. Раздел V: Учение об аффектах. Раздел VI Учение о пути благородной личности / Сост., пер., коммент., исслед. Е.П. Островской, В.И. Рудого. In Russian. СПб.: С.-Петерб. Ун-т, 2006 [Vasubandhu, *Encyclopaedia of the Buddhist Canonic Philosophy (Abhidharmakośa)*, Section V, Teaching of Affects; Section IV, Teaching on the Path of a Noble Person / Compilation, transl., commentaries, research by E.P. Ostrovskaya, V.I. Rudoy (St Petersburg : the St-Petersburg University, 2006)]

Dhammajoti K.L. 2002, *Sarvāstivāda Abhidharma*, Sri Lanka: Centre for Buddhist Studies.

(Translated from Russian by Galina Lisenco)

CHAPTER XII

COMPLIMENTARY GROWTH OF SCIENCE OF LANGUAGE AND PHILOSOPHY OF LANGUAGE IN INDIA

In this article, an attempt is made to study how Science of Language and Philosophy of Language grew hand in hand and how they benefited from each other in their growth since the early ages and how the process continues even today, in the diverse linguistic situation in India.

India has 23 officially recognized Languages.1 These Languages are divided into 4 Language families. They are: Indo-Aryan, Dravidian, TibetoBurmese and Austro-Asiatic. Apart from these, there are approximately 1500 dialects spoken in various parts of India.2 This diversity and richness in Linguistic aspect is indeed a unique feature of Indian culture. However, when we look at the Data Resources, both print as well as electronic of this vast mass of Langauges, we feel sorry, because there are not many sources available. Therefore, we say that India is Language rich but resource poor. Various attempts have been made by scholars of Languages with the support of the Government of India to rectify the situation and to create various kinds of resources, both print as well as electronic.

We witness rapid development of Language Technology in India more so in educational environment in terms of various institutions situated in different parts of India, taking lead to develop resources in respective languages.

In this development, it is observed that the Language Technology developers face various kinds of problems. Standardization of the process is very important in the matter of technology development and to agree upon something as a standard in a huge and diverse country like India is in itself a big task. Philosophical insight to meet with the Language Phenomena dealt with is another very important problem faced during this process. I will focus here on this issue which is relevant for the present discussion and

1 They are - Asamese, Bengali, Bodo, Dogri, Gujarati, Hindi, Kannada, Kashmiri, Konkani, Maithili, Malayalam, Manipuri, Marathi, Nepali, Oriya, Punjabi, Sanskrit, Santhali, Sindhi, Tamil, Telugu, Urdu and English.

2 One conglomeration of 800 such dialects was organized very recently at Vadodara, Gujarat, India, on January 6-7, 2012 under the auspicies of a nongovernmental institution *Vak* based in Vadodara.

attempt to develop it with the help of available linguistic resource and it's application in the task of development of language technology.

By availablility of Linguistic resource, we mean, indegenious linguistic resource. To be more specific, any linguistic theory, in the first place, which accounts for the facts of Indian Languages in an effective manner and later on, other resources like the dictionaries and grammars and more importantly the philosophy to look at the phenomenon of development of language technology in a proper perspective which allows absorption of technology in human life.

Here we present a case of using Paninian grammar formalism 3 in developing Parse Tree Banks for Indian Languages. Projects related to Indian Language to Indian Language Machine Translation (IL-ILMT) revolve around the idea that Paninian formalism would be helpful for processing of Indian languages. The parse structure of any given input sentence in any Indian Language which is useful for various Natural Language Processing tasks is now developed using Paninian formalism. In this formalism, the Sanskrit terms are used with their philosophical connotations intact. Panini has devised a system called *Kāraka* in order to account for the interrelationship between words in sentence, more so between words which are grammatically classified as verbs and nouns. These are different roles nouns can play with respect to the action. They are *Kartā* (Agent), Karma (Object), *Karaṇa* (Instrument), *Sampradāna* (Recepient), *Apādāna* (Point of departure) and *Adhikaraṇa* (Substratum). In order to account for certain phenomena in theory as well as in computational processing, in Hindi, for example, the philosophers have identified a new concept called '*Anubhava-kartā*' (Experiencer Agent).

We already have Parse Tree Banks for Bengali developed using Paninian formalism with new additions as shown above. Parse Tree Banks for languages like Hindi, Marathi, Kannada etc are under construction. At the same time, a philosophical way to look at Language and to understand the basic limitations of language are evident in efforts related to development of various lexical tools such as Wordnets for Indian Languages.4

We have very briefly presented a modern case where we tried to show that the Science of Language in India in the field of Computational Linguistics is growing and going hand in hand with the philosophy of language. This phenomenon is, however, not new. This has been happening since ages in Indian scenario. Language science and Philosophy of Language have developed in India hand in hand since almost 2500 years

3 For details see, Akshar Bharati: 1995.

4 Indo-Wordnet is a broad umbrella under which various institutions in India are developing Wordnets. IIT Bombay is leading the way with creation of 3 Wordnets: Hindi, Marathi and Sanskrit. For further details see, www.cfilt.iitb.ac.in

back. I try to present below in the remaining part of this article, an account of the same.

II

India can boast of the existence of great tradition of Linguistic thought 5 starting back from the Rgvedic periods when seers of Rgveda composed hymns in praise of speech and put forward questions related to the nature and form of speech. *Pada-pāṭha* can be considered to be the first commentary on Rgveda as it split words from Rgvedic sentences and demarcated the word boundary. Nirukta (700 BCE) is considered to be an important text to have dealt with the Science of Etymology so early. It has also provided guidelines for modern scholars in the field to follow. It was Pāṇini, however, who took the Science of Language to near perfection and evolved a grammar of Sanskrit which is unique and an example to follow. In what follows, in this paper, I summarise in general historical development in Science of Language in Pāṇini and after along with the development of Philosophy of Language and focus further on a specific topic of Stem determination in the same regard.

Pāṇini used the term *Vākya* meaning sentence without defining it in his grammar. It was Kātyāyana (300 BCE) who provided the definition of *Vākya* (sentence) by saying 'ekatiṅ vākyam' (A string of words containing one *tiṅ* is called a sentence). Tiṅ is a set of terminal suffixes added to a verbal root. This definition took into consideration the formal aspect of a sentence. Several centuries later Bhartṛhari provided and collected ten definitions of *Vākya*. These definitions take into considereation, apart from a formal definition, meaning as well as propositional aspect.

Pāṇini provided an analysis of a language. He assumed sentences as the base for this analysis and provided for the components of the sentences, namely, words, (*pada* for Pāṇini). This can be shown diagrammatically as follows:

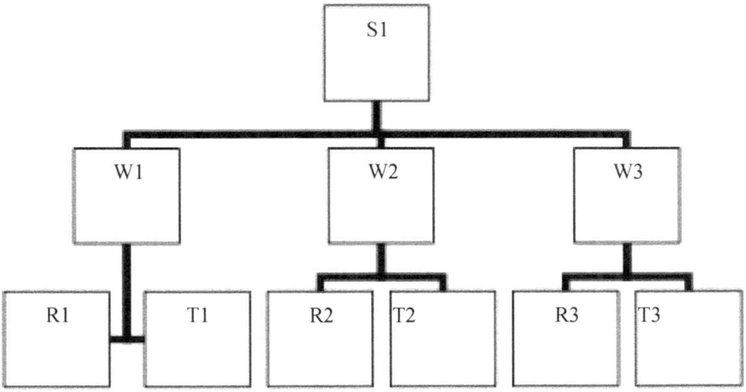

5 For details see, Belvalkar: 1976.

Figure 1: Sentence Structure (S - Sentence, W - Word, R - Root, T Termination Suffix)

This figure can be further explained with the help of the following example:

(1) Gopālaḥ grāmaṃ gacchati. Gopal
village to go es
Gopal goes to a village.

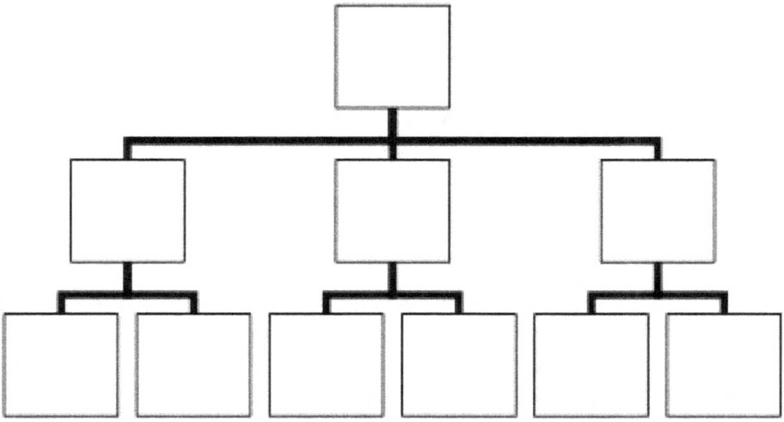

.

Based on this model, the sentence meaning model can also be shown in the following way:

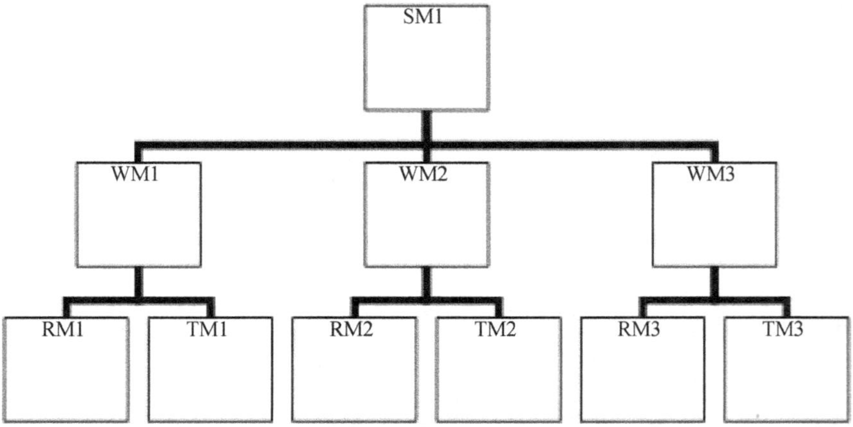

Figure 3: Structure of Sentence Meaning (SM - Sentence meaning, WM - Word Meaning, RM - Root Meaning, TM - Termination Meaning)

Below is presented the example based on this model.

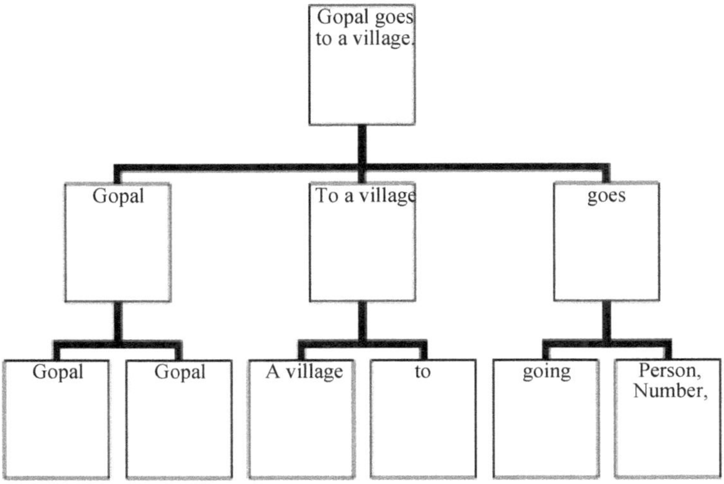

Figure 4: Example of Structure of Sentence Meaning.

In this way, all sentences in Sanskrit can be derived. These are not parse trees. The parse trees will show the exact interrelation amongst the words. They will also show the head-modifier relationship. These figures drawn above show the internal structure independent of any grammatical theory of headedness etc. Pāṇini6 classifies Roots into two broad categories: *Dhātu* (a verbal root) and *Prātipadika* (a nominal root) and Terminations into two corresponding categories, Sup (nominal terminations) and Tiṅ (verbal terminations). From another point of view, Pāṇini classifies roots as Simple and Derived. Simple verbal roots are enlisted in the appendix to his grammar and same is the case with some of the simple nominal roots. The derived roots are derived by grammatical rules. The derived nominal roots are again of various types: there are compounds (mainly of four types) and they are verbal nouns etc.

Pāṇini must have given a good amount of thought to fix the grammatical elements in each of these categories which did act as a finishing point for him in the process of segmentation and which would eventually turn out to be the starting point in the process of generation. This decision of fixing the roots must have had a close association with the decision of determining the exact phonological form of the terminations. All these decisions are closely linked in order to formulate the rules pertaining to different linguistic environment, phonological, morphological as well as syntactic. Pāṇini also laid down certain principles with the help of which conflicts arising between two rules operating in different environments would be resolved so as to be able to arrive at the desired surface level

6 For details see Cardona: 1976 and 1998.

form. Pāṇini also noted accent to the minutest details and also fitted it in, in the structure of the sentence shown above. Thus he had to assign accent to each and every grammatical element and had to devise build up rules that would take care of the dynamics of the accent in the process of word generation.

Since Sanskirt was and is found morphologically rich, Pāṇini had to devise the strategy of 'Substitution' in order to account for the relationship between the surface level forms and the base grammatical elements. He had to accept the principle of Extension of properties in between the 'Substituted' and the 'Substitution'. He also had to order the rules in sequence, in accordance with the environment that would get applied in the process of word generation. Thus syntactic rules applied first followed by morphological rules followed by phonological rules. Thus he had to say that phonological rules apply last and after their application, no morpholocial rule gets applied. With this technique in hand, he could account for a huge number of linguistic phenomena. In order to account for this huge linguistic phenomena, he declared that a certain section in his grammar is as if nonexistent for the rest of the rules. The non-existent section contains mainly the rules of Phonological changes which apply last. This truly marked the pinnacle in Pāṇini's treatment of the Science of language.

In these abovementioned figures, internal relationships between words that form part of the sentence are not distinctly shown. They are discussed in Sanskrit tradition, threadbare and various viewpoints have emerged. The viewpoint of grammarians, who followed Pāṇini, rigorously says that this relationship is nothing but *Śakti* (Capacity)7 of the meaning and together with the concept of *Vivakṣā* (desire of the speaker to speak) it amounts to saying that the relationship between the words in a sentence is nothing but the potential capacity of any meaning that can be associated with any word to perform any role in order to accomplish any action.

Another crucial contribution of Pāṇini to the science of languages is the Meta-Language and it's effective use in the constriction of a grammar of a language. He rearranged the existing alphabet to suit the purpose of his analysis and the meta-linguistic features and created a technique unparallel in the history of Science of language, namely, *Pratyāhāras*, the abbreviated technical terms which signify certain phonemes. More recently, a german scholar, named Wiebke Pietersen8 has attempted to show that the number of signs used by Pāṇini are the minimal ones that he could have used. Petersen, following Pāṇini's model, constructed a similar and effective meta linguistic technique for representation of phonemes of German language.

We notice that Pāṇini's model was followed by all the Sanskrit grammarians, at least ten, till the 19th century, then Western grammarians tried to write the grammars of Sanskrit but failed to attain the brevity that

7 For details see, Hideyo Ogawa: 2009.

8 For details see, Wiebke Petersen: 2010.

Pāṇini had achieved or to make any contribution to the meta-language, although accusing Pāṇini to have written a 'barbaric' grammar.

With this much development in the science of language, we notice that India witnessed a huge amount of philosophical discussion based on these developments. While stating the obvious feature of his meta-language, Pāṇini himself proclaimed that a word in grammar stands for it's phonological form except the technical terms specially devised by Pāṇini. Thus the word 'agni' (which means Fire in Sanskrit object lagnauge), in Pāṇini's grammar will stand for it's phonological form. Thus Pāṇini's usage of 'Agni' in the text of his grammar should be taken to mean the sequence of 'a', 'g', 'n' and 'i' and not fire. This particular statement of Pāṇini became a huge inspiration for a philosopher, Bhart ṛrhari who stated that a word has two fold function: the Signifier and the Signified (which later on the Western world came to know from Saussure). Bhartṛhari developed his theory of Śabdabrahmavāda (Word is the ultimate reality theory) by generalising the above principle that every word primarily stands for it's own form and the listener-participant in the speech act primarily bases himself upon the form of the word and the meaning as well is in the form of the word.

Bhartṛhari's thinking led to cognitive aspects coming in to explain the linguistic phenomena and the speech act. Verbal cognition was considered as distinct from perception and inference etc. in the sense that it requires the knowledge of word as a priori. Bhartṛhari went on to say that Word is essential in any cognition: be it verbal or perceptional or inferential.9 And the reality is the speech act in which the speaker of the language is involved. The grammar presents before a reader a picture of the reality which helps him grasp the reality. Grammar is real because of it's existence and not because of the picture it presents. Bhartṛhari compared Language to a picture and effectively showed that just as the picture is real in the sense that it is a picture and is unreal in the sense that what it depicts can not be associated with the physical actions that object could very well have performed.

The next question in line for discussion was the interlink between grammar and language, whether the lagnauge is pre condition to grammar or vice versa. Kātyāyana raised this issue as far back as 300 BCE and answered by saying that usage exists before grammar and determines the grammar and later on the speech acts of members of the society depend on both: the availability of the speech as well as the grammar of that language.

The more fundamental issue which caught the attention of Indian philosophers was the relationship of word and meaning. The Yogasūtras of Patañjali (150 BCE) clearly state that the domains of word and meaning and their cognition are different and in this world, we normally superimpose one on another. The yogis who concentrate on these three as separate entities are

---

9 For details see, Kulkarni and Dangarikar (forthcoming), *Word in Cognition.*

said to attain the super natural powers of knowing all the languages. 10 Bhartṛhari stated that the relation between the word and meaning can be said to be of three types: Capacity, Causal and Superimposition.11

We see that in the modern field of Computational Lingusitics in India, scientists are using the abovementioned theory of Bhartṛhari, specifically, the Capacity aspect to develop lexical resources. Sanskrit Wordnet is an example of such a resource, an online multipurpose thesaurus of Sanskrit that is being developed at IIT Bombay. 12 Not just Sanskrit wordnet but the entire Wordnet development activity in India, called IndoWordnet is benefited by this principle and other such principles stated in Sanskrit texts by philosophers like Bhartṛhari. We thus see that the philosophy of language in India was inspired by the scientific developments reflected in the grammar of Pāṇini and as a reverse process the philosophy of Language helped develop a technological tool.

Kātyāyana discussed a very important question related to the very purpose of the existing of a grammar. Kāatyāyana's discussion is relevant not only for the science of language but for any science in general. Kātyāyana said that the purpose of grammar is *dharmaniyama* (restriction for the Merit). Kātyāyana admitted openly that the so called grammatical words and the so-called ungrammatical words, both are equal in terms of communication, the basic purpose of the use of language, they do convey the meaning to the listener. However, it is the duty of the grammar to tell the speaker which utterance - grammatical or ungrammatical - is going to accrue merit for him. This way of dealing by Kātyāyana is unique in the history of Language sciences and Philosophy of Language of the world. The same argument can be extended and further applied to Science in general and can be argued that the basic purpose of Science is restriction for merit.

I think, Kātyāyana had understood the very basic nature of Science which is harmony and not devastation and we in modern world should applaud Kātyāyana for giving us this ingenious insight for dealing with Sciences on the one hand and Philosophy on the other. If we follow what Kātyāyana said more than half of the trouble of the modern world in terms of weaponry etc. will be resolved.13

III

We conclude by summarizing what was presented in the pages before.

Thus we see that there is a constant interaction in the fields of Philosophy of Language and Science of language in India. This interaction

---

10 For details see, Kulkarni Malhar (forthcoming), "Omnilinguality". 11 For details see Ogawa Hideyo (Forthcoming), "Bhartṛhari on three types of Linguistic Unit-Meaning relations".

12 www.cfilt.iitb.ac.in

13 For details, see Kulkarni Malhar: 2004.

could further be strengthened in various subfields and to deal with many philosophical questions that philosophers are resolved to address. We can also say that India witnessed a huge amount of interest on the part of thinkers, in Language, both in its Science and in it's philosophy. We get an impression that these Indian thinkers never treated these two as separate disciplines, separate from each other by all means. Rather they thought about both as sides of the same coin, one to the rescue of the other and the other for the benefit of the first, thus complimenting each other in a unique way. We propose this as the ideal way of an interaction taking place between the two fields: Science of Language and Philosophy of Language.

REFERENCES

Akshar Bharati. 1995. *NLP: A Paninian perspective*, Prentice-Hall of India. S.K. Belvalkar. 1976. *Systems of Sanskrit Grammar*. Reprint, Delhi: Bharatiya Vidya Prakashan.

Otto Bohtlingk. 1971. *Pāṇini's Grammatik*, Hildesheim: Georg Olms Verlag, 1887. Reprint, New York.

George Cardona. 1976. *Pāṇini: a survey of research*. Delhi: Motilal Benarsidass.

George Cardona. 1998. *Recent Researches in Paninian Studies*. Delhi: Motilal Benarsidass.

Harold Coward and K. Kunjunni Raja. 1990. *Encyclopedia of Indian Philosophy*, Vol.5, *The Philosophy of the Grammarians*. Delhi: Motilal Banarsidass and Princeton, N.J.: Princeton University Press.

Subramania Iyer, K.A. Bhartrihari. 1969, reprint 1997. *A Study of Vākyapadīya in the Light of Ancient Commentaries*, Poona: Deccan College Postgraduate Research Institute.

Malhar Kulkarni. 2004. *Contribution of Kātyāyana to Paninian grammar, Pāṇini to Patañjali: a grammatical march*. New Delhi: D.K.Printworld.

Malhar Kulkarni. Forthcoming: Omnilinguality.

Malhar Kulkarni with Dangarikar Chaitali. Forthcoming: Word in Cognition.

Hideyo Ogawa. 2009. "On Bhartrhari's Notion of Power (Śakti)," *Bhartṛhari Language, Thought and Reality, Proceedings of the International Seminar of Bhartṛhari*, edited by Mithilesh Chaturvedi, Delhi: Motilal Benarsidass.

Hideyo Ogawa. Forthcoming: Bhartṛhari on three types of Linguistic Unit Meaning relations.

Wiebke.Petersen. 2010. "On the Generalizability of Pāṇini's Pratyāhāra Technique to other languages." *Proceesings of the 4th Sanskrit Computational Linguistics Symposium*, Edited by G.N.Jha, LNCS, Springer Verlag, pp. 21-38.

CHAPTER XIII

ON CERTAIN SPEECH AND CULTURAL PRESUPPOSITIONS FOR THE EMERGENCE OF THE THEORY OF SCIENCE IN ANCIENT INDIA BASED ON THE PAINTING TREATISE CITRASŪTRA

The formation, in Ancient India, of a special teaching that might be defined as the theory of science was taking place in the space of an entire complex of disciplines concerned, on the one hand, with the grammatical tradition and that of the philosophy of grammar and, on the other, with the teaching on communication.

Contemporary studies investigating Ancient Indian approaches towards the understanding of knowledge (Kunjunni Raja 1990, Olenev 2004, Oberhammer 1991, Lele 1981, Shokhin 1994, 2004 *et al.*) usually proceed from the techniques of constructing a scientific text as exposed in "toolbox" lists (*tantra-yukti*) that go back to the ritual of discussion (*saṃvāda*). Lists of this type are concise treatises that are either incorporated into scientific *śāstras* on various individual branches of knowledge (e.g., into the medical texts *Carakasaṃhitā* and *Suśrutasaṃhitā*) or constitute separate chapters in such treatises (e.g., the last chapter of the treatise on policy, the *Arthaśāstra* by Kauṭilya).

The present paper is based on my study and translation from Sanskrit of the earliest Indian treatise devoted to the theory and techniques of painting, the *Citrasūtra* (the first to the middle cc. A. D.). The *sūtra*, forming part of the *Viṣṇudharmottarapurāṇa*, is prefaced with a certain type of prologue: a special theoretical treatise on the exposition of knowledge. The latter work has never been identified as such in the Purāṇic text, studied or translated into foreign languages.

This mini-treatise is a separate work, whose purpose was evidently to legitimate the creation, for the first time, of a treatise (*sūtra*) dedicated to the theory of painting.

The prefatory text consists of three chapters: Chapter One (VD III.4), *Meticulous Examination of the Saying* (*suparīkṣaṇaṃ vākyasya*); Chapter Two (VD III.5), *Merits and Demerits of the Exposition of Knowledge* (*tantra-guṇa-doṣa*); Chapter Three (VD III.6), *Purity of the Exposition of Knowledge* (*tantra-śuddhi*).

As can be seen, the prefatory treatise starts out with the teaching on the saying (*vākya*).

It should be reminded that the problem of the saying is examined in detail in the *Vākyapadīya* by Bhartrhari (5th c.) and in a number of other, later treatises. When approaching the saying as treated in a certain Ancient Indian source, it is important to ascertain whether the *vākya* in it is identical with the sentence, in which the words are usually thought to be connected via the verb (Pāṇini, the *Mīmāṃsakas*), and what the relation between the saying and the word is.

In the first chapter of prologue treatise, we are evidently dealing with a teaching in which the principal carrier of meaning is the saying/enunciation. This saying is not seen as a sentence. The words do not possess individual meanings. Thus, the first part of the mini-treatise, entitled *Suparīkṣaṇa vākyasya,* sets forth, in all probability, the *vākyavāda* concept, where the saying itself is the principal unit of communication.

Here, as in many other early Sanskrit texts, the teaching on *vākya* is constituted in the form of a classification. It should be noted that, within a single list comprising 14 items, one can clearly discern two independent classifications of the types of saying, both of them built according to the hierarchical principle.

The first of the lists is oriented towards the classifiers of the world of Brahminism. It enumerates five types of saying, organised in a sacred hierarchy:

the saying of Brahman (*vākyaṃ svayambhuvaḥ*); the saying of the *Ṛṣis* (*Ṛṣīṇāṃ vacaḥ*); the saying of the *Ṛcikas* (*Ṛcikānāṃ vākyam)*;
the saying of the sons of *Ṛṣis, i.e.* of the pupils of *Ṛṣis* (*Ṛṣi-putra vacaḥ*)
the saying of Mitras, *i.e.* of friends (*mitrāṇāṃ vākyam*)

Functioning as classifiers in the second list of sayings (*vacana*) are a number of gods, demigods and demons known from many scriptures of Hinduism. The enumeration in this case begins with the ascetic-kings, whose position in Epic texts is often higher than that of the gods, and ends with the individual human being:

the saying of the *Rājarṣis*, the ascetic-kings (*rājarṣīṇāṃ vacanam*); the saying of the *Devatās* (*devatānāṃ vacanam*);
the saying of the *Dānavas* (*dānavānāṃ vacanam)*; the saying of the *Gandharvas* (*gandharvānāṃ vacanam*); the saying of the *Rākṣasas* (*rākṣasānāṃ vacanam*); the saying of the *Yakṣasas* (*yakṣasānāṃ vacanam)*;
the saying of the *Kinnaras* (*kinnarais uktavant* - *lit.*: "said by the Kinnaras");

the saying of the *Nāgas* (*nāgānāṃ vacanam*); the saying of the human beings (*pauruṣaṃ vacanam*).

However, in order to function as an introductory chapter to the treatise on painting, these two separate lists, both of them probably having independent early prototypes, were rethought in the Purāṇic traditon as a single one, expounding the concept of *vākya*. Each item of this unified list enumerates certain features of the relevant type of saying. Among these distinguishing features, one may single out the sacredness/profanity opposition, e.g., *dīptam* "resplendent with supreme light" *vs. garbheṣu artha-pravartanam* "deriving the meaning from the foetus, *i.e.* learned from infancy." Alternatively, sayings may be distinguished by the pleasantness of their sound, the distinctness of their pronunciation, the observance (or nonobservance) of the rules of grammar in them; they may contain "little sense and many words" or "much sense and few words" or be characterized by other similar parameters.

All these features, or attributes, of sayings are correlated with certain classifiers, *i.e.* every saying belongs to a definite type of participant in abstract communication, which may be discovered in various types of texts. Thus, according to *Nyāyabindu* I.1.8., the sayings of the *Ṛṣis* belong to the world of hidden energy (*adṛṣṭa*).

Thus, these classifications of sayings represent the subjects of communication, each of them marking a certain communication strategy or communication tactics (a repertory of means, linguistic and extralinguistic). In the present case, the participants in communication are not shown as the carriers of definite, specific knowledge. The act of communication itself (dialogue, polylogue) is not shown either; the text only gives an indication of its components - verbal acts (*vākya*).

It is not our purpose here to give a detailed examination of all the attributes of sayings. Rather, our task is to elucidate the function of the *Suparīkṣaṇaṃ vākyasya* chapter in the overall space of the painting text and, in this connection, to clarify the rôle of the *vākya* notion in the three-part treatise on the exposition of knowledge.

First, it should be pointed out that the chapter on the saying (*vākya*) is immediately followed by the one entitled *Merits and Demerits of the Exposition of Knowledge* (*tantra-guṇa-doṣa*), which begins with a section on the *sūtra* (a rule expounding the basics of a certain discipline, as well as a type of treatise consisting of such rules). The section details the linear order of elements in the *sūtra*, its structure, the application of logical schemes (the syllogism) in it, etc.

Comparing the two chapters just mentioned, it is possible to conclude that the saying (*vākya*), which may possess social characteristics and be dependent on the moment and the type of enunciation, is, at base, nothing but a "one-time" utterance (or a series of "one-time" utterances). It cannot be returned to, despite the fact that it may possess an *artha-krama,* "train of thought." Neither is the *vākya* treated as a sentence. On the whole, the *vākya* may describe the speech behavior of an actor (in the improvisation format), the speech interaction of the teacher and the disciple, the dialogue of "the knowledgeable."

In sum, what I see in the first two chapters of the prefatory treatise to the text on painting, of the treatise devoted to the exposition of knowledge, is the opposition of the discourse and the text in the conception of Vladimir Admoni (Admoni 1985).

The *sūtra*, as described in VD III.5, is a text. Lying at its basis is a reproducible utterance, it may be returned to, a commentary (*vyākhyāna*) can be compiled on it; such an utterance has a linear order, a structure, a numerical model of organisation (*cf. a sūtra* made up of two, four, etc., components). As to the *vākya*, it is a saying that may be classified as belonging to one of the speech genres as defined by Mikhail Bakhtin (Bakhtin 1978).

Thus, the difference between the ten types of saying set forth in the prefatory treatise, together with the distinguishing marks that are ascribed to them, is related to the change of the speech genre, each of latter being conventionally designated by one of a set of "speech personalities" (subjects of speech in the chain of speech communication): *Svayaṃbhū,* the *Ṛṣi*, the son of a *Ṛṣi*... the human being.

This constitutes the differentiation of speech genres depending on the status (rank, prestige) of the speech subject on a scale of values relatable to the socio-confessional one (first list) or on a scale relatable to the hierarchy of mythological characters. The respective position, or rank, of such a "standard speaker" affects the genre of the *vākya* saying, determining in broad outline its form and style: the choice of the topic and the borders of communication, the standard forms of constructing the whole, the use of typical speech patterns depending on the participants and the situation of communication: question, statement, rejoinder, agreement, order, etc.

Cf. CS 4.10-11:
stutir nindā praśaṃsā ca ākrośaḥ preṣa eva ca || 10 || *praśnonujñā*
tathākhyānam āśastir viṣayā matāḥ |
"(The following types of saying) are known: praise, censure, Abuse and
convincing (speech),
Questioning, expression of agreement, answer,
The Unutterable (state), pointing out the object (of comparison)".

It should be pointed out that the discourse/text opposition (in the sense described above) has no relation, in Ancient Indian culture, to the oral/written opposition (in contrast to the point of view of Admoni, who believed the concept of text to be only applicable to written speech). *Cf.* the transmission of *sūtras* as an oral fixed text (early ritual *sūtras*) and the recording of one-time utterances of Aśoka ("Thus says King Piyadasi..."), similar to recordings of radio speeches.1

1 *Cf.* the situational context that would be required to understand an utterance (the war with Kaliṅga and the slaughter of its inhabitants necessary to explain the teaching of Dharma - Edict XIII), the occasional character of the

Thus, elaborated within the space of the painting treatise was an original approach to the investigation and exposition of knowledge that manifested itself in an original treatise that is probably earlier than the text incorporated into the *Carakasaṃhitā* and only corresponds to the final chapter of the Arthaśāstra in the subject matter of its third section. This mini-treatise, dealing with the subject "the discourse and the text," essentially constructs the relation of the discourse of conversation (one-time utterance) to the exposition of a teaching as a coherent text, the object of commentarial activities, such as the *Arthaśāstra*, the *Kāmasūtra* and the painting text being investigated by me, the *Citrasūtra*. This mini-treatise and the steps, connected with it, in the gradual building of the text on painting have every reason to be considered one of the presuppositions for the emergence of the theory of science in Ancient India.

The prefatory treatise to the *Citrasūtra* also helps to uncover certain facets of the role played by speech itself (in its Saussurean aspect of "language faculty" (*langage*)) as one of the precursors to the construction of the theory of knowledge that was taking place in Indian culture in the first cc. A. D. This problem, as does the whole text of the mini-treatise, awaits special profound investigation.

REFERENCES

Г.В.Адмони. 1985."Грамматика и текст," *Вопросы языкознания*, М., № 1
In Russian. [G.V. Admoni, "Grammatika i text", *Voprosi jazikoznanija*, Moscow, No. 1, 1985]

М.М. Бахтин. 1979. *Эстетика словесного творчества*. In Russian. M.,
[M.M. Bachtin, *Estetika slovesnogo tvochestva*, Moscow: Iskusstvo, 1979]

В.К. Шохин. 1994. *Брахманистская философия*. M. In Russian. [V.K. Shochin, *Brachmanistkja filosofija*, Moscow: Vostochnaya Literatura Publishers, 1994, pp. 208-213].

M. Biardeau. 1964. *Vākyapadīya, Brahmakāṇḍa avec le Vṛtti de Harivṛṣabha.*

G. Oberhammer. 1963. *Ein Beitrag zu den Vāda-Tradition in Indiens //* WZKSOA., Bd. 7.

Subramanya Iyer K.A. 1969. *Bhartṛhari. A Study of the Vākyapadīya in the Light of the Ancient Commentaries*. Poona.

Viṣṇudharmottarapurāṇa. Third Kāṇḍa. Vol. 3. Ed. by Priyabala Shah, Baroda (GOS 130), 1958.

---

utterances ("Whether I am in the harem or in the lavatory..." Edict VI), etc. The one-time character of utterances on the same subject is borne out by the words: "It is said again and again!" in the exhortation edicts.

CHAPTER XIV

PRESERVING OBJECTIVITY AND RECLAIMING TRADITIONAL KNOWLEDGES: PHILOSOPHY OF SCIENCE LOOKS AT THE SPIRITUAL ECOFEMINISM OF VANDANA SHIVA

INTRODUCTION

Philosophy of science, in broad terms, reflects on foundational concepts of science and its methodology. How is such reflection enhanced by looking at knowledge systems in ancient Indian cultures? Instead of exploring shared conceptual space between modern science and traditional systems or raising 'originary' questions of whether contemporary scientific concepts were anticipated in these traditions, I explore a different trajectory of relating scientific modernity to ancient cultures in this paper. 1 My suggestion is that the project of retrieving epistemic alternatives found in non-Western civilizations could deepen the very objectivity of modern science. My paper, therefore, focuses not so much on whether and how an "Indian" civilizational conception of knowledge differs from modern science but rather on the meta-question of why looking at alternative constructions of the world in pre-modern India is important for scientific objectivity itself.

In order to make my case, I draw on the efforts of Vandana Shiva, the environmental activist who has focused on reclaiming traditional Indian knowledges based on what she calls the "Prakriti principle," as well as on contemporary feminist scholarship on the nature of objectivity. The use of Shiva's work for a philosophical reflection on scientific objectivity is interesting on many registers. After all, the pre-modern concept of Prakriti for Shiva is a "Feminine Principle," an ontological trope, and a Goddess. Modern science, on the other hand, is coded as 'male', as an epistemological trope and as being the proud marker for the secular. So in claiming the relevance of Prakriti-based world views for science, we in effect, upset many standard binaries that structure our conceptual scheme. These dualisms go beyond the basic tradition/modern opposition to encompass the binaries of female/male, ontology/epistemology and sacred/secular. Further,

---

1 Though here I am speaking of Western modernity and Indian tradition, I by no means regard the concepts of *Indian* modernity and Western *tradition* to be empty.

as will become clear, the effort of retrieving Prakriti-based knowledges as part of the practice of good science intervenes in another fundamental set of dichotomies - that between truth and justice, theoretical investigation and democratic citizenship, or simply put, the divide between science and politics.

PRAKRITI THROUGH THE LENS OF 'STANDPOINT EPISTEMOLOGY'

Prakriti is a metaphysical principle with different connotations in the various philosophical systems of Classical India. Deftly side-stepping these scholastic subtleties, Shiva glosses Prakriti as a monistic principle which manifests itself as both the animate and inanimate worlds - "the primordial energy which is the substance of everything, pervading everything." This panentheistic principle which for Shiva epitomizes "ancient Indian culture" is revered as a Goddess and translates into the worshipping of forests, rivers and sacred groves. Women in rural India are said to have a special affinity for Prakriti making it a "Feminine Principle" in more than a metaphorical sense. The typical subsistence activities of village women - the activities of providing the food-fuel-fodder needs of a poor rural family to 'stay alive' depend on the continued existence and symbiosis between the different ecosystems of forests, rivers and grassland and the harmony between nature as a whole and the human populations living off it. This life-style, according to Shiva, represents Prakriti ontology: it reflects the equality of everything as forms of the same Divine Principle thereby undercutting any anthropomorphic entitlement of one form to exploit the others. Now, such a metaphysical articulation of Prakriti has been criticized as essentializing both *Indian* culture and Indian *women*. Even while agreeing with these criticisms, I do not give up on the notion. I explore a more interesting twist to Prakriti-spirituality which can be given by looking at how the concept *functions* in Shiva's work. Shiva puts Prakriti to an epistemological use.

The clue to a robust re-articulation of the concept lies in noting that Prakriti is offered as a *solution* to the environmental crisis in modern Indian society. Now, Shiva traces the problems of the Third World to a 'logic of colonization' kept in place by twin "reductionisms." These are (1) a narrow notion of *productivity*, and (2) a narrow notion of *knowledge*. 'Productivity' here is associated with generation of profit and disassociated from processes that sustain life outside the market economy. 'Knowledge' on the other hand is restricted only to what is produced in laboratories and to mechanistic understandings derived by the breaking up of a complex into discrete parts. Both these reductionisms are associated with *modern science*. Thus, the root of Third World crises lies in what Shiva calls 'reductionist science:' Prakritispirituality - as a *solution* to this problem - would need to resist such reductionisms and re-articulate conceptions of productive labor and knowledge. In fact, Shiva explicitly says that Prakriti

(a) allows a *redefinition of growth and productivity* as categories linked to production, not the destruction of *life*" (SA 13, my emphasis),2 and (b) involves an *epistemological shift* in the criteria of assessment of the rationality of knowledge (SA 28, my emphasis)

This makes it abundantly clear that the veneration of Prakriti as a Goddess functions as a device both to de-construct *economic* categories and re-conceptualize *rationality*. How is this possible?

Feminist standpoint epistemology, often used to frame Shiva's work (as for example, in the work of Sandra Harding) is helpful here. Life at the rural margins, which is a practical realization of Prakriti-metaphysics, can be cast as a 'location' from where alternatives to science become visible. Reductionist science is embedded in an ethos where the world is understood as a resource for profit-maximization. The struggles of the poor and disenfranchised living on the fringes of a market economy, however, force them into different kinds of interactions with nature. This generates alternative *understandings* of the world. From this perspective, for example, a forest is not a 'resource' for the paper industry but is the source of food, nutrition, medicine, fuel and fodder. But according to reductionisms of science, anything that does not have market value is 'waste' or 'weeds.' This ignores the fact that such alleged waste is the wealth of biomass that maintains the water and nutrient levels of the soil and is a source of nutrition and fodder for tribal communities. The rationality of a monoculture of eucalyptus in 'scientific' forestry can thus be juxtaposed with the rationality of maintaining diversity of low yielding plant-species in pre-modern life-styles. So Shiva's point could well be that rural women who depend on Nature for their daily needs become "intellectual gene pools of ecological categories of *thought* and action (my emphasis)." 3 A Prakritiorientation to Nature can therefore be 'the site through which indigenous *theories* about nature is reclaimed' making Prakriti an epistemological 'standpoint' whereby local knowledges keyed to more holistic understandings are made visible. A plethora of such indigenous knowledgesystems serve to counterbalance the oppressive homogenization of a *reductionist science.*

Scholars like Meera Nanda, however, warn us of a real danger in celebrating this epistemological pluralism. The retrieval of indigenous wisdom in the above manner can become, according to her, a route to reviving alternative 'Hindu' ethno-sciences' and to rejecting *science* as an 'ethno-science of the *West*.' Abandoning science in favor of different civilisational 'ways of knowing' leaves us with no trans-cultural universals to critique the local frameworks thus retrieved or question the host of social prejudices that they harbor. "Epistemological multiculturalism," accordingly

---

2 Vandana Shiva, *Staying Alive: Women Ecology and Development* (London: Zed Books, 1989)

3 Ibid.

helps solidify superstitions and gender/caste hierarchies historically associated with traditional Hindu world views and can even give fuel to a chauvinistic Hindu fundamentalism. Nanda forces a broader responsibility on those who blithely go about "picking and choosing those aspects of the non-Western world that help them fight their own battles against modern science, without adequate awareness of the role local knowledges play in sustaining traditional power structures in non-Western societies." 4 The 'sacralizing' of the systems retrieved through Prakriti shields them from critical scrutiny and this is not a blessing for many.

The larger debate before us here is whether culturally *situated* understandings of nature can aspire for trans-cultural objectivity. Even though modern science might be imperialistic, Nanda's appreciation of the power of enlightenment rationality to maintain secular structures in the Third World is important.5 Can critiques of science prevent the slide into a facile relativism or a museumized plethora of "ethno-knowledges"? I turn to some feminist work on the nature of objectivity to engage these issues.

OBJECTIVITY AND EPISTEMIC INJUSTICE

The authority of science is underwritten by its claims to objectivity. Philosophers of science have generally linked such objectivity to the method followed in establishing the truth-value of scientific statements. Naomi Scheman,6 however, asks us to consider a slightly different question: *why is objectivity important for science in the first place?* Attributions of objectivity, besides ensuring that the statement or theory gets the world as it is, commends it as *worthy of being accepted* by a diverse group including those outside the scientific community. Thus, personal knowledge becomes social knowledge and science gets linked to universal acceptability. But if, whatever is labeled 'objective' comes with a claim of being 'worthy of being *accepted*,' then a second move is waiting in the wings: Something which is worthy of being accepted must be *worthy of appropriate trust* and so we get a link between objectivity and *trustworthiness*.

---

4 Meera Nanda, "Response to my Critics," *Social Epistemology,* 19.1, (2005), p. 164.

5 Ashis Nandy calls modern science today a "rebel without a cause" while admitting that "the earlier creativity of modern science (which) came from the role of science as a mode of dissent and a means of demystification" which "paradoxically depended upon the philosophical pull and political power of traditions." See "Modern Science and Authoritariansim: From Objectivity to Objectification," *Bulletin of Science, Technology & Society,* 17, (1997), p. 8, 10.

6 Naomi Scheman, "Epistemology Resuscitated: Objectivity as Trustworthiness" in Nancy Tuana and Sandra Morgen, eds. *Engendering Rationalities* (Albany: State University of New York Press, 2001)

However, the important point now is that conditions of trustworthiness are wider than the conditions of a theory/statement's being true or its being generated by reliable processes. Trustworthiness is earned amongst other things, by conveying the intention not to harm and more positively, by a concern with the welfare of those who trust. We trust our friends because we believe they are interested in our well being and are committed to championing our causes; we mistrust those whose motives we think are harmful for us. Given this understanding of trustworthiness, scientific theories can be objective only when institutions within which they are produced - scientists working in research organisations - are perceived not to be harmful by those to whom the theories produced by the institutions are presented. Institutions after all, are trustworthy at least to the extent that they are not perceived as promoting injustices. Thus unfair and harmful institutional structures of generating and disseminating knowledge - their complicity with oppression and exploitation - vitiate the objectivity conditions of science. Consequently, redressing these injustices become necessary for securing objectivity.

Now, what are some of the injustices that could plague epistemic practice in general? Let us look briefly at two which have been recently highlighted by Miranda Fricker.7 First, prejudices undermine the credibility of certain groups of peoples and prevent their participation in knowledgeseeking. Fricker calls this a "testimonial injustice." A paradigmatic example is the easy dismissal of claims made by perfectly competent women because of the construction of femininity itself as being irrational. Secondly, a different but associated harm is "hermeneutical injustice." This results because the lives of certain groups are made systematically unintelligible because the interpretative categories in place reflect the experiences of only the powerful. A patriarchal conceptual scheme, for example, where the women is routinely a temptress and the work-place a level playing field, has no resources to capture the experience of sexual harassment. Not only is the self-understanding of women skewed in such a system but their needs fail to gain any foothold in scientific research programmes. It should be clear that both *testimonial* and *hermeneutical* injustice stem from power-infused habits of social perception which congeal into negative epistemic judgments regarding the credibility of some people and some experiences. These harm people qua *knowers* by preventing their full participation in the knowledgeseeking enterprise.

PRAKRITI IN THE SERVICE OF OBJECTIVITY

In this background, both Shiva's anti-science rhetoric and her insistence on reclaiming indigenous insights, acquire new connotations. Her

---

7 Miranda Fricker, *Epistemic Injustice: Power and the Ethics of Knowing* (Oxford: Oxford University Press, 2007)

critique of science is not a simple rejection but a warning that science is *untrustworthy* in certain segments of the world.

But how is State-promoted science in India untrustworthy? A case can be made that the twin reductionisms of science perpetuate both hermeneutical and testimonial injustices against the rural poor which naturally undermines their trust in science. And given the link between trustworthiness and objectivity, these injustices become a critique of its objectivity for large sections of the population in post-colonial India. The relevant *injustice* being associated with science here is not that it is yet to reach the villages of India but that it marginalizes large sections of the populace in cognitive space.

We can spell this out in the following way: Once production, growth and waste are defined in terms of profit and capital gains, there remain no "rhetorical spaces" for the radically different needs of the rural poor to figure in research agendas. Their lives become triaged out of 'scientific' forestry, water management and agriculture. In the terminology discussed above, this becomes an instance of a gross *hermeneutical injustice*. Furthermore, once knowledge is defined narrowly as what is produced in research labs alone, the know-how of peasants gets defined away as having no cognitive content. Shiva's discussions of IPRs (Intellectual Property Rights) show how the possibility of biotechnological manipulation of genes is grounded on centuries of work by peasants to preserve the diversity of gene pools. However, while bioengineers claim cognitive authority, the skills and wisdom found in subsistence economies that make such 'scientific' knowledge possible are completely erased as having cognitive content. The practice of science thus fails to recognize farmers as epistemic agents in their own right because of its reductionist prejudice about what counts as knowledge and a knower. This amounts to a *testimonial injustice* against them.

The general upshot of this is that once the reality of hermeneutical and testimonial injustice in the practice of science is granted, then we must also concede that these epistemic harms constitute historical conditions for *mistrusting* science. And given the link between trustworthiness and objectivity, they become grounds for a justified critique of its objectivity. Of course, the case that retrieval of indigenous knowledges can make science more objective (and trustworthy) hangs crucially on what is necessary to get back on track if, and once, trust is broken. Since the injustices of marginalization lead to the mistrust of science, institutionalizing the *participation* of those who have been hitherto excluded, is a way of winning back the trust. The retrieving of local knowledges through Prakriti can be seen as doing just this.

All science is associated with a cosmology. The cosmologies of indigenous people not only widens scientific imagination, but their retrieval removes the *hermeneutical injustice* against the communities that live by those cosmologies. Research can now be relevant to their lives and motivate them to buy into scientific rationality. Furthermore, taking local knowledges seriously directly counters entrenched testimonial injustices against peasants. The reductionism that had conceived their technologies of preserving biodiversity over the centuries as not 'real' knowledge is reconceptualized as epistemic activity and they become genuine epistemic participants in science.

The point here is not simply that local knowledges enhance objectivity by introducing new hypotheses. Even while alternative perspectives do bring in new theoretical content and thereby widen the circle of hypotheses under discussion, they also engage the messy issues of unjust privilege. Consideration of hitherto excluded theories does something crucial for the *agents* who uphold these positions and hence facilitates the moral and political normativity of scientific institutions. Shiva's insistence on giving indigenous insights a hearing around the table of knowledgeexchange thus becomes a move to end the epistemic marginalization of rural communities associated with these positions and thereby ensure the *trustworthiness* of science in their eyes.

The encounter between 'modern' science and 'traditional' local knowledges being staged here is dialogic and not the holding up of civilizational essences as ossified objects of curiosity. For the notion of *trustworthiness* to act as an effective bridge between objectivity and justice, it must have a foot in both the camps of *truth-seeking* and *politics*. We are not looking at simply winning over the disenfranchised through political negotiation just as we are no longer aiming at a de-contextualized search for facts. The dismantling of epistemic injustices through trust-building practices must feed into the basic epistemic goal of truth. Shiva's retrieval of indigenous knowledges is not blind revivalism aimed at isolating them from critical investigation. For instance, the aim of *Navdanya* - a movement launched by Shiva to save seed diversity - is to "build a program in which farmers and scientists relate *horizontally rather than vertically*, (my emphasis) in which conservation of biodiversity and production of food go hand in hand, and in which farmers' knowledge is strengthened, not robbed." 8 In principle, Shiva is not even opposed to trans-cultural epistemological universals. The Prakriti-principle for her is 'trans-gender' and comes with a claim to *its* being adopted across the board. However, *Prakriti*-universalization, unlike traditional science does not make dissent disappear, but is based on dialogue with different points of view. The goal is neither a forced consensus nor a facile visibility.

Democracy in science is thus not just an issue of distribution of epistemic goods nor even of equal representation, but of *engagement*. Prakriti becomes a tool for democracy by securing *epistemic justice* by expanding epistemological citizenship. The Indian anthropologist and historian of science, Shiv Visvanathan, has defined a notion of 'cognitive justice' as "the right of different forms of knowledge to coexist without

8 Vandana Shiva, *Earth Democracy: Justice, Sustainability and Peace* (Cambridge: South End Press, 2005), p. 92.

being marginalized by official, state-sponsored forms of knowledge."9 What I have tried to show is that such justice is an *epistemic* good because it enhances objectivity.

One important and deep worry remains. The *tactical* or pragmatic appropriateness of using Prakriti in a post-colonial society like India is an open question. After all, an epistemology of science based on Prakriti becomes just one more avenue of making *Hindu* symbols - the marker of a majority religion - visible in the public sphere that intends to serve other minority religions as well. Can the epistemological egalitarianism being espoused here resist a Hindu fundamentalist appropriation?

I do not have time to either elaborate on this important objection or go into the details of how Shiva would counter it. Suffice it to say that Shiva calls 'Hindutva' or a fundamentalist Hinduism, "doubly alien" and antithetical to the ethos of Prakriti. The epistemological function that I have tried to tease out of Shiva's use of the concept focuses on establishing the trustworthiness of science by engaging with past and present injustices in scientific practices. Guarding against such injustices requires a *selfreflexivity* on multiple fronts - an attention to criticisms of one's performance - and the *epistemic and cultural humility* of acknowledging one's own privileges that engender and exacerbate these injustices. Now Prakriti on the interpretation suggested here, embodies a methodology of socially and materially grounded critical awareness about power in knowledge-seeking and the constant modulation of scientific practice in the light of this awareness, then Prakriti - as a socially grounded self-reflexivity - can loop back to illumine the very 'standpoint' from which *it* is imposed it can become aware of its complicity in the trust-eroding consequences of its *own* location. This would involve taking seriously the charge of why the use of Prakriti to reclaim traditional knowledges might look politically suspicious to some and a consequent readiness to give it up altogether in the interest of trust-building. One would then have to look for different ways of bringing alternative knowledges to the scientific table. However, Prakriti as a form of *situated* and *responsible* knowing through a constant selfreflexivity and sensitivity to perceived injustices can be a form of responsible '*situated devotionalism*' which is the antithesis of any authoritarian fundamentalism.

To summarize: The insertion of indigenous first-order forms of life into epistemic space calls for a re-distribution of power at the second-level regarding who gets to speak and who is heard and what can be said. Such intervention engages with forms of violence endemic to the practice of a commerce-and-colonialism-tainted science. These are injustices of epistemic exploitation of subdominant knowers and epistemic erasure of subdominant knowledges. Because trustworthiness depends on the quality of socio-political relations within which scientific claims are generated, the

9 Shiv Visvanathan, "A Celebration of Difference: Science and Democracy in India". *Science*, 280(5360), Issue of April 3, 1998.

reclaiming of Prakriti-based knowledges becomes a constructive engagement with these injustices and thereby with scientific objectivity. The eco-spirituality of Vandana Shiva therefore, is as much an intervention in ontology as it is in methodology or epistemology because it deconstructs deep structures of epistemic power in a globalized world. By forcing a confrontation between the "logic of the nation state" and the "logic of civilizational discourse" the indigenous knowledges associated with Prakriti help us to "learn how to learn better" 10 which even according to Meera Nanda, one of Shiva's most strident critics, is the value of science.

---

10 Meera Nanda, "Making Science Sacred: How Postmodernism Aids Vedic Science," *Wrongs of the Religious Right: Reflections on Science, Secularism and Hindutva* (Gurgaon: Three essays Collective, 2005), p. 99.

CHAPTER XV

THE EPISTEMOLOGICAL AND COSMOLOGICAL FOUNDATIONS OF INDIAN ASTROLOGY AND DIVINATION

Indian cultural history, in all its diversity, attests to our enduring attention to the sky and our perennial inclination to find meaning in the heavens. In India, from their inception, astronomy and astrology have operated concurrently and in complementary fashion providing a grammar and syntax for a single semantic universe. Formal cosmological structure is coupled with a rich mythological tradition to support a living, meaningfilled cosmos. This cosmos was above all relevant to the terrestrial world, especially to the proper functioning of Aryan society. The structures and movements of celestial phenomena provide an arena in which philosophical insights and religious traditions, mythological vision, and social reality are expressed, mediated, and objectified. Therefore, to know the grammar and the syntax of the heavens - the unfolding chronology, the modulations of meaning - was essential if the order of the world and of society was to be maintained.

There exist in India and outside of it some 100, 000 manuscripts on the various aspects of Indian traditional astral sciences (*jyotiḥ-śāstra)*. At the same time, scholarship is still suffering from embarrassment about taking serious interest in the history of traditional divination systems. Despite the efforts of classical philologists and historians of Indian religion and science, such as H. Kern, A. Weber, H-G. Thibaut, since the end of the nineteenth century to preserve and to publish the long-neglected astrological Sanskrit texts and emphasize their autonomous conceptual value, the astrological texts and astrological practices are still largely ignored by mainstream of Western Indologists. Still for a long period the notion of "pseudosciences" has hindered historical investigation into phenomena like astrology and other forms of divination. Understanding the knowledge as rooted in social practice changes the way one writes the history of science. According to Richard Lemay, "Hence the effort to understand medieval attitudes toward astrology by applying to this science our contemporary paradigm (to use Kuhn's convienient term) - the usual approach to the problem - seems to foreclose in advance all avenues leading to the medieval mind, to its structural framework, and to the contents of its own different paradigm". (Lemay 1987, 58) 1 Nevertheless, it seems that the study the

1 Tamsyn Barton rightly argues that the modern opposition between rational science (*τεχνή*) and divination (*μαντική*) is a fundamentally unhelpful

earlier paradigms is possible through patient and open-minded examination of texts and their context. Historians of science are, perhaps, the only scholars who have looked at astrological practice, but they have normally been concerned only with what they could learn of contemporary mathematics or astronomy, not with astrology itself, let alone with setting it in its social or even intellectual context. Now, mainly due to the historical works of the late professor David Pingree and his immense project, *Census of the Exact Sciences in Sanskrit*, the importance of medieval astrological texts for the history of culture and the history of ideas is much more fully appreciated. 2 Thus, in the present paper I will try to reveal the epistemological and cosmological foundations of Indian astrology and divinational practices while relying mostly on early astrological Sanskrit sources.

Jyotiḥ-śāstra ("science of lights") was the branch of Indian sacred knowledge (*scientia sacra*)3 devoted to the study and interpretation of the heavens. The *jyotiṣa-vedāṅga* is known in India to be one of the six auxiliary sciences (*aṅgas*) of the Vedas. The *jyotiṣa-vedāṅga* is a general name by which one generally refers to the treatises called the *Ṛgveda Jyotiṣa* (RJ), the *Yajurveda Jyotiṣa* (YJ) and the *Atharvaveda Jyotiṣa* (AJ).4 The former two are ascribed to the sage Lagadha (around 400 BC), while the last one is anonymous. According to the medieval Indian astrological treatises, *jyotiṣa-vedāṅga* was originally revealed by *prathama muni* (first seer) god Brahma and promulgated by the eighteen mythological sages.

---

antithesis, which runs the risk of pandering to an anachronistic and, indeed, idealistic notion of science, because, this was a period in which boundaries between science and divination were fluid and negotiable, and tradition itself was an important source of legitimation for knowledge. (Barton, 1994, 15).

2 In his immense project called *Census of the Exact Sciences in Sanskrit,* D. Pingree provided a preliminary explanation and organization of the vast of Sanskrit and Sanskrit influenced literature devoted to astronomy, mathematics, astrology and divination together with brief bibliographical information concerning the treatises and their authors. Without this unique encyclopedia any serious attempt in the field of traditional Indian astrosciences would be nowadays rather impossible. (Pingree, 1994).

3 I am using here the expression and definition of the sacred science provided by Seyyed Hosein Nasr. According to him, *scientia sacra* is metaphysics as the ultimate science of the Real and lies at the heart of each tradition, and as the center of that circle which encompasses and defines tradition, is not a purely human knowledge lying outside of the sacred precinct of the various traditions. „The formal language used for the expression of *scientia sacra*, and in fact nearly the whole spectrum of traditional teachings, is that of symbolism" (Nasr, 1981, pp 131-153).

4 A detailed comparative table of corresponding verses of these oldest treatises of *jyotiṣavedāṅga* has been provided by Shankar Balakrishna Dikshit (Dikshit, 1931).

(Pingree 1981, 1)5 The purpose of this science was to provide Vedic priests with a means of computing the times for which the performances of sacrifices are prescribed, primarily new and full moons. In the following verse the purpose of the *jyotiṣa-vedāṅga* is clearly stated:

> The Vedas arouse for the purpose of use in sacrifices; sacrifices are enjoined according to the order of times; therefore he who knows *Jyotiṣa* which is the science lay in down the proper times knows sacrifices. Just as a tuft of hair stands on the head of peacocks or a jewel in the heads of cobras, so astronomical calculations (*gaṇita*) stand at the head of all the sciences that are spoken of as *vedāṅga*.6

After quoting the verse given above in his commentary on *Bṛhajjātaka* (II.I.2.) Bhaṭṭotpala says:

Now, how is it proved that astrology is Vedāṅga? It is Vedāṅga because auspicious times are described in terms of lunar and solar eclipses, sun's entry into a sign of the zodiac, [calculations] of *vyatipāta, gajacchāya, tithi,* etc; because specific times are prescribed for the sacrifices, and because times are laid down for various other activities described in the Śrutis, Smṛtis and Purāṇas.

This means that, according to Bhaṭṭotpala, astrology (*phālita-jyotiṣa*) depends strongly on astronomy (*gaṇita-jyotiṣa*). In the *Pāṇinīya Śikṣā* the science of the movements of heavenly bodies is said to be the eye of the Veda. (*Śikṣā,* 41-42) It shows that the words *jyotiṣa* and *gaṇita* are used as synonyms in the *jyotiṣa-vedāṅga.*

The famous phenomenologist of religions Mircea Eliade was one of the first scholars to respect the organic integrity of astral mythologies. He demonstrated the significance of celestial archetypes in contributing to the unity and cohesiveness of the cosmological vision imbedded within the cultural fabric. He has also examined the ontological conceptions that underlie the celestial archetypes that permit and facilitate, for traditional societies, a necessary intercourse between the conditioned and the transcendental. (Eliade 1974, 6-11)

Space and time are two of the primary categories of perception that cosmologies address. All calendrical systems mark space as well as time. M. Eliade has pointed out that the archetypes of archaic cultures belong to a

---

5 According the *Matsyapurāṇa*, the authority of *ṛṣis* is due to their knowledge of the stars (*tārakādinidarśibhiḥ*). They are also said to dwell in, or even to become, celestial bodies, for they have become gods because of their religious action (*karmadeva*) (*Matsyapurāṇa,* 142.22; 127.40-41).

6 vedā hi yajñārtham abhipravṛttaḥ kālā anupurvyā vihitāśca yajñāḥ, Tasmād idam kālāvidhānaśāstramṃ ya jyotiṣaṃ veda sa veda yajñān
Ṛgveda Jyotiṣa, 35 *Yajurveda Jyotiṣa,* 3.

"cosmic time" beyond temporality. The cosmos is homologous to cosmic time:

For just as the cosmos is the archetype of all creation, cosmic time, which the cosmogony brings forth, is the paradigmatic model for all other times - that is, for the time specifically belonging to the various categories of existing things. (Eliade 1963, 141)

In the context of Indian philosophy, the primary causality of time was often, though not universally, accepted. The *Bhāgavata Purāṇa* gives an account of the *Sāṃkhya,* one of the six major Indian philosophical systems (*darśanas*), in which time (*kāla*) is equivalent to God because, like God, time causes the three *guṇas* - the primary quantitative components of existence - to lose their equilibrium and combine. (Dasgupta 1975, 4:25, 47) From this perspective time becomes the primary cause and catalyst of a cosmos that unfolds in accord with its infinite potential for permutation.

Indian astronomers, however, believed that time itself was generated by the motions of the planets. The complex internal mechanics of the celestial system, marked largely by continuity and regularity of the planetary movements, constitute a perfect image of cosmic time made manifest. In the *Kālasamuddeśa* of his *Vākyapadīya*, Bhartṛhari, the famous seventh-century Indian grammarian, cites this same opinion in the course of his discussion on the astronomical reckoning of time: „Furthermore, the knowers of time regard time as the motion of the sun, planets, and constellations, distinguished by their different revolutions".7 According to Bhartṛhari, the divisions and designations of time are generated from a single, undifferentiated time by natural events and human activity that condition the temporal dimension.

But time in India has never been merely quantitative, that is, limited to the measurement of intervals within any temporal typology, be it solar time, lunar time, seasonal activity, ritual cycles, etc. Time in India is preeminently qualitative. In other words, time, in its differentiated state, possesses meaning - as diverse as the periodicity of time itself. Time, then, is a matter of both natural and moral fact. It is within this conceptual framework, also, that theories of karma and transmigration seek to explain both the continuity and the transformation of meaning within human existence. Determining the nature of a particular time and acting accordingly are crucial if one is to live in harmony with the cosmos and within society.

Through the language of myths and symbols, the rhythms and structures of the world reveal themselves to man, although "in cipher". Using Clifford Geertz's notion of a "cultural system", a notion from the discipline of anthropology, the need for terminology that respects the context in which symbolic meaning - the life of cultural continuity - is

7 ādityagrahanakṣatraparispandam athāpare /
bhinnam āvṛttibhedena kālaṃ kālavido viduḥ // - *Vākyapadīya,* 3.9.76.

created and sustained.8 Astrology and divination are cultural systems that use symbolic language to decipher those rhythms and structures. Concerning the practice of divination, M. Eliade comments:

All the techniques of divination pursued the discovery of "signs," whose hidden meanings were interpreted in accordance with certain traditional rules. The world, then, revealed itself to be structured and governed by laws. If the signs were deciphered, the future could be known; in other words, time was "mastered" [...]. (Eliade 1978, 83)

Similarly, astrology seeks to understand and interpret a symbolic language of signs in the rhythms of time. The astrological practitioner utilizes the stars as cipher. Bhartṛhari cites the opinion: "The stars, which, individually, have the names of constellations, are simply signs for the transformations of the elements that follow the sources of time".9 Therefore, by knowing the meaning of astrological "signs," the astrologer can know, and in some sense even manipulate, the existential transformations to which they refer. There is, in this cosmology, an explicit synchronicity of "sign" and event, and an implicit affinity between simultaneity and meaning, using the expression of C. G. Jung.10 The symbolic, multivalent language of the astrological system does provide the astrologer with a kind of calculus for interpretation and mediation; through this language the astrologer articulates a particular life-pattern and circumstances for his client and / or whole country.

The astrologer's task then is not so much to measure the elapse of time, but to mark and classify the qualitative modalities in terns of which time manifests itself in human experience. The doctrine of *punarjanma* (reincarnation) was the conceptual locus through which the astrological system could be seen to operate, both generating and prefiguring lifeexperience as conditioned by the karmic residues (*karmāśaya*) of previous existences. In turn, the astrological system, in its representational and effective operation, made individual and group experience intelligible in terms of *karma*. The same could be said for the culturally constitutive category of *dharma*. The astrological system as celestial icon was seen as the divinely regulated image of *sanātana dharma* (eternal order), but an image capable of signifying the *svadharma* (individual order) of an individual, a group, or event, for any point in time - a template for existence and activity in Hindu culture. The integration of the astrological system, and particularly of natal (*jātaka*) astrology, into Indian culture is therefore highly understandable: astrology integrated the individual's experience with an envisaged cosmic order through the cultural categories of *karma* and

8 For a detailed diascussion on the notion of "cultural system," see: Geertz 1973, chapters 4 and 5.

9 mātrāṇāṃ pariṇāmā ye kālavṛttyanuyāyinaḥ /
nakṣatrākhyā pṛthak teṣu cihnamātraṃ tu tārakāḥ // - *Vākyapadīya* 3.9.44.

10 In one of his books C. G. Jung offers an extensive discussion on the principle of synchronicity and its relevance for astrology (Jung, 1955, 69).

dharma, and provided the means for the amelioration of disharmonious experience.

Thus, the celestial world is regarded in India as a divinely regulated icon of cosmic order (*ṛta*); astrological metaphor encodes this cosmic order and proceeds to translate that order into a continuous, multidimensional, phenomenal expression of eternity. The symbolic language of astrology deciphers the synchronic rhythms imaged in the celestial world, and articulates the teleology of these rhythms in a narrative of emergent, diachronic experience, providing temporal organization and a "trajectory of events". (Friedman 1986, 327) Astrological symbols are woven into a complex relation of mutual implication and form the apparatus by means of which the teleology of events and circumstances is deciphered. Victor Turner has shown that symbols, both as sensorily perceptible vehicles and as a set of "meanings", are essentially involved in the multiple variability of the people who employ them; symbols associated with human interests, purposes, and aspirations, individual and collective, take on the character of dynamic semantic systems. (Turner 1979, 13-14) 11 The resultant mutual implication of diverse levels of cultural discourse permit the incorporation of individual experience into semantically charged patterns operative within Hindu society. The polysemantic symbols of Indian astrology function to relate ontology and cosmology to aesthetics and a morality. As Claude LeviStrauss asserts, "the assimilation of such patterns is the only means of objectifying subjective states." (Levi-Strauss 1963, 1:171-172) The Indian astrological system accomplishes the process of objectification of cosmic cycles, in part, by locating human experience within a cosmic frame of reference, by orienting human experience away from the accidental and contingent. This capacity to cosmicize the phenomena of the mundane world is, without doubt, analogous to the process by which religions, historically, have legitimized social institutions. (Das 1976, 247-252) Through the operation of "analogical imagination" (expression of B.S. Friedman), the symbols and structures of the astrological system have referents on several planes of discourse, e.g., physical, psychological, social, mythical, and religious.

An earlier generation of European scholarship had, with rationalistic bias, assumed that astrology represented the consistent application of *post hoc ergo propter hoc* ("after this, therefore because of this"), and judged the system to be little more than an antiquated and fallacious epistemology. Indian astrologers were certainly not thought to be engaged in any extended historical project of inference and deduction (*anumāna*) by which their astrological system was conceived; but in fact, such a project, individually implemented along heuristic lines - together with the faulty transmission of

11 For instance, G. Reichel-Dolmatoff also suggests that "symbolic images are always seen as chains of analogies"; different cultural systems within a society therefore gain access to common themata by the operation of analogical imagination (Reichel-Dolmatoff, 1982, 170).

astrological teachings - probably accounts for the variation in astrological traditions encountered in texts and in practice. Rather, the Indian astrological system, as system, implies its own epistemological foundations that must be understood within the broader context of an Indian cultural and intellectual agenda. The epistemological underpinnings of Indian astrology emerge through the dialectical transactions of the analogical imagination that inform the entire symbolic system of astrology, transactions that, to use the language of Levi-Strauss, "guarantee the convertibility of ideas between different levels of social reality." (Levi-Strauss 1966, 76) The result is a vitally alive, richly complex cultural system, grounded in myth, imagination, and the exigencies of everyday life, that orients the person within a meaningful and multidimensional order of being. No wonder, therefore, that according to the *Agnipurāṇa* (1212.1) knowledge of *jyotiḥśāstra* - a science which claims nothing less than complete hegemony over the entire permutable network of reality - makes the astrologer in a sense omniscient (*sarvavid*).

Formal cosmological structure together with a rich mythological tradition supports a living, meaning-filled cosmos. This cosmos is above all relevant to the human world and Indian epistemology ensured this relevance in the concept of "likeness" or "resemblance" (*sādṛśya*). The concept of "likeness" (*sādṛśya*) is fundamental to the operation of the Indian astrological system. In his seminal astrological text, *Yavanajātaka* ("*The Horoscopy of the Greeks*"), probably the oldest known Sanskrit text on horoscopic astrology (written around 270 A. D.), Sphujidhvaja asserts that the mutual interactions (*yoga*) of the planets as they pass through the various signs of the Zodiac are said to be formed in the likeness of shapes (*saṃsthāna sādṛśyakṛta*):

One sees that objects have various natures and the likeness of their shapes is infinite; these are to be recognized as belonging to the various divisions of the world and having names similar to their likeness of shape. There is a natural acquisition of qualities that arises from association with [zodiacal] signs and [celestial] embodiments of inherent nature, whose forms are similar to the shapes [of objects] (*Yavanajātaka* 36.1-4).12

12 *Yavanajātaka* is the main Sanskrit text that has preserved for us what remains of Grecco-Babylonian planetary astrology in India. The prime indisputable evidence that the *Yavanajātaka* is indeed influenced by Greek astrology is the presence in it of a large number of technical terms that are, as was proved by D. Pingree, simply transliterations of their Greek equivalents. From the concluding three verses of *Yavanajātaka* we are informed that it is a versified version of a prose translation of a Greek text, with a high degree of probability from Egypt, Alexandria, made by one Yavaneśvara, in the year 149/150 AD, probably at the court of the Western Kṣatrapa Rudradāman in Ujjayinī. The prose translation of Yavaneśvara was evidently deemed an unsuitable vehicle for the transmission of śāstraic knowledge, therefore Sphujidhvaja undertook to versify the work. It was perhaps Sphujidhvaja who

Thus, according to Sphujidhvaja, the universe of objects is characterized by various natures inherent in these objects. The names of objects are consonant with the natures inherent in them. There exists an infinity of likeness between objects that pertain to the various divisions of the world, and the names of objects reflect the likeness between them. Lastly, object in the world naturally acquire the qualities of the Zodiacal signs and of other celestial embodiments and the shapes of objects. By the way, the application of the principle of resemblance was not limited to India. Western sympathetic magic was grounded on the principle of resemblance. As Michel Foucault suggests, until the end of the sixteenth century, "it was resemblance that organized the play of symbols, made knowledge possible of things visible and invisible, and controlled the art of representing them". (Foucault 1973, 17)

The early *Taittirīya brāhmaṇa* already had suggested: "The constellations are images of the world."13 The *Yavanajātaka* reverses this relationship:

There are always an essence, condition, characteristics, and external form similar to its internal qualities and form; existing like a mirror and its image, these are produced not within its own substance but in the world of men.14

The world is then the image of the heavens, and to know the structural components and interactional dynamics of the astrological system - to know the patterns of being as these are continuously generated by this system of meanings - is, through the "correspondence" that a dialectical imagination makes possible, to know the world.

For horoscopic astrology the most essential correspondence between heaven and earth finds its nexus in man, for the human body is constituted as microcosm of the celestial world. In fact, the principle of likeness or resemblance was essential to the Indian cosmology in which the astrological system developed, beginning with the Cosmic Man (*puruṣa*) of *Ṛgveda*

---

being himself an indianized Greek further indianized the text introducing the chapters on reincarnation; the list of minerals, plants, and animals, which is influenced by the Āyurvedic *materia medica*; and the section on military astrology and other elements of Indian culture. Thus, the original Greek system was further modified so that the predictions fit the social and economic expectations of people born in India.

13 yāni vā imāni pṛthivyāś citrāṇi tāni nakṣatrāṇi - *Taittirīya brāhmaṇa* I.5.2.2.

14 antaḥ sadāsyākṛtilakṣanāṇāṃ/
samānasattvasthitiliṅgamūrtiḥ//
bimbānubimbapratimāsthito/
ayam utpadyatītyasvavasau nṛloke// - *Yavanajātaka* 28.2. As David Pingree suggests, the concept of *sādṛśya* reminds one of the
Platonic "idea" with the modification that the celestial bodies act as a bridge between the forms (*intelligibles*) and matter (*sensibles*) (*Yavanajātaka*, II.331332).

(X.90) and Upaniṣadic assertion that one who knows his microcosmic relationship to the universe attains salvation in or through the celestial world. The *Bṛhatsaṃhitā* (14.1-5) then speaks of the *nakṣatra-puruṣa* ("man of the constellations") whose body is formed from the twenty-seven lunar mansions. The *Bṛhajjātaka* of Varāhamihira (1.4) describes the *kālapuruṣa* ("man of time") whose body is composed of the twelve zodiacal signs beginning with Aries and ending with Pisces, his head and feet, respectively. The analogical operation of the Indian astrological system permits this cosmic man and the human body to be regarded, in the words of Brenda Beck, as "related topological spaces." (Beck 1976, 241; see also: Wayman 1982) As planetary lords pass through the body of the *kālapuruṣa*, the bodies of men are correspondingly affected. The *Yavanajātaka* (51.6) insist that the good or evil influences which reside in the mind (*manas*) as the body (*tanu*) possess the strengths and weaknesses of their lords (*īśvara*), as these latter are variously conditioned by their passage through the constellations. Thus, human experience, in its mental, emotional, and physical modalities, is seen to depend on influences from the celestial world; through principles of similitude and correspondence man is fashioned in the image of the heavens. According to B.S. Friedman,

> *Sādṛśya* guaranteed that the terrestrial world, reflecting the order of heaven, could be known and ordered according to principles of similitude and correspondence. The astrological system, informed by *sādṛśya* comprehends the grammar and syntax of the heavens - the modulations of meaning imaged there - and validates the interconnectedness of human experience. (Friedman 1986, 327)

To know *jyotiṣa*, therefore, is to know the order of the world, the system that generates and prefigures life-experience as it is conditioned by *karma*. The astrological system thus objectifies human experience and ensures a universe of participation in which the individual and the cosmos are fundamentally relevant to each other. An Indian astrologer is provided with a kind of calculus with which to locate an apparently chaotic and meaningless social and individual situation within an integrated and intelligible web of meanings.

The distinction between unconditioned and conditioned time, or "real" and „human" time is, as Indian psychologist Sudhir Kakar sugests, reminiscent of the distinction between reality and cosmic illusion (*māyā*). "Human" time, then, with its fluctuation and periodicity, is only an apparent phenomenon; *saṃsāra* ("universal flux") is a wordly manifestation of absolute time. (Kakar 1978, 46) It is this view of time that has given rise to the image of *kāla* ("time") as a fearful god of death and inexorable fate. Sudhir Kakar has emphasized the relevance of the conceptions of time and destiny - these essential dimensions of experience - for an understanding of individual psychology: "The way in which a culture estimates and elaborates ideas of time and destiny provides insight into the psychological organization of its individual members." (Kakar, 1978, 45) A person lives in a unitary life-world in which numerous influences are naturally active, and he has a destiny that is manifested in the experiential milieu of daily life. The cyclical movements of heavenly bodies produce cyclical patterns of influence on the terrestrial world and on the life of the person. These celestial cycles create a progression of auspicious (*śubha*) and inauspicious (*aśubha*) periods of time. Celestial cycles do not simply mark the passage of a homogenous time: they create fluctuations in the quality of time that influence the possibilities of human action. Changes in life-experience are often expressed in patterns of fluctuation that mark the person's physical and psychological conditions and also mark the quality of his relationships in his family and community. So, the theory of cycles is a basic feature of Hindu cosmology, with its accounts of cosmic cycles of creation and destruction, and with the fundamental place of the theory of rebirth (*punarjanma*), in which the life-time of the person is merely one phase in an ongoing cycle of death and rebirth.

Eclipses, predictable astronomical conjunctions that are said to be caused by the mythical planets Rāhu and Ketu swallowing the sun and moon, produce a state of inauspiciousness, which may be countered by worshiping the planets or donating gifts, but misfortune would still befall anyone who started a ritual or new venture, or even ate a meal, during their occurrence. However, eclipses also pollute people who try to counteract the effect by bathing during them, as well as bathe the deities' images, which calls for extra rituals of purification and appeasement before normal worship can be resumed. Thus, the natural, inevitable occurrence of eclipses causes a general disturbance of the whole human and divine order, which demands appropriate ritual counteraction, although these astronomical events also have to be lived through while they last. It is common for traditional Hindus to argue that every misfortune caused by divine or personified agencies is ultimately determined by natural phenomena - time itself or the inauspiciousness emergent from the natural order.

Thus, the "fault of the planets" (*graha-doṣa*) refers to an impersonal planetary force, but it also refers to its effect, a defect in human beings productive of misfortune that can connote ritual pollution and moral failing as well. In the words of C. J. Fuller:

> The partial overlap among concepts of impersonal inauspiciousness, physical or mental illness, ritual pollution, sin and immorality reflects the fact that in popular Hinduism etiology natural phenomena can affect the whole human condition. (Fuller 1992, 244)

In concluding - the Indian astrological system, therefore, provides a theory of experiential contiuity and accounts, conversely, for *saṃsāra* as personal flux. Capable of an infinite permutation of its symbilic components

- a constantly changing celestial icon - the astrological system both generates and prefigures karmic conditions: an individual's *karma* and *dharma* are reified in the horoscope. Astrology in its entire operational schema becomes a language that is used not only in constructing a myth of the self but also in connecting such myths to society, thus creating a dialectics of self and society. The very act of choosing and consulting an astrologer or diviner can be considered a rite by itself in which particular selves and their worlds and hence society itself are re-created and confirmed. The structural analogies between consulting an astrologer and listening to his words and going to a temple and having a *pūjā* done are obvious enough. They become weak only in the degree of comprehension achieved in the *pūjā* as opposed to that achieved through consultation of the spoken word, insofar as the former is likely to be in archaic Sanskrit. A close inspection of horoscope reading will reveal the nature of their significance as ideology; it will show how myths of the self and society are parallel to the structures of the ideology of *karma* and *dharma*.15

Opposing the common assumption that astrology is merely an expression of archaic - and degrading - superstition, my paper concludes that the Indian divinational system - as cultural system - is based on a particular cosmic vision and lends human experience value and meaning. Astrological practices cannot be differentiated from other social practices on the basis of their symbolic exchange or their rhetorical powers. The specificity of astrology lies in a particular cosmological perspective. All human life is lived symbolically and in conformity to various theories, mythologies and ideologies, so the ready availability of a symbolic statement about one's own life, containing both explicit and implicit structures that denote continuity with other areas of symbolic life such as religion, medicine, and human relationships, seems a credible and worthwhile exercise.16

REFERENCES

Sanskrit Sources:

Agneyamahāpurāṇa. ed. by Khemraj Krisnadas, Bombay: Venkateshwar Steam Pres., 1900.

Bṛhatsaṃhitā with Bhaṭṭotpala's Commentary. ed. By Sudhakara Dvivedi, Varanasi, Vols. 2, 1895-1897.

Bṛhajjātaka with Bhaṭṭotpala's Cintāmaṇi Commentary. ed. by Sitaram Jha, Varanasi, 1934.

Dikshit, Shankar Balakrishna. 1957. *Bhāratīya Jyotiṣa* (2nd printing, Poona, 1931; Hindi trans., Publication Bureau, U.P., Prayag,. English

---

15 See more Perinbanayagam 1982, p. 170.

16 On the relation between two traditional Indian sciences - astrology and Āyurvedic medicine, see: Beinorius, 2008, pp. 189-208.

translation of part 1, *History of Astronomy during the Vedic and Vedanga period,* tr. by R. V. Vaidya, Delhi, 1969).

Kālasamuddeśa of Bhartṛhari's Vākyapadīya. Peri Sarveswara Sharma, ed. and trans, New Delhi: Motilal Banarsidass, 1972.

Matsyapurāṇa. ed. by Jivananda Vidyasagarabhattachayya, Calcutta: Sarasvati Press, 1876.

Taittirīya brāhmaṇa. eds. Godabole and Narayanasastri, Anandasrama Sanskrit Series, vol. 37, 2 vols., Poona: Annadasrama Sanskrit Press, 1934.

Vedāṅga Jyotiṣa. ed. with corrected readings and interpretations in his commentary, by Himmatram M. Yajnik (Jani), Ahmedabad: Vedhashala, 1985.

Yavanajātaka of Sphujidhvaja. ed,, translated and commented on by D. Pingree, Vol. I-II, Harvard University Press, 1978.

Secondary Literature

Tamsyn S. Barton. 1994. *Power and Knowledge: Astrology, Physiognomics, and Medicine under the Roman Empire*, Ann Arbor: Michigan Press. Brenda E.F Beck. 1976. "The Symbolic Merger of Body, Space and Cosmos in Hindu Tamil Nadu," *Contributions to Indian Sociology* 10, pp. 213243.

Audrius Beinorius. 2008. "Astral Hermeneutics: Astrology and Medicine in India", in *Astro-Medicine: Astrology and Medicine: East and West* (Micrologus' Library 25). Edited by Anna Akasoy, Charles Burnett and Ronit Yoeli-Tlalim. Firenze-Sismel: Edizioni del Galluzzo, pp. 189208.

Clifford Geertz. 1973. *The Interpretation of Cultures,* New York: Basic Books.

Veena Das. 1976. "The Uses of Liminality: Society and Cosmos in Hinduism," *Contributions to Indian Sociology* 10.2, pp. 245-263. Surendranath Dasgupta. 1975. *A History of Indian Philosophy*, 5 vols., Cambridge: Cambridge University Press, 1922; Reprint. New Delhi: Motilal Banarsidass.

Mircea Eliade. 1963. *Myth and Reality*, trans. William R. Trask, New York: Harper and Row.

Mircea Eliade. 1974. *The Myth of the Eternal Return*, trans. by Willad R.Trask, Princeton: Princeton University Press.

Mircea Eliade. 1978. *A History of Religious Ideas*, trans. By Willard R. Trask, Vol. 1: *From the Stone Age to the Eleusinian Mysteries*, Chicago: University of Chicago Press.

Michel Foucault. 1973. *The Order of Things: An Archeology of Human Sciences*, New York: Vintage Books.

Barry Steven Friedman. 1986. *Negotiating Destiny: The Astrologer and His Art in Bengali Cultural History,* Ph.D dissertation, University of Chicago.

C.J.Fuller. 1992. *The Camphor Flame: Popular Hinduism and Society In India,* Princeton: Princeton University Press.

Carl Gustav Jung. 1955. *Synchronicity: An Acausal Connecting Principle*, trans. R.F.C. Hall, (Bollingen Series 20) New York: Pantheon Books. Sudhir Kakar. 1978. *The Inner World, A Psycho-analytic Study of Childhood and Society in India,* New Delhi: Oxford University Press. Richard Lemay. 1987. "The True Place of Astrology in Medieval Science and Philosophy: Towards a Definition", in *Astrology, Science and Society: Historical Essays*, ed. Patrick Curry, Woodbridge: The Boydell Press, pp. 57-73.

Claude Levi-Strauss. 1963. *Structural Anthropology,* trans. By C. Jacobson and B.G. Schoepf, New York: Basic Books.

Claude Levi-Strauss. 1966. *The Savage Mind*, Chicago: University of Chicago Press.

Seyyed Hosein Nasr. 1981. *Knowledge and the Sacred. (The Gifford lectures*), New York: Crossroad.

R.S. Perinbanayagam. 1982. *The Karmic Theater: Self, Society, and Astrology in Jaffna,* Amherst: University of Massachusetts Press. David Pingree. 1981. *Jyotiḥśāstra: Astral and Mathematical Literature*, A History of Indian Literature, Vol. 6, fasc. 4, ed. Jan Gonda, Wiesbaden: Otto Harrassowitz.

David Pingree. 1994. *Census of the Exact Sciences in Sanskrit,* Philadelphia, American Philosophical Society, Vol. I-V.

R G.eichel-Dolmatoff. 1982. "Astronomical Models of Social Behaviour among Some Indians of Columbia," *Annals of the New York Academy of Sciences* 385 (May), pp. 165-182.

Victor.Turner. 1979. *Process, Performance and Piligrimage,* New Delhi: Concept Publications.

Alex Wayman. 1982. "The Human Body as Microcosm in India, Greek Cosmology, and Sixteenth-Century Europe," *Journal of the History of Religions* 22 (November), pp. 172-190.

(Translated from Russian by Galina Lisenco)

CHAPTER XVI

SOME BUDDHIST IDEAS OF REALITY AND THE "EXTENDED EVERETT'S CONCEPT" BY M.B. MENSKY

On September 10th 2010 here, in the Institute of Philosophy of the Russian Academy of Sciences [RAS], well-known Russian scientists were discussing with the Buddhists a problem of mind and reality. On the level of the leading scientists of the country such meeting took place for the first time.1 What brought the eminent Russian physicists, neurophysiologists and philosophers together with the Buddhists at the round table?

The prehistory of this meeting goes back to the very beginning of quantum mechanics when Nils Bohr took notice that "in search for the parallels to the atomic theory lesson of limitations in applicability of the ordinary ideations, we are to refer to quite different areas of science like psychology, or even to specific philosophical problems - like those problems addressed by such thinkers like the Buddha or Laotse when trying to correlate our position of both observers and actors in the great drama of being."2

V. Pauli used to discuss these problems with C.G. Jung, 3 HH the Dalai-Lama XIV used to study quantum physics together with C. von Weizsecker and D. Bohm as well as to hold series of conferences with physicists on this subject.4

It is most likely that at the deepest level the general idea of modern physics and Buddhism is to grasp falsity of the ordinary ideas about internal self-sufficiency of phenomena and their independence from each other, to understand that reality should be regarded from the viewpoint of

---

1 See "Consciousness in Buddhism and Quantum Physics - Discussion in the Institute of Philosophy of the Russian Academy of Sciences," *Buddhism of Russia*. In Russian. No. 43, (2011).

2 N. Bohr, *Selected Scientific Works*. In Russian (Moscow: Nauka, 1971), p. 256.

3 For more details see, e.g.: K.V. Kopeikin "Souls" of Atoms and "Atoms" of the Soul: Wolfgang Ernst Pauli, Carl Gustav Jung and "three great problems of physics," *Tribuna* [Tribune] UFN; 0812.

4 There are a lot of publications on this subject. As for a Russian-speaking reader, one may point out, for instance, a book of V. Mansfield, *Tibetan Buddhism and Modern Physics* (Moscow: Novy Akropol, 2010) and, in particular, a book of HH the Dalai-Lama "The Universe in a Single Atom" printed by the "Otkrity Mir" [Open World] publishing house.

interconditionality not only in terms of gnoseology but of ontology as well. Taken all around, that is likely to be clear to everybody. However, it seems that some recent interpretations of quantum mechanics correspond in much more specific manner to the Buddhist (first of all, Mahāyāna) ideas of the world.

The Buddhist thinkers distinguish two levels of reality: *vyavahāra* ordinary reality of phenomena, illusive in the sense that we imagine all the phenomena and events as really existing the very way we perceive them within the frame of the karmic conditionality of our consciousness and as if "objectively independent" from each other and our consciousness; and paramārtha - real "supreme" reality - "*dharmatā*" or "*tathātā*" wherein the phenomena and events do not exist as separate entities, and are "empty" of any "self-being": they exist only in their interconditionality. Perception of reality - at the lower or higher level - is determined by the level of our consciousness: it is for the sake of transition to the higher levels of comprehension that the training of consciousness is performed in Buddhism.

The Teaching of the Buddha is based on the two levels of being (*satya*):

ordinary manifested being and essence of being. Those who do not understand the differences between these levels of being,

Do not understand the deep reality (*tāttvaṃ*) discovered by the Buddha.5

And Nāgārjuna continues further on [*Ibid.*, 24:10]:

Without relying on the ordinary [as a base], the supreme cannot be grasped

Without reaching the supreme, *nirvāṇa* cannot be reached. This means that *nirvāṇa* is reached by means of spiritual practice resulting in direct perception of *emptiness* which enables one to cognize the essence of being - *dharmatā* or thusness, *tathātā*.

The definition of *dharmatā* is suchness (*tathātā*), 6 indivisible into object and subject, into expressed and expressing.7

---

5 Nāgārjuṇa, Mūlamadhyamakakārikā 24:8-9.

6 "Suchness" (sanskr. *tathātā*) is the essence of phenomena unperceivable by an individual who has not reached the level of ārya (direct cognition of "emptiness"), and this "essence appears" (as Hegel used to say), i.e. appears in the phenomena and, besides, does that in full. That is, both profane and 'real' levels of reality are true, but each one in its own way.

Tathātā, dharmatā (as well as *dharmadhātu*, etc. - in different Buddhist thinkers these terms sometimes obtain slightly different meanings) may be considered as a kind of ontological correlate of emptiness as universal interdependence.

And now, the interpretation of the Everett's quantum mechanics developed by Professor M.B. Mensky of the Lebedev Physical Institute at the RAS, seems to come to the same: our physical world which we are accustomed to consider to be "real" is only one of innumerable "aspects" in the *truly real* "quantum world" - an aspect chosen by an act of our consciousness, and it is only by mistake that we take it for the whole of reality.

Such interpretation proceeds from a known fact that according to quantum mechanics, a state of microscopic system may represent a superposition (sum) of two or more other states of this system. It means that such system, for instance, a micro-particle, is physically (and not only mathematically!)8 present at the same time in several points of space: the state of the particle may represent a superposition of its states in two or more different points. When the microscopic system is undergone to a measurement, the correlation arises between its state and the state of a microscopic device which also represents a quantum system. If before measurement the microsystem is in the state of superposition, after the measurement is over, the composite system (micro-system + macro-device) also must be a superposition. This follows from the circumstance that the process of quantum measurement consisting only in collision and interaction of particles of a system being measured and a micro-device, changes the nature of these particles in no way.

However, as a result of measurement, the components of superposition become microscopically discernible for us. For example, the states of device characterizing different components of the superposition, after the measurement is over, differ in the position of the pointer which is

7 Maitreya/Asaṅga. Dharmadharmatāvibhaṅga, 5. See full Russian translation [version] with commentaries of Vasubandhu in the book "Otnositelnoye y absolyutnoye v buddisme [The Relative and Absolute in Buddhism]". In Russian. (Moscow: Ganga, Svatan), 2012.

8 This is a decisively important moment. The specificity of "quantum reality was first disclosed in the famous work of Einstein, Podolsky and Rosen (1935) and then stated in the theorem of John Bell (1964). Nevertheless, there could still be attempts to assign the probabilistic nature of measurements, for example, to the lack of full information on initial state of the objects being measured - i.e. to assume that in essence, the quantum measurement is in everything similar to the classic one. However, in the course of Aspect's experiments (Aspect, 1981) verifying Bell's theorem, it was experimentally confirmed that it was the quantum reality which ruled in our real world. See more details, for example: M.B. Mensky, "Concept of Consciousness in the Context of Quantum Mechanics," *Uspekhi Fizicheskikh Nauk*. In Russian. (Moscow: Russian Academy of Sciences, 2005), 48(4), p. 394.

fraught, as in case of the known example with "Schrödinger's cat", with the superposition of the states with the "alive cat" and with the "dead cat" being unbearable for our intuition.

The paradox of "Schrödinger's cat" is as follows: the cat is placed in a closed box with a radioactive isotope counter of disintegration products and a device which breaks the ampoule with poison in the cat's mouth when the counter is actuated. While the atom has not disintegrated the cat is all right, but when it disintegrates, the counter is actuated and the cat dies of poison. We do not know when the atom disintegrates, but in every moment there is a certain probability of disintegration. For a quantum system this is described as superposition, i.e. in every given moment an atom is in superposition of two states: the state when it has not disintegrated yet and the state when it has disintegrated. Consequently, approaching the closed box, according to the laws of quantum mechanics, we should believe that the system "atom+cat" is in superposition of two states: (non-disintegrated atom + alive cat) + (disintegrated atom + dead cat). However, having opened the box, we would always see the cat either alive or dead! Why?

In order to solve such questions various hypotheses were proposed. In compliance with so called "Copenhagen Interpretation", when a measured system is interacting with a microscopic device, the linearity of quantum evolution is violated. Thus, if the position of a point particle is measured, then prior to the measurement the particle could have been in superposition of two localized states (i.e. with different probabilities to be in different points), while after the measurement it is found only in one of these points, meaning that superposition disappears.

Owing to what could the state of particle have changed so radically? This could mean that at the moment of measurement the particle lost its quantum-mechanical properties. However, the process of measurement has not created any qualitatively new situation for the being of this particle - the collision with particles of the measuring micro-device in no way differs for it from the collision with any other particles. Therefore such hypothesis is contrary to both common sense and the equation of Schrödinger, which is why some physicists believe the Copenhagen Interpretation to be incorrect.

Evidently, this paradox could be explained by accepting that the system description depends on whether we have opened the box or not that is wether an observer has realized the result of measurement. So, in 1957 an American physicist H. Everett suggested an interpretation wherein the linearity of evolution is maintained in the course of measurement. Correspondingly, he came to an unavoidable conclusion that the superposition which existed before the measurement should remain after the measurement too. But this means that in the world there should also exist superpositions of microscopically distinct states, for instance, superpositions of the two states with the alive cat and the dead one (as in the above mentioned example).

In order to make the Everett's interpretation more visual, J.A. Wheeler and B. DeWitt proposed to describe the superposition state of microscopically distinct configurations of the quantum world as coexistence of different "Everett's worlds". Say, the cat is alive in one of the Everett's worlds and the observer in this world perceives the cat being alive, while in another Everett's world the cat is dead and the observer sees that the cat is dead.

It means that the "twins" of one and the same observer in different worlds watch different classical realities. Herewith, it is important to remember that such "Everett's worlds" are not physical worlds but only a visual conventional designation for the components within the superposition of the quantum world.

Instead of the 'Everett's worlds', M.B. Mensky suggests speaking about the "alternative classical realities" or simply "classical alternatives" which are in superposition (coexist) though the mind perceives them separately. This is a description of the same situation but it is more convenient due to the absence of the notion of "twin" which is not quite clear. According to Mensky, different classical realities (i.e. the "Everett's worlds") objectively coexist in superposition but are *separated in consciousness* so that, perceiving one of them, an observer does not perceive the rest.

But both descriptions entail the radical conclusion that a picture of a sole classical reality, to which we are accustomed, is just an *illusion* emerging in the mind of observer.

In the wording "alternative classical realities are separated by the consciousness of observer", there is no exact definition of the two key notions, "separation of alternatives" and "consciousness". In 2000 M.B. Mensky proposed the "Extended Everett's Concept" (EEC) wherein these two notions are identified: herewith, instead of two primary concepts there remained only one separate perception of alternatives, understood as an act of consciousness. In this way, Mensky assumes that the real quantum world, we see in the form of one classical alternative, is the very realization of the animate beings' ability to perceive not all the quantum superposition as a whole, but only its components - the alternative classical realities.9 It means that our usual classical world IS our "ordinary" consciousness.

In principle, we know that for a long time,10 and Marx used to say practically the same: "Bewusstsein ist immer bewusste Sein", but in the context of quantum-mechanical understanding of reality this old wording about identity of being and consciousness obtains absolutely new meaning.

But how does the "real" quantum world wherein we are living, looks like from the viewpoint of physics? It is difficult and, strictly speaking, even

---

9 On the basis of this proposal M.B. Mensky states a whole number of interesting hypotheses that we are not going to discuss here. They are given in sufficient detail in his books and articles.

10 Let us recall, for example, the approach of Spinoza who was speaking of ONE Substance acting in the aspect of both extention and intelligibility.

impossible for us to imagine, because as Mensky11 explains, in a quantum world "there are correlations between the any remote domains and in virtue of these correlations the future of local system depends on the present in all of the remote domains… This means that knowing the state of some space domain, one cannot even approximately forecast which would be the state of this domain in the future". In other words, in a quantum world there is a cause-effect dependence of everything upon everything, therefore it turns out to be impossible to single out, perceive and designate the independent individual things and phenomena (*dharmas*) - they are just missing.

In Buddhism such a state is denoted by the term "emptiness" understood as interconditionality and as "The Heart Sūtra of Prajñāpāramitā" says: "...in *emptiness*… there are neither eye, nor ear, nose, tongue, body, nor mind, nor forms nor sounds, nor smells, nor tastes, touch nor *dharmas*…."12

Reality, the quantum world, as distinct from *saṃsāra*, the world of phenomena (dharmas), is called "*dharmatā*" - that is what represents *nirvāṇa* as Maitreya said:

That which one names dharma here, is *saṁsāra*, while *dharmatā*

is *nirvāṇa* in [all] the three Chariots.13

Saṃsāra - the world of phenomena and *nirvāṇa* - the world of "piece" - are the widest ontological categories of Buddhism (if it is possible to speak about the "Buddhist ontology" at all). In order to understand these categories, it is necessary to remember that the Buddha was not engaged in an abstract ontology, he considered only the world of phenomena as the human world, the world of human experience.

This world, *saṁsāra*, is described for instance in the categories of five *skandhas*, 12 *āyatanas* or 18 *dhātu*. This very *saṁsāra* in the course of mastering its *emptiness*, i.e. interconditionality of all the phenomena and their non-existence as independent entities beyond this interconditionality, is called *nirvāṇa*. These two layers of being - *nirvāṇa* and *saṁsāra* - may be tentatively designated as the world of absolute reality and the world of relative reality.

In Mahāyāna Buddhism this is worded already as an identity of *saṁsāra* and *nirvāṇa* where this "superposition of classical alternatives" is designated with such words as *tathātā*, *dharmatā*, etc., while the "classical alternatives" themselves - with the terms of *vyavahāra*, *saṃvṛti-satya*, *saṁsāra*….In both cases, consciousness is a significant aspect but as some

11 Personal letter to the author of 08.09.2010.

12 See full translation: A. Terentyev, "The Heart Sūtra. Sanskrit and Tibetan texts, translation and commentaries," *Buddhism. History and Culture*. In Russian. (Moscow: Nauka, 1989), pp. 4-21.

13 Maitreya/Asaṅga. Dharmadharmatāvibhaṅga, 3.

Mahayana philosophers state, with regard to *tathātā* or *dharmadhātu* it is better to use the term Knowledge/primordial knowledge (Sanskrit: *jñāna*) while to *saṁsāra* - the consciousness (*vijñāna*), the decomposition of this full, primordial knowledge under the influence of *ignorance*.14

It is via the notion of *emptiness* as the Sanskrit term "*śūnyatā*"15 is translated into Russian, that they are associated. Division between these two

levels of reality - essential, *paramārtha*) "absolute" (Pāli: *paramattha*; Sanskrit: (Pāli: and conventional, "r *saṃmuti* или *samuti*; elative"
Sanskrit: *saṃvṛti*) is usually translated into the European languages as the theory of the "two truths".16

Only relative truth - the relative world is accessible for ordinary perception and thinking because only here introduced are the division of reality into subject and object (which are false in relation to the essence of being, "*paramārtha*") as well as discursive thinking. While *paramārtha* the real "supreme" reality - is comprehended by the individuals who have attained the direct perception of *emptiness*, i.e. by the "saints" (Sanskrit: *ārya*) on the "path of vision" - the third of five steps of perfection on the Buddhist path. It is important that like in the Everett' concept:

14 See, for example Third Karmapa Rangjung Dorje. *Distinction of Consciousness and Initial Realization* [*Sensing*]. In Russian. (Moscow: Ganga/Shechen, 2008)

15 It has to be mentioned that this is not a felicitous translation because of which an important Buddhist philosophic notion is often confused with physical notions such as vacuum or space. F. I. Stcherbatsky, for example, proposed to translate "*śūnyatā*" as "relativity" using the terminology of physical theories that emerged in his time, but more accurately, *śūnyatā* is, first of all, interdependence, absence of independent self-being of any thing or idea.

16 Much more than "emptiness" this translation is likely to disorient a European reader. In the European philosophy what we call "truth" is, first of all, correspondence of a notion to its object while here the point is very different: two levels of being. Such translation evidently appeared because the Sanskrit word *satya* (which is usually translated as "truth") is derived from the root *sat* being or existence. In other words, satya is literally "what is [present]" - which sometimes but not in all the contexts, could be translated as "truth". Probably, for more felicitous translation of the pair of categories *saṃvṛiti-satya* and *paramārtha-satya* (Tibetan: kun dzob bden pa, don dam pa'i bden pa), denoting the relative world of phenomena and the real "true" world behind it, it would be better to use the paired European categories "phenomenon and essence": "The truth of being is essence" Hegel used to define (G.V.F. Hegel, *Science of Logic*. In Russian. (Moscow: Mysl. 1971), vol. 2, p. 7. In Indian philosophy, as far as I know, there is no relative pair of categories - essence and phenomenon.

By the way, the use of such translation would also enable to avoid the homonymy in the name of this Indian doctrine and the Western "theory of the two truths" - medieval teaching on autonomy of truths in philosophy (i.e. [of] rational cognition) and theology.

These two [truths] are neither one nor separate as between the existing and non-existing there is and there is no difference.17

Thousands of pages have been dedicated to the theory of Two Truths, however, what matters here for us is only the very principle of two layers' reality: ordinary existence which all of us know to some extent and true non-dual reality which is behind it; weather we call it *nirvāṇa, dharmatā, tathātā, dharmadhātu*, "superposition of classical alternatives" or by other names (its essence, the same as Kantian "thing-in-itself", cannot be expressed or described in any case).

In terms of cognition both Science and Buddhism are pursuing one goal: to find out the real state of things. The physicists say that one of the quantum world's features is interdeterminability of ALL the events in it. In other words, we live in the quantum world and the *superposition of alternatives* is the very true state of things. There are no individual entities with their own nature but everything exists in an interrelative way. In Buddhism such "true" state of affairs, a state of interdependent emergence is called "*dharmatā*" or *thusness* - "*tathātā*". The person who has reached the level of *ārya*, i.e. the one of direct cognition of *emptiness*, no longer sees individual things and phenomena as we do. What does he see? Evidently, what he sees is this "superposition of classical alternatives", i.e. metaphorically speaking, all the separately non-existing phenomena of all the probabilistic "Everett's worlds" - simultaneously and in all their interrelations.

Therefore, it seems to be heuristically interesting to correlate the quantum-mechanical idea of "classical alternatives" by Everett-Mensky with the Buddhist notion of relative reality as the world of phenomena, and the idea of superposition of classical alternatives - with the notion of *dharmatā, tathātā (dharmadhātu*, etc.) as "essential" reality in Buddhism.

How far could this parallel be drawn?

(Translated from Russian by Galina Lisenco)

---

17 Maitreya/Asaṅga..., 7.

PART III

FAR-EAST TRADITION

CHAPTER XXII

CHINESE CULTURE AND ATOMISM

The atomic theory is one of the prerogative examples demonstrating fundamental and general differences between Chinese and Western scientific and philosophical traditions and cultures. Chinese physicists would stubbornly reject atomism while staying loyal to the philosophical prototype of the wave theory, as was shown by J. Needham (1900-1905). Apparently, Chinese thinkers did not create any version of atomism themselves. Dominated by continuous-wave notions of matter, they would usually conceive all substrate states of both material and spiritual phenomena as continuous and homogeneous ("pneuma" - *qi* 气, "seedspirit" - *jing* 精).

Meanwhile, in the literature originating from Christian missionaries, who were brought up in the tradition of mechanistic atomism of the 17th18th centuries, one comes across erroneous interpretations of the continual field-forming "pneuma"-*qi* and its subtle (essential) form, "seed-spirit" *jing* (cf. "spermatic logos" of the Stoics) as atomized matter ("particles-*qi*" and "particle-*jing*"). Quite an absurd point was made, for example, by Father S. Le Gall (1858-1916), who interpreted the thickening and thinning of *qi* in the *Great Void* (*tai xu* 太虛) as a concentration and dispersion of atoms, which Zhang Zai 張載(1020-1078) compared with the solidification and melting of ice in water; the latter comparison was based on the popular Chinese philosophical analogy of the metamorphoses of *qi* and water, which Wang Chong 王充 (*Lun-heng* - *Weighing of Judgments*, VII, 1 / ch. 24, XX, 3 / ch. 62) made in the 1st century AC.

According to the just remark of *A.C.* Graham (1919-1990), S. Le Gall did it "in spite the fact that the comparison with water shows clearly that the ether (*qi*. - AK) is a continuum and not an aggregation of atoms" (A. C. Graham. *Two Chinese Philosophers*. L., 1958, p. 34). It would indeed be strange if the Chinese associated the idea of discrete elementary particles with air (*qi*), which classical atomism (Leucippus and Democritus) considered as an opposite of atoms, i.e., as continual emptiness (S.A. Lurie, 1970, fr. 176, 200-203).

Common for both Chinese philosophy and science, the concept of universal substance as an air-like pneuma-*qi* was also used to determine other, more specific scientific theories; in particular, it affected the selection of wind instruments (*lü* 律 denoted a set of tubes of different sizes resembling a flute) as a material model for acoustics and musicology - not strings as was the case in the West.

A number of researchers from the Peoples' Republic of China (Feng Qi 冯 契, 1915-1995 and Liu Wen-ying 刘文英, b. 1939) find the concept of the atom in the three terms used in ancient Chinese philosophy: *duan* 端 - "beginning, end, extremity, base" from *Mo-zi* (5th-3rd centuries BC, ch. 40, def. 61/62), *xiao yi* 小一, or "little unit" of Hui Shi 惠施 (*Zhuang-zi*, 4th-3rd centuries BC, ch.33), and *xiao tian-xia mo-neng po yan* 小 天下 莫 能 破 焉, or "a little that can not be broken/disclosed by anyone/anything in the whole world" from *Zhong-yong* (*Mean and Stability*, 5th-4th centuries BC, *zhang* 12). Yan Fu 嚴復(1853-1921) used the last mentioned term to convey the European concept of the atom.

Though it allows different interpretations and corrections, the term as used in *Mo-zi,* reads: "*Duan* is that [something] in the body that has no previous/thickness/dimension (*xu/hou* 序/厚) and is the first." Chen Li 陈 澧 (1810-1882) identified *duan* with a geometric point (*dian* 点) in the Western sense (*Dong-shu du-shu ji* 东塾读书记 - *Notes by Dong-shu on Reading Books*); for example, this interpretation was presented in a consistent manner in the classic comment by Gao Heng 高亨 (1900-1986) entitled *Mo-jing jiao-quan* ("*Mohist Canon" with Editorial Comments and Annotations*, 1958). Liang Qi-chao 梁啟超 (1873-1923) identified *duan* in *Mo-jing jiao-shi ("Mohist Canon" with Editorial Comments and Interpretations*) with both a geometric point and the smallest and indivisible physical body - the Indian atom (*ji wei* 极微 or "extremely small/subtle", Skt. "*paramāṇu*") and an electron, which was then considered the ultimate divisible part of an atom in the West.

According to Feng You-lan 馮友蘭 (1895-1990) and Needham, the definition of *duan* in *Mo-zi*, which is reminiscent of the paradoxes "Dichotomy" and "Achilles" by Zeno of Elea (5th century BC), is close to the definition of the Euclidean geometric point and is directed against the aphorism by the "dialecticians/sophists" Hui Shi and/or Gongsun Long 公 孫龍 (4th-3rd centuries BC), describing the futility of dividing even a short stick in half every day (*Zhuang-zi*, ch. 33). On the other hand, Hu Shi 胡适 (1891-1962) and Graham argued that in *Mo-zi*, as in "dialecticians/ sophists", infinite divisibility is postulated as the opposite to atomicity. This discrepancy in authoritative opinions was due to the indivisibility of physics and geometry, which was characteristic of Chinese science in general and Mohism (*mo-jia*), in particular, and which, moreover, did not, in the absence of a developed idealistic theory, impart a special ontological status of pure ideas to geometric objects. This circumstance underlies, for example, the problem of interpreting the term *zhong* 中 ("middle/center") in Mohist descriptions of optical characteristics of the concave mirror (*Mo-zi*, ch. 41, def. 14/15 or 22/23), because in this context, stands for the focus, though in the preceding chapter (ch. 40, def. 54/55, 58/59) it is defined as the center of a circle, and, hence, must mean the center of curvature here as well.

Therefore, although the definition of *duan* is found in the "geometric section" of *Mo-jing* (*Mohist Canon*, i.e., ch. 40-45 of *Mo-zi*) and definitely has a corresponding meaning, the term also means a physical point, as in the example cited by the Mohists (ch. 42, def. 2) - the "starting-point of a measured length (*chi* 尺)." This "explanation" (*shuo* 说) refers to the definition of *ti* 体 ("body/entity") as meaning "a part, element, or member of [the whole]," i.e., a clearly physical meaning. Graham justly remarks that *duan* is not any but the initial and/or end point. Such "initial points" are both ends of a stick, which is confirmed by the binomial *liang duan* 两端 ("two/both ends") used in ch. 63 of *Mo-zi*. In *Zhong-yong* (*zhang* 6), the term received a more general meaning, a "dyad of opposites," with the specification in the form of goodness (*shan* 善) and evil (*e* 恶), and then in the Neo-Confucian teachings of Zhang Zai, when it came to be used as one of the main world-descriptive categories representing the binary manifestations of the Way-*dao* 道. Also testifying to the extreme improbability of the atomic interpretation of *duan* is an "explanation" (ch. 42) of the original definition in *Mo-zi* (ch. 40, def. 61/62), namely, "the absence of a similar/identical" (*wu tong* 无同), which indicates the uniqueness of the object in question that is not associated with the concept of the atom.

The only thing known about the "little unit": it is "extremely little, not having the internal" (*zhi xiao wu nei* 至小无内; tr. by D. Bodde: the smallest has nothing within itself); and opposed to the "great unit" (*da yi* 大一), which is "extremely great, not having the external" (*zhi da wu wai* 至大无外; tr. by D. Bodde: the greatest has nothing beyond itself) (*Zhuang-zi*, ch.33). It is unclear whether this is any kind of substance. In chapter 36 of *Kuan-tzu*, now recognized as the treatise of Hui Shi's contemporaries Song Jian 宋鈃 and Yin Wen 尹文, the similar expression "little, not having the internal" (*xiao wu nei*) used in the same combination with "great, not having the external" (*da wu wai*) describes the "Way-*dao* between heaven and earth," i.e., a single entity, procedural and continual, and not something multiple, substantial, or discrete as atoms. In *Lü-shi chun-qiu* (*Springs and Autumns of Mr. Lü*, 3rd century BC, XV, 3), these formulas are applied to describe "a person who has attained Way-*dao*" (*de dao zhi ren* 得道之人). In *Huainan-zi* (2nd century BC, ch. 2), similar expressions described the continual proto-being in which "the presence and absence (*you wu* 有无) had not yet begun to be present". It is an unlimited "space" (*yu* 宇) for which no depth or width "can be external" (*bu ke wei wai* 不可为外), nor even a chipped bristle or chipped bone "can be internal" (*bu ke wei nei* 不可为内). Sometimes, scholars following Zhang Ping-lin 張炳麟 (1869-1936) (*Ming-jian pian*, or *Chapter on Keen Vision*) and Hu Shi, interpret the term *xiao yi* as a designation of time and *da yi* as space and time (I. Kou Pao-koh. *Deux sophists chinois Houei Che et Kong-souen Long*. P., 1953. p. 72, note 2), which cannot in any way be associated with the atomic. Hui Shi can hardly be considered an atomist as his famous aphorism, "If one takes away half from a stick of one *chi* [in length] a day, one cannot see the end of it not in 10,000 generations," is apparently anti-atomistic, like the paradoxes of Zeno of Elea, according to the concept of P. Tannery (1843-1901) published in *Pour l'histoire de la science Hellène* (P., 1887).

An analogue of this aphorism in *Mo-zi* (ch. 41, 43, def. 59/60) was noted by the creator of its first modern edition, Sun Yi-rang 孙诒让 (18481908), which read: digging a field requires pre-digging of its half, and before that of another half, and so on, which ultimately makes it impossible to move forward and makes one stay at the starting point (*duan*). Graham supported this analogy as an expression of a general anti-atomistic position. For his part, Wu Yu-jiang 吴毓江 (1898-1977) found similarity between these judgments and the definition of a "little unit" and "a little that can not be broken/disclosed by anyone/anything in the whole world", which negates all attempts to discover the ancient Chinese atomism. Mei Rong-zhao 梅 荣 照, among some other specialists, argues, however, that *Mo-zi*, far from confirming, in fact refutes the thesis of Hui Shi / Gongsun Lung about the infinite divisibility through the concept of *bu-ban* (不半), or the "nondivisibility into haves" of *duan*, or "point."

Interestingly, both paradoxes, as well as the "Dichotomy," refer to dividing in half. Graham, like Tannery in the case of Zeno, explained this as a simple convenience; there is probably a deeper and more general reason to this, namely, a special role of binarity in ancient Chinese methodology as in ancient Greek atomism and Pythagoreanism, which Zeno argued against.

The expression from *Zhong-yong* characterizes the ultimate secrecy/incomprehensibility (*yin* 隐) of the Way-*dao* (perhaps a 'teaching') of a noble man (*jun-zi* 君子), and is associated with his "greatness, which can not be incorporated/carried by anyone/anything in the whole world" (*da tian-xia mo-neng zai yan* 大天下莫能载焉). This passage gives rise to at least two enticing associations. First, the image of a "secret noble man" (*yin jun-zi*), which is the main characteristic of Lao-tzu in his seminal biography, included by Sima Qian 司馬遷 (135-87/86 BC) in *Shi-ji* (ch. 63). As the mysterious image of Lao-zi suspiciously resembles that of the Buddha (A.I. Kobzev, 2009, 2010), one is entitled to look for traces of Buddhist atomism here. Even more interesting is the epithet "unbreakable/unsplittable," which points not to India, where the term "atom" (*'aṇu', 'paramaṇu'*") contained the notion of "the finest/smallest," associated with the opposition "subtle rough state of matter" (*sūkṣma - sthūla*) (V.G. Lysenko, 1986), but to Greece, where it meant precisely "indivisible/uncuttable" - in opposition to the void. Proceeding still further, one can see here not so much a semantic

"atom" as an Latin "individual" (*individuum)*, especially given the rather ancient links between China and Rome. Although it seems at first glance that the expression from *Zhongyong* is chronologically related to the "atomic bodies" (*atoma sōmata*) of

(5th

4th centuries BC), or to "indivisibles"

(*adiaireta*) of Metrodorus of Chios (4th c. BC; **Theodoretos**, IV, 57, 9, S. J. Lurie, fr. 199), and not to "individual" of Cicero (106-43 BC) in *De Finibus Bonorum et Malorum* (*About the Ends of Goods and Evils*, 45 BC, I, 6 17), which is identified with the "atom." The dating of the Chinese text is quite uncertain, however, and comes to about the 2nd - 1st centuries BC, when it was included in the canon *Li-ji* (*Notes on Decencies / Book of Rites*); hence, there is no fundamental contradiction in comparing it with the somewhat younger Latin term. The anthropic connotation of "individual" is considered to have come into being later, but if one is to follow to methodological principle of "human anatomy as the key to the anatomy of the ape," one may suppose that it had a similar semantic potential from the very start, especially since Cicero himself operated with the "atom," which indicates that some additional meaning had been installed in its duplicate. But even if this bold hypothesis were backed with documentary evidence, the unshaken historical fact is that there had been no further Chinese intellectual movement toward atomism of the physical or mental world.

Along with Buddhism, Indian atomism began its entry into the Middle Kingdom. *Abhidharma-hṛdaya-śāstra* (*Apitan xin lun*, or *The Shastra of the Heart of Highest Dharma / Teaching of Law*, II c. AC), which contained "the first explicit formulation of the idea of material atom" (V. G. Lysenko, 2009), was translated in 391, but to the 7th century the Chinese already had a representative picture of the apology and criticism of Indian atomism. Moreover, Chinese Tripiṭaka, *Da zang jing* (*Great Treasury of Canons*), includes the treatise of the Vaiśeṣika school (*sheng [lun] zong* 胜[论]宗), which created the most advanced atomistic doctrine in India, the *Vaiśeṣika-nikāya-daśa-padārtha-śāstra* (*Sheng-zong shi-ju-yi lun* 胜宗十句义论, or the *Shastra/Judgements on the Ten Categories of Vaiśeṣika/School of Winning [Opinions]*). Its author Candramati (Hui-yue 慧月) supposedly lived in the 5th century AC. The text was brought to China and translated in 648 by the famous Chinese Buddhist pilgrim Xuan-zang 玄奘 (600/602664). That treatise was preserved only due to the fact that it was translated into Chinese, as in its motherland, India, no traces of it were found. Vaiśeṣika explained the transformation of atoms into perceivable objects with the help of numerology based on combinations of dyads (*dvyaṇuka*) and triads (*tryaṇuka*), i.e., numbers 2, 3 and 6, which is very similar to Chinese numerology of *Yi-jing* (*yi xue* 易学 - "teaching about [*Canon of*] *Changes*") and the "teaching about symbols and numbers" (*xiang shu zhi xue* 象数之学) (A. I. Kobzev, 2011).

At the beginning of the *Sheng-zong shi-ju-yi lun,* Hui-yue states that "thin/small body/entity" (*wei ti* 微体) and "short" (*duan ti* 短体) are atomically binary (*er wei guo* 二微果), and "large" (*da ti* 大体) and "long" (*chang ti* 长体) are atomically ternary (*san wei ti* 三微果). Moreover, this theory was presented by Kui-ji 窥基 (632-682) in the subcomments to the commentary of his teacher Xuan-zang to the famous treatise of Vasubandhu

(Shi-qin 世亲, approx. 316-396) *Viṃśatikā* (*Twenty Verses*) - *Wei-shi er-shi lun shu-ji* 唯识二十论述 记 (*Notes of Interpretations to "Shastra in Twenty [Verses] of Only Consciousness"*). According to Kui-ji, the primary element is the atomic pair ("father" and "mother"), generating a "son", i.e., attaching the atom and becoming a triad. Then, two triads are coupled, creating a sixfold combination to which the seventh atom is attached. Next, two sixfold combinations are coupled and to them the fifteenth atom is attached. See the Figure 1.

The comment of Kui-ji has correlation with the binary generative structure that is central to Chinese methodology (see Figure 2). Its presentation is the description of the 15 phases of the transformation from the Supreme Ultimate (*tai ji* 太极) to the eight trigrams (*ba gua* 八卦) in the *Yi-jing* (*Xi-ci zhuan - Tradition of Connected Aphorisms*, I, 11) as well as its illustration in the 15 members of the "Image of the Linear Sequence of Eight Trigrams According to Fu-xi" ("Fu-xi ba-gua ci-xu tu", Fig. 3). In both cases, the total number of described structural elements is 15, embodying the most important Chinese numerology structure *san wu* 參伍 ("3 and 5 / triad and pentad/trinity and quinary")

Fig . 2

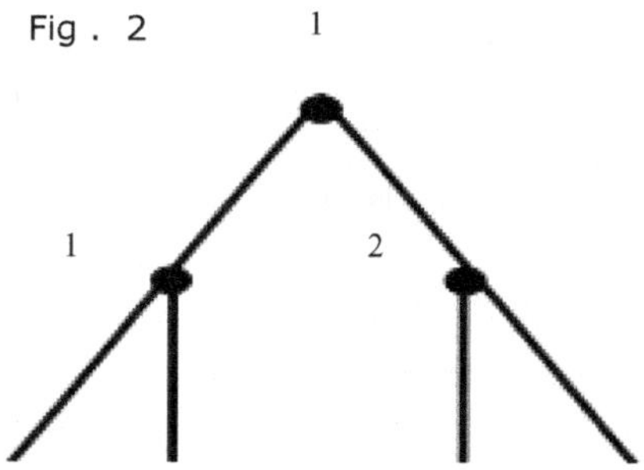

Figure 3

Kun	*Gen*	*Kan*	*Xun*	*Zhen*	*Li*	*Dui*	*Qian*
(15)	(14)	(13)	(12)	(11)	(10)	(9)	(8)
Tai yin		*Shao yang*		*Shao yin*		*Tai yang*	
(7)		(6)		(5)		(4)	
Yin (3)				*Yang* (2)			
Tai ji (1)							

The mechanism for the formation of the bodies from their constitutive atoms is as follows: one atom of the first (top) gives rise to the level of the dyad (two atoms of the second level), which together with it becomes a triad. Two triads (two atoms of the second level and four atoms of the third level) engender a sixfold combination becoming a sevenfold together with an atom of the first level. Two sevenfold combinations (two atoms of the second level, four of the third and eight of the fourth levels) give rise to a combination of fourteen atoms together with the fifteenth atom on the first level. That concept of the Vaiśeṣika may have been under some Chinese influence, particularly it's most powerful and original numerologeme - the hexagram (*gua* 卦), built on the numbers 2, 3 and 6 (2 species traits, 2 trigrams, 3 diagrams, 6 positions). Maybe by this way (through the prophets of other hometown) the atomistic potential of hexagrams, marked by J. Needham, was realized in foreign teaching.

The Vaiśeṣika tradition has two schemes of atom-based production of bodies. One is exposed in the *Sheng-zong shi-ju-yi lun*, according to which, two atoms generate a dyad, three atoms - a triad, etc. The other one is presented by Shridhara (X c.) in his commentary on the most authoritative Vaiśeṣika treatise *Padārtha-dharma-saṃgraha* (*The Collection of the Characteristics of Categories*) of Praśastapāda (VI c.) - two atoms constitute a dyad, three dyads - a triad as 6 elements like a hexagram. It is not clear who introduced this innovation - Praśastapāda or Śrīdhara himself, and whether this innovation was connected with the impact of the Chinese interpretation. The study of *Sheng-zong shi-ju-yi lun* and the developments of Buddhist atomism in China shows that Chinese thinkers, even as Buddhists, remained within the traditional numerological framework of hexagrams and assimilated atomism through their prism.

On the other hand, one may glimpse here a resemblance to the Pythagorean-Platonic mathematical atomism, in which the numbers were considered indivisible entities, therefore, dyads and triads were allowed to maintain their atomic nature. This parallel appears even more intriguing in the light of theories of atomic triangles of Plato (427-347 BC) (*Timaeus*, 53c-57d; Criticism: Aristotle. *De Caelo - On Heaven*, III, 1) and "indivisible/atomic lines" of Plato/Xenocrates (396-314 BC) (Aristotle. *Metaphysics*, II, 9, 992a 19-22; Aristotle/Theophrastus. *ΠΕΡΙ ΑΤΟΜΩΝ ΓΡΑΜΜΩΝ / De Lineis Insecabilibus - On Indivisible/Atomic Lines*). In Plato's smallest "single bodies," which form the four elements (*stoicheia*: fire, air, water, earth), stereometric corpuscles in the form of regular polyhedra (tetrahedron, octahedron, icosahedron, and cube), which in turn are composed of geometric shapes - triangles that make up "any flat surface." The "fairest" of them, the "initial" of the "original" and the simplest elements - fire, is a right-angled triangle, a half of an equilateral one, with legs and the hypotenuse in the proportion of: x, x √ 3, 2x.

Six of these triangles, i.e., three pairs connected by the hypotenuses form an equilateral triangle that becomes a basis of the initial threedimensional body - the pyramid-tetrahedron. Obviously, this construction is based on numbers 2 and 3 and the formula 2 x 3 = 6. It deliberately highlighted the doubling and tripling of geometric atoms - the right-angled triangles with sides x, x √ 3, 2x, since they formed an equilateral triangle that would be easier to describe as an object divided by three medians. Xenocrates's "indivisible/atomic lines" appear as a natural deepening of the mathematical concept of atomicity of his teacher Plato - a transition from the ternary two-dimensional triangle to a binary (defined by two points) one-dimensional line, which seems strikingly consonant with the modern physical theories of superstrings as one-dimensional branes. It noteworthy that the Greek word "gramma" ("line") also has the meaning of "a written sign, a letter."

In China, Indian atomism did not take root because of its completely alien nature, or, alternatively, it became completely dissolved in the native conceptual milieu. The terms "*aṇu*" and "*paramāṇu*" were translated mainly with the help of the character *wei* 微 ("thinnest/smallest," 1 *chi* 尺: 106 = 30: 106 cm) and its derivative binary *ji wei* 极 微 ("very thin / fine," an intelligible atom), or *chen* 尘 ("dust", 30: 108 cm, 10-8) and *lin xu* 邻 虚 ("close to void"). The latter term vividly demonstrates the absence of the fundamental European opposition of atoms to void. Vasubandhu's treatise *Abhidharma-kośa-śāstra* (*Apidamo jushe lun - Shastra Containing Highest Dharma / Teaching of Law*), which enjoyed great popularity in China and was translated at least twice - by Paramārtha (*Zhen-di* 真谛, 499-569) in 563-567, and Xuan-zang in 651-654; chapter (*juan*) 12 of that treatise says: "Division of all *rūpa*/colorforms (*se* 色) to the end leads to very thin/fine one (*ji wei*), therefore, very thin/fine one is a very small (*ji xiao* 极小) *rūpa*/color-form". It also contains a striking assertion, which requires a special study, namely that the size of the "extremely thin/small" one is 1/280 millionth of the length of the middle phalanx of the index finger, that is, of about 10-8 cm, which corresponds to current data on the size of an atom. These atoms are joined in "clusters of the finest/smallest" (*ju wei* 聚 微), and those form in the "thinnest/smallest dust" (*wei chen* 微尘), which can be seen. *Apidamo juishe lun* (*juan* 11) also quotes dimensions of the atoms of two of the five elements (*wu xing* 五行) - metal and water: "Seven of extremely thin/small (*ji wei*) [ones] equal one of finest/smallest (*wei*). When joining to form a seven, the finest/smallest amount to a dust (*chen* 尘) of metal. Seven joined dusts of metal equal the size of a dust of water. By joining, seven dusts of water make up a dust of a rabbit's hair".

Favorable conditions for the development of atomic theory were the use of phonetic transcription of *a-nu* 阿拏 to render the term "*aṇu*," because it was indicative of the recognition of its principal novelty. In particular, the encyclopedia *Da-sheng fa-yuan yi-lin zhang* (*Reflections on a Forest of Meanings of a Park of Dharmas of the Mahayana / Great Chariot*, v. 5), composed by Kui-ji, says: "Among those having a body/entity (*ti* 体) and a function/manifestation (*yong* 用), the extremely small (*ji xiao*) is known as *a-nu* and also extremely thin/small (*ji wei*)." This designation did not prevail, but moreover, lost its atomistic specifics, becoming a designation of one level of refinement of being and not its ultimate subtlety. *A-nu* are corpuscles of the sensual world (*wu-shi jing* 五 识 境, a "sphere of perceptions of the five [senses]") that could be perceived visually by deities and bodhisattvas; each of these corpuscles is formed by an accumulation of seven "extremely thin/small [ones]", i.e., atoms of the supersensible world which are correlated with the first ones as "abilities/potentials" (*neng* 能) correlate with "provisions/places" (*suo* 所). Perhaps that is why another phonetic transcription of "*aṇu*" - *a-nou* 阿耨, came into being later (in particular, in Part 1 of Hu Ying-lin 胡应麟 (1551-1602), *Introductory Judgments about Nine Streams, Jiu-liu xu-lun* 九流绪论, included in *Assembly of Manuscripts from a Solitary Abode of Small Capacity, Shao-shi shan-fang bi-cong* 少室山房笔丛 along with *wei chen*). On the contrary, the concept of a "very fine/subtle" level of being, in particular, the Way-*dao*, had been present primary in Chinese philosophy and has determined the victory of the semantic calques of *wei*. It appears as one of the basic definitions of Way-*dao* in *Dao-de jing* (*Canon of Way and Virtue*, *zhang* 14): "Grabbing (*bo*) and fail to reach, [so it] called the smallest (*wei*)." Hinting rather pointedly in this maxim at the meaning "atom" that the character *wei* acquired at a seemingly later date, is the meaning of "cutting" implicit in *bo* 搏 and the possibility of reading this piece as "Cutting (*bo*) and failing, [hence you end up with what is] called atomic (*wei*)."

In 1962, simultaneously with the publication of the famous book by H. M. McLuhan (1911-1980) *The Gutenberg Galaxy*, which asserted that the Greeks made their discoveries in art and science after the assimilation of the alphabet, J. Needham pointed directly in Part 1, v. 4 of his *Science and Civilization in China* at the link between atomism and alphabetic writing. Irrespective of this, I developed in the 1970s-1980s a theory of two opposite-alternative types of philosophy: on the one hand the Western (Mediterranean and Indian) substantivizing ontology of discrete essences and idealizing methodology of logical connections, which are based on inflectional languages and an analytical alphabet-phonetic writing, on the other hand, the Eastern (Chinese) naturalistic ontology of continuous process and numerological methodology of correlative relations, which are based on isolating languages and synthetic-visual hieroglyphics.

In developing this theory and by relying on McLuhan's concept that the Chinese, by using a non-phonetic writing, retain a holistic and profound perception of experience, and on Vyach. Vs. Ivanov's research into the asymmetry of brain and sign systems in his book *Odd and Even* (1978), I made the following points in 1989: "In contrast to hieroglyphic characters, letters as phonetic abstractions atomize experience fixed in writing of an even elementary level. The very fact of dismembering words into letters suggests a similar partitioning of beings and of finding in it pre-experience and post-experience bases. That was the path that ancient Greek philosophy took....Desemantization of the primary linguistic element - the letter resulted in the absence of "secondary" sensory qualities in the ontological primary element - an atom or idea. Traditional Chinese culture, which did not use desemantizied linguistic units, developed neither the concept of atoms, nor that of ideas. Accordingly, there was no distinction between "primary" and "secondary" qualities, i.e. in the linguistic projection - the qualities and characteristics of letters and of words. Since the notion of writing became ontologized (character *wen* 文 could mean a cosmological structure and a bird's footprints on the ground), the world was conceived similarly to a set of characters - as a finite collection of sensible things (*wan wu* 萬物 and *wan you* 萬有)." This theory received the most complete expression in my 1993 monograph *The Teaching about Symbols and Numbers in Classical Chinese Philosophy*.

First, this is an historical, i.e. empirical, fact that atomism evolved only in two authentic scientific and philosophical traditions: European and Indian, which both used alphabetical letters of common descent. Second, there is an obvious logical relationship between the two: letters are the primary elements of writing as atoms are those of the universe. Genetically, the initial formation of alphabetic writing, which occurred about half a millennium before atomism, apparently led to the emergence of the latter, becoming some kind of an heuristic prototype for it - something that its ancient Greek and ancient Indian creators were conscious of when they were comparing atoms with letters (Leucippus and Democritus, Aristotle. *Metaphysics* I, 4, 985b 15-20) and the sounds they expressed (Indian phoneticians). Moreover, Posidonius (139/135-51/50 BC) traced the "the ancient doctrine of atoms," to the Phoenician Mokh of Sidon, "who lived before the Trojan War" (Strabon. *Geography* XVI, 2, 24; Sextus Empiricus IX, 363), that is, actually linking its origin with the place and time of birth of alphabetic writing.

Both cultural phenomena, moreover, share one fundamental philosophical position - ontological idealism - that distinguishes Europe and India from China. Born of a large "Greek miracle," the small "miracle" of alphabetic writing consists in that out of insignificant letters significant words are formed, i.e., an act of creation of something out of nothing is taking place: letters not endowed with any direct physical referents and meanings of their own, or with other aspects of meanings or referents (numerical, phonetic, etc.) add up to form words with meanings and values. In the words of McLuhan, Western man himself was formed on the basis of ties between a meaningless character and a meaningless sound. Similarly, things are made up from ideas or atoms, acquiring fundamentally new qualities in the course of this transformation. Indicative in this respect is a community of ideas and atoms, which Democritus, incidentally, called *ideai*, or "indivisible/atomic ideas" (S. J. Lurie, fr. 198, CXVI).

It was that initial proto-idealistic notion of doubling the world and the recognition of otherness as primary and perfect that generated not only Platonism, but also the alphabetical writing and atomism. It was rooted in the archaic Indo-European custom of cremating the deceased ancestors and was manifested in the recognition by Democritus of the atoms of the soul as fire, the identification of fire with the soul among the Pythagoreans and with the Logos in the adherents of Heraclites and the Stoics; finally, it manifested itself in the self-determination of the Christian Logos inspired by Greek philosophy: "I am the Alpha and the Omega" (Rev. I, 8, 10, XX, 13). Its development was also reflected in the western understanding of personality as an indivisible spiritual atom - literally "individual," because, like the human soul, it is, in the words of A. Pushkin's, "eternal and indivisible," as opposed to the Chinese understanding of the psychosomatic body *shen* 身, which is easily divisible and not eternal at all.

Dominant in China was another naturalistic and holistic worldview tradition, one that did not allow an independent emergence of mature idealism or atomism; that tradition correlated with the all-powerful hieroglyphics, which epitomized all *wen*-culture. Being full-fledged words not derived from any primary written signs, hieroglyphs are primary themselves, just like letters in an alphabetic piece of writing. Most of them can be naturally broken down to their elements, but these, too, are hieroglyphs. Moreover, the opposition of simple letters/complex words does not work here because some hieroglyphs are simpler than any letters as they consist of one line only. Generally speaking, the alphabet as a product of the "left-hemispheric mentality" is analytic and logical and, therefore, oriented to atomism and discreteness; conversely, hieroglyphs as a product of the "right-hemispheric mentality" is synthetic and figurative (Gestaltung), and, therefore, is oriented to holism and continuum.

Also important for our agenda is a problem of numerical nomination. One of the major sources of Platonism, it will be recalled, was Pythagoreanism, which considered numbers as analogues of ideas among the primary substances of the world. This philosophy originated in a cultural context where numbers were denoted not only with ordinary words, but also with letters - written prototypes of ideas, which led later to the formation of a specific digital alphabet. No such need to denote numbers with special characters that differ from regular hieroglyphs ever arose in traditional China. For classification purposes, the Chinese used two sets of cyclical signs: the decimal "celestial stumps" (*tian gan* 天干) and the duodecimal "earthly branches" (*di zhi* 地支) (similar to the well-known practice of duplicating Arabic numerals with Roman numerals); they also used 60 coupled combinations of these signs and *One-Thousand-Word Text* (*Qian-zi wen*, 521), consisting of 1,000 different characters. In all these cases we deal with usual hieroglyphs not atomic signs, or letter-like figures.

The fundamental discovery in ancient Greece of irrational numbers by establishing the incommensurability of the diagonal of the square and its side (or the hypotenuse and the isosceles of a right triangle) dealt a crushing blow at the Pythagorean number theory and stimulated the geometrization of ancient Greek mathematics. The Chinese mathematicians, for their part, seemed to have overlooked the qualitative specificity of irrational numbers, which, according to Needham, was due to their use of decimal fractions. In solving problems related to the Pythagorean theorem, they confined themselves to obtaining approximate numerical values and to selection of triples of Pythagorean numbers, i.e., the integers. The fundamental difference with regard to irrational numbers may reflect a fundamental difference between ancient Greek somatism and Chinese processualism, i.e., the comprehension of the world in images of discrete entities (bodies or ideas), on the one hand, and continuous processes (changes, events, affairs), on the other. In the context of Chinese naturalism, which was unaware of any individuality (literally, indivisibility) of atoms or the individuality of ideas/eide, and which relied on its processualization of reality and its conceptualization as a multitude of continuous masses, the infinite decimal fraction did not appear as something extraordinary and could be interpreted as a reflection of the infinite divisibility of any material object or phenomenon, such as a "stick [as long as] a *chi*" from the aphorism of Hui Shi / Gongsun Long.

The standard Western association of the world's primary elements with letters is supported by the meaning of "letter" in the Greek word "stoicheion" (see, for example, Plato. *Timaeus*, 48s and *Cratylus*, 422A), which has a worthy etymological parallel in the European "element." The Latin "elementum" stands for a fragment of the alphabet: L M N, i.e., is constructed in the same way as the "alphabet" or "ABC." Somewhat similar to this is the Chinese term *xing/hang* 行, meaning not only the five elements (water, fire, wood, metal, soil), but also a hieroglyphic line, or, to be exact, a vertical column of hieroglyphs. However, here again we are talking about hieroglyphs, not letters that correlate with ideas or atoms. Etymologically, the Greek and Chinese terms are very close: both *stoicheion* and *xing/hang* represent a number of elements as a sequence formed by materialized results of motional processes (shifts). In this regard, both differ significantly from their Indian counterpart *bhūta*, which has an ideal philosophical origin - from the verb "to be" (*bhū*), which is also associated with a process through a shade of its meaning of "becoming." By and large, *stoicheion* as a philosophical concept is much closer to *bhūta* than *xing/hang*, which points not to the ontological nature of elements but to their hierarchical status in the global classification.

(Translated from Russian by Serge Gitman)

CHAPTER XVIII

SOME FEATURES OF LATER MOHIST INTERPRETATION OF SHI (實) "OBJECT"

1. The School of Later Mohism (flourished in 4th-3rd century BC at the very height of the "Warring States" period 1) was truly unique. It opposed the whole of the "mainstream" of ancient Chinese philosophy on many issues, and thus when examining Later Mohist teaching we constantly stumble across all kinds of strange and unusual features.

First of all, Mohism *is the only true school of ancient Chinese philosophy* in all senses of the word. It is generally known that the classical six (or ten, according to another version) schools of ancient Chinese philosophy - Confucianism, Mohism, Legalism, Taoism, Sophists and Naturalists - are a mere reconstruction made by Han historiographers much later than the "Warring States" period on the basis of similarities in ideas and conceptions used by philosophers, and also perhaps on the tradition of transferring knowledge. However the Mohists were a "school" not only in the sense of a group sharing common course of ideas or tradition of succession; they were *a full-fledged organization* (often referred to as the "Mohist Order") with a strict discipline and clearly defined, structured doctrine.

Second, it is *the most obscure school* of ancient Chinese philosophy. Many things concerning it are quite unclear. These include the meaning of the name of the school, the origin of its members, the biography of the school founder - Mo-zi, the history of its development and finally, the causes of the demise of such a powerful structure at the end of the "Warring States" period followed by nearly total oblivion of its efforts.

And of course very sophisticated Later Mohist philosophy is also not yet fully clarified. The Later Mohist magnus opus, *Mo-jing* 墨經 "Mohist Canon/s" is literally larded with the most complicated technical terms which are hard to understand due to the broken tradition of interpretation; moreover the extant text of *Mo-jing* is very mutilated and corrupt (not least caused by the lack of understanding of technical terms by the scribes and commentators of medieval China).

However our current knowledge about Later Mohist philosophy stands for the following (third) thesis: the Mohist school was *a school of the most marginal and paradoxical interests*. In a quizzical form we can name Mohism a peculiar nursery of strange, unnatural and marginal forms of thought for Chinese philosophy. Indeed, Confucianism and Taoism were the

1 It is justly called the "Golden Age" of Chinese philosophy.

mainstream of Chinese philosophy. They can be designated as organic and natural because as styles of thought they survived and continued to evolve until the present day after the "Judgment Day" of all ancient Chinese philosophy, the brief reign of the Qin Dynasty in China. All other alternative forms of discourse that had emerged during the "Warring States" period have disappeared. *Legalism and Chinese Sophists* (similarly marginal in the view of general history of Chinese philosophy) are convincingly shown by modern scientists either to have an origin in Mohism or to be ideologically associated with it.

The Mohists had a very unusual range of interests. They explicitly developed methods of cognition and justification of knowledge, topics that were not as popular among ancient Chinese thinkers as, for example, reflections on the moral qualities of an ideal ruler and the causes of order and disorder in the state (i.e., on ethics and politics). Moreover, their method had an influence on the major non-Mohist thinkers of the time such as Zhuang-zi and Xun-zi. If one may put it this way, the Mohists introduced fashion in the methodology of traditional ancient Chinese science and philosophy.

Furthermore, the Later Mohists were, to the best of my knowledge, *the singular group* among the ancient Chinese who developed what may be called ancient Chinese science. They did it in a specific manner also atypical for the rest of ancient Chinese philosophy. The Early Mohists had been Chinese "theologians" (in the full sense of the term with respect to the understanding of "Heaven"; unlike the vast majority of ancient Chinese thinkers who thought "Heaven" synonymous to impersonal processes in Nature, Early Mohists stated unambiguously that "Heaven" was endowed with will and intentions and punished bad people while rewarding good people). Later Mohists were Chinese "positivists".

Indeed, the Later Mohists position reveals very interesting parallels with the three most salient characteristics of this 19th - early 20th century school of Western philosophy - (1) an anti-metaphysical enthusiasm, (2) a tendency toward scientism and (3) various types of reductionism.

"Metaphysics" in the strict sense did not exist in ancient China because all ancient Chinese philosophy was naturalistic and dealt with a range of issues and concepts related to the sensuously perceived world around; nevertheless, it did include the concepts such as *dao* 道 "The Way", *tian* 天 "Heaven", *tian ming* 天命 "Mandate of Heaven", *xing* 性 "[individual] nature", *xin* 心 "heart-mind", *qi* 气 "pneuma" (see below), *yinyang* 陰陽 "the Dark and the Light" etc., which could be considered "protometaphysical" according to some facets of their meaning. The later Mohists deliberately refused to operate with all these notions in their doctrine. A peculiar parallel to positivist scientism as a deification of the scientific method, science in general and scientific knowledge in particular formed by Mohists' penchant for specific science problems as well as by their elaboration of procedures of making justified propositions about things, names and actions was unprecedented in the history of ancient Chinese philosophy. At the same time, the Mohists being brilliant reductionists tried to simplify and clarify everything possible in the teachings of Confucius whose main opponents they were. Thus, they simplified his ethical theory by abandoning the idea of *li* 禮 "ritual behavior" that was part of the concept *yi* 義"duty / justice / morality" in fact reducing it to *li* 利 "benefit". They also simplified the term *zhi* 智 "reason / wisdom" reducing it to *ming* 明 "enlightenment / clarity".

While reviewing the results of the Later Mohists' efforts it should be noted that they had given Chinese philosophy an alternative form of rationality. The Mohists opposed their "protological" methodology to the simultaneously progressing and subsequently dominant form of rationality called "numerology" or "correlative thinking".2 Concerning specific science results of the Later Mohists, here, too, they have formed an original and alternative conception to the prevailing view of the rest of ancient Chinese philosophy on the term "thing" (more precisely - "object"), what it consists of and how it is formed.

2. The traditional view on the nature and constitution of "things" was, apparently, born at the same time that the Mohists proposed their alternative version. Unlike the Mohist version the view further developed in Chinese philosophy was that *wu* 物 "things" are made up of *qi* 氣 "pneuma".

Qi 氣 is a cornerstone for the whole of Chinese philosophy, and thus has many meanings. Etymologically it is a "vapor rising over cooking [sacrificial] rice", i.e. some "evaporation" or in a broader sense, a "wind flow", a "general state of the environment", an "atmosphere" or "ambiance" (as, for example, in the phrase "atmosphere/ambiance of the place").

Apparently since the earliest antiquity these meanings of the word began to be associated with the states of "Heaven" and "Earth", the two cardinal poles between which the whole world is located. Thus, in one of the earliest references in *Guo yu* the chief dignitary of the Kingdom of Zhou explains the causes for the earthquake by referring to *qi*:

> In the second year of You-wang's rule an earthquake took place in the three rivers district in Western Zhou. Bo Yang-fu said: "Zhou is on the eve of death! For *qi* (氣) of heaven and earth should not violate their sequence. If the sequence is not followed, it will lead to discord among the people. The light element *yang* is at the bottom and cannot move outside; the dark element *yin* suppresses it and would not let it go up - that

---

2 Cf. *Duchovnaya kultura Kitaya,* in 5 vol. In Russian (Moscow: Vostochnaya Literatura Publishers, 2006), vol. 1, pp. 82-125; and also cf A. I. Kobzev. *Uchenie o simvolach I chislach v kitaiskoi klassicheskoi filosofii. I*n Russian (Moscow: Vostochnaya Literatura Publishers, 1993)]

> is why earthquakes occur. Now the area of the three rivers was hit by an earthquake - the light element lost its habitual place and is being depressed by the dark element. If the light element is not where it should be, but below the dark element, the sources of rivers are drying up. And when the sources are running dry, the state would die.3

Evidently Bo Yang-fu thought of the two states of *qi* (*yin* and *yang*) as of the different types of the "ambiance" (consisting of "vapor"?) which can rise towards Heaven or descend to Earth and depending on their position vis-à-vis each other bring harmony or natural disasters to the country.

Subsequently *qi* with the meaning of "atmosphere", or "ambience", or even in the sense of "spirit" (as in the phrase "spirit of the time") was extended to the four seasons. Each season had its own particular *qi*. Cf. *Guan-zi*, ch. 40:

> The East is the stars. Its time is spring; its life force (氣) is the wind. Wind produces wood and bones. <...> The South is the sun. Its time is summer, and its life force is *yang*. *Yang* generates fire and steam (氣). <...> The West is Chen. Its time is autumn, and its life force is *yin*. *Yin* produces metal and claws. <...> The North is the moon. Its time is winter; its life force is the frost. Frost generates water and blood.4

So, spring is windy, summer is clear and hot (*yang*), autumn is dim and damp (*yin*), winter is frosty. These are different states of the *qi*ambience of seasonal periods, which is spread all over the world.

However, *qi* characterizes not only the state of the world as a whole. *Qi* could mean not only "evaporation", "ambience" and "atmosphere" between Heaven and Earth, but also the "evaporation", "medium" and "atmosphere" *in human being*.

Qi (氣) is what fills (充) [the] body [of man] (身), 5 says another passage in *Guan-zi*, ch. 37. *Qi* in this sense is some kind of general filling of human body that circulates through its veins with the blood (hence the binomial *xue qi* 血氣 "blood and pneuma/blood pneuma/blood flow" frequently appear in Chinese texts), penetrates human body thus animating it, and *often is deemed as a conductor of its mental functions* (in this sense, *qi* can be compared to the "animal spirits" of European philosophy). Yet this kind of *qi* retains the meaning of "vapor" and, therefore, can be compressed

3 *Drevnekitaiskaya filosofiya.* In Russian (Moscow: Mysl, 1973), vol. 1, pp. 295-296].

4 Ibid., vol. 2, pp. 43-46.

5 *Drevnekitaiskaya filosofiya*, vol. 2, p. 31.

to a point or expanded far beyond human body (cf. the famous passage from Mencius about *qi* which "if <…> is nurtured with directness and is not spoiled <...> fills everything between Heaven and Earth",6) surrounding it with a peculiar "micro environment" that can influence other people. In this sense *qi* could be appropriately understood as "character", "presentation of self" and "energy" (as in the phrase "he seems to be full of energy today"). Chinese military treatises commonly use *qi* in the sense of "fighting spirit/morale" (cf. *Sun-zi*, ch. 11):

> When robbing fertile fields, have abundance of food for your own army, take good care of soldiers and do not tire them, rally their spirits (氣) and unite their strength.7

Finally, the classical philosophic understanding of *qi* that would thread through the entire Chinese philosophy has crystallized by the midlate period of the "Warring States" based on the meanings described above. *Qi* according to this is not only the atmosphere in Nature, or a life-giving filling in a person, but the "pneuma" which either constitutes all things or originates them (cf. *Zhuang-zi*, ch. 18; *Xun-zi*, ch. 9):

> <...> A change occurred (變) and a pneuma (氣) was formed, pneuma changed and a shape (形) was formed, a shape changed and a living (生) was formed, then [the living] changed again and became dead (死) <...>.8

Water and fire have *qi* but have no life, herbs and trees have life but do not have [the ability] to learn; birds and beasts have [the ability] to learn but lack a sense of duty; man has *qi*, has life, is able to learn and also has a sense of duty, therefore, he is the most precious of all under Heaven.9

Thus after a certain time *qi* came to be understood as a kind of substance: everything is made of *qi* or all was *qi* at some time (that is original *qi* that forms Heaven and Earth themselves, called *yuan qi* 元氣). "Everything" includes Heaven and Earth (*yin* and *yang* "evaporations" spread between them and interacting with each other), human body (the blood and "animal spirit"), animals, plants, soil and stones in that soil, physical bodies and non-physical souls etc. Sometimes one may find that *qi*

---

6 *Kofuzianskoe "Chetveroknizie" ("Si schu").* In Russian (Moscow: Vostochnaya Literatura Publishers, 2004), p. 272.

7 *Drevnekitaiskaya filosofiya*, vol. 2, p. 208.

8 My translation. From: *Чжуан-цзы цзии* (*Чжуан-цзы с собранием толкований*), *Чжуцзы цзичэн* (Пекин: Чжунхуа шуцзюй, 1985), t. 12, p. 615.

9 V.F. Feoktistov. *Filosovskie traktati Sun-zsi.* In Russian (Moscow: Natalis, 2005), p. 228.

is translated as "particles", but this is not right. The Chinese thought of *qi* as a homogeneous continuous medium which can condense and dissipate. Condensations of *qi* constitute "rigid", tangible things; its subtle, refined and dissipated states (the so-called *jing qi* 精氣) constitute souls. *Qi* is the universal substrate of all things, but since etymologically it means "vapor" one can say that *the ancient Chinese considered everything around consisted of some kind of air in one or another transformed state or quality.* Due to its potential perceptibility (while in "condensed" state) and an explicit connection to the material world around us, *qi* ("air") is often translated as "matter / materia". But this translation is only partially correct. *Qi* is a "materia" in the sense as modern French materialists or the Stoics in the Hellenistic period put it - an active self-organizing and mobile substance capable of spontaneous change. Therefore, a more appropriate translation of the term is "pneuma".10

So the point of view declaring that everything consists of or originates from a single substance, the *qi*, that is congener to "air" has become classic in Chinese philosophy. We would call it the ontology based on *qi*, or the *qi*-ontology. The Later Mohists offered an alternative view on how things are formed.

3. For Later Mohists, the whole world is *yi shi* 異時 "different times" and *yi suo* 異所 "different places". *Mi* 彌 "pervasion" of "different times" is *jiu* 久"duration" (A 4011); "pervasion" of "different places" is called *yu* 宇 "space/extention" (A 41). The Mohists consistently emphasized the difference and separateness of "duration" from "space" in so far as this was possible. Contemporary Chinese philosophers designated similar concepts with the binomial *yu zhou* 宇宙 , where *yu* 宇 stood for the notion of "space", same as for the Mohists, while "time" was designated with the graph *zhou* 宙. As for the rest of classical Chinese philosophy, these two concepts were closely intertwined and implied one another.12 In an attempt to break the symmetry of space and time the Mohists first split the fixed combination of *yu zhou* 宇宙 (in which both members imply each other) on the linguistic level by replacing the second of the two characters with the neutral *jiu* 久 being syntactic complementary to *hou* 厚 "thickness / dimension", but not *yu* 宇. Second, they argued at the conceptual level that *yu* 宇 "space / extention" and *jiu* 久"duration" are *bu jian bai* 不堅白 "not

10 On critique of erroneous understanding of *qi* see A.I. Kobzev. *Filosofiya kitaiskogo nejkonfuzianstva* (Moscow: Vostochnaya Literatura Publishers, 2002), pp. 307-315.

11 Here and below, symbols and citations from the original *Mo-jing* text are from A.C. Graham *Later Mohist Logic, Ethics and Science* (The Chinese University Press/The Chinese University of Hong Kong, 1978, 2003).

12 On connection between *yu* and *zhou* cf. A.I. Kobzev. *Filosofiya kitaiskogo nejkonfuzianstva* (Moscow: Vostochnaya Literatura Publishers, 2002), pp. 304-307.

[like] hardness [in respect to] whiteness [in stone]" (B 14). Conversely, *wu jiu* 無久 "the durationless [i.e. the moment] " and *yu* 宇 "space/extention" are *jian bai* 堅白 "[as] hardness [in respect to] whiteness [in stone]" (B 15).

The technical term *jian bai* 堅白 "[like] hardness [in respect to] whiteness [in stone]" is a generalization or a representative abstraction for instances when two objects *bu xiang wai* 不 相 外 "are not excluding each other" (A 66). In the case of *shi* 石"stone" (cf. B 37) its *jian* 堅"hardness" and *bai* 白"whiteness" - *bi xiang yin* 必相盈 "necessarily fill each other" (cf. explanation to B 15). If *yin* 盈 "to fill / be filled" means *mo bu you* 莫不 有 "to be nowhere absent" (A 65), then the white stone is hard and white everywhere in its bulk at the same time, i.e. its hardness and whiteness are mutually intertwined. Where there is hardness in the stone (that is everywhere in the stone), whiteness is nowhere absent either. The case of "extended space" and " the durationless [i.e. the moment]" is similar.

As the greatest contemporary authority in the interpretation of the Later Mohists works A. C. Graham puts it, the Mohists separated space and time in order to eliminate any possibility to deduce the constancy of the principles of government in time from their immutability in space, i.e. they pursued ethical and political rather than purely scientific goals. This separation may have had a mere logical sense: dimension does not in itself imply duration, but only lack-of-duration or moment.13 But this is not as important to us as an introduction of the term *jian-bai* to justify this thesis.

Indeed, this term seems to divide the Mohist world into two different types of objects, some of which "are not excluding each other" ("hardness"

"whiteness;" "durationless" and "space"; perhaps, "shape" and and "intelligence/consciousness/mind" etc.) while others "are not filling each other" ("different positions" etc.). It is tempting to interpret the first type as a distinctive feature of attributes such as "color" etc., in which case *jian-bai* 坚 白 becomes an original Mohist definition of "properties": they differ from each other as long as they can simultaneously occupy the same place

(cf. B 37 on "hardness" and "whiteness" in the "stone", A 22 on

---

13 One can see some similarities between the Mohist conception and the conception of absolute (i.e., independent of anything: from things or from each other) space and time by I. Newton. What alienates this conception from the Newtonian one is the definition of time and space, which are close to the alternative relativistic conception of G.W. Leibniz, according to which space is the order of coexistences, and time is the order of the sequences. Duration for the Mohists is "pervasion" of the various "places", while duration is "pervasion" of different "times"; thus, they are reduced to something other, namely, their own parts, which reminds of non substantial and nominalistic character of time and space postulated by G.W. Leibniz. However, the Mohist position differs from the position of G.W. Leibniz. Whereas G.W. Leibniz reduces space and time to things (as would be later done by A. Einstein), the Mohists, as we shall see below, *rather reduce things to places*.

combination of "consciousness" (but not "heart" as an organ and a "shape"). Another temptation is to interpret the second kind of objects as indeed individual objects or aggregates of objects - in contrast to properties (such aggregates are *jia* 兼 "whole", which consists of *ti* 體 "units" (*fen yu jian* 分 於兼 "portions in a whole" (A 2)), which may themselves be a new "whole" at a new level for new "units"; in A 67 such "units" "do not wholly cover each other" unlike "hardness" and "whiteness" in stone).

The Mohists have a special word *shi* 實 that usually denotes "[concrete] object". However, the Mohists always refer to *shi* 實 in correlation to *ming* 名 "names" and never say, for example, *zai shi** 在實 "is in the object" or *shi zhong** 實中 "[what is] in the object". Yet we find in their treatises *zai shi* 在室"in the room" and *shi zhong* 室中 "[what is] in the room" (B 70). In A 86 and A 87 *shi* 室 "room" is compared to *chu* 處 "position / to occupy" and *suo* 所 "place" as if they were synonymous. A. C. Graham assumes that the Mohists could have used *shi* 室 (literally "room") as a technical term to designate not only a room filled with something, but also an object filled with its own properties (see explanations to B 70 *zai shi zhe zhi se* 在室者之色 lit. "the color of what is in the room"; one can assume that the authors of B 70 do really speak about some object in the certain place, for example, about a hard "stone" in the "room", but they may be talking about *two properties in one object*, for example "hardness" completely filled with "color" in a "stone"). So if the interpretation is correct, then *shi* 室 is a technical term for an "empty object" without reference to its properties, while *shi* 實 is a technical term for "complete object" *filled with its properties.*

This reconstruction is hypothetical, but if authentic it could lead to a conclusion that Later Mohists deemed "[concrete] objects" as various "places", "positions", "containers" (i.e., parts of "space") that are not filling each other, but are filled with pervasive properties in turn. In Later Mohist world there are mutually pervasive properties and places for properties that did not fill each other. But the Mohists do not have a substrate or substance different from the places and space as constellation of places.14 That is to say, Mohist "objects" do not consist of the "pneuma".

---

14 The Mohist idea of *jian-bai*, i.e. mutually pervasive properties, *can be compared with the Stoic idea of* κρᾶσις δι' ὅλων *or "mixing entirely-andcompletely"*, the case of interacting bodies penetrating each other entirety, forming one body but at the same time do not losing their unique attributes (i.e., remaining two different bodies). At one point, the Mohists say that "different positions" (*yi chu* 異處) "are not filling each other", and, hence, "are excluding each other" simply because they are *xiang fei* 相非 "not being each other" (cf. explanation to A 66). This suggests that objects related to each other "[as] hardness [to] whiteness [in stone]" are, in a sense, one and the same thing, i.e. hardness and whiteness of piece of stone are one thing in some sense. But B 37

The Mohists had no special term for "properties" that penetrate one another in one place, thus forming an "object". Such a term was put in circulation by their successors, Xun-zi and Han Fei-zi. Xun-zi writes in *Xun-zi*, ch. 22:

> Among things some are identical in appearance (狀) but are present in different places (所); others are not identical in appearance but are in the same places; it is possible to distinguish this! Although two things identical in appearance but located in different places may be called by one name, in fact they should be referred to as two real [things] (實). When the appearance of a thing is changed, but its real [content] stays the same, not giving rise to a new thing different from it, it is called change (化). When [appearance of a thing] is changed, but its [content] remains the same, one should talk about the same real [thing].15

So Xun-zi keeps and develops Mohist intuition. He says that something should be called "two" things when their "places" are different, but one thing if only their properties are different (e.g., they change in time but not in "places"). At the same time he names such mutually pervasive properties *zhuang* 狀, but this term has not been further used in Chinese

---

emphasizes that hardness and whiteness are *er* 二 "two", but *zai* 在 "are in" "stone" (in *yi* 一 "one"). The Mohist conception of "objects" deemed as places filled with properties is, in a sense, analogous to the Platonian conception of χώρα "space" as something on which the demiurge imprints ideal forms and from which sense-perceptible things arise, but with the following important difference: there is no place for "ideas" in the Mohist doctrine. According to A. Einstein, any thing has an absolute spacetime interval, the number of which is invariant and remains unchanged for all observers, while its spatial or temporal components may vary with respect to a certain observer. To put it other way, a body will be shorter for one observer, but the time will run slower for it; it will be longer for another observer, but the time period for it will be shorter (the time will run faster). Yet the sum of these parameters, will, roughly, be constant. On the other hand, the essence of Einstein's theory, as he understood it himself, was that if you remove all the things from the world, spacetime won't be there either. The Mohists disagreed that if you remove the things there will be no space-time. Conversely, if you remove the space there will be no things. That view is consonant with modern physical theories which reduce some of the fundamental interactions and physical properties of objects to spatial geometry. As we shall see later on, attempts to reduce many properties of things (including the sense-perceptible properties) to spatial geometry were undertaken by Han Fei-zi, who followed the later Mohists in this respect.

15 V.F. Feoktistov, *Filosovskie traktati Sun-zsi* (Moscow: Natalis, 2005), p. 295.

philosophy. Xun-zi's former apprentice Han Fei-zi would later introduce another term for "properties", which gained much more popularity. In *Han Fei-zi*, ch. 20 he writes:

> If there is a shape (形), then there are short and long; if there are short and long, then there are small and large; if there are small and large, then there are square and round; if there are square and round, then there are hard and fragile; and if there are hard and fragile, then there are lightweight and heavy; if there are lightweight and heavy, then there are white and black. Talking about the short and long, large and small, square and round, hard and fragile, lightweight and heavy, white and black, one says "These are *li*" (理).16

Han Fei-zi reduces hard and white as well as many other properties to *xing* 形 "shape" (the same "shape" which appears in the case of "changing" of "pneuma") and refers to them as *li* 理 "principles".

Thus, *the Later Mohists and partly Xun-zi and Han Fei-zi have presented an alternative ontology* based not on the concept of *qi*, i.e. some air-like proto-substance with its transformations giving rise to things possessing different qualities, but an ontology based on the concept of "properties", jian-bai, li, or zhuang. It does not introduce any special substance, but uses the notions of "places" and the compatibility or incompatibility of different qualities in one and the same place. We would call it the ontology based on *li*, or the *li*-ontology.

4. However both Xun-zi and Han Fei-zi lived in an age, when it was possible to review the accumulated accomplishments of the predecessors, and philosophers in China were becoming more and more obsessed with the thought that the truth is a kind of comprehensive synthesis. Specific doctrines of hundred schools are not completely wrong but rather one-sided, while synthetic approach, the "Way" is required to connect all the good parts from different teachings. They lived in a time of syncretism, hence they actively used *qi* along with *zhuang* and *li* in their philosophy (cf. the quote from Xun-zi in paragraph 2).

In the course of further evolution of Chinese philosophy the concepts of *qi* and *li* (although not directly in the same sense as used by the Later Mohists) *have merged into a single doctrine*. On the one hand, the *qi*ontology, indeed, presupposes some kind of a substance, but says nothing about how its properties are formed. The Mohists, on the other hand, did talk about properties, but saw no problem in that some "places" allow properties to penetrate each other, while others do not. If one associate them together postulating that *li* determines and specifies *qi*, everything falls into place immediately.

---

16 *Drevnekitaiskaya filosofiya* (Moscow: Mysl, 1973), vol. 2, p. 254.

The idea of relationship between *qi* and *li* would develop into its classical form in medieval Neo-Confucianism, where *li* would become the main category, though in a sense different from discussed above. "*Li* has come to designate an initial substantial element that constitutes the nature of things and determines their structure. The whole sum of the myriads of "principles" of individual things constitutes the "Supreme Pole", i.e. the origin and the primary source of *li*, which shapes the amorphous "pneuma" and commences the process of cosmogenesis." 17 But the doctrine of the structure of "object" in the form proposed by Later Mohists has gone into oblivion.

(Translated from Russian by Serge Gitman)

---

17 Duhovnaya cultura kitaya: encicklopedia. In Russian. (Moscow: Vostochnaya Literatura Publishers, 2006), vol. 1, p. 296. For the detailed review on relationship of *li* and *qi* cf. A.I. Kobzev. Filosofiya kitaiskogo neokonfutsianstva. In Russian (Moscow: Vostochnaya Literatura Publishers, 2002), pp. 164-175.

CHAPTER XIX

ABOUT PRINCIPLES OF "FEMALE ALCHEMY" IN "XIWANG MU NÜXIU ZHENGTU SHIZE" (TEN RULES OF THE QUEEN MOTHER OF THE WEST ON THE PROPER PATH OF WOMEN'S CULTIVATION)

During recent decades an appreciable interest to gender problems is observed among the researchers of the Chinese culture. The problems of the female health, the new methods of treatment of the female illnesses, the ways of the rejuvenation and strengthening of an organism based on the principles of traditional Chinese medicine are in the centre of the experts' attention (see [14; 15; 21]). In the paradigm of the daological researches there appeared some works devoted to "the female internal alchemy" (*nü gong nei dan* 女功內丹) (further - "the female alchemy") - to the Daoist's methods of self-perfection focused on women (see [1; 2; 4; 5, vol. 5, p. 789791; 10; 11; 19; 20; 22; 23; 24; 25; 26]). "The female alchemy" - is one of the specific psychophysiological directions in Daoism which has gender specialization and erects the sources to the ancient "teaching about immortality" (*xian xue* 仙學).

The principles of the "female alchemy" are based on the connection of the cosmological concepts "*Yijing*" (Book of Changes), the therapeutic traditions of the ancient Chinese doctors fixed in "*Huangdi neijing*" (The Yellow Emperor's Classic of Internal Medicine) and the methods of the "internal alchemy" (*nei dan*).

The allocation of the methods of self-perfection for the women into a separate direction in the historical development of the Daoism leads to the fact that ungenderic in its essence the doctrine of the "internal alchemy" starts to subdivide into two traditions oppositional to each other - the "male" and "female" alchemy (*nan dan* 男丹 and *nü dan* 女丹) [24, p. 150]. The cosmological and psychophysiological distinctions between men and women which in their turn, have caused the distinctions in the practical methods fixed in Daoist works of the XII-XVII centuries were laid down in the basis of this division. In the XVIII-XIX centuries there begins the active formation of the tradition of the "female alchemy" - the conceptualization, systematization and unification of the methods focused on the daoists nuns. The works describing these methods were created and gathered by the daoists in the monastery cloisters. According to the tradition, it is considered, that they have been given to the inhabitants of heaven, immortals and patriarchs of past times.

Modern researchers allocate four main centres where the female internal alchemical classics were formed:

1. On the mount of Jin'gai 金蓋山 in Jiangxi provinces. This centre is connected with the name of Shen Yibing 沈一炳 (1708 - 1786), who received the daoist doctrine from a mysterious wise man Li Niwan. His schoolmate and in a consequence the XI patriarch of school Longmen 龍門 派 (Dragon Gate) Min Yide 閔一得 (1758 - 1836) collected and edited some books which contained manuals on the "female alchemy" created on Jin'gai mountain.1

2. On the mount of Zhaoyang 趙阳山, in the province of Sichuan where the daoist Temple Qiftgyang 青羊宫 is located. Here Fu Jinquan 傅 金銓 (1765 - 1845) and He Longxiang 贺龍驤 (? - 1906) collected and published some works devoted to the female methods of perfection.2

3. On the mount of Qingcheng 青城山 in the province of Sichuan. The supervisor of the monastery Tianshi dong 天 師 洞 (the Cave of Heavenly Masters) Yi Xinying 易心瑩 (1896 -1976) collected about ten works on the "female alchemy."3

4. In the city of Shanghai where the daoist master Chen Yingning4 陈 樱宁 (1880 - 1969) edited and commented on the texts devoted to the female practice [11, p. 203].

On the whole, about thirty works completely devoted to female methods of self-perfection have remained till our time in which the main principles of *nü dan* have found their reflections [11, p. 202]. These principles are based on the distinctions of the male and female congenital nature (*bing xing*), the physical form (*xing ti*) and practical methods (*gong fa*).

Borrowing the symbolical language of "*Yijing*" the "female alchemy" as well as the "internal alchemy", represents men and women as a part of cosmological process where the beginnings of *Yang* and *Yin,* the trigrams of

---

1 You can read in detail about the tradition of the formation "the female alchemy" in mount of Jin'gai and its representative sources in our publication, see [4]. About Shen Yibing, Min Yide and the development of Daosism in mount of Jin'gai see [4; 13].

2 E. Valussi has written in details about the activity of He Longxiang and his contribution to the tradition of the development of the "female alchemy", see [21].

3 About Yi Xinying see [12, pp. 207-208].

4 About Chen Yingning and the history of the development of Daosism in the XX century you can find in the work of the Chinese researcher of the daosism Liu Xun [18].

Qian and *Kun*, *Li* and *Kan* the Sun and the Moon correspond them and allocate the following distinctions in their congenital nature:5

- A man personifies "light" *Yang*, and a woman personifies "dark" *Yin*;

- Hardness is inherent in the male nature, softness is inherent in the female nature;

- The feelings of a man are agitated, the feelings of a woman are quiet;

- Man's thoughts are confused, female thoughts are clear; - A man constantly stays in movement, and the movement promotes waste of *Qi*, a woman constantly stays in stillness, and stillness promotes accumulation *Qi*.

- A man is connected with trigram "*Li*" and its life cycle corresponds to the Sun making full circulation in the sky for one year; a woman is connected with trigram "*Kan*" and its life cycle corresponds to the Moon making full circulation in the sky for one month;

- It is more difficult for a man to supervise the *Qi*, but for a woman it is easier [23, p. 178 - 179].

Besides that the male body differs from the female body in its physiology. The distinctions in physiology and the internal nature lead to the distinctions both on the first stage of the internal alchemical process, and in practical methods as a whole.

These principles are closely connected with ideology of "*Xiwang mu nüxiu zhengtu shize*" (Ten Rules of the Queen Mother of the West on the Proper Path of Women's Cultivation). This is one of the earliest works on the "female alchemy", created in the mountains of Jin'gai.6 The prospective time of its occurrence is 1799 [11, p. 203]. The text has received a short name - "*Nüxiu zhengtu*" 女修正途 (The Proper Path of Women's Cultivation). It was originally known under the title of *Nü jin dan jue* 女金丹訣 (Manuals on Female Alchemy). This work has been commented and published by Min Yide in "*Gu Shuyinlou cangshu*" 古書隱摟藏書 (*Collection from the Ancient Hidden Pavilion of Books*). This scripture is also present in "*Dao zang xu bian*" 道藏續編 (Addition to "Daoist Cannon"), in "*Dao zang jing hua*" 道藏精華 (Best of "Daoist Cannon") and in modern collection of daoist texts "*Zangwai daoshu*" 藏外道書 (Daoist Books outside the Cannon) (see: [27]).

5 About the principles of dichotomy *Yin-Yang* in the ancient Chinese conceptions of the male and female beginning, their interconversion, see A. I. Kobzev's article devoted to the Chinese erotology [5, vol. 5, pp. 430-474].

6 About this scripture also see in [19, pp. 237-239; 11, pp. 301-302]. The French translations of "*Xiwang mu nüxiu zhengtu shize*" is made by M. Esposito, see [13, pp. 317-346].

In the preface to the "*Zangwai daoshu*", reflecting the legendary history of this work, it is told, that the master Chunyang 純陽 (I.e. Lü Dongbin 呂洞賓 - *I.B.*) has sworn to rescue all reasonable beings and has transferred "Cinnabar Scripture of Nine Emperors" 九皇丹經 (*Jiu huang dan jing*) with the help of which a man can improve himself in transcendent. However he could observe indifferently how women, who have turned all their thoughts to the Dao, not having true manuals, go in a false roundabout way and become an entertainment for phantoms-*gui*. Therefore, in the year under a cyclic sign of *yi-wei*, on the first day that has fallen on the first winter month, he has handed over the transmitted orally lectures to Sun Buer 孫不二 which Xiwang mu7 has transferred to Primordial lady Wei (i.e. Wei Huacun - *I.B.*). Further the preface says, that the real name of this scripture is *Nü da jin dan jue* 女大金丹訣, and the history of its transference is connected with Wei Huacun8 魏華存, He Xiangu9 何仙姑, Ma Gu10 麻姑, Fan Yunqiao11 樊雲翹 and Feng Xiangu12 鳳仙姑. Later on after several hundreds years these scripture began to be transferred with errors which have led to still greater errors. Therefore he ordered Sun Buer13 to edit them carefully and to transfer them in the world of people so that the female tradition to self-perfection not be interrupted (see: [27, p. 533; 23, p. 169]).

However, in the initial preface to this text from "*Gu Shuyinlou cangshu*" (as it is resulted in *Zangwai daoshu*), there appear not only its legendary authors, but there are also instructions to its real composers and

---

7 About Xiwang mu see B. L. Riftin's encyclopedic inquiry [5, vol. 2, pp. 568-569].

8 Way Huacun is the semi legendary tutor of the doctrine of the Highest Clarity 上清 (Shangqing). You can read in detail about her life and selfsacrifice in S. V. Filonov's researches, see [8, pp. 85-113].

9 He Xiangu is one of Eight Immortal 八仙 (*ba xian*) of the daosist's pantheon. See about it in B. L. Riftin's encyclopedic inquiry [5, vol. 2, p. 675].

10 Ma Gu (the Hempseed maiden) is the character of the late Chinese mythology, esteemed as the immortal fairy helping people. See about her in B. L. Riftin's encyclopedic inquiry [5, vol. 2, pp. 521-522].

11 You can get acquainted with the short biography and the poetic creativity of the daosist tutor of the III century Fan Yunqiao by name in T. Cleary's work [10, pp. 59-62].

12 About Feng Xiangu see [3, p. 31].

13 About the life, creativity and the spiritual way of the daosist tutors of school of Complete Perfection (Quanzhen 全真) Sun Buer (1119-1182) see the researches of the author of these lines in [3, pp. 28-32; 4, vol. 5, pp. 843-845]. About the role of Sun Buer in the tradition of the "female alchemy» see [1, pp. 74-75]. A reader interested in her poems can get acquainted with their translations in our article [2], and also in English - in T. Cleary's version [10, pp. 7-54; 74-78]. The fullest information about Sun Buer is presented in theses of the Chinese researcher of daosism Ye Yijing [27].

commentators - Shen Yibing and Min Yide. It is said in it, that the name of this composition was written by Lü Zu (Lü Dongbin), Shen Taixu (Shen Yibing) owned it, the lady Sun (Sun Buer) supplemented it and the comment was made by Min Yide (see [27, p. 533]).

"*Nüxiu zhengtu*" represents ten rules (*shi ze*) of the female internal alchemical practice, stated in the strict sequence of their performance. The first step on the way to the female alchemical art is the observance of nine precepts-instructions (*jiu jie*), reminding in their form the traditional Confucian code:

1. To show filial esteem and to respect seniors, to [be] soft and kind, not to speak superfluous and not to show jealousy.

2. To keep oneself clean and calm, not to make bad acts. 3. To protect all living beings, to [be] merciful and compassionate,
not to kill.

4. To execute diligently and correctly the ceremonies (*li*) and recitations (*song*), not to use meat food and wine.

5. The articles of the clothes [should be] simple and clean, not to be fond of dresses and jewels.

6. To bring to harmony the feelings and the internal nature, not to give way to irritability and anger.

7. It is impossible to visit crowded places often. 8. It is impossible to allow cruelty in treatment with servants. 9. It is impossible to humiliate good and to encourage bad [14, p. 534].

The one who strictly observes all nine precepts, adheres to them, not receding, will have an opportunity, as promises a source, "to rise in the Purple justice" (*zi fu*) and to take a place among Transcendents.

"Nine precepts-instructions" from "*Nüxiu zhengtu*" practically word for word quote the earlier daoist work - "*Chuzhen jie shuo*" 初真戒說 (Description of the Precepts of Initial Perfection) [28]. This work has been written by the seventh patriarch of school Longmen (Dragon Gate) Wang Kunyang 王崑陽 (aka Changyue 常月) (1622-1680), the prior of Temple Baiyunguan, one of the most significant figures in the daoist movement of Complete Perfection of the XVII century.14 Among the numerous rules and precepts-instructions for the daoist monks there are in the text the preceptsinstructions for the women, entitled "*Nü zhen jiu jie*" 女真九戒 (Nine Precepts for the Women's Perfection).

14 About Wang Kunyang and his contribution to the development of the subtradition of the doctrine of Complete Perfection (Quanzhen) - schools Longmen (Dragon Gate) the most comprehensive investigation belongs to M. Esposito, see [14].

The difference of the earlier source from "*Nüxiu zhengtu*" only in the final point - the ninth precept from "*Nü zhen jiu jie*" says: "Do not steal other people's things" [28, p. 29; 17, p. 263].

After the mastering of moral and ethical rules, the basical methodological principles *nü dan*, based on dual cultivation of Inner Nature and Destiny (*xing ming shuang xiu*) are explained to the devotees. Chapters "Destiny Root" (*ben ming*) and "Source of the Inner Nature" (*xing yuan*) are devoted to these principles. After this, women pass to the fulfillment of the practical methods, which begin with "Regulation of the Menstruation" (*xiu jing*) and "Returning and Restoration" (*fu huan*) of health and youth. Further the practice of the "female alchemy" concentrates on "Breast" (*ru fang*) where the process of the internal alchemical smelting of blood and its transformation into a liquid begins. Chapter "Jade Fluid" (*yu ye*) describes the exercises on the transformation of the cleared liquid discharges of an organism into *Qi*. "Embryonic Breath" (*tai xi*) pays attention to the special daoist respiratory practice. The exercises on visual meditation "[on a method] of the goddess of Tara" and the reading of mantras to which chapter "Southern Absence" (*nan wu*) is devoted, finish the complex of the female methods of self-perfection. In the final part of the composition entitled "Prudence to the End" (*shen zhong*) is once again underlined the fact,that the main thing at the fulfillment of all methods is to store the emptiness and silence in mind, and to observe the cleanliness and stillness in heart, or all efforts are in vain! [See 27, p. 533 - 540].

Special attention in the text is given to a complex of the exercises connected with "bridling" (*duan*) and "decapitation" (*zhan*) "red dragon".15 The idea of the age changes occurring in the female body is still presented in "Huangdi neijing" - "The Scripture of the Yellow Emperor about the Internal" - the work of the III-II century BC which, is traditionally carried to the Chinese medicine, is put in their basis.16 The "red dragon" (*chi long*) - in the daoist source of the Qing dynasty, is a symbolical name of the menstrual blood which, according to the late daoist representations, along with *Qi*, is necessary to the woman for cultivating a Transcendent in herself.

According to "*Xiwang mu nüxiu zhengtu shize*", a woman personifies the *Yin*, and the moon is its image. At the age of 13-15 the Primordial *Qi* (*yuan qi*) reaches its plenitude and the Perfect blood (*zhen xue*) is in abundance, as the full moon, which light is especially bright. It is that about which is said "inside *Yin* contains *Yang*". When menstruation start to descend, the Primordial *Qi* damages and destroys, and the Perfect blood

---

15 You can read in detail about the method of "the decapitation of a red dragon", see [20, 22, 26].

16 About the influence of the principles of "Huangdi neijing" (The Yellow Emperor's Classic of Internal Medicine) on the traditions of the "female alchemy", see the master-theses of the Chinese researcher of the daosism Li Cuizhen [26]. The Russian translations of chapters from "Huangdi neijing" are made by B.B. Vinogrodsky [7].

pours out. After the woman marries and gives birth to children the gradual harm is done to the Primordial *Qi,* and the Perfect blood decreases gradually. And though every month they are restored, every month they decrease again, and harm is done to its Inner Nature. Therefore it is said, that the perfection of the Inner Nature 性 (*xing*) is necessary to begin with the saving of the Destiny 命 (*ming*). The woman should make so that her monthly flow did not undergo changes because her Destiny (*ming*) is concluded into the monthly flow [see "Destiny Root", 27, p. 534].

In the third instruction about the woman it is said, that water is her Inner Nature, and flowers are her quintessence. If a girl has reached the understanding of things since her young years then she should protect the cleanliness of the internal nature - not to abandon herself to entertainment, not to listen to immodest speeches, to be silent and modest, and to follow internal foundations (*nei ze* 內則 - i.e. to behavior rules - *I.W.*). At this time the first monthly flow, drop by drop, gather together in her "internal female" (*nei pin* 內牝) (i.e. in a womb, the other name is "a palace of children" (*zi gong*) - *I.W.*) similarly "to stars or pearls". Only then one thing separates it from the returning to the Heavenly Nature (*xing tian*) and to Primordial Unity (*yuan yi*): it "Treasure of the Greatest Superior Heaven" (*xian tian zhi bao*) which is stored over a stomach, in the centre of "median-yellow" (*zhong huang*), should not become "a red pearl" (*chi zhu* 赤 珠) and turn to the monthly flow. If she indulges in entertainments, her *Qi* will be excited, her heart will be disturbed, the essence-*jing* and spirit-*shen* will come in the disorder, and Primordial *qi* will lose durability. Then the "stars" of her Heavenly Treasure begin to boil and melt as oil. Their heat is similar to fire. They aspire to break downwards through the "gate", break doors and follow outside and all world names it "monthly flow" ("Celestial water" *tian gui* 天 癸). And even if subsequently the girl will observe chastity, she for ever remains only usual woman [see "Source of the Inner Nature", 27, p. 534535].

If a girl has resolved to find immortality, she should prevent the process of decrease of the basic components participating in internal alchemical transformation. For this purpose it is necessary for her to be engaged "in the regulation of monthly flow" (*xiu jing*) and "to decapitate a red dragon" (*zhan chi long*).They reach it by means of massage of the waist and the bottom area of a stomach with the help of certain breathing gymnastics and visualization which techniques is described in details in the fourth instruction. However if in the course of performance of these exercises she does not observe full stillness then she can easily plunge into "the Sea of feelings" and her essence-*jing* will stream outside. In this point of practice as it is said in the comment, the ways of immortal and worldly disperse. If a woman has reached advanced years, but has not returned yet to "Primordial Unity", and her "red dragon" "is already killed", it is necessary to "restore" it at first, and then again to "decapitate" [see "Regulation of the Menstruation", 27, pp. 535-536].

That, who has already "decapitated a red dragon" all the same should continue her practice in order to return to a primary condition and to assimilate to the virgin (*chu nü* 處女). For this purpose she needs to carry out a special massage of the breast and visual exercises which are resulted in the fifth instruction. According to "*Xiwang mu nüxiu zhengtu shize*", the girl who practices these techniques will have "body as a little boy". The woman will be harmonious as the man, she will return "her beauty", her breasts will be involved, like a little girl has and will become "as hard as a walnut [shell]" [see "Returning and Restoration", 27, pp. 536-537]. After "the weak will become stronger, and the old will return [herself] gradually to youth", it is possible to start to the higher methods of self-perfection which begin with the "transformation of a red dragon into a white phoenix" [see "Breast", 27, pp. 537-538].

Further, in the chapter "Jade Fluid" (see [27, pp. 538-539]) the explanations about the distinctions in the performance of this method among men and women are given, and this is what said about it:

After all they say, that when a man starts to comprehension of [methods] of cleanliness and stillness (*qing jing*) … his Perfect essence-*jing* (*zhen jing*) will be saved up much and will not stream from the Mysterious Pass (*xuan guan*), it will direct upwards to [his] top. [Having reached the brain], it will irrigate the Heavenly valley (*tian gu*) and will fall down as moisture in the Flower pond (*hua chi*). It is also named 'Jade fluid' (*yu ye*). This is the way *Yin-shen* appears. Then the Sunlight souls (*hun*) go to Jade justice (*yu fu*) and the Moonlight souls (*po*) are on an audience to [heavenly] Lords and Perfections. The shining aura surrounds the top of the head.The waves of the inflow cover the Mysterious Sea (*xuan hai*).The sounds of the surf reach the [heavens] of Jade Clarity. It is, truly, a cinnabaric circular motion of Jade fluid! …As for the female Jade fluid, then it is the ancient essence of [this practice] to transform the liquid from 'a red dragon' into 'a white phoenix' [27, p. 538].

We cannot unconditionally give superiority to the method of "decapitating of the red dragon" as the key techniques in the female internal alchemical art. Nevertheless, it expresses the specificity of the female methods of self-perfection.The expressions "*zhan chi long*" 斬赤龍 or "*duan chi long*" 斷赤龍 are the markers with the help of which we can precisely define, that this work belongs by tradition to the "female internal alchemy".

To reach the result in the "decapitating of the red dragon", as it is said in the text, is very simple. It is enough only to carry out each exercise that is described in the fifth and sixth precepts within one hundred days. However it is not enough to become the Transcendent. According to the doctrine of Complete Perfection (*Quanzhen*) to which the subdirection of this source belongs, the higher principle of the returning to Dao is the cherishing of the cleanliness and stillness of mind and it is reached by means of a special respiratory practice. The breath and the expiration through a nose when there are even no thoughts about the breath, is called as "embryonic breath". It is said in the text that the "embryonic breath" is "the highest Way of Dao and a ladder to the Sky". In "*Xiwang mu nüxiu zhengtu shize*" the exclusive importance of the application of such type of breath in the practice of the "female alchemy" for the reaching of the Transcendent is underlined: "After the woman has finished 'cinnabar circular motion', her essence-*jing* and *Qi* are in the prosperity, and the body becomes similar to the man's. But if she does not go in for the 'embryonic breath' then she will not rise into Heavens (letters. 'To return to emptiness', *huan xu*) is never fated to her!" [27, p. 539]. The purpose of this method, as the source says, consists in the reaching of the limit of the emptiness and stillness [see 27, p. 539]. As it is considered, this method of "the embryo" or "womb breath" was known in the Han dynasty. About it the description in 8 ch. has remained "*Baopuzi*" (Book of the Master Who Embraces Simplicity), belonging to the brush of Ge Hong and in the other scriptures of the VI-VIII centuries [see 6, pp. 49-54]. Practicing the "embryo breath", the daoist devotee "as though comes back to an embryo condition, refusing from rough external *Qi* of Posterior Heaven", gradually filling the body pure *Qi* of Superior Heaven which the child in a womb of a mother breathes and finds qualities of the inhabitant of Celestial Transcendent [6, pp. 50-51]. The respiratory exercises played an important though an auxiliary role in the "internal alchemy" on the way to self-perfection.17 However the tradition of the "female alchemy" to work with breath, and along with "*zhan chi long*" becomes one of the basical methods of the achievement of the immortality.

The principles of the "female alchemy", described in "*Xiwang mu nüxiu zhengtu shize*" had received their development in the subsequent works on *nü dan*. The methods stated in it have been laid down in the basis of sanitation practices for the women known under the name of the "Female *Qigong*", which have got great popularity in modern China.18

REFERENCES

И. В. Белая. 2009. "Формирование техники женской алхимии на основе даосских мировоззренческих концепций о роли женского начала," *Религиоведение*, № 3, In Russian [Belaya I., "Formorovanie techniki zenskoi alchimii na osnove daosskich mirovozzrencheskich konzepzij o rolo zenskogo nachala, " *Religiovedenie*, No. 3, pp. 70-76].

---

17 About respiratory methods in early daosism see S. V. Filonov's article [9].

18 It is known, that in Beidaihe there is a school of the "Female Qigong" (*nü zi qigong* 女子氣功) under the guidance of Liu Yafei, the daughter of the foundress of the modern Qigong Liu Guizhen. In spite of the fact that "the Female Qigong" is based on the methods of "the female internal alchemy", unlike daosism they are presented as the technique of the improvement of a female organism, instead of the religious practice for the achievement of the immortality [23, p. 190].

И. В. Белая. 2008. "Практика женской алхимии, изложенная в семи стихах Верховной Владычицей Сунь Бу-эр," *Материалы докладов XV Международной конференции студентов, аспирантов и молодых ученых «Ломоносов».* In Russian [I. Belaya. "Prktika zenskoij alchimii, izlozennaja v semi stixax Verchobnoij Vladichizei Sun Bu-er," *Materiali dokladov XV Mezdunarodnoj koferenzii studento, aspirantov i molodix uchenix "Lomonosov"* (Moscow: 1 CDROM, 2008)]

И. В. Белая. 2010."Жизнеописание наставницы Сунь Бу-эр в даосской традиции," *Вопросы культурологи,* № 1, In Russian [I. Belaya. "Zizneopoisanie nastavnizi Sun Bu-er v daosskoij tradizii," *Voprosi kulturologii*, No. 1, 2010, pp. 28-32].

И. В. Белая. 2011."О развитии традиции «женской алхимии» (*нюй дань*) в горах Цзиньгайшань," *Сборник докладов XLI научной конференции «Общество и*

Vostochnaya Literatura Publishers, 2006-2010)]

Путь золота и киновари: Даосские практики в исследованиях и переводах Е.А. Торчинова. In Russian. [*Put zolota i kinovari: Daosskii practiki v issledovanijax i perevodax* (St. Petersburg: Azbuka-klassika, 2007), pp. 49-54].

Трактат Желтого Императора о внутреннем. Ч. 1: Вопросы о простейшем; Ч. 2: Ось духа

, transl. Б.Б. Виногродского. In Russian [*Traktat zeltogo Imperatora o vnutrennem, Part 1-2* (Moscow: Profit-Steil, 2007)]

С.В. Филонов. 2006. "Шанцинский даосизм: у истоков традиции: по материалам работы Тао Хун-цзина «Чжэнь гао»," *Религиозный мир Китая, Альманах'*2005, Труды Ин-та восточных культур и античности. In Russian [S.V. Filonov. " Schanziskij daosism...," *Religioznij myr Kitaya, Almanax'2005*, (Moscow: RGGU, 2006), vol. IX, pp. 85-113].

С.В. Филонов. 2008. "Концепция «сань у ци цзю» («три, пять, семь, девять») в ранних памятниках даосской религиозной традиции," *Религиоведение,* № 2, In Russian [S.V. Filonov. " Konzepziya « san u zi zu » (tri, pyat, sem, devyat) v rannix pamjatnikax daosskoi religioznoj trdizii," *Religiovedenije*, No. 2, 2008, pp. 48-62].

T. Cleary. 1996. *Immortal Sisters: Secret Teachings of Taoist Women.* California: Berkeley

C. Despeux. 1990. *Immortelles de la Chine ancienne: Taoïsme et alchimie féminine*. Puiseaux: Pardès

C. Despeux, L. Kohn. 2003. *Women in Daoism*. Cambridge

M. Esposito. 1993. *La Porte du Dragon - L'école Longmen du Mont Jin'gai et ses pratiques alchimiques d'après le Daozang xubian (Suite au canon taoïste)*, Ph.D. diss., Université Paris.

V. Esposito. 2004. "The Longmen School and Its Controversial History during the Qing Dynasty," *Religion and Chinese Society. Volume II: Taoism and Local Religion in Modern China*, A Centennial Conference of the École française d'Extrême-Orient., pp. 621-698.

C. Furth. 1986. "Blood, Body and Gender. Medical Images of the Female condition in China 1600-1850, " *Chinese Science*, 7, pp. 43-66. C. Furth. 1999. *A Flourishing Yin: Gender in China's Medical History*, Berkeley: University of California Press, pp. 960-1665.

L. Kohn. 2003. *Cosmos and Community: the Ethical Dimension of Daoism*. Cambridge.

Liu Xun. 2001. "In Search of Immortality: Daoist Inner Alchemy in Early Twentieth Century China," ph.D. diss. University of Southern California, pp. 367-368.

J. Needham., et al. 1983. *Science and Civilisation in China, vol. 5: Spagyrical Discovery and Invention - Physiological Alchemy*. Cambridge: Cambridge University Press.

E. Valussi. 2003. "Beheading the Red Dragon: A History of Female Inner Alchemy in China," ph.D. diss. University of London.

E. Valussi. 2008. "The *Nudan hebian* (Collection of Female Alchemy), Its Editor and His Women," *Nannu: Men, Women and Gender in Early and Imperial China*, 10, pp. 242-278.

E. Valussi. 2008. "Blood, Tigers, Dragons: The Physiology of Transcendence for Women" *IASTAM, Journal of Asian Medicine*, 4.1, pp. 46-85.

E. Valussi. 2008. "Female Alchemy and Paratext: How to Read nudan in a Historical Context," *Asia Major*, 21.2, pp. 153-193.

E. Valussi. 2009. "Female Alchemy: In Introduction," *In Internal Alchemy: Self, Society and the Quest for Immortality*, ed. by L. Kohn & R. Wong, Three Pines Press, pp. 141-162.

Suping Li. Nü shen, nü dan, nü Dao (Women's Goddess, women's alchemy, women's Way to Dao). Beijing: Zongjiao wenhua chubanshe, 2004. 李素平《女神女丹女道》, 北京: 宗教文化出版社, 2004 年。

Cuizhen Li. Zhan chilong yanjiu: daojiao yu tiandijiao jingzuo xiulian zhi bijiao (Researching of the methods of "decapitation a red dragon": Comparative analysis of meditation practices in Daoism and Tiandijiao's teaching), diss. ... Magister. University of Nanhua. [Taibei], Min guo 96 [2007]. 150 c. 李翠珍. 斬赤龍研究 - 道教與天帝教靜坐修煉之比較: 碩士論文. 指導教授為李豐楙 / 南華大學. [台北], 民國 96 年 [2007]. 150 頁.

Yijing Ye. Quanzhen nüguan Sun Buer ji "Sun Buer yuanjun fayu" zhi yanjiu (About daoist nun Sun Buer of Quanzhen school and works "Dharma Saying of Primordial Lady Sun Buer"), diss. ... Magister. State

University of Chenggong. [Taibei], Min guo 92 [2003]. 185 c. 葉怡菁.
全真女冠孫不二及 «孫不二元君法語» 之研究: 碩士論文. 指導教授 為丁煌/ 國立成功大學. [台北], 民國 92 年 [2003]. 185 頁.

Xiwang mu nüxiu zhengtu shize (Ten Rules of the Queen Mother of the West on the Proper Path of Women's Cultivation) 西王母女修正途十則. ZWDS, № 356, T. 10, pp. 533-540.

Chu zhen jie shuo (Description of the Precepts of Initial Perfection) 初真戒說 ЦВДШ, № 404, T. 12, pp. 14-31.

ABBREVIATION

ZWDS - *Zangwai daoshu* 藏外道書 (Daoist Books outside the Cannon). Ed. Hu Dao-jing: In 36 vol. Chengdu, 1992-1994.

CHAPTER XX

SOME FEATURES OF THE DEVELOPMENT OF SCIENCE AND TECHNOLOGY IN THE 17TH19TH CENTURY JAPAN IN THE CONTEXT OF NATIONAL SPIRITUAL TRADITION

This paper will be primarily concerned with the development of natural science knowledge in the context of Japanese culture.

Japan's historical and geographical conditions developed in a way that kept it for a very long time in the position of a student; hence, it can be designated as a catch-up culture. Finding itself on the periphery of Chinese civilization, it was in the beginning in the realm of Chinese cultural influence. Its cultural development was largely determined by the centripetal movement, a striving to learn and borrow as much as possible from China.

The "student" situation repeated itself when the Japanese began to develop contacts with European civilization. The need to acquire and master achievements of West European civilization became highly acute in the second half of the 19th century, when Japan found itself in danger of colonization. Similarly after its defeat in World War II, the shortest way to economic recovery was a scientific and technical re-equipment through the use of foreign achievements.

The tradition of borrowing knowledge from outside has historical roots. For a long time, the name 'scholar' designated a man who studied Chinese and, later, Western sciences. In a way this led to the appearance of a certain inferiority complex when foreign achievements were *a priori* perceived as something of a higher value than anything created in Japan. According to Kawajiri Nobuo, the Japanese obviously perceived new knowledge as knowledge of a higher order, even before they had a chance to comprehend or evaluate its true nature. 1 The underlying reasons are primarily historical and geographical.

Several noteworthy issues arise in connection with this situation. Firstly, the formation of cultural and adaptive mechanisms that helped to smoothly combine borrowings with local traditions and develop them in a certain direction.

---

1 Kawajiri Nobuo. "The Characteristic Features of Japanese Culture in the Field of Science in the Eighteen-Nineteen Century," *Indian Journal of History of Science,* 17(2), 1982, p. 278.

Secondly, the place of these borrowings in Japanese culture. Did imported scientific and technical knowledge that emerged elsewhere and was inevitably imbued with a certain different worldview tend to force out local tradition? How did they relate to each other? If the Japanese were compelled, due to certain circumstances, to import scientific knowledge, does it follow that in a way the Japanese spiritual tradition impeded the development of scientific knowledge?

Most researchers in Japan say that the genius of the Japanese consists not in invention, but in adaptation of new cultural elements - first from China and Korea, then from Europe and the US. As a result, borrowed elements start an independent life of their own, often changing beyond recognition in the process.2 This fully applies to the development of science and technology in Japan.

How can one explain it with reference to the specifics of Japanese culture and its worldview?

Below is an outline of some approaches to finding answers to these questions.

The method of borrowing Chinese scientific and technological achievements was summarized in the 9th century in a formula *wakon-kansai* ("Japanese spirit - Chinese skills") attributed to poet and statesman Sugawara Mitizane (845-903).

In the 19th century, philosopher and political activist Sakuma Syosan (1811-1864) refashioned it into *toyo dotoku - seiyo geijutsu* ("Eastern morality - Western skills"). Both slogans eloquently indicate that in the first as well as the second cases borrowed knowledge was perceived as technically necessary, but alien with respect to national spiritual tradition.

The Japanese world view was indeed hardly compatible with the philosophical underpinnings of classical western science. The Japanese perceived things as a process, not as something static; the world was seen as a single living organism as opposed to the mechanistic world view current in the West. Whereas the Western thought of the New Times focused primarily on objects, the Japanese, under the influence of Mahayana Buddhism in the first place, saw as priority connections and interrelationships. The Europeans attached importance to structure; the Japanese - to function. Japanese spiritual tradition was characterized by spatio-temporal thinking in contrast to the spatial and temporal thinking in the West; it merged subject and object, and made no division between spiritual and material; and it relied on a logic that was different from classical Aristotelian logic, with its law of non-contradiction. This ideological division lost its significance with the advent of non-classical science in the late 19th century and even more so of post-non-classical

2 See for example: J. J. Tobin, "Introduction: Domesticating the West," *Re-Made in Japan. Everyday Life and Consumer Taste in a Changing Society* (London: New Haven, 1992), pp. 3-4; *Japanese Systems. An Alternative Civilization*? (Yokahama: Sekotac, Ltd., 1992), p. 54.

science in the 20th century. How did the Japanese manage to combine such different things: to accept Western science without destroying their own non-modernist form of rationality and their values?

Exerting some influence on the formation of the adaptation mechanism in Japanese culture was the Buddhist concept of "two truths" unconditional, perceivable only in the experience of enlightenment and conventional and relative.

If Japanese Buddhism, particularly Zen, could, on the one hand, conflict with scientific thinking by proclaiming the cerebral incomprehensibility of true being through everyday logic and the impossibility of expressing its essence with concepts, it still allowed, on the other hand, the existence of some conventional truths. Undoubtedly a very special contribution to the elaboration of the doctrine of plurality of truths was made by the Tendai school, whose basic text is "Lotus Sutra."

Assuming the possibility of many conventional truths of instrumental nature paved the way for accepting all kinds of new knowledge and teachings without renouncing the Buddhist teachings.

Thus, the mechanism of adaptation consisted, first, in placing new information in a different plane and in a different context. For example, the attainment of truth through enlightenment occupied its plane and functioned in one context, the regulation of social relations operated in another, while empirical-rational knowledge was used in the third one. This implied multiplicity and fragmentation of the truth. Its criterion was a capacity to solve specific practical problems. This fact drew the attention of the American Japanese scholar T. Kazulis, who writes that whereas the West initially sought to create a single coherent theory that would reflect the "one great truth of the highest order," the Japanese, following their tradition, have not sought anything of the kind. They were after a set of truths of a lower order that could help accomplish daily tasks. For the Japanese, he goes on, "truth is not monolithic, but plural, not holistic but fragmented. Truth varies depending on the context. Without a context there can not be any truth".3

This paradigm opened the door to the unity of the three doctrines Shinto, Buddhism and Confucianism. For example, a syncretist thinker from the 17th and 18th century, Isida Baigan (1685-1744), expressed it this way: "Buddhist law is useful for the purification of the heart from evil. Confucian teaching is good to foster good conduct, correct family order, and manage the country properly. A ship is good for crossing the seas and rivers. The most suitable way of moving on land is a horse and palanquin. Trying to follow Buddhist law with the aim to maintain order in the world is like trying to cross the seas and rivers with a horse and palanquin".4

---

3 Th.P. Kasulis, "Sushi, Science and Spirituality: Modern Japanese Philosophy and Its Views of Western Science," *Philosophy East and West,* vol. 42, No. 2, 1995, p. 234.

4 *Ishida Baigan Zenshu* . In Japanese. (Osaka: Seibundō Shuppan, 1972), vol. 1, p. 56.

Fitting the same paradigm is the Rangaku school (a school of Dutch learning), which arose in the 18th century in Nagasaki; many of its adherents, including Sakuma Syosan mentioned above, combined neoConfucian world-view principles with Western knowledge. Initially, it comprised physicians whose primary motivation was to gain more knowledge in the field of medicine; later, the spectrum of their scientific interests expanded. In the 19th century, the authorities, too, started to show interest in Western science and technology in a bid to strengthen the country's defense. For this purpose, a special institute, *Bansho Shirabesho* (Office for Studies of Barbarian Books), was organized in 1855, which was engaged in translation and studying Western works on science and technology. The strategy worked out by the founders of this institution, Katsu Kaishu (1823-1899) and Oda Matazo (1804-1870), relied on neoConfucian philosophy of the school of Hayashi Razan (1583-1657) as its ideological basis.

2. Creation of ontological systems that served as a precursor of natural sciences in the West was not initially on the agenda for the Japanese. During the Tokugawa period (1603-1868), Japan perceived western scientific knowledge through the lens of neo-Confucian ontology and cosmology, a nearly unique systematic ontological and cosmological theory in the history of Japanese thought, which gained currency only in the 16th19th century (that is, apart from Kukai's attempt to create a Buddhist ontology in the 8th-9th century). Neo-Confucian philosophy in Japan was a rather open system with many trends and modifications. While preserving a relative structural integrity of the Chu Hsian scheme, various thinkers filled it with new meanings by incorporating some elements from other religious and philosophical systems, with the resulting shifts in emphasis that inevitably occurred and changed the original hierarchy and direction of the doctrines. Familiarity with the works of Chinese neo-Confuccianist Lo Ch"in-shun (1465-1541) promoted the establishment of philosophical NeoConfucianism in Japan, which was characterized by empiricism and rationalism associated with the names of Hayashi Razan of the Chu Hsian school and a number of thinkers who created independent neo-Confucian teachings, in particular, Yamaga Soko (1622-1701), Ito Jinsai (1627-1705), Kaibara Ekken (1630-1714), and others.

Lo Ch'in-shun was the first in China who shifted the emphasis from the "principle" (li) to the "pneuma" (qi). Hayashi Razan, one of the most established and officially recognized Confucian scholars of the Tokugawa Era, accentuated after Lo Ch'in-shun the meaning of "life energy" or "pneuma" as a starting element embodying "the principle" of specific forms of physical and mental phenomena, while stressing the unity of the two principles. Hence, coming to the forefront of his teaching were studies of phenomena of the external world and of texts, which in Chu Hsi's system qualified as an "achievement of knowledge." The ideological line of Hayashi Razan concentrated on the consideration of the heavenly principle above all as a reality that was immanent in the world and that was embodied by the psychophysical element *qi*, and on the study of "the principle in things;" it was continued by some of his students, undergoing some transformations in their teachings. In particular, it was interpreted in the writings of Kaibara Ekken (1630-1714), who created an empirical and rationalist doctrine in the Chu Hsian philosophical line.

Among his achievements one may mention the building of bridges between Zhu xian philosophy and the natural sciences.

Like Hayashi Razan, Kaibara Ekken adhered to the notion of the indivisible unity of *ri* and *qi* since the "principle" was the law of the existence of the form-building element. 5 He called for a study of the "principle" in real transformations of the pneuma, and pointed to the need to correlate such studies with a specific time, place, country and people. 6 One of the most important aspects of neo-Confucianism that acquired special significance and, in fact, determined the direction of intellectual dynamics in the Tokugawa Era, was a "practical" or "real" doctrine, the doctrine of "concrete things" (Chinese *shih-hsueh*, Jap. *jitsugaku*), which aimed at concrete goals and served as an antipode of abstract knowledge. Later, this term, once invented by Chu Hsi, was used by ideologues of Japanese education with regard to Western scientific knowledge.

In the Tokugawa period, science was designated in Japan in the neoConfucian key as *kyuri*, or "a study of principles."

It is also noteworthy that originally western scientific knowledge was assimilated in Japan only occasionally, not in conjunction with the scientistic worldview. As a result of the policy of isolation and limits on information channels scientific books fell into the hands of translators and scholars mostly by chance. Moreover, this knowledge occupied a niche of its own without conflicting with the existing ideological system.

Whereas during the Tokugawa period Western science was embedded in the Confucian scheme of research of things and principles, after the Meiji Restoration (1868), Western science and technology fitted into the ideology of nation-building under the slogan "Rich Country - Strong Army" (*fukoku kyohei*). They appeared as an extension of Japanese values that supported the government policy of modernization.

When the Japanese became acquainted with modern Western philosophy they perceived it as something radically different from their own spiritual tradition yet something that needed to learn in order to compete with the West.

The fundamental difference between the two worldviews explained why the name *tetsugaku*, invented to designate Western philosophy, was not applied to Japanese thought for quite some time, thus creating a false impression that Japan did not have its own philosophy at all.

---

5 Kaibara Ekken Zenshu (Collected works of Kaibara Ekken). In Japanese. (Tōkyō : Ekken Zenshū Kankōbu, 1939). Vol. 2, pp. 172-173.

6 Kaibara Ekken Zenshu, vol. 3, p. 560.

3. The establishment of science in Japan as part of the process of assimilation of foreign scientific achievements and technologies posed a major problem of creating a new scientific language and a new vocabulary in the Japanese language itself, a process that was complicated by differences in the cultural foundations. Yet the language is one of the important factors of adaptability of Japanese culture and has played a role in the assimilation of Western science and technology. Translation of scientific terminology based on the existing meanings in Japanese culture and the linguistic image of the world, contributed to a certain degree to their conservation in the formation of a new conceptual system transmitted through hieroglyphs. In the absence of equivalents in the native Japanese language for new terms, they had to be invented, and the hieroglyphic writing both helped to preserve the original meaning and simultaneously create a new one. Thus, the general term for science was *kagaku,* a "teaching of changes;" *kuri* meant a "study of principles;" and *butsurigaku* denoted physics, or in a word-for-word translation, a "teaching of the principles of things."

Hieroglyphs create additional adaptive capabilities. In the dominance of the centrality stereotype of Chinese civilization, the adaptive mechanisms in China did not develop, in our opinion, to the extent it did in Japan. Furthermore, additional opportunities for rendering scientific and technical knowledge arose in the Meiji period (1868-1912) with the appearance of scientific and technical terms in *katakana* (a syllable system of writing used primarily for borrowing) when it was difficult to adequately convey them with hieroglyphics. Moreover, transliterations appeared, as a rule, in an abridged form that differed from the original words, which helped them to become words of the Japanese language and embedded in Japanese grammar. At the same time, loaned words were easily recognized and separated in their writing from the Japanese proper, although they followed the general grammatical rules of word-building, conjugation, etc.

Meanwhile, their encounter with Western culture produced a "logical complex" among the Japanese intellectuals. The peculiarity of western languages is the central position of nouns, whereas in Japanese the central position is reserved for verbs. When translating, the logical structure of a sentence can vary somewhat because the grammatical subject is often merely implied and is defined by the predicate.

Therefore, a rather wide-spread opinion in Japan has it that the Japanese can not think logically, and that the Japanese language as such is alogical. In fact, some intellectuals have held this view from the Meiji era (1868-1912) to this day. For example, these men included the thinker, educator and first minister of education Mori Arinori (1847-1889); the writer Shiga Naoya (1883-1971), and the researcher of French philosophy of the 17th century Mori Arimasa (1911-1976). Thus, Mori Arinori would say that it was impossible to master Western science in Japanese, nor could the new laws use the Japanese language; for his part, he began to write papers in English.7

However, calls voiced by some supporters of the For Civilization and Enlightenment movement (*bummei kaika*) at the beginning of the Meiji era, to abandon the native language and not only use the same machines with the people of the West, but also to think the same way, were quickly found to be Utopian.

In our opinion, the Japanese language, with its linguistic image of the world and its own logic, perhaps did make it difficult to translate and understand works of Western scientists, but, at the same time, it certainly contributed to the adaptation of alien knowledge and its conversion into Japanese.

4. The Japanese worldview, established in the frameworks of the Shinto-Buddhist-Confucian ideological complex, regards this world as perfect, on the one hand, and as being in constant motion, on the other.

The Japanese processual ontological paradigm is fundamentally different from the substantial ontological paradigm, which goes back to Aristotle and underlies classical modern Western science. The continuous movement of the world in Japanese spiritual culture is denoted by the concept of *onozukara*, which implies spontaneity. Man's actions are perceived in this framework as an integral component of this natural selfmotion and denoted by the concept of *mizukara* (spontaneity of an individual), which coincides with the hieroglyphic writing of the word *onozukara*.

It is not accidental, in our view, that, historically, Japanese behavior has been characterized by a specific and short-term pragmatism. That they do not tend to establish strictly defined laws and regulations for all times, is due to their deep-rooted view that this motion of the world is for ever inherently spontaneous and unpredictable. On the contrary, rules keep varying depending on time and place, and this view, imbued with certain fatalism, is present in many works of Japanese thinkers.

Similarly, the Japanese are adept at short-term planning, but are not inclined to drawing up long-term plans and forecasts. With reference to scientific research, they have historically shown interest in the development of concrete problems and areas of learning that could be put to a specific practical use today or in the foreseeable future. Knowledge is not obtaining a certain amount of abstract conclusions about the world, but learning to adapt to this world.

Another point that may explain to some extent the highly pragmatic orientation of Japan's technological development is the distinct empiricism of Japanese intellectual tradition. Empiricism also distinguishes Japanese Buddhism, which maintains there is complete coincidence of absolute being with the phenomenal world one experiences through one's sensations, and

7 Tsukimoto Hiroshi, *Nihongo wa ronriteki de aru* (Tokyo: Kōdansha, 2009), p. 2.

most of the Japanese Confucian teachings, and the Shinto worldview. The approach that the ultimate reality is what we perceive in concrete things in everyday life, did not encourage search for something hidden behind phenomena, or abstracting and theorizing that might destroy immediate perception of life. Characteristic of Japanese culture, an orientation toward the world perceived in its concrete manifestations partly explains the fact that the concept of science as such did not even exist in Japan for a long time. The focus was set on the task of how to handle things, with the amount of knowledge that might arise in connection with this task falling under the concept of *geijutsu*, which means "technique," "skills," and/or "art." This was how traditional mathematics *wasan* was perceived.

Thus, whereas the 16th-17th century scientific revolution in Europe began with physics and then spread to other areas of knowledge, in Tokugawa Japan, medicine was the main science, which situation persisted until 1920; even the study of Western science in Japan began with medicine. 8 In addition to medicine, some development efforts went to astronomy, which was necessary for verifying calendars and in shipping. The Japanese of the Tokugawa and Meiji periods considered Western scientific knowledge and technology as a single entity, foreign but valuable for the development of their own country and its defense, but not in terms of knowledge for the sake of knowledge. Thus, the perception of science from the very beginning was biased toward regarding it as a skill rather than pure knowledge.

Incidentally, even today the share of basic research in Japan's innovative development falls behind that of the U.S. and in many areas behind the European countries.

Imports of foreign technologies remain a most important resource for innovative development. According to Yu. Denisov, "the Japanese concentrated all their scientific and technical potential on improving foreign technologies and adapting local facilities to their mass production".9 This may be the formula of Japanese scientific and technological creativity. Having evolved over centuries and partly going back to the cultural archetype, these thought patterns make it possible, in our view, to trace to some extent the origins of the formation in 17th-19th century Japan of that peculiar form of pragmatism in relation to scientific and technical knowledge that subsequently enabled it to achieve high economic growth.

This does not imply that creative scientific thinking is alien to the Japanese in general. Suffice it to mention the accomplishments in traditional mathematics, *wasan*, of Seki Takakazu (1642-1708), who invented the method of accelerating slowly convergent sequences and created the theory of determinants that anticipated the discovery of Leibniz. Moreover,

8 See J.R. Bartholomew, *The Formation of Science in Japan. Building a Research Tradition,* (New Heaven/London: Yale University Press, 1989), p. 5.

9 U.V. Denisov, "Japonskaya innovationnaya sisteme - ispitanie mirovim krizisom," *Mirovoi krizis i yaponija* (Moscow: AIRO-XXI, 2009), p. 148.

Japanese inventors of the Tokugawa period are credited with creating the prototype of today's famous Japanese robots, the automatic Karakuri dolls, which stagger one's imagination even today. And the list can go on and on.

(Translated from Russian by Serge Gitman)

CHAPTER XXI

SCIENTIFIC PROGRESS AND THE SEARCH FOR REDEVELOPMENT FOLLOWING THE AFTERMATH OF THE 2011 EARTHQUAKE IN EAST JAPAN

In this paper I would like to analyze the situation based on the data collected by May 2012 in Japan in response to the triple natural disaster of March 11, 2011. The tragedy of March 11, 2011 that hit the Japanese East coast, and in particular the Fukushima 1 Power Station disaster, has presented Japanese society with a need to seriously and fundamentally reconsider attitudes towards its scientific and technological so-called achievements.

It is still difficult to speak with either real perspective or certainty concerning the path of future community development, because several serious problems have not been fully resolved. Reconstruction and rehabilitation work is still in progress, more than three hundred thousand local citizens have to live in evacuation centers. Answers to the problem of Fukushima 1 have not been found and moreover it is still not truly known what further problems it will bring. Unbridled forces of nature and the tremendous damage that advanced technology brought to our country, forced us to focus on two vital questions: What was the true reason for the tragedy? Are we living our lives generally in the correct way?

This paper attempts to provide an accurate picture of the opinions and moral-psychological condition of Japanese society today which contemporary Japanese philosophers, writers and scientists reflect. We will try to represent their ideas concerning the scale and direction of future development, and the current rising zeitgeist of the Japanese nation.

In point of fact, the dominant theme of all utterances is the attitude of the Japanese nation towards its so-called scientific and technological success in general, and to nuclear power and nuclear power stations in particular, as well as the question about the moral standards that guide progress and safety measures within society.

After a series of Fukushima 1 breakdowns, one can observe in our country a tendency towards public active protests - both among average citizens and famous figures in science and culture. They speak against governmental nuclear policy and against the policies of reconstruction and rehabilitation of the ruined districts and areas.

Author and Literary Nobel Prize winner Kenzaburo Oe asked with bitterness: “How could you deceive us, the people of Japan, so coldheartedly?" He considers his civil duty as "to call for an immediate end to the nuclear power generation", insisting on judging nuclear power engineering not from a perspective of economic effectiveness, but rather from one of honesty and concern for life.

Author Haruki Murakami, exposing governmental and business circle lies about the safety of nuclear stations, says that rehabilitation of the ethical standards of life will take considerable time. Reminding us that the Japanese nation has a deep and inherited mistrust of nuclear power after the atomic bombing of the Second World War but have nevertheless lately permitted and tolerated increasing numbers of nuclear stations on its territory (now ranking first in the world by number), he asks the direct question: "Why did it happen? Has the feeling of disgust for nuclear power with which we were possessed for all those post war years vanished completely from our memory? What could really destroy and deform a peaceful and wealthy society to which we've all aspired? The answer to the last question is one and simple: the power of economical effectiveness."

Murakami further points to the fact that the government and scientists, wanting to exploit nuclear power, falsely proclaimed "comfort" to be "a life necessity". And the writer goes on: "We Japanese should not have kept silence, but screamed "No to nuclear power!"

In fact the Japanese yielded to propaganda, and were convinced by politicians and scientists of the necessity of nuclear power as a source of clean energy, and so voted for such a program, albeit with a slight apprehension. But immediately after the catastrophe of March 11 voices against nuclear stations were raised again. In that period 16 leading Japanese nuclear scientists made the usual, public, self-chastising speeches and begged the nation for forgiveness.

What does the Japanese nation think about this matter now? According to the Asahi Shimbun newspaper referendum after Fukushima, 41% of Japanese people now vote for a reduction of nuclear stations or their full liquidation. Mainichi Shimbun newspaper also published the results of its referendum in which 54% of respondents voted against nuclear stations while 40% still consider that electricity demands make nuclear stations a necessity. The last opinion is probably connected to the fact that, according to official quotas, nuclear power provides 30% of the sum total of electricity, thus making nuclear stations a certain necessity in the minds of some. Their thinking is that more traditional means of generation cannot match consumption.

But some specialists hold different opinions. For example Mr. H. Koide argues that Japan can survive without nuclear stations because the 30% in the quota appears as a result of intentional action - increasing the exploitation coefficient of nuclear stations and reducing heat capacity of thermal power plants. Mr. Koide considers that if the quota of the thermal power plants could be raised from 48% to 79% then Japan would receive the full amount of energy with no need for nuclear power. If Mr. Koide's analyses is right, then the warning to the Japanese nation issued by Kenzaburo Oe and Haruki Murakami about being deceived is also true.

Nowadays, in the Japanese media and periodicals, one can more often find negative attitudes to nuclear stations, as well as people's strong indignation of deceptive governmental information and policy surrounding nuclear power and rehabilitative actions in tsunami struck areas. But simply analyzing opinion polls does not make certain which side will win in the nuclear debate. The Fukushima 1 catastrophe raised, in the psyche of the Japanese, people a vital question about attitudes towards scientific and technological achievements in the very near future. Neither science nor technology themselves can dictate opinions; free choice has always been the prerogative of a human being.

The Fukushima tragedy, where modern technology caused serious consequences for people's health and lives, is now examined by progressive minded Japanese citizens from a moral point of view. They are trying to find an adequate attitude towards technology, but there are many among those who feel very worried about the possibility of technology gaining the whiphand over humankind. Mr. T. Yoshimoto, who in previous decades was excessively critical about the Japanese mistrust of nuclear power, is now pessimistically speaking about the inevitability of humankind walking a dangerous tightrope.

Latest publications and speeches offered by Japanese scientists and writers are typically scathing in their accusations against the government and energy companies. Kenzaburo Oe said: "A big amount of fraud was unmasked lately. It appeared that the foundation of democracy was fragile." And in the words of Murakami: "We must rebel and accuse ourselves that we allowed such deformed structures to exist." So the Japanese nation is both a victim and the guilty party. As the famous writer continues, the situation has seen "the defeat of Japanese moral standards". Murakami encourages the world wide community to be utopian dreamers but to create a "spiritual community" which will be open to all nations and cultures.

The Psychological Changes in Japanese Society

As noted in the psychological and spiritual changes in the Japanese society after March 11, 2011 the importance of interpersonal relationships is now growing rapidly. Continuing this thought we should remember that the most frequently used words in Japan currently are "human bonds". Certainly the death of relatives and loved ones is an irreplaceable loss, but our shared tragedy gives us the possibility to remember that the things which tie us together are most valuable in life. This is mirrored in the active voluntary work and participation of young Japanese people to help in the earthquake struck areas, and collections and donations for tsunami affected zones. Among the young generation there is a preference to create families rather than to free style relationships. Rebecca Solnit, in her book "Paradise Built In Hell", writes about the strange communities which appear in time of mutual danger.1 In an interview during her visit to Japan she speaks about the lesson of disaster, which teaches us that everyday normal life can be destroyed so easily, and how strongly people need solidarity and interaction, and that the creation of human bonds touches people's souls. Her words are proven true by the social interviews given in the last year in which 70% of respondents in the affected areas said that they were convinced, most of all, in the importance of interpersonal relationships. In other prefectures of Japan more that 50% of citizens gave the same answer.

But others have contrasting opinions about strong empathy. Mr. N. Sakai warns about the danger of mutual sympathy because it gives people the feeling of mutual spiritual comfort and makes them forget about the need to investigate the true reasons of tragedy as well as to find workable solutions. He gives an example of such a situation when the emotions of survivors are used by the government to raise in people's minds the feeling of duty to the state and to unite and support the general political course which Japanese politicians have chosen. In this case the course is increasing the rates of consumption for the sake of restoring the economy of the country post-disaster.

Mr. Nakai, on his side, expresses the concern that the call to unite the nation might lead to negative social consequences, and as an example uses the vanishing of the democratic mood in the Kanto area after the earthquake in Japan in 1923. It begs the question: is the historically inherent Japanese collectivism, by itself enough, and the only force which must be the spiritual core of further development in Japan?

Reminding us about the works of I. Berlin, a thinker who saw himself as a refugee of the world, Mr. Zturumi urged the Japanese people to consider themselves as refugees of civilization and to start a new life based on mutual help and natural exchange among neighbors. Haruki Murakami in his reception speech for the Catalonia International Prize also talked about his dream to create a spiritual community without state borders and cultural differences.

The modern Japanese philosopher Daisaku Ikeda put forward an idea based on the Buddhist concept of interdependent occurrence, which can be an example of moral code for the development of society and the key to an attitude towards scientific and technological achievements as well as the identity or substance of human relationships. In his article "Peace Proposals of 2012: The Concept of Human Security and Sustainable Development of Society; Worshiping Life" Mr. Ikeda quotes "Risho Ankoku Ron" - the treatise "Securing Peace for the People by Establishing the Ultimate Law" written by the 13th century Japanese philosopher Nichiren Daishonin. "If you care anything about your personal security, you should first of all pray for order and tranquility throughout the four quarters of the land, should you not?" Interpreting the meaning of these words Mr. Ikeda stresses the importance for people to realize the impossibility of gaining one's own true

1 http://www.asahi.com/culture/news_culture/TKY201203290216.html

happiness and prosperity in isolation from the world around one, in isolation from other human beings. This is an exact definition of the concept of interdependent occurrence according to Mr. Ikeda. He goes on to say: "Any living being and/or phenomenon occurs thanks to the existence of other living beings and/or phenomena. Nothing is able to appear or survive separately in a vacuum apart from the universe. Absolutely everything we can experience now in an infinity of forms is the result of interdependent occurrence of anonymous "cause" and "effects"."

According to this Buddhist Cosmology, all and everyone collaborate with each other in interdependent occurrence. These strong ties we can easily see in all spheres of life such as the biosphere of the Earth where plants, animals and micro-organisms play their own roles, and none can survive without the other two. And on this fundamental concept Mr. Ikeda suggests adopting the famous ultimate moral code: "Don't build your happiness on the unhappiness of others". In an ideal world when each and every one of us fully realizes that we all depend on each other and can't simply exist in a personal vacuum, it would be unlikely that we could cause harm to others. From this point of view he suggests examining the problem of nuclear stations in Japan. If we take into consideration the geographical fact that Japan is situated in a very seismically active zone of the Earth and where 10% of all earthquakes with tsunamis happen - it is over optimistic to believe that the nuclear station disaster won't happen again. The probability of catastrophe assumes the probability of victims. And if it is so, nuclear power engineering is inconsistent with the above mentioned moral principle.

Let us consider the possible lever of influence and morals Mr. Ikeda's idea could provide. Though unlikely, this moral code "Don't build your own happiness on unhappiness of others" will meet objections from society. We cannot say that it will be respected implicitly by everyone everywhere. Unfortunately we can see the exact opposite quite often.

But what exactly prevents people from working towards its realization? According Mr. Ikeda's way of thinking it could be a lack of faith. That is why the Japanese philosopher, in his above mentioned article, stressed the importance of belief in the unlimited potential of each and every human being. And from such a perspective he ties the phenomenon of "human being" with two Buddhist concepts - "interdependent occurrence" and "ku". The Sanskrit word "*śūnyatā*", translated in Japanese as "ku", covers the scope of two concepts - "existence" and "non-existence". Shakyamuni Buddha used it to explain the causes of suffering, which human beings experience because of their attachment to the world which they consider to be always unchanged and constant. In his turn, Nāgārjuna, when criticizing the teaching of Sarvāstivāda Buddhist Scholasticism, considered dharma as possessing valid ontological status, and developed this concept in conjunction with "interdependent occurrence". Mr. Ikeda, in his explanation of the Buddhist concept of life, interprets "ku" as follows: "Ku - "*śūnyatā*" is not an emptiness, as it is often falsely taken to be, but the real state of life where vital energy exists in its latent form. This latent form of life is invisible to the eye. That's why "ku" can be taken as nonexistence. But in contrast to nonexistence "ku" has the potential force to provide new life if connected to the eternal influence. That's why "ku" is not emptiness. Buddhism proclaims that the essence of life phenomena cannot be explained by two usual definitions as existence (to be) and nonexistence (not to be)." 2

Examining the concept of "self" or "the self of individual" according to "*śūnyatā*" teaching, Mr. Ikeda says: "Anātman does not mean the absence of "self" but the absence of constant unchangeable "self"." He looks at this concept from the opposite side: there is no unchangeable "self", but there is constantly changeable "self" instead. In this the Japanese philosopher sees the infinite possibility of self-improvement for a person. Coming from such an understanding of an individual, Mr. Ikeda considers empowerment as a key to the "spiritual rehabilitation" of Japan after March 11. Here we should take into consideration that he uses the English word "empowerment" not in the meaning of gaining worldly skills which are necessary for our social and private life but only in the meaning of improving the personality and spiritual capacity of an individual; a human revolution. Nevertheless selfimprovement and human revolution are much more difficult that the improvement of technology. A man needs moral support and human bonds of trust.

Conclusion

Since March 11, 2011the rehabilitation period has been going intensively in Japan and it is still unknown when and how the Fukushima disaster consequences will be solved. At this crucial and short time, it is still difficult to give a full analyses of psychological and moral level of the Japanese society. One thing that can be said for sure is that Japan is standing at crossroads. But there is no doubt that we should unite all efforts to rebuild the stricken areas and to rehabilitate the soul and life of everyone there.

2 D. Ikeda, *Izberi zizn.* In Russian. (Moscow: Moskovsky Universitet Publishers, 2007), p. 311.

PART IV

ISLAMIC TRADITION

CHAPTER XXII

HOW CAN ISLAMIC PHILOSOPHY CONTRIBUTE TO A COMPARATIVE STUDY OF PHILOSOPHY

In the Name of God, the All-Good, the Compassionate In a global age when different cultures have come to know each other
in an unprecedented way and in which deep-delving and penetrating studies have been made regarding the philosophies of other civilizations, the significance of comparative philosophy becomes increasingly evident and in the recent decades it has become the focus of attention in some philosophical circles.

But there are some philosophers who deny the possibility of such a discipline as comparative philosophy, arguing for example that different schools of philosophy are autonomous totalities like independent circles or like parallel lines which do not have elements in common. Even if there might seem to be similar issues in different schools, but each should be understood and interpreted within its peculiar and proper context and solely in relation to its initial principles. To make a comparative study of philosophical issues, in other words, is to take them out of their proper context which would ultimately belie their intended purpot. But to argue in this way is to say that both philosophy and philosophical issues are so equivocal that a common understanding among philosophers becomes almost an impossibility. Even one might say that philosophy, which by its nature demands a deeper penetration into reality, loses it reason of being. It could be moreover said that, this point of view, which ultimately ends in a sort of relativism, makes the search for truth that has traditionally been regarded as the sole objective of philosophical endeavor, something redundant and futile. Philosophy moreover, is said to deal with certain questions considered to be ultimate and perennial which have been posed in all ages and in different cultures whose people had reached a certain level of intellectual maturity. The history of philosophy shows us many examples of such first and primordial questions.

In order to do comparative philosophy certain conditions are required. First, one should have a profound knowledge of two philosophical traditions or at least two philosophical schools, with an emphasis on a special philosophical problem. A superficial discussion of the issue, needless to say, does not suffice. A knowledge of the historical development of the problem under consideration is also necessary. This knowledge will help us to see, for example, what changes a certain idea or philosophical term has undergone in the course of history and will forestall dilapidated and quite marginal comparisons sticking to the literal and outward form of philosophical issues, and will hinder rather than help the comparative study of philosophical issues. Showing undue concern to the letter kills the spirit of philosophy. How often it happens that one might think that there are wide discrepancies between philosophical issues in two different schools or a total difference between two philosophical terms, which on a closer scrutiny will evaporate.

There are also different methods for doing comparative philosophy. One might, for example, make a comparative study of a single issue, in two philosophers who not only belong to one school of philosophy, but also to one single tradition. One might, for instance compare the theory of substance in Aristotle and Alexander Aphrodisias (who belong both to the Peripatetic school and again to the Western tradition.) Again, one might compare an issue between philosophers belonging to the same school but to two different traditions: one might for instance make the same study between Aristotle and Avicenna. A third alternative would be to make a comparative study of a problem between two philosophers who belong to two different schools of thought but, nonetheless, to the one and the same tradition (As a case one might, for example, mention, different stages of knowledge in Plato and Kant.) A fourth possibility would be to study a philosophical issue between two philosophers who belong to two different schools of thought and two different traditions, which nevertheless have philosophically influenced each other (one might, for example, compare and contrast, the being of the copula, in Aristotle, Kant and Mulla Sadra.) A fifth possibility would be to compare issues in two different thinkers who belong to different schools and to two various traditions where moreover there is no evidence to show that there has been the least trace of philosophical influence and counter - influence between their respective traditions (Prof. Izutsu has for example, compared the metaphysical systems of the Muslim mystic Ibn Arabi and the Chinese sage Lao Tzu.) Here it would be surreptitiously vain to talk about historical influence and an appeal to historicism and historicistic explanations would mull over the issue.

After these introductory remarks let us turn to our initial problem about the possible contribution of Islamic philosophy to comparative philosophy. A few allusions and remarks about the nature of Islamic philosophy would again aid us in providing a satisfactory answer to this question.

Islamic philosophy is the intellectual heir of multifarious and diverse traditions. One could for example mention the tradition of Greek philosophy. As is well-known, a very great and stupendous movement in translation from Greek into Arabic took place in Baghdad where almost all major works in philosophy and science together with main commentaries were translated, which provided sufficient material for philosophical reflection and scientific experimentation. It is enough to consider that philosophers such as Avicenna and Averroes, most probably did not know any Greek but nonetheless they were well-versed in the Peripatetic tradition.

Considering the fact that none of these works, except two, had been translated into Latin, and that some centuries later these works were translated first from the Arabic translation and commentaries and then from the original Greek into Latin, one can safely conclude that the Islamic civilization was the true inheritor of Hellenic and Hellenistic intellectual tradition and that Europe and the West, inherited them through the Islamic civilization.This fact which makes a comparative study of many disciplines specially philosophy between the two respective traditions both feasible and an urgent necessity. Islamic civilization, moreover, being situated, symbolically and geographically speaking in the middle belt of our globe, has been a golden bridge for the transmission of Eastern cultures to the West, which did not know anything of significance about the East in the Middle Ages. The Islamic contribution in this regard far exceeds the introduction of the Arabic numerals, paper mills, gun powder and the compass and does not fall within the limited scope of this paper.

Let us mention one more point in this connection so far as a comparative study with Islamic philosophy is concerned. When we talk about Islamic philosophy, we should make a clear-cut distinction between Islamic philosophy proper and Islamic philosophy in a general sense. When we treat a certain philosophical issue in Avicenna, we are no doubt talking of philosophy in the proper and specific sense; but when we compare, for instance, Ibn Arabi with Shankara, Meister Eckhart or Lao-Tzu, here we are taking philosophy in its broader and more general sense. In my humble view, for the purpose of a more fruitful and profitable execution of comparative philosophy, we should not restrict our studies to issues which fall within the scope of the narrow conception of philosophy. There are also many issues of philosophical significance which lie outside its more proper domain. Missing these would deprive us of many interesting discussions in comparative philosophy. Islamic intellectual history is suffused with many themes in speculative Sufism, rational and dogmatic theology which a modern lover of comparative philosophy would not be inclined to condone.

PROBLEMS IN ONTOLOGY

Some orientalists who have taken the trouble of studying Islamic thought, often come up with the almost worn-out cliché that Islamic philosophy is nothing but an anachronistic repetition of Greek philosophy which has been brushed up and embellished with some unfortunate theological issues, as if it has been transplanted in quite an alien soil. To say the least, this is very far from the truth. Even a very cursory glance at one philosophical issue such as ontology which we have chosen to discuss below will disprove the above claim.

Plato taking as his starting-point the famous Parmenidean principle "Tauto gar estin to einai te kai to noein: for it is identically the same thing both to be and to intellect" as stated in the eponymous dialogue, came to the conclusion that true being (*ontos on*) is synonymous with intellection, both in the sense that it can be truly grasped by the intellect and in the additional sense that true being belongs to a special realm which he called the intelligible universe which was the abode of the Divine and eternal Ideas. A logical corollary of this view was first that our material and physical world, that is the world of becoming (rather than being itself) could not deign to belong to that world of true and eternal being; and more important, the One (*to hen*), that is the originating principle of all entities is beyond being (*epekeina tes ousias*, as stated in the allegory of the cave in the Republic). True being, in other words, belongs to the world of Ideas and it cannot be predicated either of the Divine principle which is called the Good (*to Agathon*) or the One (*to hen*), nor to the world of becoming which is below the dignity of such a sublime reality.

This is quite different when we come to consider the metaphysics of Aristotle where the idea of substance (*ousia*) is the pivotal term round which all other philosophical concepts revolve. Being, in the sense of substance is analogically predicated of both God, the highest being and of the physical substances such as the four elements. The theory of substance, as one of the ten categories, as the latter term implies, has been derived from the theory of logical predication and hence substance is defined as "that of which everything else is predicated and it is predicated of nothing". In sum, in Aristotle being is equated with its primary instance, i.e, substance. In some passages in Metaphysics, he has voiced this metaphysical equation of being with substance.

In Islamic philosophy, starting with Al-Farabi and consummated in Avicenna, metaphysics is not based on the theory of substance; it is rather founded on the more basic and intellectual distinction between essence (*almahiyyah*) and existence (*al-wujud*) a distinction which has on the one hand altered the mainstream of philosophy, and on the other hand has influenced its development to the present day.

It might be objected that this essence-existence dichotomy implicity existed in the Aristotelian philosophy. So what was the Islamic contribution in this particular problem? Answering this objection we might say that it is true that such a distinction existed implicity in Aristotle but even so, it was not used as a metaphysical foundation for a new metaphysics as we find among Muslim philosophers such as Avicenna.

A corollary consequent upon this essence-existence distinction, is the one known in Islamic philosophy as the occurrence (*urud*) of existence and known in western Medieval philosophy as the accidentality of being. In Islamic philosophical parlance, this means that these two concepts (essence and existence) are quite independent from each other and their alterity (*alghayriyyah*) means that the concept of the one does not necessarily entail that of the other. In the western philosophical tradition thanks to the misinterpretation of Averroes and his quite erroneous understanding of *urud* (occurrence) of being, in the sense of being an accident, being has been misconstrued as an accident and Medievals have wrongly accused Avicenna of unnecessarily adding one accidental category to the Aristotelian list.

Another corollary of such distinction is that resting on the contingency and necessity of being. If we predicate being of all things or quiddities in the world, such predication does not entail any kind of necessity. Such quiddities, in other words, are contingent in the sense that they are indifferent with respect to being or to not-being. Were not this the case, they would be either impossible (necessary not to exist) or necessary (impossible not to exist.) All beings of the World being contingent, they cannot of themselves come into being and the chain of contingent causes, to avoid an infinite regress, should ultimately end in a necessary being (*wajibal-wujud*) This necessity-contingency proof for the existence of God, is one of the major contributions of Muslim philosophers.

Unlike the other cosmological proofs it rests on purely rational (and not empirical) premises; it is moreover presupposed by the other proofs (the Aristotelian proof from motion demands an ultimate necessary mover in the chain of contingent movers; an uncaused cause is the necessary cause from among the contingent causes and so on.) It provides a purely metaphysical distinction between God and the world. In addition it can be proved that the world (the totality of all entities other than God) which is contingent in nature, derives, by definition, all its perfections from the necessary being.

METAPHYSICA GENERALIS AND METAPHYSICA SPECIALIS

Very few, even among experts in Islamic philosophy, know that the distiniction between Metaphysica Generalis (*Ilahiyyat bi-l mana al-a`amm*) and Metaphysica Specialis (*ilahiyyat bi-l mana al-akhass*) starts and is first encountered with in the works of Avicenna. This distinction is the Avicennian solution to a perennial question in Aristotle hinging upon the question of the subject matter of what later came to be known as metaphysics (this word was never used by Aristotle, for which he used the alternative terms: first philosophy, Sophia or wisdom and theology or he Divine Science.) To the question as to the subject matter of metaphysics, Aristotle gave three different answers; sometimes he said it is being as being (on he on); elsewhere he said it is the first principles and causes (Prote aitiai kai archai); Still in other places he would mention the first substance, i.e. God as the proper subject-matter of metaphysics. Considering the fact that according to Aristotle, a science cannot have more than one subject-matter, the question immediately arose as to which of the three was the proper subject-matter of metaphysics. Almost all the commentators prior to Avicenna, and almost all the modern scholars, believed that, these were different aspects of one subject-matter and tried to prove this fact by appealing to certain principles of the Aristotelian metaphysics. Some argued for example, that as the three different names of metaphysics, referred to, are denominations for one single science, so too, these three apparently different subject-matters point to three different aspects of the one science of metaphysics. Others, in order to prove the unity of the first philosophy, resorted to such well-established metaphysical principles as the analogy of being according to which analogical realities such as the reality of being, have a first instance which ontologically is prior to the rest and which is the cause and the first principle of being as such and in this way tried to unify the three subject-matters into one. According to this theory the first substance (i.e. God) being prior in the order of being, was the supreme cause in the hierarchy of beings and was considered to be the being of all beings.

Avicenna, on the other hand, having studied Aristotle's metaphysics more than forty times was quite skeptical about the solution of his predecessors and offered his own peculiar solution with regard to the mentioned problem. After having axiomatized the science of logic and turned it into a very sharp and rigorous tool for the science of demonstration, he used the methodology of apodictic sciences to find the proper solution of the problem at issue. According to the principles of Avicenna's axiomatized science of logic (which is also the logic of axiomatization), the subject-matter of a science should either be self-evident or should be taken for granted and not to be demonstrated in that science. Two of the themes mentioned to be the subject-matter of metaphysics (God as the first substance; and the first causes and principles of all beings) are the objects of demonstration in metaphysics and so cannot function as its subject-matter. There remains the third option i.e. "being as being" which also being self-evident can be the only subject-matter of the first philosophy. For the first time in the history of philosophy "being as being" is made the subject-matter of what came to be known as Metaphysica Generalis. The existence of God is proved first as a problem in this science and then it is made the subject-matter of another branch of metaphysics called Metaphysica Specialis. Each branch treats about the essential attributes (*al-awarid al-dhatiyyah*) of its proper subject-matter.

The division of metaphysics into Metaphysica Generalis and Metaphysica Specials was accepted by medieval philosophers specially by those who accepted Avicenna's interpretation of the Aristotelian metaphysics particularly by St. Thomas Aquinas. Regarding the fact that Christian Wolff used the term ontologia as an equivalent for general metaphysics and the term theologia as synonymous with the special metaphysics one can safely say that Avicenna was the founder of apodictic science of ontology.

SUHRAWARDI

In Suhrawardi, the problem of being and essence takes a new turn. One might wonder why many ontological distinctions emphasized so much in Avicenna or in peripatetic philosophers are either shelved or are totally obliterated in the illuminationist scheme of metaphysics founded by Suhrawardi. One reason might be that Suhrawardi does not hold that the ratiocinative (*Istidlali*) or the discursive (*bahthi*) philosophy is the highest type as the peripatetic philosophers maintain. Higher than it stands a philosophy which is based on the knowledge by tasting (al-Ilm al-dhawqi) or sapiential knowledge (from the Latin word sapere meaning to taste). Sapiential wisdom which finally ends in theosis (*Ta`alluh*) is much more elevated and exalted in rank than the one based on purely discursive reason. So one might say that the peripatetic metaphysical distinctions such as existence and quiddity, matter and form and the like are obliterated as soon as we leave the domain of ratiocination and conceptualization and rise to the domain of intellectual intuition and sapential cognition.

THE BEING OF SYMBOLS

According to Suhrawardi, sapiential philosophy is distinguished from the discursive by several characteristics which are lacking in the latter:

(a) By the use of what he calls *ramz* (symbolism)
(b) By the theory of illumination;
(c) By their tripartite cosmology;
(d) By their more rigorous and staunch adherence to the metaphysical principle of unity;

(e) By their reinterpretation of ancient philosophers from the new perspective of sapiential philosophy.

A distinctive feature of sapiential wisdom in contrast to discursive philosophy is the use of mythology or symbolism. As in Plato in the Republic where the ascension from *dianoia* to *noesis* requires that we employ the knowledge gained in the former stage as a symbol or as a myth (a word which is cognate with "mystery", and "mystic" and derived from he Greek infinitive "*muein*", to get silent, to stop the psychic activity) in order that by the use of the dialectical method, we may attain to the higher reality, so too in the viewpoint of Suhrawardi, we should make use of *Rumuz* (pl. of *Ramz*) in order to lift ourselves to the vision of the intelligible realities. Again as in Plato, a *Ramz* can never be refuted and its refutation betokens a lack of comprehension on the part of the literalistic demythologizer. One of the criticisms of Suhrawardi against peripatetics and Aristotle in particular, revolves upon the fact that they have made a literal interpretation of ramz found in ancient philosophers and that they have, so to say, demythologized them.

Another characteristic feature of the Sapiential philosophy, according to Suhrawardi, is the use of the theory of illumination for explaining both the origination of the cosmos and the human knowledge. Being itself is interpreted as comprising multiple levels of light from its primordial source which he calls the light of lights (*nur al-anwar*) down to the nether confines of utter darkness.

A third distinctive feature of sapiential philosophy or theosis is their belief in three longitudinal (*Tuli*) worlds (*al-awalim al-Thalath*), emanating from their primordial principle, a theory which according to Suhrawardi was shared by all ancient sages and which is lacking in the peripatetic cosmology.

Another characterstic mark of the companions of theosis (*ashab altalluh*) is their more staunch adherence to the principle of unification (*altauhid*). Could this mean that their metaphysical system is based, not on the concept of being and substance, but rather on the principle of unity and its multiple stages as in Plato and some presocratics who tried to expound all reality on the basis of one ontological principle (*arche*)? Is it not a criticism of Aristotle and the peripatetcs who considered the first principle to be the nous nouon (the intellecting intellect) which already implies some kind of multiplicity? Can it refer to Plato who differentiated between the absolutely simple one (*to hen*) and what he called the "one and many". Be that as it may, this is a very important difference between the two methodologies in philosophy.

Again it makes an obvious difference whether we read, interpret and compare philosophers in the light of sapiential wisdom or in the shadow of discursive philosophy. Viewed from the latter perspective, philosophy started with the Greeks and culminated in Aristotle as Aristotle himself and some of his Muslim commentators especially Averroes believed. From the former viewpoint, which started with Avicenna's oriental philosophy and culminated in Suhrawardi's philosophy of the Orient of Light, philosophy is universal in the sense that it is not the monopoly of a single nation and community and God, the bestower of wisdom is not stingy to deprive all nations but one, from such extremely precious Divine blessing. Viewed from such a vast and glorious panorama, philosophy gets a new lease of life. The presocratics, for example who were considered by Aristotle as elementary physicists (*physilogoi*) who like small children quite haphazardly and by random hit the mark, are regarded by Suhrawardi as the great companions of theosis and prominent representatives of sapiential wisdom and even the companions of Divine ambassadorship. Suhrawardi, moreover, regards all the great Muslim Sufis such as al-Hallaj, Bayazid, Junayd and Sahl-al-Tustari as perfect adepts in sapiential wisdom.

History of philosophy, if written from the sapiential and not merely discursive perspective and as depicted and delineated by Suhrawardi, would, no doubt, be quite different from the present historiography of philosophy as prescribed by Aristotle and Hegel, and would without doubt comprise the great sages of the East as the great representatives of sapiential wisdom.

SADRA'S TRANSCENDENT PHILOSOPHY

The transcendent philosophy is the culmination of the problem of ontology in Islamic philosophy which synthesizes all the main currents with regard to being in almost all schools of thought available to him. Mulla Sadra, the founder of the school has revisited all problems related somehow or other to this issue and after a very critical analysis of the problems, has either offered a very novel solution, has criticized the unacceptable theories before him; has elaborated on the ambiguous premises, or at least reformulated the solution in a more rigorous and philosophical fashion. Many are his great contributions to the problem of ontology. Owing to the shortage of time and space we will have to do only with a few of them.

Mir Damad, Mulla Sadra's mentor and tutor had raised a new problem in ontology. If all entities in the world are rationally analyzable into being or existence (*wujud*) and quiddity (*mahiyyah*) the problem naturally arises as to which of the two is prior in the order of intellection considering the fact that both of them cannot share in priority. Mir Damad is said to have opted for the priority of the quiddities, a theory which came to be known as *asalah al-mahiyyah* (the principiality of the quiddities). Mulla Sadra on the contrary has opted for the principality of existence and has offered some proofs for his claim including the fact that a quiddity is identically the same both in the mind and in the external world. What differentiates the two, is their mode of existence in the mind and of the external existence outside the mind.

Again in Mulla Sadra a distinction is made between the notion (*mafhum*) of existence and its reality. The notion of existence as a secondary intelligible is the most universal of concepts, very rich in connotation but extremely poor in extension and denotation. The reality of existence, on the contrary, is the richest and the most concrete in denotation. With regard to the issue at stake, that is the principality of being, the priority should be predicated of the reality, rather than the mere notion of existence.

Man occupies a very special and distinctive rung in the ladder of existence. Mulla Sadra has proffered a very superb account of Dasien or the existence of man which can be considered the best of its kind which unfortunately has been cast in utter oblivion. A major theme in Mulla Sadra's ontology of Dasein is that in man too, his existence takes precedence over his essence. Mulla Sadra time and again reiterates the fact that man as such has no fixed and stereotyped essence. He is what he makes of himself. In reference to a Quranic verse which refers to the fact that man was created in the best constitution and stature and then he was cast into "the lowest of the low", Mulla Sadra comments that man can decide to become anything from the "highest of the high" to "the lowest of the low". In other words man is the maker and the artificer of his own essence, a theme taken over, out of its context, by the modern existentialists.

For Mulla Sadra, the transcendent philosophy (*al-Hikmat alMutaaliyah*) is the best way to reach up from the lowest of the low to the "highest of the high". Another way is a sapiential understanding of the esoteric wisdom embedded in religions. In order to attain to this supreme wisdom four intellectual journeys are necessary:

1. A journey from the creatures to the creator (or from multiplicity to unity or from the manifoldness of phenomena to the Absolute Reality (*alhaqq*))

2. A journey in the Real by the Real (in God through and by God) 3. A third journey which in contrast to the first one is from the Real to the creatures by the Real (from God to creatures by God)

4. The fourth journey which in contrast with the second one, is a journey in creatures with God. By accomplishing the four intellectual journeys, one gets a Divine vision of things and one gets assimilated unto God as much as it is humanly possible. For Mulla Sadra like for Plato, the way of philosophy presupposes, but is quite different from that of all sciences. For Plato as for Mulla Sadra all sciences somehow or other use discursive reasoning. But for the one, the four intellectual journeys and for the other the practice of dialectics are not requisite for the sciences, but are essential and absolutely necessary for practicing philosophy. Ontology, epistemology, eschatology, cosmology and philosophical anthropology, which constitute the main sections of Mulla Sadra's books and treatises find a new lease of life when understood in the light of philosophy in the abovementioned sense.

THE PHENOMENOLOGY OF MIND

One of the greatest pitfalls which Muslim philosophers have always been on their guard to avoid was the problem of subjectivism. Mulla sadra opened a new chapter in ontology under the rubric of "existence of the mind" or simply "mental existence" (*al-wujud al-dhihni*).

Some schools of thought in Islam, such as the Asharites and some of them in the West as some dogmatic theologians and generally speaking almost all philosophers who deny the validity and the authenticity of reason, (i.e. all anti-rationalists) and again all epipheno-mentalists deny the independent existence of the mind. Mulla Sadra gives some proofs to demonstrate that the mind is an independent reality quite different from the body and the bodily functions.

There are many things, for example, which we conceive in our minds which by definition cannot exist in the external world. For example, to state the principle of non-contradiction we have first to conceive it in our minds and evidently the principle does not exist outside the mind, so the mind should have a prior existence in order to conceive it. Such is again the case with the concept of non-existence which by definition cannot have an extramental reality. There are moreover universal and necessary propositions which are always and everywhere true. They cannot be derived from mere experience, because empirical propositions are contingent. So universal propositions, being rational, rather than empirical, are always perceived by our intellects, or in other words by our minds. Such is the case again with the universal concepts which are essential for the possibility of their being an apodeictic and demonstrative science. Mulla Sadra expatiates on the subject and responds to all the putative objections. Mulla Sadra has perused a vast literature regarding the question at issue, which is rather sporadic and sparse and our philosopher has meticulously analyzed the texts and has answered all their real or supposed objections. The upshot is demonstrative proofs for the existence of the mind and the laws governing it. But the problem of the mind can be viewed from another angle, that is from the viewpoint of transcendent philosophy. Viewed from this vantage point, the human soul is an exemplification of the Divinity. It belongs not to the world of corporeal substances, but to the world of Divine command and hence being Divine it is able to create ex nihilo. The human soul has all attributes of God such as knowledge, power, volition, life and speech. There are even some sages and saints who can create things in the outer world through mere intentionality just as common people can create images in their faculty of imagination.

ANTI-VOLUNTARISM

Voluntarism, in my understanding of the term, is the belief in the priority or the precedence of the will (or volition) over knowledge. The problem first started in Islamic thought as a theological question. God has infinite attributes of which seven, called the Mother of Names (*ummahat alasma*) are the most significant (comprising life, knowledge, volition, power, speech, seeing, hearing). Even if all the infinite Names are actually present in God, but the question is: which of them is logically prior to the rest in the sense that it is presupposed by them. All philosophers and almost all Sufis believe in the primacy of knowledge. Most dogmatic theologians especially the Asharites believe in the logical priority of the Divine volition. A corollary of this theory is that there are no eternal truths, because eternal truths are not the objects of Divine knowledge but rather of Divine volition; he could have willed them otherwise.

This problem can be traced back to Plato's Euthyphro which is a dialogue on piety. In response to Socrates' question as to what piety is, Euthyphro answers by saying that "piety is that which all the gods like." Then Socrates poses the further question: "is piety good because gods like it or do gods like it because it is in itself good?" to which Euthyphro rejoins by saying that piety is good because the gods have willed them.

Essences or quiddities as well as eternal verities are the objects of Divine knowledge and God could not have made them otherwise. In Islamic philosophy this problem is known as j`al (or making). The principle states that the objects of Divine volition are not the reality of things which eternally exist in the Divine mind. Divine volition only wills the being of things or existentiates the realities which eternally pre-exist in the Divine knowledge.

There has been a tortuous trend of voluntarism in modern western philosophy. In an interesting article by Emile Brehier entitled "The Creation of Eternal Truths in Descartes' System" he has convincingly shown by producing copious illustrations that according to Descartes God has created the eternal truths and he could have created them otherwise. In other words eternal truths are the objects of Divine volition and not his primordial and eternal knowledge, a theory which would have been repugnant to Muslim sages. Similar kinds of voluntarism can be detected in Kant, Hume, Schopenhauer, Nietzche and many others.

CHAPTER XXIII

KORAN EPISTEMOLOGY AND SCIENTIFIC DISCOURSE

In contrast to the Christian world where concordism had not received official support and, in fact, disappeared from the scene from the middle of the last century, modern and contemporary Islam is characterized by ever more loud statements about the unity of the Koran and science and the essential harmony between them. Scientistic interpretations of the Scripture are becoming ever more widespread, with more finds of the anticipation of some or other scientific discoveries, which is sometimes seen as further evidence of its divine origin. Vigorous efforts are being made to develop a "theology of science", "Islamic philosophy/epistemology of science," and similar plans for "Islamization of science" and "Islamization of knowledge". The initial guidelines here are primarily appropriate passages in the Koran regarding the relationship between faith/religion and reason/knowledge that were developed in the prophetic Tradition (Sunna) and the work of Muslim thinkers of the classical age. Below, we will focus on some of these major guidelines, considering them from the reformistmodernizing point of view.

The Cult of Knowledge

Arab-Islamic literature designates science/scholarship by the term *'ilm*, which also refers to knowledge in general. Contributing to the flourishing of science in the Muslim world of the classical age was the cult of knowledge, which had come into being thanks primarily to the intellectualist provision of the Koran and Sunna.

Symbolically, the first word uttered by Archangel Gabriel to Muhammad as he called upon him to start his prophetic ministry, was "Read!" and that the initial lines of the first (in chronological order) chapter of the Koran praised God as the creator who taught man to read and write (96:1-5). The next chapter (68th), too, opens with God's oath with the weapons of writing - ink and pen.

Expressions like "contemplate", "delve", "do they not understand", "for people who understand" appear in the Koran like a refrain, and, moreover, the word *'ilm* and its cognates appear in more than 750 verses of the Scripture (with its total number of verses being 6,236). Still more, there are there hundreds of instances of the use of words with close meanings, such as *'aql, fiqh, fikr*, etc.

God points to the superiority of knowledge/reason in such Koran revelations as "Are those equal, those who know and those who do not know?!" (39:9); "God will raise up, to high ranks, those of you who believe and those who have been given knowledge" (58:11). Commenting on the last verse, one of the Prophet's companions, Ibn-Abbas, said that "the knowers (*'ulama'*) are superior to the believers (*mu'minun*) by seventy steps, with a five hundred years of walking between each of them."

Also noteworthy is a story in the Koran about the creation of the first people which presents Adam as a person endowed with great knowledge in "naming beings;" this, according to some interpreters, symbolizes the ability of the human race to comprehend rationally the nature of things. It was due to this ability of his that God commanded the angels to bow down before Adam (2:30-34).

Fairly common (although not included in the six canonical sets) is the "tradition about intellect" (*hadith al-'aql*), whereby the first thing God created was intellect. And he said to him: "Turn around to face me", and he turned. Then he said to him: "Turn your back to me", and he turned. And God spoke: "I swear by my majesty that I did not create anything that was closer to me than you. With you I take away, with you I bestow, with you I reward and punish".

The Prophet called scholars (*'ulama'*) heirs of the prophets. He declared the search for knowledge/science "the duty of every Muslim man and woman", and spoke about studies as a continuous process that lasts "from cradle to grave" and requires courage in the search for wisdom, "even in far-off China". Widely circulated among the people of classical Islam was also the following of his sayings: "An hour of reflection (*tafakkur*) is better than a whole year of worship (*'ibada*)"; "On Judgment Day, the ink of scholars is equated to (version: 'outweighs') the blood of martyrs."

These commandments of the Koran and Sunnah account, first and foremost, for the fact that American researcher F. Rosenthal remarks in the conclusion to his book *Knowledge Triumphant*: "In Islam, the concept of knowledge enjoyed an importance unparalleled in other civilizations".1

Koran intellectualism found a vivid expression in the main trend of Islamic philosophical theology, *Kalam*, the two schools of which (Mutazilites and Asharites-Maturidites) held that the first duty of a Muslim was to practice rational speculation (*nazar*). Such a revival of pietism for knowledge/intellect and, simultaneously, for science, is what contemporary modernists-reformers have been advocating.

Rationality of Doctrine

Underlying the basic tenets of reformed theology of science is the premise that the Koran/Muslim faith does not encompass any provisions

---

1 F. Rosenthal. *Knowledge Triumphant.* Leiden: Brill, 1970. P.334.

that could not be justified by human reason2.

In its polemics with the pagans, the Koran demanded from them "evidence" (*burhan*) in favor of their (21:24; 27:64) doctrine of the plurality of gods (21:24, 27:64). A maximum willingness to accept any conclusive opinion is expressed in the Koran revelation to the effect that the Prophet was commanded to declare: "If...God had a son, I would be the first to worship" (43:81). It is also noteworthy that verse 23:117 threatens those appealing to other gods besides God with the Lord's punishment in the event that evidence of their existence is not provided.

The Scriptures also commanded its followers "to call into the Lord's path with the help of wisdom" (*hikma*) (16:125), i.e., with methods of rational persuasion. In fact, the Koran lists rational arguments in favor of the main principles of faith, such as the existence of God (e.g., 2:164, 50:20, 67:1-4), His uniqueness (17:42, 21:22, 23:91), the revelation of Books, the erection of prophets (2:213; 5:19; 6:91), the resurrection of the dead (18:48, 36:78-79, 46:33), and the afterlife reward (10:4, 20:15; 38: 28). A purely intellectual and philosophical basis underlies the Muslim doctrine created by the Mutakallims (masters of Kalam).

The Koran *intellectualizes* miracles (*mu'jiza*), which is a traditional way of corroborating the truth of prophetic missions and their heavenly origin. Although the Muslim Scripture does mention the supernatural miracles revealed by the earlier prophets (in particular, the staff of Moses that was transformed into a dragon, the healing by Jesus of the desperately ill and even the resurrection from the dead), the founder of Islam flatly refused to submit to his pagan opponents similar miraculous signs that violated the natural order of things; instead, he preferred signs of a completely different kind - the Book, the Koran (2:23, 11:13, 17:88).

In line with this rational reorientation, the modernists-reformers interpret the Koran description of the Prophet Muhammad as *khatam annabiyyn* (litteraly: "seal of the prophets", 33:40), i.e., the one who closed the long line of prophetic messages. Islam came into the world when mankind had already reached a degree of intellectual maturity that no longer called for the old and rather primitive ("prophetic", "sacred-revelatory") forms of communion with God and the attainment of truth. From that time on, mankind had to rely on reason and its ability to adequately read and interpret the Great Book, the Book of Nature.

In using the word *ayat* to denote not only the verses of the Koran, but also an individual natural phenomenon (e.g., 2:164, 41:53), the Muslim Scripture seems to be pointing at the unity of the two scriptures - the Koran and the cosmos, as two forms of God's revelation. Also symbolically, the Koran uses the word '*ilm,* indicating science, is also used in reference to God's revelation for the benefit of the prophets (e.g., 2:120, 247; 3:19, 19:43, 27:42).

---

2 This fact has been already noted, although in polemical context, by Thomas Aquinas in his "Summa contra gentiles" (I:6).

Being united at their source, these two scriptures - together with religion and science - cannot conflict with one another. In the case of apparent contradiction between the revelational / scriptural and rational/scientific, one has to appeal to the methodology of allegorical interpretation (*ta'wil*) sanctioned by the Koran (see 3:7).

The World's Orderness

One of the most fundamental principles of the Koran worldview is the idea of improving the Universe and its consistent pattern.

According to the Koran, God is "the Best to create" who "disposed of all things in perfect order» (23:14; 27:88). In his creation, "no want of proportion wilt thou see. So turn thy vision again: seest thou any flaw? Again turn the vision a second time: thy vision will come back to thee dull and discomfited, in a state worn out" (67:3-4).

The Scripture emphasized repeatedly that God created all phenomena of nature as "signs" (*ayat*) of His wisdom and all-good. He proportioned all things (25:2, 54:49), has invested in them "guidelines" (*hidaya*) and "nature" (*fitra*) (30:30; 50:20; 87:3), i.e., laws of behavior. And these laws are constant and unchanging (30:30, 35:43, 48:23). In this sense, nature is autonomous, but not autocratic, as it has existence only through God, who can destroy it at will.

The order prevailing in the world is a reliable prerequisite for scientific and cognitive activity. In revealing this order all the deeper, science, in turn, is intended to establish in the minds the idea of God as its giver. One can assume the order in the universe without believing in God the Creator, of course. But it is difficult without the idea of God to explain the existence of such an order.

Vice-regency of Man...

The need for scientific knowledge is dictated by the main principles of the Muslim view of man's destination and mission in the world.

First of all, it is the principle of vice-regency (*istikhlaf, khilafa*): man is created as a vice-regent (*khalifa)* of God on earth, and control of the outside world has been given to him in trust (*amana*) (2:30, 6:165, 10: 14, 35:39). Therefore, man is called to transform the world, to bring civilization to it (*'imara*, 11:61), to create conditions for a more secure life and a greater freedom from natural factors - all in order to rise and come closer to the Creator. And this is only possible in case of an orientation toward scientific methodology and technology that pave the way to discovering the laws of nature.

Closely linked with the idea of vice-regency is the principle of subservience (*taskhir*). For the sake of serving man, God provided "all things in the heavens and on earth" (31:20; 45:13); the sun and moon, day and night (14:33, 16:12), the sea and the rivers (14:32, 16:14, 45:12), etc. It is only through science that man can adequately implement this principle.

The most fundamental of Islamic principles regarding life is the principle of moderation (*wasatiyya*)/balance (*tawazun*) between the spiritual and corporeal. The Koran calls the Muslim community (*umma*) a just moderated community (2:143), because it is designed to avoid extremes that had befallen other religions and civilizations which cultivated either materialism or spiritualism/asceticism. In line with the Koran admonition to "seek the Home of the Hereafter, nor forget thy portion in this World" (28:77), the Prophet Muhammad taught: "The best of you is not the one who neglects the earth for the sake of heaven, nor the one who does the opposite; the best of you is the one who takes from both." Achieving the right balance is only possible with the help of scientific methods and facts put to practical application.

Universalism

Koran monotheism (*tawhid*) involves the concept of the unity of mankind: in metaphysical terms (people as creatures of one God are called to serve him), in ethnic terms (all come from the common ancestors - Adam and Eve), and in prophetological/soteriological terms (the prophets were established to all the peoples, and following them ensures happiness in this world and in the other). Consequently, the revelational element is present not only in the three monotheistic religions (Islam, Christianity, Judaism), but also in other religions, which creates favorable conditions for openness in relation to them.

In addition, the Koran points out that religious, ethnic and cultural pluralism was established by God and thus - forever (2:213, 11:118-119, 30:22). Such a variety helps to promote a situation "that you may know [better] one another" and "so compete with one another in good works", human solidarity, harmony and mutual enrichment (2: 148, 5:2, 48; 49:13), including the scientific sphere. Meanwhile, the Prophet Muhammad taught: "Wisdom is a cherished dream of the faithful, wherever he may find it he ought to take it", and "Take wisdom from the lips of even the heathen". His saying about searching for knowledge "even in China" can be understood in terms of teaching science and other secular disciplines.

With this universalist orientation, classical Islamic civilization accumulated the scientific achievements of other cultural areas. It is in the framework of this civilization that for the first time in human history, science has become international, having united under its banner scientists of different nationalities and faiths.

Freedom of Intelligent Search

Freedom of scientific work ensues from the principle of freedom of belief/religion, as enunciated, inter alia, in verse 2:256, "Let there be no compulsion in religion: truth stands out clear from error", and 18:29, "Say: [it is] truth from your Lord. Whosoever will, let him believe and whosoever will, let him reject [it]".

The Koran also requires that its followers exhibit goodwill to the dissenters and avoid suspicion, "Oh, ye who believe! Avoid suspicion as much [as possible]: for the suspicion in some cases is a sin" (49:12). Quite widespread in classical theology was the following principle: "If the opinion of an opponent admits ninety-nine possibilities of interpretation in terms of heresy (*kufr*) and at least one possibility of denying it, one ought to give in to the latter".

In addition, starting from the Koran revelations ("On no soul doth God place a burden greater than it can bear...Our Lord! Condemn us not if we forget or fall into [unconscious] error", 2:286); "There is no blame on you if ye make a [unconscious] mistake: [what counts is] the intention of your hearts", 33:5; etc.) and the Sunna ("If a judge, applying [all his cognitive] efforts, takes the right decision, he is [entitled to] a double reward, if he makes a wrong decision, he [is entitled to one] award - [for the hard work]"); theologians of the classical era formulated the position: *almujtahid ma'zur, "mujtahid* (i.e., a man who takes all his cognitive efforts) deserves an apology [if he makes a mistake]".

However, such a tolerant attitude is usually related only to matters of practical theology (*fiqh*) or secondary provisions of dogma. Yet there were theologians lenient to any *mujtahid* no matter what the issue might be practical or theoretical, fundamental or private. Following in their footsteps, many modern reformers advocate a tolerant attitude towards all diligent seekers of truth. Sometimes, they interpret in this sense verse 29:69, "And those who strive in searching Us, - We will certainly guide them to our paths".

As for scientific fields proper, Islamic civilization did not know the practice of limiting anyone's freedom to seek knowledge on account of incompatibility with religion.

Methodological Skepticism

The Koran calls upon its adherents to think critically and decry epigonism (*taqlid*), i.e., blind adherence to views inherited from the past (2:170, 43:22-24) or propagated by opinion leaders (33:67).

The principle of methodological doubt is founded in the following Koran verse describing Abraham's desire to ascertain the truth of resurrection: "My Lord! Show me how Thou givest life to the dead./ - Dost thou not then believe!?/- Y ea! But to satisfy my own heart./- Take four birds; cut them into pieces, then put them on every hill, and call to them: they will come to thee [flying] with speed", (2:260). "To doubt (*shakk*) we have more rights than Abraham", ran the comment on this verse by the Prophet Muhammad at some time.

The Sunna also tells us how some Muslims complained to the Prophet about doubts that sometimes plagued their souls, to which he remarked: "This is the true faith!"

Based on these provisions, the Mutakallims (Mutazilites and Asharites-Maturidites) taught that doubt was a necessary precondition of genuine faith and true knowledge. Some of them, moreover, even declared skepticism the first religious duty of Muslims.

Even Mutazilites applied, in their time, the principle of doubt to the scientific field proper.

Thus, al-Jahiz conducted experiments on animals to test some of the provisions of Aristotelian zoology, al-Jubbai wrote several treatises in refutation of the same natural views of Aristotle. It was in this context that al-Biruni said: "The Mutazilites tend to refute what is generally accepted".

Practical Orientation

The fundamental importance of the practical (moral and ethical as well as technological) side of science derives from the Koran's central idea of the unity of belief (*iman*) and deeds (*'amal*). The prophet Muhammad instructed his companions to pray to God for the gift of "beneficial knowledge" (*'ilm nafi'*), and himself often cried, "God, forbid me from knowledge that is not good!"

True learning involves high morality and piety. In this sense, the Koran teaches: "Only the scholars / learned among his people truly fear God" (35:28). Hence, the imperative of the moral responsibility of men of science (35:28).

Following the Koran guidance on useful knowledge, scholars of classical Islam sought to overcome the largely speculative nature of ancient Greek science and to join science and practice, theoretical knowledge and technical activities. Related to this was their interest in experimentation. Some Mutazilites were even accused of "preferring experiments on dogs and roosters to prayer and reading the Koran". In fact, the foundation of experimental science were laid in the work of Mutazila scholars (al-Jahiz and an-Nazzam) and later the Asharite ones (Ibn-al-Haytham and al-Biruni) long before they appeared in Western Europe.

(Translated from Russian by Serge Gitman)

CHAPTER XXIV

PHILOSOPHY AND SCIENCE IN ISLAM: AN OUTLOOK

The worl 'Islam' in the title denotes both Islam as religion and as civilization; because Islamic religion and Islamic civilization are essentially connected with each other from every point of view. Two sources of Islam, the Qur'an which is God's revelation and Prophet Mohammed's Tradition (Sunnah) which is a firsthand interpretation of the Qur'an, are two main sources of that is called today Islamic Philosophy and Islamic Science; and no doubt they are deeply rooted in those sources. For, from the very beginning the Muslims have regarded it as the project of civilization. The Qur'an is an admonition to all people for ever. Islamic philosophy is profoundly rooted in it; obviously it is not a book of philosophy, nor one of science. Nevertheless Muslim philosophers made considerable use of it to lend weight to the philosophical views and doctrines. The Qur'an was and still is considered to be rational and to contain a message inviting people to reason and speculate; as it is well known.

Franz Rosenthal very rightly pointed out that undeniable fact by saying that "'Ilm (knowledge) is Islam."1 And that we could add without hesitation: Islam is knowledge. Since the Qur'an, being a very different, in content, of any sort of holy books, does not only speak of religious matters as such but also nearly all things of universe from small things like a mosquito to a biggest thing like sun, stars, oceans and so on. So, as we have mentioned above we Muslims consider the Qur'an as the project of civilization. Undoubtedly, the Qur'an is not a book of philosophy or of science as such, but it gives a lot of information concerning man, nature, and natural and human histories. Then it asks man to think about God, nature and history by and with every like the eye, ear, reason and heart in order to understand that which is. Therefore many verses of the Qur'an end: to look at, think about, reason on, understand, mediate, and remember?

But, despite this, some western thinkers of the nineteenth century like V. Cousin, for example, denied the very existence of Islamic Philosophy and Islamic Science and maintained that the teachings of Islam opposed to all free discussion and investigation, and therefore Islam has never risen to aid philosophy and science throughout the centuries of its existence.2 No doubt those western thinkers have simulated Islam to the Christianity of Medieval

---

1 F. Rosenthal, *Knowledge Triumphant* (Leiden: E. J. Brill, 1970), p. 2. 2 V. Cousin, *Cours de l'Histoire de la Philosophie* (Paris: Didier, 1841), pp. 48-49.

Popes with a great ignorance. In fact knowledge, philosophy and science, was the very foundation of the rise of Islamic civilization. That is why, as Franz Rosenthal again said, knowledge is one of those concepts that have dcompared Islam as religion and as civilization, and given it their distinctive characteristics and complexion. In fact there is no other concept that has been operative as a determinant of Islamic philosophy and science in all their aspects to the same extent as *Ilm* (knowledge).3

This is not to deny the fact that Islamic Philosophy and Science have been influenced by foreign sources, mostly by Greek philosophy. But this is not simply imitation and repetition of Greek philosophy as some orientalists have wrongly pretended; the first of these was a French orientalist E. Renan, who had said once that Semitic race has no ability to produce philosophy and science.4 But when he wrote an "Avertissement" for a later edition of his famous book "Averroes et l'Averroisme" he said the Arabs have an original philosophy. Thus Renan contradicted himself like many others. It is unfortunate that it was not Renan's later judgement, but his previous racial prejudice, which had an effect on other later generation orientalists, including Léon Gauthier, Th. J. De Boer, R. Rudolf Walzer and J. David Carson.

Fortunately there are a number of orientalists who did not in the past and do not today share that fallacious opinion of the first group of orientalists. One among them is Henry Corbin, he finds even worth talking of any foreign source for Islamic Philosophy other than the Qur'an itself; and speaking of the origins of Islamic thought says "La question ne sera pas de discuter ce que les occidentaux trouvent ou ne trouvent pas dans le Qur'an mais de savoir ce que les Musulmans y ont trouvé en fait..."5

Islamic Philosophy can be differently defined, but as the name implies it refers to the philosophy produced by the Muslim thinkers within the framework of Islamic culture and milieu. The birth of speculative thought in the Muslim World began as early as the lifetime of the Prophet Mohammed himself. After the death of the Prophet Muhammed in 632, early Muslims were faced with so many religious and socio-political problems, and in order to solve them they put forward so many different thoughts and there came into existence different sects. Their birth paved the way for more philosophical thinking.

But the pure philosophy (*al-falsafa*) which is in fact an Arabic rendering of the Greek world "philosophia" started to flourish with the establishment of the Baytu'l Hikma by the Abbaside caliph al-Ma'mûn in 829; and from this date onward the translation movement into Arabic was

3 F. Rosenthal, *Knowledge Triumphant* (Leiden: E. J. Brill, 1970), p. 2. 4 E. Renan, *Historie Générale et Systeme Comparé des Langues Sémitiques* (Paris: Imprimerie impériale, 1855), pp. 3-10.

5 H. Corbin, "La Philosophy Islamique des Origines a la Mort d'Averroes," *Historie de la Philosophy,* ed. by B. Parain (Paris: Gallimard, 1969), vol. I, p. 1048.

accelerated under the patronage of the same caliph. Mainly Greek philosophical and scientific texts had been translated into Arabic. That translation movement enriched, no doubt, the rising Islamic thought in terms of quantitative and qualitative development in the following centuries. Islamic Philosophy in its broader sense can encompass pure philosophy, theology (*kalâm*), sufism and methodological aspects of Islamic jurisprudence; and its main schools of philosophy can be classified as follows:

- Rational Theology: What is call today Islamic theology was from the very beginning a rational movement. Although religiously motivated Islamic theology dealt with so many problems of the times from economic to philosophical. Especially with the rise of Mu'tazila it became a philosophically oriented theology. It is true that many theologians have criticized the Greek way of philosophizing and philosophy mainly for its metaphysical assumptions. Nonetheless, Islamic theology can be regarded as an original and creative philosophy. Indeed, some Muslims and orientalists, like G. Dugat and Ibrahim Madkhur for example considered Islamic theology as an original creation of Muslim thinkers and Islamic culture. Amongst the most important schools of theology are Mu'tazilisme, Asharitisme, Maturidisme and Shiisme.

- Peripatetic Philosophy: This is what is properly called alMashshâ'iyya. Peripatetic philosophy as the name implies refers to the Aristotelian way of philosophizing in the Islamic milieu. Of course, this does not mean that Muslim Philosophers have only been influenced by Aristotle; in addition, Socrates, Plato, Plotinus and some of the Hellenistic philosophers were well known to Muslim philosophers. The majority of eminent Muslim philosophers, such as al-Kindi, al-Farabi, Ibn Sina, Ibn Bajja and Ibn Rushd are representatives of this school.

- Illuminative Philosophy: Another important school of philosophy is al-Ishrâkiyya initiated by a famous philosopher Shihabu'd-Din Yahya asSuhrawardi, in the twelfth century. We could incorporate in it intellectual mystical movements such as *wahdat al-wujûd* (unity of excistence), *wahdat al-shuhûd* (unity of witnessing) and *wahdat al-Qusûd* (unity of willing). Illuminative philosophy is qualified by some modern scholars as perennial philosophy. Ibn al-Arabî, Dawûd al-Qaysarî, Isma'il al-Ankarawî, al-Jilî and Molla Sadra as sufis and philosophers are some of the important thinkers of this school.

Although Islamic philosophy, especially the peripatetic school took many ideas from the Greek heritage, Muslim Philosophers have developed, reshaped and enriched those Greek ideas in such way that they became Islamic as they themselves originated and created uncountable new concepts, ideas and thoughts. Here, of course, we have not enough time and space to recall all of their original contributions. We will restrict ourselves to a few examples.

As it is known, Muslim peripatetics took the principle of causality from Aristotles for example; but they inverted the order of Aristotle's four causes, by puting on the top the efficient cause as the first cause, being in the third rang the Aristotles. For them it is God who can be the first and ultimate cause of everything. Some Muslim thinkers, like Abû Hâtim alRazi, have added to the four causes one more, which they had named as "instrumental cause". Ibn Sinâ (Avicenna) and al-Farabi, for example, adopted Plotinus' cosmology; but changed the nature of the absolute One of Plotinus into Allah. The absolute One of Plotinus does not think of nothing, even of himself whereas al-Farabi and Ibn Sina's One is necessarily thinking as having the necessary attribute of thinking; He thinks Himself as well as the created beings. Otherwise the One could not be active and efficient; the One of Islam or Allah cannot be in potentiality. As Th. J. de Boer pointed out, 6 al-Farâbi was the first to bring to our attention the problem of "ante rem", "in re" and "post rem". When this idea of al-Farâbi passed to western Middle Age theologians and philosophers, they started to discuss the issue whence such movements as realism, conceptualism and nominalism came into existence. Again al-Farâbi was the first to make the distinction between analytical and synthetical concepts long before Leibniz and Kant. No doubt al-Farâbi is the pioneer of Kant for the idea that existence is not predicative at all. Ibn Sinâ has also many contributions and innovations. He was the first to make a clear distinction between essence and existence. For Ibn Sinâ, the center of thinking man's personal identity is soul or spirit. In order to prove this Ibn Sinâ used a parable of flying man (al-insânu'tâ'îr), the same parable is also used by Descartes for his "cogito ergo sum" and we could say that Descates was inspired by Ibn Sina.7 And here is one more example from Ibn Sina; in order to refute the inniatism of Plato he says that man's mind is by birth empty like a white sheet of paper. This is nothing but J. Locke's "tabula rasa".

As for al-Gazâli, he is also a very innovative philosopher or theologian philosopher famous for his severe criticisim of peripatetic metaphysics. Among his original ideas and thoughts is occasionalism, which is indeed very similar to that of Malebrache. The existential and ethical optimism of his "This world is the best possible world," is verbally repeated by Leibniz. And there is no doubt, al-Ghazali is the pioneer of Pascal's "Pari de Pascal". Al-Ghazali is also famous for his rejection of the theory of natural causality. Like D. Hume later on, Al Gazali maintains that what is called cause or causality is but a mere impression deriving from the habit of observing phenomena as being necerrariliy linked. These few examples show how Islamic thought is original and independent from Greek heritage in many respects.

---

6 Tjitze J. de Boer, *De, History of Philosophy in Islam*, eng. transl. by E. R. Jones (New York: Dover Publ., 1967), p. 113.

7 S. van den Bergh, *Die Epitome der Meta physiks des Averroes* (Leiden: Brill, 1924)

Among interpretations of Islamic philosophy by contemporary western scholars is that of Henry Corbin, which seems too allegorical, esoteric and mystical. One consequence of his interpretation is that everything must be read rather in sacred terms in the sense of Shiite and especially Isma'ili concept. The second interpretation is put forward by Leo Strauss, according to whom everything must be read in a negative sense. He imagines that Muslim philosophers were normally persecuted for their ideas by theologians and *ulamâ*. This led Muslim philosophers to disguise their true opinions either by paying lip service to religious truths or through a technique of writing designated to divert the hostile attentions. Third is the interpretation of some of the USSR's orientalists, Russian and Muslim who represented many Muslim philosophers, from al-Farabi to Ibn Khaldûn, as socialists, materialists and atheists. Of course for us no one of such interpretation is is acceptable and correct as a general interpretation of Islamic philosophy or Muslim philosophers.

It is not possible for us to adequately discuss the relationship of Islamic philosophy with modern European philosophy here and speak of the chain of ideas that relate these two.

4. Philosophy of Science: Let us now return to Islamic science and to say few things concerning its nature and characteristics. Islamic science in its formative period in the ninth century was also influenced from foreign heritages, especially from the Greek. But Muslim scientists rejected sooner the Greek philosophy of science which they found very theoretical and speculative; a scientist like al-Birûni even found it mythological. Therefore, they established a new philosophy of science, whose minute methods and approaches are observation, experiment and quantitative empiricism. As a matter of fact they have not only corrected some Greek scientific theories but also accomplished many new scientific ideas, discoveries and innovations in medicine, mathematics, astronomy, physics, chemistry and technology.

We cannot enumerate here all the valuable scientific contributions of Muslim scientists. But in order to show their creativeness in different fields of science we would like to give some examples. The famous mathematician al-Kharizmi was the first to use "zero" as number. By proving the wrongness of the fifth postulate of Euclid, Nasiru'din Tûsi established anti-Euclidian geometry long before modern mathematicians. Some north african Muslim mathematicians, such as Ibnu'l Banna and alQalasadi invented modern numerals that Europeans called "Arabic Numerals", as well as algebraic signs and denotations. Spherical trigonometry, which properly speaking did not exist among the Greeks was introduced and developed by al-Battani and Thabit ibn al-Qurrâ.

Al-Birûni and other Muslim astronomers severely criticized Ptolemy's planetary model and almost established a new model which is very similar to that of Copernicus; that is to say a heliocentric system. AlBattani discovered the movements of the sun's apogee. Ibn Rush is the first scientist to observed solar spots. Ibn Sina is said to have employed an air thermometer. And Ibn Yunûs certainly did use the pendulum for the measurement of time. The Muslim astronomers determined with remarkable accuracy the procession of the exquinoxes and the movement of planets which were quite unknown to the Greeks. As Columbus himself said it in one of his letters, his voyage was made possible by Ibn Rush's geographical and astronomical teachings and with al-Battani's Tables Regiomontanus that constructed the Ephemerides.

As to the field of physics and optics Muslim scientists also made many important contributions. Ibnu'l-Haytham (Alhazan of Latins) Haytham) was the first to established the correct theory of vision; and he was the pioneer for Kepler's Laws of reflection and refraction of light. AlBirûni was the first scientist to speak of universal gravitation.

In the field of chemistry, the first name to be mentioned is Geber of westerns, Jâbir ibn Hayyam. He made chemistry as an empirical science and was to first to discover nitric acid, sulphuric acid, silver nitrate and aqua regain in which gold and silver could be dissolved. Here let us remember again the name of al-Birûni; because he was the first to use a kind of hydrostatic balance, known as "Picnometer" in the West, for the determination of specific gravity of minerals.

Muslims, scientists also contributed a lot to medicine and pharmacology. The eminent physician Abû Bakr Zakariyya ar-Râzî (Rhazes of Latins) was the first to distinguish between small-pox and measles. The princes of physicians Ibn Sinâ was the first to make distinguish the kinds of meningitis. And his famous disciple Ibn Nafs discovered the small blood circulation, which is transmitted by Michal Servitor to the West in the sixteenth century. Small-pox vaccine has been practiced since the fifteenth century in Istanbul. Lady Montagu has transmitted it from Istanbul to London in 1718 as she herself narrated in her Letters. As far as we know, to cure some mental desires, al-Kindi and Ibn Sinâ are said to have used music.

These few examples that we have just mentioned suffice to show that like Islamic Philosophy, Islamic science is also original and not merely a repetition of Greek heritage. Though some orientalists have pretended that after the death of Ibn Rushd in 1198 philosophical investigation in the Muslim World is died. What is true is that no real Aristotelian, like Ibn Rushd, who has spent his whole life to interpret Aristotles, emerged any more in the Islamic World. But philosophical and scientific activities survived long after his death that so many historians said, the period between the tenth and fifteenth centuries was the Golden Age of Islamic Philosophy and Islamic Science.

On the other hand, both Islamic Science and Philosophy have played twofold undeniable important role in the history of mankind and notably in the history of Europeans. The first is that Islamic philosophy and science preserved the Greek heritage in Arabic translation from loss and transmitted it to medieval Europe through Latin translations. Since early western Christian authorities found Greeco-Roman thought pagan and then dangerous for the Christian faith, they did not permit its teaching in schools; and in the year 529 they asked the emperor Justinianus I to close the Athenian School. Indeed he exiled seven Neo-Platonist philosophers from Athens.

The second and most important role of Islamic philosophy and science is that the translation of Muslim thinkers' works into Latin, Hebrew and some vernacular languages, awakened Europeans from their dark and long sleep. This translation movement was started by Pope Slyvesrter de Sacy II himself in the tenth century; he opened like Baytu'lHikma a school of translation in the city of Rippol. As a result of this Europeans, Christian and Jew, learned again philosophy and science from the Muslims. It was under the influence of Islamic culture that the European Renaissance took place firstly in Spain and Italy. In speaking of Ibn Sina's influence upon Medieval Europe A.-M. Goichon said this: "Cette philosophie Arabe venait comme un soufflé tout chargé d'effluves nouvelles, grecques et orientales, vivifiant le jeune esprit de l'Europe, tout ouvert."8

R. Briffault expressed his view on how Islamic philosophy and science is the driving force behind modern Europe. He says: " It is highly probable that but for the Arabs modern European civilization would never have arisen at all; it is absolutely certain that but for them, it would not have assumed that character which has enabled it to transcend all previous phases of evolution. For although there is not a single aspect of European growth in which the decisive influence of Islamic culture is not traceable, nowhere is it so clear and momentous as in the genesis of that power which constitutes the paramount distinctive force of modern world and the supreme source of its victory - natural science and the scientific spirit. The debt of our science to the Arabs does not consist in startling discoveries or revolutionary theories; science owes a great deal more to Arab culture; it owes its existence. The ancient world was, as we saw, pre-scientific.What we call science arose in Europe as a result of a new spirit of inquiry, of new methods of investigation, of the method of experiment, observation, measurement, of the development of mathematics in a form unknown to the Greeks. That spirit and those methods were introduced into the European world by the Arabs."9

---

8 A.-M. Goichon, *La Philosophie d'Avicenne et Son Influence en Europe Médiéval* (Paris: A. Maisonneuve, 1944), p. 91.

9 R. Briffault, *The Making of Humanity* (London: G. Allen and Unwin, 1919), pp. 190-191.

CHAPTER XXV

SOME ASPECTS OF AVICENNA'S EPISTEMOLOGY

Ibn Sina (Avicenna, 980-1037) merits a special place of honour among intellectuals of classical Islam, a group distinguished by their encyclopedic knowledge of Renaissance type. A major representative of *Falsafa* (Hellenizing philosophy of Islam), Ibn Sina combined monotheistic revelationism with the scientific and philosophical tradition of Antiquity, which later inspired Judaic (Moses Maimonides) and Western Christian thinkers (Thomas Aquinas) to undertake such synthesis as well.

A great philosopher Ibn Sina was also a great physician, whose name is on a par with Galen, Hippocrates and Dioscorides. Significantly, the Latin translation of his seminal work *Canon of Medicine* was a handbook for European doctors until the 17th century, while his physics concept of inclination (*mayl*) formed the basis of Jean Buridan's teaching of impetus, thus anticipating the theory of inertia known as Newton's first law.

Not only was Ibn Sina's work *The Book of Healing* a landmark in the history of the Aristotelian tradition, but even today it is still the largest volume to come from the pen of a single philosopher. This encyclopedia was the first to present a systematized scientific and philosophical legacy of Aristotle and, as some researchers noted, this systematization underlay the success that Aristotelian teaching enjoyed in the Latin West. Encompassing all disciplines of the day, Ibn Sina united, for the first time, all three kingdoms of nature - minerals, plants and animals, into one whole. Another first was his suggestion of the great chain of being as a metaphysical basis for the integration of all sciences, from the "natural" to the "divine".

Ibn Sina begins his encyclopedia with the classification of sciences, to which he dedicated a separate treatise "On the Division of Rational Sciences". Following the Peripatetic tradition, he brings together all fields of knowledge under the banner of philosophy as a "science of sciences". But whereas Aristotle primarily distributed sciences in three large groups according to their objectives - "theoretical/speculative", which focused on

knowledge itself (physics, mathematics, and metaphysics), "practical" designed to regulate human behavior (ethics and politics), and

"creative/productive" aimed at creating something (art, crafts, and applied sciences), Ibn Sina actually does away with the third group when he includes rhetoric and poetics, which Aristotle attributed to this group, into the section of logic, while listing applied sciences/ arts and crafts in the "secondary" sub-categories of theoretical philosophy. Ibn Sina stressed that the aim of the theoretical part of philosophy is to attain the truth (*haqq*), and that of the practical part - to achieve good (*khayr*).

The hierarchy of the three parts of theoretical philosophy - physics, mathematics, and metaphysics - is structured in accord with the degree of abstractness of their objects, i.e., their detachment from matter and motion. The practical disciplines - ethics, politics, house holding (economy) - vary in their application.

As for logic, which Aristotle did not consider either as part of philosophy or as a separate science, but merely as a methodological tool, Ibn Sina's teachings regarded it, as will be discussed below, rather as a theoretical science and an independent part of philosophy while simultaneously serving as its tool. The logical corpus of Ibn Sina's teachings consisted of nine disciplines corresponding to Porphyry's Isagoge and to eight Aristotelian treatises: *Categories, On interpretation, Prior Analytics (Syllogism), Posterior Analytics (*Demonstration/Apodictics*), Topics, Sophistical Refutations, Rhetoric,* and *Poetics.*

Contact between the theoretical and practical sciences is provided by dividing them into the primary (*asliyya*) and secondary (*far'iyya*), which corresponds to their present-day division into "pure /fundamental" and "applied". Thus, the primary branches of mathematics are arithmetic, geometry, astronomy, and [theoretically] music, which adjoin corresponding applied disciplines: the Indian method of addition and subtraction and algebra; the science of surveying; the science of mechanical inventions; the science of pulleys; the science of weights and scales; the science of graded instruments; the science of optics and mirrors; hydraulics; the science of making astronomical and geographic maps; the science of making musical instruments.

Pure physics encompasses eight disciplines that correspond to the natural-philosophical writings of Aristotle: *Physics; On the Heavens; On Generation and Corruption; Meteorology* (the first three books); *On Minerals* (the fourth book of *Meteorology*); *On Plants*; *On Animals* (this and the previous book are pseudo-Aristotelian); and *On the Soul*. The seven disciplines belonging to practical physics are medicine, astrology, physiognomy, dream interpretations, the science of talismans, the science of magic (*nayranjiyyat*), and alchemy.

Pure Metaphysics is divided into five disciplines, the first of which explores the concepts common to all that exists; the second deals with the first elements of individual sciences (physics, mathematics, and logic); and the third is devoted to proving the existence of the First Principle, His unity and attributes; the fourth is concerned with primary and secondary "spiritual substances" (i.e., minds and souls of the celestial spheres); and the fifth explores ways of subordination of heavenly and earthly bodily substances to spiritual substances mentioned above. Applied disciplines are the science of revelation/prophecy and of afterlife.

Even this list indicates what was characteristic of medieval Islam: a particular differentiation of sciences, the need to strengthen their ties with everyday life, and the development of trade and commerce; the latter called for the development (to a much greater extent than in antiquity) of empirical knowledge and for research that focused not only on the qualitative, but also on the quantitative aspects of the processes under study.

Ibn Sina structured his encyclopedic work *Healing* according to a hierarchical sequence of four theoretical sciences - logic (in nine books), physics (in eight books), mathematics (in four books), and metaphysics (in one book). The latter also dealt in relative detail with prophetology and eschatology, and gave in the conclusion a succinct survey of political and ethical issues: moreover, Ibn Sina promised to devote a separate essay to the subject later on.

In contrast to Porphyry's *Isagoge*, conceived as an introduction to Aristotle's *On Categories*, the first of nine books of logic in *Healing*, entitled 'Madkhal' ('Introduction'), appears to be rather an introduction to logic in its entirety, and to philosophy in general. In proposing a general classification of sciences, Ibn Sina stops to consider the old issue of the relation between philosophy and logic and whether logic is a tool or part of philosophy. Platonic tradition holds logic to be both. The peripatetics considered logic only as a "tool" of all sciences. As for the Stoics, they held that logic was only a part of philosophy.

To answer the question of the relation between logic and philosophical sciences, Ibn Sina drew attention to the fact that the essence (*mahiyya*) of things could be viewed in three ways: as [embodied] in specific particulars, as a general concept in the mind, and by itself, i.e., regardless of the previous two modes of being - neither as universal/common or as particular/individual. Logic studies such modes of mental concepts as subjectiveness and predicativeness, universality and particularity (in predication), the essential and accidental (in predication).

This being the case, Ibn Sina concludes that the traditional debate about the inclusion or non-inclusion of logic in philosophy is purely verbal. If one regards philosophy as a science of extra-mental essences, then logic is not a philosophical science in this sense but only a tool. But if philosophy is considered a science about what is and irrespective of what the nature of that is in general (whether extra-mental or mental), then logic is one of philosophical sciences in so far as it examines the mental essences (*Madkhal*, I, 3).

Interestingly, Ibn Sina offers a clear definition of the subject-matter of logic not in the logical section, but in the section dealing with metaphysics (*Ilahiyyat*, I, 2). For the first time, he distinguishes terminologically the first intelligible intentions (*ma'ani ma'aqula ula*) and the second intelligible intentions (*ma'ani ma'aqula thaniya*). Logic studies the second intentions, but not in the sense in which they appear as intelligible intentions, nor in terms of their intelligibility and their existence in the mind, but in the sense in which they can be used to help advance from the known to the unknown. Later tradition firmly established even in the Latin West not only Ibn Sina's understanding of the subject-matter of logic, but also the very terms - the first intention (intentio prima) and the second intention (intentio secunda).

It is also noteworthy that *Madkhal* would later consider the three above-mentioned aspects of essence as three modes of the existence of the universals: 1) the eternal existence in the Active intellect (along with the forms of things and human souls), until [the realization in] plurality [of things] (*qabl al-kasra*); 2) in the plurality (*fi al-kasra*); 3) in the mind, after the plurality (*ba'd al-kasra*), as they appear in the mind, and based on particuars. Ibn Sina refers to these three categories of universals, respectively, as intellectual (*'aqli*), natural (*tabi'i*), and logical (*mantiqi*) terms that, as a philosopher, he, presumably, regards as not entirely successful. Therefore, he does not use them in his subsequent works (although this terminology is widely used in post-avicennian tradition). Following the translation of *Madkhal*, European scholasticism adopted this division (Albert the Great and Thomas Aquinas), in particular, genus naturale, genus mentale, and genus logicum, as well as relevant qualifications: ante res ("before things"), in rebus ("in things"), post res ("after things").

The next fundamental question is how may methods of logic, whose objects (i.e., the second intentions) are purely mental, be applied to other sciences, in particular, to mathematics and physics, involved as they are in the study of extra-mental things of the world and of their causal relationships. Although Ibn Sina did not clearly articulate the problem and its solution, all of his arguments suggest an attitude common to Muslim peripatetism in general - a belief in the unity of objective and subjective logic. From Ibn Sina's perspective, the order and connection of things in the world is the same as the order and connection of ideas in the mind. Therefore, a correct proof reflects the causal structure of the world.

The idea of common ground between logic and the sciences of nature stems from the above-mentioned teaching of Ibn Sina of the three aspects of essence: the universal essence in the mind and the universal essence outside the mind are united in an essence as such (for example, "humaneness," which as such is neither universal nor particular).

If the Latins viewed logic as a linguistic science, which formed the famous trivium along with grammar and rhetoric, Muslim culture did not know this. When one spoke of the "three arts" (*sina'at thalatha*), one referred to the three sections of logic: apodeictic, dialectic and rhetoric (with sophistry typically attached to dialectic and poetry - to rhetoric). The methodology of science (mathematics and physics) was developed specifically in the section on apodeictic, which set out the rules leading to certain (scientific and epistemic) notions and judgments. Reliable notions are achieved with the help of definitions and reliable judgments - due to apodeictic inference/syllogism.

Ibn Sina discussed these rules in the fifth section of the book on logic - *Burhan*/Demonstration, which corresponds to Aristotle's *Posterior Analytics*. But if modern scholars disagree whether that book is devoted to science in general or to individual sciences, or whether Aristotle describes in it only a way of formalizing (for pedagogical purposes) acquired knowledge, the author of *Burhan* makes it clear that the purpose of his book is the development of a general methodology of science applicable to all sciences. Supporting such a global orientation of Ibn Sina is the fact that the philosopher continually uses examples from all specific sciences medicine, physics, mathematics, and metaphysics.

According to Ibn Sina, scientific knowledge (Arabic 'ilm; Greek. episteme) is of two types: knowledge of the first principles of any given science and knowledge acquired with the help of [apodeictic] proof (*burhan*). The first principles are notions that are part of this science and are not determined in the framework of this science, and judgments that are not proved. Similar to Aristotle (*Second Analytics*, I, 18), Ibn Sina stresses the role of sensory perception in the acquisition of such basic assumptions of science. However, he makes the following significant adjustments that I would like to point out. First of all, they concern the role of senses in acquiring the first principles of science through techniques such as abstraction, induction, and [methodological] experience.

In the interpretation of abstraction (*tajrid*), Ibn Sina found a fundamental difference with Aristotelian epistemology. Abstraction facilitates the attainment of intelligibles by our mind, but these intelligibles come from outside - from the Active Intellect, the tenth in a series of cosmic intelligences emanating from the First Principle (Necessary existent, God). It is this reason, a kind of the world's Logos, a notion of which was introduced in Islamic philosophy by Alfarabi, and which was designed to ultimately ensure the necessity and universality of scientific knowledge.

In an aside, we would also like to point to the following epistemological aspect of the East Peripatetic doctrine of active intellect. By identifying this intellect with the archangel Gabriel, who in Muslim theology is the messenger of God's revelation to the prophets, Ibn Sina and other Islamic Peripatetics emphasized the unity of revelation-prophetic and scientific and philosophical truth: the first truth, clothed in images, is given to a prophet - through his imaginative power, while the second, in the form of concepts, is attained by a scientist-philosopher - through the mind. This ensures an onto-noetic base for allegorical interpretation of sacred texts the literal meaning of which is not consistent with the arguments of scientific knowledge.

As regards induction (Arabic *istiqra'*; Greek. *epagoge*), Aristotle attributed to it an ability to establish the first principles of science, which, in his understanding, is a method that includes not only generalizations, but also a formal syllogism (as in his well-known example of the *First Analytics*, I, 23, where he states that "every long-liver is gall-less"; as a major premise of the syllogism, he uses the judgment that "all horses, mules, people, etc. are gall-less", and as a minor premise: "long-lived animals are horses, mules, people, etc.").

Sceptical about the heuristic ability of induction, Ibn Sina proves that the reliability (i.e., the universality and necessity of knowledge) can be maintained neither by the sensory component of the induction procedure, nor by the rational, nor by the combination of both of them (*Burhan*, I, 9). He is convinced that induction is incapable of justifying the universal provision, and can only contribute to its restoration (*munabbih*), through the senses, in the mind (*Burhan*, III, 5).

Ibn Sina replaces induction as a method of approving the original elements of science with technical experience (*tajriba*). Similar to induction, this method includes the sensual and the rational components. Also as in the case of induction, Ibn Sina believes that monitoring regularly recurring phenomena in a methodic experience does not reveal direct causal relation. It is assumed, however, that in a methodic experience, causality itself is revealed by the recorded regularity of the phenomena in question (e.g., the attraction of a magnet to iron), though this regularity is linked to an essential (*zati*) and natural (*tabi'i*) aspect of this phenomenon (because only the essential can be repeated on a regular basis). Thus, a methodic experience can help discover universal principles of science that are based on senses. Such a conception of experience, as outlined in *The Book of Healing*, anticipates inductive logic and the scientific method that emerged in Europe of the Modern Age.

The Canon of Medical Science, where Ibn Sina makes extensive use of the experimental method, formulated methods of agreement, difference, and concomitant variation, whose establishment in the West is associated with the name of J. St. Mill. It was for the first time in the Mediterranean scientific tradition that the *Canon* developed and applied the holistic healing principle stemming from understanding health as a "vertically" balanced combination of mind, spirit and body, and a "horizontally" combination in man of elements of the natural world.

(Translated from Russian by Serge Gitman)

CHAPTER XXVI

VISIONS OF TIME IN ISLAM

Today the world of Islam is estimated to count more than one billion people, almost one fifth of humanity. Islam occupies the center of the globe. It stretches like a broad belt across the map from the Atlantic to the Pacific, encircling both the "haves" of the consumer North and "have-nots" of the disadvantaged South. It sits at the crossroads of America, Western Europe, and Russia on one side and black Africa, India and East Asia on the other. Islam is not contained in any national culture; it is a universal force. Stretching from Morocco to Mindanao, it is built of five geographical blocks, the Muslims of black Africa, the Arab world, the Turco-Iranian lands, the Muslims of South Asia, and the inhabitants of the Indonesian archipelago.

Islam is also at a crossroads in history, destined to play an international role in politics and to become the most prominent world religion in the decades to come. In the seventh century of the Common Era, Islam entered the global scene with Muhammad at a turning point in time. With spectacular conquest and organic growth, it expanded through the centuries and became stretched taut in a bow of tension between striving for God and struggle for dominion. As we have entered the third millennium of the Common Era, Islam looks back nostalgically at its medieval glory, when the Judaeo-Christian West studied at its feet, and sees fundamentalism as the fulcrum of its future in the struggle for preeminence with the secular and technologically superior West.

How does Islam understand the ideas of past and future, of time and temporality, in which it strives to realize its eternal destiny? Picture yourself in a downtown McDonald's in Pushkin Square taking a short lunch break at the office or grabbing a bite to eat between errands. Now picture yourself in an Arab coffee house nursing an espresso after your siesta. We all know from lived experience that these two settings carry with them quite different senses of time. In the first scenario, time pushes relentlessly onward; in the second, it lazily winds its way forward in the afternoon sun. Move from fast food to edification of a more intellectual sort and check the entry on the philosophy of time in a major encyclopedia. What you will find there are learned articles contrasting the linear progression of time predominant in Western culture with the cyclical concept of time prevalent in India. Both conceptions, we are told, belong to the defining characteristics of these two cultural worlds. With regard to Islam their geographical neighbor, however, the same sources of reference identify no such characteristic notion of time.

Does the world of Islam, occupying the center of the globe, possess a concept of time characteristically its own, or can the Islamic notion of time be exhaustively explained by a cluster of borrowings from its neighbors and cultural ancestors? Is there a unity to the Islamic notion of time, or is Islam a universal culture encompassing many languages and ethnic groups, each with its own notion of time? Can one only speak of a spectrum of ideas on time in Islam or are there constants that would provide parameters defining Islam authentically as a religion and culture? On the one hand, are there distinct and perduring elements in the Islamic notion of time that challenge the current clash-of-civilization theories to articulate a definition of Islamic civilization upon which to base their axioms? On the other hand, do developments in the Islamic concept of time reveal the monolithic claims of Muslim fundamentalism to rest upon an idealized and homogenized vision of the past?

The search for defining characteristics of Islamic culture and religion might begin with many notions, including monotheism, revelation, prophethood or religious law. I have chosen the concept of time for two reasons: first, time appears to provide a more neutral point of comparison than other more religiously charged notions; second, time is not limited to one particular field of Islam, but can be traced in a broad cross-section of Islamic writings. Time is pervasive in Islamic history, central to language and poetry, indispensable in Islamic astronomy and music, constitutive for Islamic ritual and law, and crucial in Islamic theology, cosmology and philosophy. From the great range of these fields I would like to select four points for my reflections in the present paper: the vision of time in the Qur'ān and Muslim tradition, the atomism of time peculiar to Islamic theology, the paradigm of time prevalent in the medieval mystical philosophy of Islam, and the rhythm of the Muslim calendar that provides the basis for Islamic historiography.

In the pre-Islamic era, Arab time was characterized by fatalism, dahr, which erases human works without hope for life beyond death. Also called the "days" or the "nights," dahr is the cause of earthly happiness and misery; it is death's doom and the measure of destiny; it changes everything, and nothing resists it. While dahr held sway like fate, it could be transcended by a moment marked out in tribal memory and often preserved in poetry. Dahr was thus punctuated by the Days of the Arabs, ayyām al'Arab, the days of vengeance in combat and tribal prowess, when memorable events placed markers in the recollection of the course of events.

The Qur'ān rejects the pre-Islamic fatalism of dahr. Instead, it explains time from the perspective of a transcendent monotheism promising paradise and threatening eternal damnation. Just as the pre-Islamic Arabs had their days of victory and vengeance, so Allāh had His days of deliverance and punishment. God's personal command, "'Be!,' and it is, kun fa-yakūn" obliterated the spell of fate. God gave His command when He formed the first human being and made the heavens and the earth. He determines the beginning of a person's life and calls each individual to a final account after death. There is no place in the Qur'ān for impersonal time; each person's destiny is in the hands of the God who creates male and female, gives life and brings death, and grants wealth and works destruction. God is active even in a person's sleep, for "God takes the souls unto Himself at the time of their death, and that which has not died in its sleep. He keeps those on whom He has decreed death, but looses the others till a stated term" (39:42). From the "Be!" of a person's creation to the time of death, human existence falls under the decree of God: Allāh is the Lord of each instant; what He has determined happens.

Muslim tradition, or Ḥadīth, amplified the divine determination included in the Qur'ān, and transformed Muhammad's stress on divine omnipotence into a rigid predeterminism. Saving dahr from Qur'ānic condemnation, Ḥadīth identified dahr with God through a powerful divine utterance and warned against slandering dahr through a famous saying of the Prophet. In order to establish that Allāh's unalterable decree is invariably fulfilled, another strand of Ḥadīth introduces the notion that everything that happens is written in a heavenly book. While each embryo is still in the womb, an angel writes down the daily ration, the works, the moments of misery or happiness, and the hour of death of the man or woman it will become. Combining pre-Islamic notions of all-pervasive time with the idea of God's decree in the Qur'ān, Muslim tradition saw time as a series of predetermined events binding divine omnipotence to the certain occurrence of each instant of a person's life span. Unavoidable as fate and irreversible as time, each instant happened solely through God's very own action.

The most common Islamic term for time, zamān, does not appear in the Qur'ān, nor does qidam, its counterpart for eternity. The Arab lexicographers, however, had a great variety of terms for time. In general, they distinguished dahr, time from the beginning of the world to its end, from *zamān*, a long time having both beginning and end; *'aṣr*, a span of time; *ḥīn*, a period of time, little or much; *dawām*, duration; *mudda*, a space of duration; *waqt*, a moment in time; *ān*, present time; *awān*, time or season; *yawm*, a time, whether night or day; and *sā'a*, a while or an hour. *Abad* was duration without end and *azal* duration without beginning, to which *qidam*, time without beginning, corresponded in its primary sense as distinct from sarmad, incessant continuance. Khulūd, perpetual existence, was implicit in the Qur'ānic day of eternity, the entrance to *dār al-khulūd*, paradise. It is obvious that these distinctions do not reflect a quasi-technical usage of each term to the exclusion of others, but rather an approximately predominant meaning that often blends with the neighboring terms in the actual literary use. When it came to translating Greek philosophical texts into Arabic, the most commonly employed correspondences were *chrónos*, translated by *zamān, aión* by *dahr*, *kairós* by *waqt*, and *diástasis* by *mudda*.

Through the exposure to Greek thought, the philosophers of Islam became familiar with two powerful und mutually opposed philosophical notions of time. For those who followed the Aristotelian view, time was an accident of motion, while for those who espoused the Plotinian concept, time had no extra-mental reality; rather it was the stream of consciousness of a thinking mind, a duration existing independently of motion. Aristotle had attempted to prove the eternity of the universe from the nature of time. In the Plotinian view, time did not come into existence with the creation of the universe, but existed from eternity as the duration of God's infinite consciousness.

While Islamic philosophical notions of time oscillated between Aristotelian motion and Plotinian duration, it was the atomism of Democritus that appealed most strongly to the creators of normative Islamic theology. Atomic theory opened a way to link the immutability of reality with the observable changes and manifold forms in nature by describing reality as composed of simple and unchangeable minute particles, called atoms. The atoms and their accidents exist for only an instant. In every instant, God is creating the world anew; there are no intermediate causes. God can be thought of as continually creating the universe from nothing. Subverting Greek "materialistic" atomism, the Muslim theologians made atomism an instrument of divine providence and held that each moment within time is the direct creation of the eternally active God. Of itself, creation is discontinuous; it appears continuous to us only because of God's compassionate consistency.

Islamic atomism may be illustrated by the famous example of a person engaged in writing. Allāh creates within the human being first the will and then the capacity to write, creating both will and capacity anew in every instant. Then God creates, anew in every instant, the movement of the hand, and finally, the motion of the pen concurrent with it. Every instant and action in the process of writing is independent from every other; all stages of the process issue from God alone. It is only in appearance that there is a coherent action of writing. Similarly, a self-consistent world in space and time, working harmoniously, is only an appearance. The one true actor is God alone. The link of causality that appears to rule the world and human life becomes subordinate to Allāh, and natural causes give way to divine will. As a rule, God does not interrupt the continuity of events, though He is able to intervene at any moment by what is commonly termed a miracle but simply means an interruption of His customary activity. Atomism was not only most congenial to a vision of God acting instantaneously in the world as the sole true cause, it also proved most closely akin to Arabic grammar, which lacks genuine verbs for "to be" and "to become." Neither does Arabic employ the tenses of past, present and future. Instead, it uses the verbal aspects of complete and incomplete, marking the degree to which an action has been realized or is yet to be realized without distinguishing precisely between present and future.

While Muslim philosophers and theologians sought to explain time, the mystics of Islam set out to experience it. For the Sufi mystics the paradigm of time is suspended between two days, the Day of Primal Covenant at the dawn of creation and the Day of Final Judgment when the world comes to its catastrophic end. Time resembles a parabola stretching from infinity to infinity, an arc anchored in eternity at its origin and end that reaches its apex in a mystic's ecstatic moment of memory and certitude. The early Sufis discovered the decisive religious moment for humanity in preexistence, when all human beings heard and understood God's selfrevelation for the first time at the very birth of creation. By recognizing the pre-existential origin of all humanity on the Day of Covenant, the Sufis established a dimension of time that traces the present moment back to eternity in the past and balances the eschatological thrust of the Qur'ān from the present to eternity in the future, reached at the Day of Judgment. Through a distinct meditational technique, known as dhikr, recollection of God, the mystics return to their primeval origin on the Day of Covenant, when all of humanity (symbolically enshrined in their prophetical ancestors as light particles or seeds) swore an oath of allegiance and witness to Allāh as the one and only Lord. Breaking through to eternity, the mystics relive their waqt, their primeval moment with God, here and now, in the instant of ecstasy, even as they anticipate their ultimate destiny. Sufi meditation captures time by drawing eternity from its edges in pre- and post-existence into the moment of mystical experience.

The medieval Sufi, Ibn 'Arabī analyzed the concept of time on the basis of the Prophet's tradition that Allāh is time or dahr. Just as God's being is everlasting, so is God's time; it is eternity, beginningless and endless. Human beings, who are called in Sufi language sons of their moments, may also be understood as being, not having, time or waqt. Human time is momentary. Each moment is the reflection of God's eternity in the person's receptivity to the divine action at each and every instant. Seen in this way, there are two levels of time: that of God, *dahr,* and that of human beings, *waqt.* Yet both levels are inconsistent with our ordinary conception of time, because God's time stretches out to eternity while the time of humans shrinks to a mere instant, a dot without duration. Caught between these two modes, divine everlastingness and mortal momentariness, we human beings construct a notion of time, *zamān* or chrónos, that is imaginary and subjective, though inspired by the real and objective time of *dahr* and *waqt.* The imaginary *zamān* can be understood through two principal models: that of cosmology and that of relativity. The cosmological model is based on an image of the universe that is largely derived from the Ptolemaic system of the spheres and the story of creation known from Scripture. Its central notion is the idea of the complete day, *yawm,* a sequence of night and day that complement each other like male and female or like activity and passivity. Night and day come into being with the revolution of the spheres setting the universe in motion, but become discernible only through the creation of the sun and its course. In the model of relativity, however, God and the world are seen as the two terms of a quasi-temporal relation between Creator and creatures. Time viewed from the side of God is real but has no existence apart from God. Perceived from the vantage of human beings, time is imaginary and lacks any existence of its own. Whether conceived from the human or the divine side, time is a mere relation. Yet this mere relation is infinite, just like empty space. It can be divided into ever smaller or larger time-segments in a duration that has neither beginning nor end. There is, however, an implicit link between our imaginary time and God's real time which can be aptly described by one of Ibn ʿArabī's images: Any point along a circle may be seen as the point separating past from future. While having no extension whatsoever, this point of the "now" is still part of the actual extent of the circular line. In other words, although a product of our imagination, time is, in each moment, the virtual and actual object of interaction with eternity. Eternity belongs to God alone, but God's creature participates in the present moment.

The theocentric vision of time in Qur'ān and Ḥadīth, the theological atomism of time governed by an eternally active God, and the Sufi paradigm of time coupled with imaginary relativity give expression to the vertical dimension of Islamic thought: the individual's overpowering dependence on the Creator. The horizontal dimension, one's autonomous self-realization through one's earthly interactions with other human beings, seems to be diminished in these theoretical doctrines of time. The picture changes dramatically, however, when the focus is shifted to the immensely practical aspects of Muslim thought. Islam possesses a strong sense of law and ritual on the one hand and the order of history and society on the other. One of the most characteristic ordering principles created by Islam to define its ritual and measure its history was the Muslim calendar, its own measure of time in the horizontal realm.

Long before Muhammad, the Arabs observed a solar year and at times also followed a lunar reckoning. Their acquaintance with a solar year is indicated by the Arab months, named for definite seasons, such as the dead of winter or the grazing season, as well as by the festivals and markets. The Arabs, however, had no firmly established calendar or a uniform method of counting the years, but reckoned on the basis of particular events, such as the fire of Abraham, the building of the Kaʿba, the tribal emigration from the Tihāma, or the death of a pre-Islamic lord of Mecca. The inhabitants of Mecca knew two most notable starting points, the sacrilegious war of Fijār, toward the end of the sixth century CE, fought over tribal control of the trade routes, and "the year of the elephant," in which the expedition, led by the king of Yemen to curb the commercial power of the Meccan sanctuary, ended in disaster in about 554 CE. The pre-Islamic Arabs also used a cycle of 28 time periods, reckoned according to the setting of a star and the heliacal rising of its opposite, which suited the nomads in predicting periods of rain and good pasture grounds. They also learned to distinguish the mansions of the moon and adjust them to their time periods and the solar zodiac, thereby following a type of lunisolar year with the day beginning at sunset.

The lunar year, peculiar to Islam, was established when Muhammad gave a solemn address during his last pilgrimage to Mecca. In it, he arranged for the year to consist of 12 lunar months. He also proclaimed the divine injunction against intercalation, which is the procedure of correlating the cycle of lunar months with the solar year of the seasons by inserting a thirteenth month into a lunar year at certain intervals. Muhammad's motive for the interdiction of intercalation, cited in the Qur'ān as an expression of unbelief, may have been twofold. On the one hand, the interdiction unflinchingly maintained Allāh's rule over the order of time, manifested and observed in nature through the appearance of the moon's crescent. On the other hand, it deprived an Arab clan of its traditional rights to proclaim publicly the intercalary years and to preserve the pagan festivals and markets within the seasons of the solar year. The Prophet's interdiction killed two birds with one stone. First, it drew the believers away from pagan cults and turned them to Allāh, the true creator, cause and preserver of all things. Second, it allowed Muhammad to wrest economic power away from tribal interest groups by detaching the festivals from their pagan moorings in the seasons.

Not simply a matter of adjusting the lunar year to the seasons, intercalation also had an impact on tribal warfare. The Qur'ān upheld the Arab tribal custom of four inviolable months that were not to be disturbed by internecine battles. One month fell in the middle of the year, but the other three followed one another as a block of time at the turn of the year. Since the intercalary month was most likely inserted at the end of the year, it either interrupted the time block of the inviolable months, or it changed the status of a sacred month to profane. In either case, the intercalary month disturbed the sacred order of time. This manipulation appeared to Muhammad's eyes as a sacrilegious intervention in the divine order because it facilitated warfare and bloodshed within a period of time ordained to be an inviolable season.

While Muhammad introduced the Muslim lunar year, he did not establish the uniform Muslim calendar. Its innovation is traditionally attributed to 'Umar, the second caliph. According to tradition, 'Umar called a council to resolve the confusion of reckoning time in the light of difficulties with raising taxes and collecting tribute. After lengthy discussions the decision was made to adopt the standard Muslim calendar that remains in use today. A coin struck at Damascus during 'Umar's reign and, shortly thereafter, a papyrus of Egypt and a tombstone of Cyprus provide solid evidence for the calendar's existence. 'Umar's role in its uniform establishment, however, may be overstated in the sources since early Muslim biographers and historians continued to quote different sets of dates in random fashion.

With the increasing conquests of Islam, the standard Muslim calendar, based on the observation of a pure lunar year, no longer responded to all circumstances of a vast empire. A consistent calendar was required for the administration of state and the collection of taxes and tribute. This need led to the concurrent use of different types of calendar. The popular lunar year, based on the actual observation of the moon's crescent, found support among the scholars of law and religion. The Muslim astronomers, however, established a mathematically computed standard lunar calendar of 354 days that added one day to the last month in an irregular sequence of leap years. The astronomers also substituted uniform hours of equal length for the formerly variable hours of the day, 12 during the period of daylight and 12 during nighttime. By contrast, Muslim rulers resorted to a kind of adapted Sassanid solar calendar. This makeshift adjustment was required to overcome the incongruity of the lunar calendar with the agricultural cycle, which created periods of many years when the tax came due before the crops could be harvested. One way to resynchronize with the lunar calendar was to drop a tax year every 32 years. Over the centuries a number of attempts were made by Muslim rulers to administer the empire efficiently by introducing solar calendars that fixed the beginning of the calendar year at the vernal equinox.

As I come to my short conclusion, you realize, that I stressed the role of atomism in my reflections on Islamic theories of time and highlighted the practical implications of the calendar that measures time in Islamic history. Seeing the theoretical side as the vertical dimension of Islamic thought and the practical side as its horizontal dimension, Islam appeared as categorically theocentric in tying the individual irrevocably to God, while being immensely down to earth in determining the course of its communal history. The powerful atomistic conception of time expressed the vertical dimension of the individual as marked by a series of flashes of existence with momentary breakthroughs to eternity in ecstasy. These flashes foreshadowed the final moment that freezes time in irreversible ultimateness, when the individual stands alone before God in the trial of the last judgment. At the same time it recalled the moment when all of humanity heard God's self-revelation for the first time at the dawn of creation. In the horizontal dimension, however, the community of believers, a galaxy of individual atoms, was forcefully conscious of shaping its own temporal framework through the calendar as it began a new and ultimate era of human history.

I have not talked about the intricate timing of ritual prayer in Islam, the complex literature on time in Islamic astronomy, the work of al-Bīrūnī's Chronology, al-Ṭūsī's work on the duodecennial animal cycle, the reflections of Islamic historians on their use of time in annals and biographies, or the role time plays in poetical meter and musical mode. I also neglected aspects of time brought to light by anthropologists and sociologists in the myriad ethnic traditions of Islam. One thing, however, I hope to have conveyed: there are parameters of Islamic time that give its culture and religion cohesion and structure in theory and practice. The four points of analysis I selected in elaborating an Islamic concept of time integrate cross-cultural borrowing with original inspiration. The vision of Islam they reflect is not a monolithic phalanx moving through history but rather a dynamic religion imparting a distinct form and content to its civilization.

CHAPTER XXVII

ABOUT THE CLASSIFICATION OF SCIENCE: ARISTOTLE, EASTERN PERIPATETICS, AND AL-GHAZALI

The problem of sciences classification in the Classic Arab Muslim philosophy included the two dimensions in the context of culture: the philosophical and methodological (Eastern Aristotelians), and the philosophical and religious (al-Ghazali). These approaches both complemented each other, and at the same time were in opposition, both within the development of philosophy, the sciences and humanities, and during the confrontation, both within and between different schools of *kalam*, philosophy and Sufism. The key issue of classification of the sciences was the problem of the ratio of theoretical and practical reason.

As known, Aristotle's classification of sciences is based on the difference between theoretical and practical sciences. Theoretical include: physics, mathematics and metaphysics, and practical - the ethics, economics and politics. Both were prefaced with logic, which was considered a purely instrumental science - "Organon." The influence of Aristotle's classification is found in the works of the founder of the Eastern peripatetism al-Farabi (870-950). In his treatise "The Book of the enumeration of the Sciences" (Makala fi ihsa al-ulum), he considers the "well-known sciences" in five chapters, each devoted to one of the disciplines: the science of language, logic, mathematics, physics and metaphysics ("Divine Science"), as well as political science, *fiqh* (Islamic law) and *kalam* ("speculative theology"). Al-Farabi was among the first who tried to combine the two approaches in his classification of sciences, Aristotle's approach, which belonged to the so-called "newly appeared" science and the "Arabic" approach, which was associated with the traditional sciences. On the one hand, al-Farabi attributed to the theoretical sciences logic, mathematics, physics and metaphysics, and to the practical sciences - political science, *Kalam* and *Fiqh*. Thus, between the "divine science" and Kalam is political science, which for al-Farabi as a whole meant the science of antiquity, setting out in the "State" of Plato and the "Politics" of Aristotle, and not containing an agenda of prophecy, religion, or "speculative theology "and *fiqh*. The most important problem of the Arab-Islamic philosophy, formulated by al-Farabi is the problem of the ratio of practical and theoretical reason. And given the fact that Ibn Sina (9801037) in his classification of sciences also distinguishes theoretical and practical sciences, the intent of the Eastern Peripatetics to include newly "appeared" sciences," in particular ancient philosophy, into the cultural tradition of medieval Islam.

They faced a difficult task of bringing secular and religious knowledge and theoretical and practical reason to a non-contradictory accordance. And if the Arab Aristotelians considered the possibility of subordination of practical reason to theoretical one based on the theory of emanation, the criticism of their teaching on the part of al-Ghazali is quite fair, al-Ghazali claimed that they hadn't been unable to confirm in apodictic way those metaphysical terms, for which they sacrificed religious faith, which was the basis of the moral principals of the Arab-Muslim society. On the other hand, the problem of the correlation of theoretical and practical reason can be viewed in the aspect of the fact that the mind is the property of the "elite", philosophers, and faith is the sphere of "the masses", "public at large." In the same time knowledge that is available for "elite", was considered as an esoteric knowledge (*batin*), and the "masses" had to be content with exoteric knowledge (*zahir*). In addition, among the philosophers, it was widely believed that philosophical knowledge is not to be given "to the public at large." Hence the idea that al-Ghazali would later call "Madnun bihi ala gheiri ahlihi" that is esoteric writing. This idea was developed by the al-Razi, and especially by al-Farabi. It is not accidentally that Ibn Rushd blamed al-Ghazali for the fact that his work "Tahafut al falasifa (The Incoherence of the Philosophers)" brought the problems of philosophical knowledge into the court of the "public at large".

Al-Ghazali was well familiar with Aristotle's classification of sciences. This is evident from the content of his work "Maqasid al falasifa" (The Intentions of the Philosophers), in which philosophical science (al-ilm al-Hikma) is divided into practical and theoretical parts. We can assume that al-Ghazali used the Aristotelian dichotomy while considering the religious sciences, i.e., religious knowledge is divided by him into theoretical and practical - and this classification is central in the teachings of al-Ghazali. We are talking about the science of revelation or contemplation (*'ilm almukashshafa*) and behavior science (*'ilm al-muamala*). However, Aristotle's influence can already be seen in his work Mizan al-'amal (The Balance of Action), and taking into consideration the cultural and religious context philosophical terminology of classification of the sciences has been replaced by the religious. However, comparison of the definitions of "ilm almuamala" in the book "Knowledge" and "ilm al-Amalie" in the "Ihya' 'ulum al-din (The Revival of the Religious Sciences)" shows that in this area the differences between Aristotle and al-Ghazali are very considerable, although in theoretical knowledge in both these works they are characterized almost as the same. Apparently it is no coincidence that in the "Book of knowledge" of the three practical disciplines listed in the Mizan al-'amal (The Balance of Action) he preserved only ethics.

We should not forget that in the "Mizan al-'amal (The Balance of Action)" theoretical science is identified with metaphysics, a subject of which is formulated in religious terms, such as the knowledge of God, His angels, His prophets. If we talk about the difference in the approaches to the criteria of science classification, then Aristotle, and generally eastern Peripatetics proceeded from epistemological nature of sciences and different levels of being of the objects of study, and al-Ghazali proceeded from a different criterion - the degree of benefits that this or that science can bring in order to achieve religious goals, which are not identical to the achievement of the sciences themselves, but are beyond and above them.

Cultural and historical context of the classification of sciences by alGhazali allows him to talk about three categories of science:

1. Purely rational from the permitted (*mubah*), that is optional (*gheir wajib*) and not-recommended (*gheir mandub*), which in turn can be blameworthy (*Munkar*), or even banned (mahzur). Why? "This are sciences, which lead either to false opinions, or to true, but useless knowledge" - he says and explains: "The benefit is not in satisfaction of existing desires and not in the acquisition of material wealth: these things are ephemeral, transient. The real benefit is in the rewards in the hereafter."1

2. Purely traditional - Hadithology, Tafseer, "both the young and the old can equally well deal with these sciences, because they are mainly associated with memory and little for reason."

3. Combined Science (*muzdavvadzha*), the most noble - and they involve the personal opinions (ray), and divine law. This includes the *fiqh* (and Usul, and furu').

Ghazali supports "mukayyad ijtihad" - it is not that *ijtihad*, which would discover the truth behind the formed schools, but ijtihad of a lawyer, which is within his school can develop a reasoned opinion in all areas of the law. "Mukayyad ijtihad" does not apply to only a part of the Law, in which the lawyer is incompetent.

The subject of believing knowledge, which does not lend itself to rational knowledge, is God. Believing knowledge is based on intuition/"taste" (*Zauk*), it is here that the logic of the mind is giving way to the logic of love. At the same time the concept of love is not an aspect of the philosophy of Al-Ghazali - it is the essence of his philosophy.

In his general attitude to the philosophical sciences, described in his book "Maqasid al falasifa (The Intentions of the Philosophers)" al-Ghazali starts from prevailing in his time classification of sciences. 2 Here we encounter an initial positive assessment of philosophical sciences by alGhazali, which in its general form will remain in all his subsequent writings and works. So, here he asserts the importance and necessity of mathematics,

---

1 Al-Ghazali, *al-Mustafa min 'ilm al-usul* (The Essentials of the Islamic Legal Theory). In Arabic. (Bulaq, Egypt: al-Mtbaat al-Amiriah, 1324 H), vol.1, p.3.

2 Al-Ghazali, *Maqasid al falasifa* (The Intentions of the Philosophers). In Arabic. (Cairo: Dar al-Maarif, 1961), pp. 3 - 4.

logic and science, appreciates the views of a number of philosophers in matters of society, politics and ethics.

In the "Tahafut al falasifa (The Incoherence of the Philosophers)", he also stresses the importance of mathematics and logic, names attempts to deny or downplay their importance as not just meaningless, but contrary to the nature of true Islam, because the logic is a way to "review the mechanism of thought with regard to comprehended by reason. 3 "In his book "Mi'yar al-'ilm (The Standard Measure of Knowledge)" al-Ghazali tries to declare the logic as a necessary tool of *fiqh*, stressing that knowledge of the truth is impossible without reliance on logic.4 Hence his desire to prove that without logic, thought can not attain power. He tries to justify this idea deeply, including an attempt in his last great theoretical work, "alMustafa min 'ilm al-usul (The Essentials of the Islamic Legal Theory)."5

In his common position al-Ghazali proceeds mainly from what he calls a specificity of the reason, based on the comprehension of the essence of things. His approach towards such sciences as politics and ethics is based on the same issue. Thus, political science, according to his point of view, goes back mainly to the pragmatics associated with the mundane aspects of public life and society. As for ethics, it mainly considers issues related to the soul, manners, its correction and education. In the political and ethical views of the philosophers, he sees something similar to the ideas of the prophets and Sufi sages.

The achievements of philosophical thought in various areas alGhazali perceives as the result of true development of knowledge. He recognizes the contribution of philosophical sciences to the formation and development of the methods of searching the truth, though it does not mean that they always render a logically precise judgments. The findings can be changed and adjusted, but the essence of the truth lies in its absolute power. This approach al-Ghazali lays in the basis of his general attitude towards philosophy, saying that he calls "a huge difference in the degree of remoteness or proximity to the truth" of the philosophers.

Thus, in the work "Maqasid al falasifa" (The Intentions of the Philosophers) al-Ghazali only points to the likelihood of ideological differences with the philosophers in connection with the problems of kalam and natural science. The same idea he repeats in the "Tahafut al falasifa" (The Incoherence of the Philosophers), pointing to the existence of what he calls the twenty topics or issues on which he can not agree with the philosophers. This means that in fact he deals with philosophical problems, in the approach and the decision of which he sees the logical contradictions

3 Al-Ghazali, *Maqasid al falasifa* (The Intentions of the Philosophers), p. 87.

4 Al-Ghazali, *Mi'yar al-'ilm* (The Standard Measure of Knowledge). In Arabic. (Damascus: Dar al-Hikmat, 1993), p.26.

5 Al-Ghazali, *al-Mustafa min 'ilm al-usul* (The Essentials of the Islamic Legal Theory), vol.1, p.10.

of the eastern Peripatetics or which do not stand the test at the level of apodictic judgments. In this regard, he considers the forms or types of critical reason and criticizes the philosophical-theoretical reason (contemplative and scholastic) in the case of many polemical issues. In his discussions al-Ghazali highlights that many of the issues and approaches that are considered by philosophical thought, particularly in regard to the "theological" (metaphysical) problems do not envisage the need for a rational, conceptual position, just as there are many opinions that would be impossible in the case of rational consideration. As a result, al-Ghazali concludes that the reason in its arguments often leads to contradictory and dubious judgment, which it is impossible to rid. In this regard, he concludes that it is necessary to distinguish between clear judgments and reliable truth.6

Such an approach he puts into the basis of his position, opposing what he calls the vice of consent and the vice of objection", i.e. position of rejection of tradition in both cases. Admiration for the harmony of philosophy, scientific and philosophical arguments, especially in mathematics and logic, says al-Ghazali, leads some people to the uncritical acceptance of such argumentation and belief in the validity of all relevant findings. From the point of view of al-Ghazali the absolute truth is wider and deeper and more precise than the situation when it can be linked to a particular philosophical school or doctrine of any particular philosopher. Philosophical truth, attained in a particular field, does not mean necessarily that the philosophers are right in all matters. While appreciating the logic, al-Ghazali at the same time seeks to reveal the ambiguity of its use by philosophers. In other words, the criticism of philosophers is directed by him not so much against the truths of philosophical thought, as against what he calls the inability of philosophers to adhere to the basis, developed by them as the initial assumptions. Most of the philosophical views, according to al-Ghazali, in their essence are based on "conjectures and assumptions without research and evidence."7 As for their claim that they rely on logic and mathematics, it is unfounded. How else could the differences in opinions of philosophers in judgments, conclusions and opinions be explained, although in the arguments they don't disagree?

Differences in opinion and a lot of controversy among philosophers al-Ghazali regards as specific examples that they do not adhere to strict rules of logic. Realizing the rationalistic difficulties associated with theoretical science, he at the same time tries to discover the lack of suitability of formal logic for developing of convincing judgments on issues of life, knowledge, society, politics, law and ethics, and religious issues.

---

6 Al-Ghazali, *Mi'yar al-'ilm* (The Standard Measure of Knowledge), pp. 162 -170.

7 Al-Ghazali, *Tahafut al falasifa* (The Incoherence of the Philosophers). In Arabic. (Cairo, Dar al-Maarif, 1972), p. 76.

Thus al-Ghazali seeks to counter what could be called a philosophy's monopoly on knowledge. He argues that the philosophers logically contradict themselves, indicates that they do not fully adhere to the requirements and rules of logic. In this regard, he criticizes logic computations of philosophers, that are trying to use them in order to prove the truth of their designs. Meanwhile, in such constructions, he sees more of the hypothesis, rather than reliable knowledge, leading to the truth.

In criticizing the views of philosophers on various issues, al-Ghazali tries to prove that their logic (especially in the problems of divine metaphysics) will inevitably lead to countless errors. Philosophical views and judgments based on intuition, can not contain the absolute truth, he says. On this basis, al-Ghazali does not accept that it is right to put the discoveries of the natural sciences in the basis of ideological beliefs. In this regard in "Tahafut al falasifa" (The Incoherence of the Philosophers) he considers four issues upon which there are disagreements: the notion of causation, the human soul, the meaning of death and resurrection. In addition to these doctrinal issues, says al-Ghazali', religious thought should not be in conflict with the natural sciences.

Al-Ghazali wants to say that the achievements and discoveries of natural science, as such, do not contain worldview content. However, the problems of religious dogma in the Kalam can be comprehended by reason. Nevertheless, the true knowledge (certain knowledge) is attainable only by means of "the sublime instincts". His concept of transition from feelings to the mind and on to "what is beyond reason" is linked to this. For al-Ghazali, this process is identical to the ascent to the "certain knowledge" as knowledge in which the "knowable is being disclosed in such a way that there is no place for doubt, there can be no mistakes and illusions, and the heart can not contain an assessment of that."8 In turn, this is nothing like knowing that coincides with the original axioms - for example, such as the whole is greater than the part, that are the postulates of logic.

In this regard, al-Ghazali thinks that the commitment to logic rules is a basis for achieving reliable truths. As for the contradictions that arise in logical (rational) evidence, they not so much indicate that it is impossible to achieve true authenticity, as point to the fact that lack of adherence to the rules of logic and reason leads to confusion, making it difficult to achieve reliable truth. The contradictions that prevent the achievement of reliability (logic), are related to the fact that they can not be resolved by the evidence. Mostly it is explained by the fact that the applicable preconditions are either not credible or are well-known and generally accepted. As a source of denial of reliable truth can serve a consideration of trustworthy preconditions as not-initial. In this approach, al-Ghazali relies on the general methodological idea that there are seven components of comprehension of significant (undeniable) truth: rational initial preconditions, sacred contemplation, the

8 Al-Ghazali, *al-Munqidh min al-dalal* (The Deliverer from Error), (Beirut: Dar al-Andalus, 1996), p. 82.

external sense, experience, consistency, imagination, and fame. 9 For "achieving genuine authentic knowledge, suitable to serving as precondition for evidence", he thinks that only the first five components are usable.

This type of inner relationship of the reason (Universal acquired, active, etc.) can not be considered in isolation from the new orientation of al-Ghazali, or from the nature of its ideological synthesis, in which the unity of knowledge and action has become the essential foundation of knowledge. Meanwhile he not only seeks to build some structures, to approve the artificial unity of the individual parts of Sciences (Philosophical), but sees in their inner coherence "natural" mechanism of evolution and internal dynamics of cognition, which in its ultimate aspiration formulates the real and proper essence of reason.

From the above it is clear that al-Ghazali identifies certain knowledge and absolute truth, or intuition and rational axioms. The great merit of al-Ghazali is in his attention to the question of the possibilities of practical reason, that is the in-depth view of the logical and cognitiveoriented nature of reason, oriented on peripetia of public spirit. In other words, al-Ghazali considers the essence of reason not using the criteria of abstract knowledge, not as something identical to evident truths, or even as an abstract reflection of the acquired rational-theoretical knowledge, but through the prism of a new unity of knowledge and action. Thus, reason for him is not something that exists by itself. To reason he gives congenitallyacquired ability to accept single as a whole. And this whole is detected not by a variety of forms and types of reason, but in its internal organic unity.

---

9 Al-Ghazali, *al-Mustafa min 'ilm al-usul* (The Essentials of the Islamic Legal Theory), vol. 1, pp. 44 - 49.

CHAPTER XXVIII

ON THE CRITICISM OF REASON IN PHILOSOPHY OF AL-GHAZALI

One of the tasks facing Islamic research is to provide an objective assessment of the role of the Muslim thinker, faqih, or jurist, and Sufi, Abu Hamid al-Ghazali (d. 1111), in the drama of the rationalist tradition in the Muslim world. Still current is the notion that the reason for the Islamic world's lagging behind the West consists in subordination of the secular element to the religious, of science to religion. Al-Ghazali is believed to have played a significant role in subduing the potential of rationalism among the Muslims, and in their immersion in mysticism. The Russian philosopher Maytham al-Janabi, a renowned expert on al-Ghazali, gives a long list of assessments of al-Ghazali's role in the intellectual life of the Islamic world. Al-Ghazali is an irrationalist (E. Renan); destroyer of philosophy (Hegel); an enemy of Arab-Muslim rationalist philosophy (B. E. Bykhovskii); the main opponent of Ibn Sina in theology (A. V. Sagadeev), a representative of philosophical and reactionary obscurantism (H. Ley); a philosophizing theologian (G. Hourani), etc. 1 Not surprisingly, al-Ghazali had come to be known as a man who was almost personally responsible for the weakening of rationalism in the Muslim world.

This view was formed on the basis of two propositions. The first one claimed that al-Ghazali joined Sunni Islam and Islamic mysticism (Sufism). This view goes back to the beginning of classical Islamic studies. Even Ignaz Goldziher asserted that al-Ghazali was responsible for the link between Sufism and the Islamic religion.2 The second position asserted that al-Ghazali contributed to finalizing Muslim theological "orthodoxy". R. Nicholson writes that it was thanks to Sufi al-Ghazali, that Muslim "orthodoxy" acquired its current shape.3 R. Nicholson, like many Western scholars of Islam, maintains that Muslim "orthodoxy" is identical to the Kalam (theology) in the Ash'arite version, and because al-Ghazali shared

---

1 Maytham al-Janabi, "Teologiya i filosofiya al-Gazali," *Al-Ghazali's Theology and Philosophy*. In Russian (Moscow: Mardjani Publishing House, 2010), p. 26.

2 Ignaz Goldziher, *Al-'Aqida wa al-shari'a fi al-Islam* (Cairo: Dar al-kutub al-haditha bi-Misr, 1959), p. 179.

3 R.A. Nicholson, *The Mystics of Islam* (London: Arkana Penguin Group, 1989), p. 24.

many Ash'arite views, he calls them "orthodox".4 This vision of classical Islamic scholarship is widely accepted by scholars writing about the Islamic East, and it has even been mentioned in books on the history of Islamic philosophy.5 A modern American scholar of Iranian origin Seyyed Hossein Nasr shares the view of Western Islamic scholars of Ash'arism as Islamic theological "orthodoxy".6

This approach has inevitably influenced estimates of al-Ghazali's attitude to philosophy and rationalism as a whole. There has gradually come into being the view that in order to protect Sunni theology, which was incapable of holding its ground against philosophical arguments, al-Ghazali studied the latter and then subjected it to a devastating refutation (W. M. Watt).7 A similar position is upheld by D. B. Macdonald who claims that alGhazali completed the work of the Muslim theologian al-Ash'ari (d. 935) of introducing Greek dialectics into Muslim thinking. 8 Hence the prevailing view that al-Ghazali defended, initially as an Ash'arite mutakallimtheologian, the foundations of religion using arguments of reason (Aristotelian logic), and then, becoming completely disillusioned with the possibility of rationalism, turned to mysticism. Thus, due to its popularity, al-Ghazali became an embodiment of Islamic "orthodoxy" in the ash'arite Kalam 9 form, while his work was more and more associated with the wilting and decline of rationalism in the Muslim world.

This approach to assessing the impact of al-Ghazali on Islamic thought had already been questioned in the scientific literature. 10 For example, Russian researchers T. Ibrahim, A. Ignatenko, N. M. Kirabaev and M. al-Janabi are on record defending al-Ghazali from charges of promoting the decline of rationalism in Muslim culture.11 This accusation, according to

---

4 R.A. Nicholson, *Studies in Islamic Mysticism* (Richmond: Curzon Press, 1994), p. 80.

5 Majid Fakhry, *Islamic Philosophy. A Beginner's Guide* (Oxford: Oneworld, 2009), p. 90.

6 S.H. Nasr, *The Heart of Islam* (New York: Harper One, 2004), p. 81. 7 W.M. Watt, *The Influence of Islam on Medieval Europe* (Edinburgh: at the University Press, 1972), p. 42.

8 D.B. Macdonald, "Al-Ghazzali," *Shorter Encyclopaedia of Islam* by H.A.R. Gibb and J.H. Kremers (Original English edition published by E.J. Brill, Indian edition published in arrangement by Pentagon Press, New Dehli, 2008), p. 160.

9 Kalam is one of the fundamental trends in Arabic-Muslim philosophy; Islamic speculative theology was elaborated within the frameworks of Kalam.

10 Eric Ormsby, *Ghazali* (Oxford: Oneworld, 2007), p. 56.

11 T. Ibragim, "O kalame kak «ortodoksal'noi filosofii» islama (On Kalam as Islamic theological "orthodoxy")". *The Religion in a changing world* (Moscow: Nauka, 1992), pp. 205-212; A. Ignatenko, *Zerkalo islama (A Mirror of Islam)*/ In Russian. (Moscow: Russian Institute, 2004), p. 95; N.S. Kirabaev and M. Al-Janabi, "Znanie i vera v filosofii al-Gazali (Faith and Reason in the Thought of al-Ghazali)," *In Comparative philosophy: Knowledge and Belief in*

their point of view, stems, firstly, from misinterpretations of al-Ghazali's attitude to philosophy, rationalism, and the erroneous assessment of Ash'arism as Islamic orthodoxy (T. Ibrahim), and, secondly, from the erroneous identification of al-Ghazali's criticism of doctrinaire attitudes inherent in philosophy with his criticism of rationalism in general (A.A. Ignatenko, N. Kirabaev, and M. al-Janabi).

T. Ibrahim believes that the basic philosophical question in the Islamic Middle Ages was, given the dominance of religious ideology, the relation of God and the world, while the reason for the creative development of Islamic religious and philosophical thought was the opposition of rationalism (*'aklāniyya*/rationalism) and fideism (*'imāniyya*/fideism). Contrary to the stereotypical idea, popular in the literature, which claims that the Kalam (especially Ash'arism) as a backlash to free-thinking on the past of Islamic orthodoxy, he puts forward a thesis that the rationalistic attitudes of Mu'tazila in Ash'arism continued, albeit in a weakened form. Therefore, one cannot, in his view, refer to Ash'arism as Islamic "orthodoxy" in general, and to al-Ghazali as an "orthodox" in particular.12

To support the thesis of the insolvency of the stereotype claim regarding the Ash'arite teaching as "orthodoxy," T. Ibrahim points to the famous "Kadirit Creed," which was aimed not only "against the Shi'ism, but also against Kalam, both of the Mu'tazilite and Ash'arite".13 However, the Hanbalite theologian and jurist Ibn Taymiyya (d. 1328) writes that during the reign of Caliph Al-Qadir (991-1031) Asharites were not classified as "people of innovation" (*mubtadi'a*). Hence, they were spared the brutal persecution that befell the Mu'tazilah, Ismaelites, Shi'ites and Jahmites, with murders and curses in the mosques.14 During the reign of Caliph al-Qa'im next (1031-1075), however, the Ash'arites were designated as "people of innovation" (*mubtadi'a*) and they were also cursed in all mosques.15 It did not help Ash'arites that their teacher, al-Ash'ari (d. 935), after the disengagement from Mu'tazila, openly sided with the followers of Ahmad ibn Hanbal (d. 855), the main systematizer of Islamic

---

the Dialogue of Cultures. Institute of Philosophy. In Russian. (Moscow, Vostochnaya Literatura Publishers, 2008), pp. 163-171; N.S. Kirabaev and M. Al-Janabi, "Faith and Reason in the Thought of al-Ghazali," *Knowledge and Belief in the Dialogue of Cultures*, edited by Marietta Stepanyants (Cultural Heritage and Contemporary Change Series IVA, Eastern and Central Europe; vol. 39, 2011). pp. 143-150.

12 T. Ibragim, "O kalame kak 'ortodoksal'noi filosofii' islama (On Kalam as Islamic theological 'orthodoxy')," *The Religion in a changing world.* In Russian (Moscow: Nauka, 1992), pp. 205-212.

13 *Ibid.*, p. 207.

14 Ibn Taymiyya, *Al-Fatawa al-kubra'* (Cairo: Dar al-rayyan li-al-turath, 1988), vol. 6, pp. 650-651.

15 *Ibid.*, p. 652.

traditionalism. 16 In light of the above historical facts, Ash'arism was not what one can definitely refer to as an "orthodox theology" of Islam.

Presentation of al-Ghazali's position as anti-philosophical is also based on the belief that al-Ghazali fully shared the occasionalism of Mutakallims, especially Ash'arites, according to Majid Fakhry. 17 Meanwhile, the Russian philosopher T. Ibrahim already came up with a critical assessment of Maimonides' (d. 1204) interpretation of Kalam, which was adopted by the Europeans, as a system of atomistic indeterminism and occasionalism. According to T. Ibrahim, there is an obvious ideological bias in the interpretation of Mutakallims' atomistic occasionalism as an expression of the "spirit" of the agents of the Arab-Muslim civilization opposed to the "synthetic "European "spirit".18

We would like, if we may, to express some arguments against Majid Fakhry without going into the depths of an extremely complex question concerning the nature of thinking in agents/practitioners of Islamic culture. In discussing the issue of causality, al-Ghazali uses two concepts: the "divine sentence" (*Qada'*) and the "destiny" (*Qadar*). The second concept of "destiny" (*Qadar*) allows al-Ghazali to depart from straight occasionalism, i.e., explaining natural events and human acts through direct (voluntaristic) intervention of God. Al-Ghazali argues that the "sentence" (*Qada'*) that God makes as he desires, does not contradict "destiny" (*Qadar*), which, in turn, should be understood as an expansion in time of divine sentence (*Qada'*). He writes: "On the contrary, the cause and effect relationship is the first sentence (*Qada'*), which [took place] like in a blink of an eye, or even faster. The gradual and detailed organization of consequences according to an exact order of causes is "destiny" (*Qadar*)".19

Thus, al-Ghazali interprets divine predestination as an attempt to reconcile the traditionalist understanding, which, in essence, is occasionalism, a form of indeterminism, or recognition of God's voluntaristic attitude to people and events in the world, and the Mu'tazilite understanding, which may be reduced to determinism. The Mu'tazilah attribute acts of God to his knowledge, and this excludes the possibility of unfairness on the part of God toward his creatures.

Russian researcher M. al-Janabi believes that al-Ghazali was not an Ash'arite conservative but a thinker who though shut in the range of traditional problems, was trying to break away from the limitation of

---

16 Ibn Taymiyya, *Al-Fatawa al-kubra'*, vol. 6, p. 660; Adam Mez, "Musul'manskii Renessans," *The renaissanse of Islam*. In Russian (Moscow: "ViM" Publishers, 1996), p. 199.

17 Majid Fakhry, *Islamic Philosophy. A Beginner's Guide* (Oxford: Oneworld, 2009), p. 90.

18 T. Ibragim. "O kalame kak "ortodoksal'noi filosofii' islama (On Kalam as Islamic theological 'orthodoxy')", p. 205.

19 Al-Ghazali. *Ihya 'Ulum al-Din* (Beirut: Dar al-kitab al-'arabi, No date of publication), vol. 1, p. 592.

Kalam. 20 According to him, al-Ghazali did not reject philosophy on the whole, he rejected philosophers' claims to possess absolute truth; namely, he challenged Plato on the basis of Aristotle's positions, etc. "The negative attitude of al-Ghazali to the rationalism of philosophers was expressed in his denial of their ability to make absolute judgments".21 It was important for him to fight against any claim of this kind, of all sorts of authoritarianism, even those attired in a philosopher's toga.

The above presumably explains the purpose of al-Ghazali's writing the work *Deliverence from the Error* (Al-Munqidh min al-Dalal): He was not disappointed in Kalam as a whole, or Falsafa (Islamic Peripatetic Philosophy), fiqh (law), and Sufism; he was dissatisfied by the claims made by proponents of each of these creeds (Kalam, Falsafa, fiqh, and Sufism) to possess the ultimate truth, which led their representatives toward doctrinairism, narrow-mindedness, professional isolation, and fanaticism.

It's hard not to agree with the above arguments that defend al-Ghazali from the charge of rejecting rationalist philosophers from the standpoint of unreasoning faith. Indeed, in some cases, al-Ghazali disagreed with Ash'arism and defended the rationalistic line more persistently. This is evident in his criticism of Kalam (including Ash'arism) and Sufism. In criticizing Kalam, especially in his monumental *The Revival of Religious Sciences* (Ihya 'Ulum al-Din) and in *Deliverence from the Error* (Al-Munqidh min al-Dalal), he censured the Mutakallims for their fanaticism, blind adherence to their teachers, and the propensity to initiate doubts and shake the faith of common people.22 In criticizing Sufism, he challenged its opposition of reason to mystical knowledge. He believed that the mind needs to be supplemented by mystical knowledge, but not be replaced with it. In criticizing philosophers, he did not question the value of reason, but always pointed to limits of its use. After all, he was a Sufi, and the latter, while not denying the value of rational knowledge, at the same time pointed out its limited capabilities.23 In the chapter on Intellect in *The Revival of Religious Sciences* (Ihya 'Ulum al-Din), he defends what he calls the dignity of the Intellect. 24 According to al-Ghazali, the solution of intractable problems of metaphysics and theology from the standpoint of reason is possible only by addressing them in the plane of ethics. This is

20 M. al-Janabi. *Teologiya i filosofiya al-Gazali (Al-Ghazali's Theology and Philosophy*). In Russian (Moscow: Mardjani Publishing House, 2010), p. 93.

21 *Ibid.*, p. 104.

22 Al-Ghazali, *Ihya 'Ulum al-Din,* vol. 1, p. 167; Al-Ghazali, *Al-Munqidh min al-Dalal* (Cairo: Al-Fajr al-jadid. No date of publication), pp. 10-12.

23 M. Stepanyants, "Sufizm: misticheskoe mirovospriyatie (Sufism: mystical Perception)," *Mir Vostoka. Filosofiya: Proshloye. Nastoyashcheye. Budushcheye (Oriental World. Philosophy: Past, Present, Future).* In Russian (Moscow: Vostochnaya Literatura Publishers, 2005), p. 55.

24 Al-Ghazali, *Ihya 'Ulum al-Din,* vol. 1, pp. 140-144.

what compelled him to create a comprehensive religious and ethical system in *The Revival of Religious Sciences* (Ihya 'Ulum al-Din) 25 . A similar attempt was undertaken by the 20th-century philosopher E. Levinas who sought to create an "ethical metaphysics".26

In assessing al-Ghazali's position vis-à-vis rationalism one should consider his view of the issue of human cognition. To him the learning process is endless. "It is a continuous process in which it is impossible to achieve any absolute or ultimate result".27 In the row of knowledge seekers there is room for a philosopher (*hakim*), though the extent of his communion with // proximity to the truth is smaller than that of a prophet. "The highest degree is the degree of the prophet,"28 he writes.

Those considering al-Ghazali an anti-rationalist who, moreover, occupied an anti-philosophical position can refer to his *Deliverence from the Error* (Al-Munqidh min al-Dalal), of course, where he writes that all philosophers bear the brand of disbelief.29 But then this work is of a purely polemical nature. In it he also criticizes Kalam (including ash'arite Kalam). Most likely it was an essay written for the same purpose as another piece of his, *Reining back of the Commonalty from the Science of Kalam* (Ildjam al'awwam 'an 'ilm al-kalam), namely, to protect the uneducated masses of believers from religious and theological speculation, too abstract for them to understand and capable of confusing them and undermining their faith.

This is illustrated by his positive criticism of philosophy in the treatise *The Incoherence of Philosophers* (Tahafut al-falasifa), where he examines twenty "issues" discussed by philosophers and finds that only three of these issues or assertions are a clear expression of "unbelief" (*kufr*): recognition that the world is eternal, the claim that God knows only universals, and the denial of bodily resurrection30. The purpose of his work, he says, is not about setting out his doctrine of truth (*madhhab al-haqq*) as an alternative philosophy. The main purpose of composing *The Incoherence of Philosophers,* by his own admission, is to prove the failure of philosophers' claims to be in possession of absolutely truthful arguments for solving metaphysical problems.31

---

25 M. al-Janabi, *Teologiya i filosofiya al-Gazali (Al-Ghazali's Theology and Philosophy),* p. 137.

26 Richard A. Cohen. "Introduction," Emmanual Levinas. *Humanism of the Other*, trans. from the French by Nidra Poller (University of Illinois Press. Urbana and Chicago, 2003), p. XXVI.

27 M. al-Janabi, *Teologiya i filosofiya al-Gazali (Al-Ghazali's Theology and Philosophy*), p. 148.

28 Al-Ghazali, *Ihya 'Ulum al-Din*, vol. 3, p. 1358.

29 Al-Ghazali, *Al-Munqidh min al-Dalal* (Cairo: Al-Fajr al-jadid. No date of publication), p. 13.

30 Al-Ghazali, *Tahafut al-falasifa* (Cairo: Dar al-ma'arif, 1972), pp. 307 309.

31 *Ibid.*, p. 123.

He argues that all attempts to solve metaphysical and philosophical problems (God, theodicy) on the basis of Aristotelian logic will inevitably lead to irresolvable antinomies (George McLean).32 Rational thinking which can only move forward by means of definitions, is powerless in the face of the transcendent realm because of the indeterminacy of God. Russian expert on Islam A. Ignatenko also writes: "He (al-Ghazali - I.N.) proves the incoherence and flaws in metaphysical provisions advanced by philosophers from the standpoint of Aristotelian logic, protected by these same philosophers, and demonstrates the subjectivist fantastic nature of their utterly groundless philosophical postulates". 33 In other words, al-Ghazali criticized not reason and the rational, but claims of absolutization of the mind.34 "The mind has its own contradictions and limitations in the infinite pursuit of knowledge. Accentuation of the inabilities of reason does not justify irrationality". 35 Al-Ghazali in *The Incoherence of Philosophers* argues that it is impossible to solve metaphysical and theological problems with the help of, say, geometric evidence.36

Yet he does not think that we should abandon attempts to formulate and solve metaphysical and philosophical questions. According to him, the search for rational justification ought to proceed not in the realm of formal logic, but in the revealed source - the Qur'an. He refers to the rationalism of Islamic culture, which we interpret as the Quranic intuitive certainty of the superiority of knowledge over faith. Some knowledge always precedes faith. This idea is reflected in the Qur'an's constant appeal to the mind of man, to his reason when accepting revealed truths. "The irradiating clarity of truth is a basic Qur'anic intuition which permeates Islamic culture".37 AlGhazali relies on the tradition of the majority of believers to adhere to the

---

32 G.F. McLean. "Editor's Introduction," Al-Ghazālī. *Deliverance from the Error and Mystical Union with the Almighty (Al-Munqidh min al-Dalāl / alGhazālī) critical Arabic text established by Muhammad Abūlailah and Nurshīf Abdul-Rahīm Rif'at*, English translation with introduction by Muhammad Abūlailah; introduction and notes by George F. McLean, (Washington, D. C.: Published by the Council for Research in Values and Philosophy, 2001), p. 39.

33 A. Ignatenko, *Zerkalo islama (A Mirror of Islam)*. In Russian (Moscow: Russian Institute, 2004), p. 95.

34 Sulayman Dunya, "Introduction to the 3rd Edition," Al-Ghazali, *Tahafut al-falasifa*" (Cairo: Dar al-ma'arif, 1972), p. 37.

35 M. al-Janabi, *Teologiya i filosofiya al-Gazali (Al-Ghazali's Theology and Philosophy)*, p. 151.

36 Al-Ghazali, *Tahafut al-falasifa*, p. 181.

37 A. Smirnov, "Spravedlivost' (opyt kontrastnogo ponimaniya) (Understanding justice in the context of classical Islamic thought: some points of contrast with Western theories)," *Medieval Arabic philosophy: Problems and Solutions*. In Russian (Moscow: Vostochnaya Literatura Publishers, 1998), p. 255.

Qur'an in considering that faith (*'iman*) is a function of knowledge (*'ilm*).38 Hence, in order to protect reason, the dignity of reason, and to justify the need for rational search, he turns to those passages in the Qur'an that refer to the exceptional importance of knowledge to faith.

Knowledge is one of the most important concepts of the Islamic religion. Islam establishes a new type of knowledge, which is expressed in the language of religion and oriented toward reasonableness and rationality. The reasons for the special status of knowledge in Islamic culture are to be found in the foundations of this culture, the text of the Qur'an. The Qur'an links man's responsibility for his actions with his reason and knowledge of the law. Hence the important role of the mind (*'aql*) for the faith. In the future, the doctrine of predestination and the freedom of human choice, which goes back to the Qur'an, would become a subject of heated debate of Muslim theologians and philosophers, which stimulates the process of the conceptualization of knowledge.39

Al-Ghazali, as we have seen, was developing the rationalist line of al-Ash'ari, who devoted a small work, *The Favour of Pursuing the Science of* Kalam (Istihsan al-khawd fi 'ilm al-kalam), to a revelational justification of rational search 40 . Meanwhile, al-Ash'ari's effort in the revelational justification of the rational search was deeply organic to the religious tradition of Islam. Even the earliest Islamic traditionalism, Hanbali, was not alien to theological discussion and even debated issues of natural philosophy, and later actually contributed to the development of these issues, as is attested by such scholars as L. A. Garde, A. Laust, and J. Maqdisi.41 Ahmad ibn Hanbal, the founder of Islamic traditionalism and the eponym Hanbali, actively contested the Jahmites, who denied the existence

---

38 F. Rosenthal, *Torzhestvo znaniya. Kontseptsiya znaniya v srednevekovom islame (Knowledge Triumphant. The Concept of Knowledge in Medieval Islam).* In Russian. (Moscow: Nauka, 1978). pp. 108, 117. (Russian ed. of: Franz Rosenthal, *Knowledge Triumphant. The Concept of Knowledge in Medieval Islam* (Leiden: E. J. Brill, 1970)

39 Evgenia Frolova, *Arabic Philosophy: Past and Present.* In Russian (Moscow, Publishing House «Languages of Slavonic Culture», 2010), pp. 2630.

40 Abu-l-Hasan al-Ash'ari, "Odobrenie zanyatiya kalamom (Istihsan alkhawd fi 'ilm al-kalam) (The Favour of Pursuing the Science of Kalam). Introduction, translation and commentaries by T. Ibrahim," *Medieval Arabic philosophy: Problems and Solutions.* In Russian (Moscow: Vostochnaya Literatura Publishers, 1998), p. 368.

41 See L. Gardet, *L'Islam: religion et communauté* (Paris, 1967), p. 201; H. Laoust, *Essai sur les doctrines sociales et politiques de Taki-d-Din Ahmad b. Taimiya* (Le Caire, 1939), p. 2; G. Makdisi, "L'Islam hanbalisante, " *Revue des études islamiques,* vol. 43 (Paris, 1975), fasc. 2, p. 75. Quoted from T. Ibragim, "O kalame kak 'ortodoksal'noi filosofii' islama (On Kalam as Islamic theological 'orthodoxy')," *The Religion in a changing world.* In Russian (Moscow: Nauka, 1992), p. 212.

of God's attributes, and passed a severe "test" (*mihna*), defending the thesis of Islamic Salafi-traditionalists about the uncreated nature of the Qoran. He asseverated that the words in the Qur'an are "God's speech and that it is uncreated".42

While recognizing al-Ash'ari's profound knowledge of Mutakallims' views and their differences, Hanbali jurist-theologian Ibn Taymiyya (d. 1328) reproached him for his poor knowledge of the traditions of the rational search of the proponents of Muslim traditionalism (*ahl al-Sunna wa ashab al-hadith*). Ibn Taymiyya says: "He (al-Ash'ari. - I.N.) gives information about the Mutakallims' differences concerning the smallest particle (*daqiq*) but he does not mention the controversy of the "people of tradition" (*ahl al-ḥadith*) about the smallest particle. Meanwhile, the [latter were] engaged in extremely subtle arguments about things like, for example, 'the expression' (*lafz*) [and sense], and 'decrease of faith' [and its increase]; the preference [as a caliph] of 'Uthman ibn 'Affan [to 'Ali ibn Abi Talib, a cousin of the Prophet Muhammad,]; some *hadiths*43 about the attributes (*Sifat*) [God]; the prohibition to use the term "coercion" (*jabr*) [regarding human actions]; and other subtle things".44 It is noteworthy that there is no evidence (in the form of translations into Arabic) of direct connection between Mutakallims and antique atomists.45 This makes even more striking the existence of a stratum of original atomistic views of the pre-Kalam period among the early Muslims.

Moreover, the same Ibn Taymiyya demonstrates, in a discussion by correspondence, with the "unifiers" (*ittihadiyya*), proponents of the unity of existence, an excellent mastery of the art of Kalam (the arguments). Responding to a question about the meaning of the *hadith* (saying) by Prophet Muhammad, "Do not blaspheme against the Age (*dahr*), because God is the age," he refuses to accept the literal meaning of these words. He states that God is not the time. Time, in his opinion, is a characteristic of motion, or accident (*'arad*), which requires a substrate (or substance) (*jawhar*). But God does not need anything else to support his existence.46 And this from one of the Hanbalites who are typically described in the

42 Ibn Taymiyya, *Al-Fatawa al-kubra,'* vol. 5, p. 20.

43 "The word *hadith* means primarily a communication or narrative in general whether religious or profane, then it has the particular meaning of a record of action or saying of the Prophet [Muhammad] and his companions". Th.W. Juynboll, "Hadith," *Shorter Encyclopaedia of Islam* by H.A.R. Gibb and J.H. Kremers. (Original English edition published by E.J. Brill, Indian edition published in arrangement by Pentagon Press, New Dehli, 2008), pp. 166-167.

44 Ibn Taymiyya, *Al-Fatawa al-kubra'*, vol. 6, p. 662.

45 Al Noor Dhanani, *The Physical Theory of Kalam. Atoms, Space and Void in Basrian Mu'tazili Cosmology* (Leiden/New York/Koln: E.J. Brill, 1994), p. 5.

46 Ibn Taymiyya, *Al-Fatawa al-kubra,'* vol. 5, pp. 65-66.

literature as enemies of the allegorical interpretation of the Qur'an and the Hadith!

Even more amazing is that Ibn Taymiyya, in his criticism of pronouncements by philosophers (*mutafalsifa*) regarding Platonic ideas, eidos, that are free from forms of primordial matter (Hayula), speaks approvingly of the "intelligent among philosophers" for their rejection of real existence of "pure universals" outside of the mind, and for their moderate nominalism.47 Moreover, this is not, in his view, an expression of his personal likes and dislikes, but an expression of the position of the "people of the tradition of Muhammad and the consensus" (*ahl al-sunna wa al-djama'a*)48 that is those who are habitually referred to as one of the most zealous followers of Islamic traditionalism. A noteworthy kind of tolerance for other people's views demonstrated by a supporter of Hanbali, which is regarded as the source of the ideology of Wahhabism, an Islamic fundamentalist.

The following conclusions sum up the subject matter. In the struggle between rationalism and fideism of the traditionalists,
Al-Ghazali sided with rationalism. He relied on the potential of rationalism in Kalam, whose chief characteristics were the assertion of the priority of reason over faith; the rejection of blind adherence to tradition (*taqlid*); and the denial of any belief whose acceptance is not preceded by doubts about their veracity.49 He is not responsible for the weakening of the rationalist tradition in the Islamic East. The Muslim world's lagging behind the West (including the intellectual lag) is due to a whole range of socio-economic and political reasons. Among them - the discovery by Europeans of alternative sea routes to the East as a result of the 15th-17th-century Great Discoveries, the subsequent economic decline of the Muslim countries, the invasion of the Tatars (Mongols), etc. But that is a different topic for discussion.

(Translated from Russian by Serge Gitman)

---

47 Ibn Taymiyya, *Al-Fatawa al-kubra'*, vol. 5, p. 67. 48 Ibn Taymiyya, *Al-Fatawa al-kubra'*, vol. 6, p. 662.

49 A.V. Sagadeev, "Kalam (obzor) (Kalam (review)," *Collection of Reviews*, ed. and compiled by A.V. Sagadeev. In Russian. (Moscow: ISISS RAS, 1988), p. 82.

CHAPTER XXIX

INTERFAITH DIALOGUE IN THE CONTEXT OF NEW THEOLOGICAL LANGUAGE

We, Muslim intellectuals, need to be aware of the fact that we live in societies, which are not constituted by Islamic cultural dynamics. In such a socially constructed world, on the one hand we need to manage to remain spiritually intact as Muslims; on the other hand we need to initiate and engage in communication with the adherents of other faiths. In this paper, I am not able to explicate all the modern social, cultural and institutional forces that socially threaten the spiritually intact Muslim. This is another issue and needs a special study. My task here, in this paper, is to explore the potential of Islam and Islamic culture to develop a feasible ground for establishing inter-faith dialogue and communication.

In the Middle Ages, the relationship between religions was often in a hostile atmosphere; for instance Christians' conflict with Muslims had often ended on the battlefield. Christian theological argument with regard to the 'heathen world' and 'heretics' at that time was orchestrated by the Church. Such attitudes not only separated Christians and non-Christians but also Catholics and heretics. As a consequence, the motto *'Extra ecclesiam nulla salus'* (there is no salvation outside the Church) became a central principle of the Catholic Church.

In the Middle Ages, a Christian theology of religions was dominated by exclusivism, that is, all people, [whatever race, colour or religion] must be Christian if they are to be saved. For instance, in the decree of the Council of Florence in 1438-45 it was stated:

No one remaining outside the Catholic Church, not just pagans, but also Jews or heretics or schismatics, can become partakers of eternal life; but they will go to "everlasting fire which was prepared for the devil and his angels", unless before the end of life they are joined to the Church.1

In the Protestant world, such an exclusive the attitude was also predominant. Luther in his *Large Catechism* asserted:

Those who are outside Christianity, be they heathens, Turks, Jews or false Christians [i.e. Roman Catholics], although they may believe in only one true God, yet remain in eternal wrath and perdition.2

---

1 Henry Denzinger, 468-9, *The Church Teaches: Documents of the Church in English Translation* (St. Louis/London: B. Herder Book Co., 1955), p. 165.

2 Martin Luther, *Large Catechism*, II. iii, trans. H. Wace and C.A. Buchheim in *Luther's Primary Works* (London: Hodder and Stoughton, 1896), p. 106.

In the mediaeval period, the world was divided into different religious camps. The governing power in those days sought to justify itself through the way it displayed enmity towards the opposite religious camp.3

In this century, in spite of the dominance of such an exclusivist attitude in the Christian world, there has appeared a notable shift from religious exclusivism to the religious inclusivism or even pluralism as a result of the impact of liberal values in the West. One might state that it would have been more fruitful if the Church had reached such a form of inclusive attitude through its own development rather than through the pressure of the dominant secular culture. The Catholic Church's recent but significant paradigm shift made in the Second Vatican Council of 19631965 is arguably the result of such a cultural imperative. In its Dogmatic Constitution on the Church, promulgated in 1964, the Council declared:

The Catholic Church rejects nothing which is true and holy in these religions. She looks with sincere respect upon those ways of conduct and of life, those rules and teachings which, though differing in many particulars from what she holds and sets forth, nevertheless often reflect a ray of that Truth which enlightens all men.

If one compares this passage with the statement of *'extra ecclesiam nulla salus'* one can surely realise the progress made towards a more tolerant and better understanding of other religions in the Catholic Church.4

ISLAMIC POTENTIAL FOR INTER-FAITH DIALOGUE

It is interesting to note that in early and medieval Islam, Muslim scholars approached the issue of the adherents of other faiths within the context of Islamic jurisprudence not that of *Kalam*, Islamic theology. They often thought that the issue of determining the status of those who lived within the domain of Islam was a practical problem, i.e. it arose when a certain group of people or individuals were classified for administrative purposes.

On the other hand, I believe that the basic principles exhibited by the Qur'an and the *Sunnah* can offer a tangible account of Islamic theology of religions. In addition to this we also see the historical implementation of those principles in Muslim societies throughout Islamic history. Now, I would like to enumerate the Quranic principles with regard to the issue of

---

3 C. Philip, Almond in his *Heretic and Hero: Muhammad and the Victorians* (Wiesbaden: Otto Harrassowitz, 1989) gives an interesting account of the Victorians' image of the Prophet of Islam.

4 As far as the attitude of the Catholic Church toward Islam is concerned, The Vatican Council II has not yet produced a meeting point between Muslims and Christians. What Muslims expect to see from the Christian world is a fair understanding with regard to both the nature of the Qur'an and the personality of the Prophet. Such an understanding seems quite crucial if there is to be any hope of a Muslim-Christian dialogue.

inter-religious dialogue as propositions, which aim to suggest an account of 'Islamic potential'.

- First, in the Qur'an, the universality as well as the diversity of God's revelation to humankind is affirmed. Islam explicitly endorses the universality of God's revelation, which plays a significant part in the Islamic understanding of other religions. The God of the Quran is not only the God of the Muslims but the God of all humankind. The Qur'an illustrates this point by stating: 'Unto Allah belong the East and West, and whithersoever you turn, there is Allah's countenance. For Allah is All-Embracing, Allknowing' (2:115). The God of all humankind did not leave any nation in the dark, rather he illuminated them by sending messengers. 5 Therefore Muslims receive a Qur'anic sanction that enables them to expand an Islamic account of prophecy in such a manner that it could include those messengers who are not mentioned in the Qur'an, including Gautama the Buddha, and the *avatars* of the Hindus. Although all the messengers spoke about the same reality and conveyed the same truth, the messages they delivered were not identical in their theological forms. That is simply because the message was expressed in the specific forms which should accord and make sense for the culture it was sent to. Thus, a messenger is to speak within the cultural context of the community to which the message is revealed.6

- Second, in Islam multiplicity of races, colours, communities and religions is regarded as the sign of God's mercy and glory exhibited through his creatures.

Plurality in this sense is accepted as a natural phenomenon. The Qur'an states: "O Humankind! Verily we have created you of a male and female; and we have distributed you in nations and tribes that you might know one another and recognise that, in the sight of God the most honourable of you is the most pious. Verily God is wise and all knowing" (49:13). But what Islam aims to do is to integrate such diversity into unity through the sacred principles of the Qur'an; it explains the reason and purpose for such racial and religious multiplicity. God created such religious, racial, and other forms of diversity in order to distinguish those who can appreciate the majesty of God and see his purpose from those who

5 The Qur'an states: "To every nation (was sent) a messenger (10:47); and verily we have raised in every nation a messenger, (proclaiming) serve Allah and shun false gods (16:36); there is not a nation but a warner had paseth among them (35:24)".

6 The Qur'an endorses this view: "We sent not a messenger except in the language of his own people in order to make things clear to them (14:4)".

ignore the signs of God as such. Otherwise God could have created only one nation.7

One of the prime tasks of Islam is to eliminate discrimination based upon race or colour by proposing a single Islamic brotherhood, which aims to unite all the different people under one faith. It has partly achieved this during its history. Beyond this, Islam even managed to establish a unity among all the subjects including the Christians and Jews that it governed. Furthermore, one might even claim that diversity, whether religious or racial, is considered in the Quran as the means to unity.

-Third, it is possible that every revealed religion can be named as *islam,* when it is seen as 'a state of submission to God' (literally *islam*). Expanding the term *islam* in a manner that could envelope all other revealed religions is not something produced in order to counter the quest for a pluralistic approach. It is a Quranic endeavour, which aims to show all revelations as the part and parcel of God's plan. Muslims believe that *islam* is the name of the basic mission of all prophets throughout history.

-The fourth principle is that there is no compulsion in religion. This is one of the unique principles of the Quran which was initiated in order to regulate freedom of religious belief in Islam. The Quran reads: "Let there be no compulsion in religion: Truth stands out clear from Error: whoever rejects Evil and believes in Allah has grasped the most trustworthy handhold, that never breaks. And God hears and knows all things (2:256); Say 'The Truth is from your Lord': let him who will, believe, let him who will, reject (it) (18:29); If it had been the Lord's Will, they would all have believed - All who are on earth! Will you then compel mankind against their will to believe! (10:99).

This verse itself has functioned as a law by safeguarding the freedom of religious belief throughout Islamic history. 8 It was such Quranic

---

7 The Qur'an simply states this point: "If your Lord had so willed, he could have made mankind one nation: but they will not cease to dispute (11:118).

8 Vardit Rispler-Chaim compares the verse 2:256 with the other verses in the Quran that speak of the regulation of war and concludes that the verse that propagates religious tolerance was not intended in the first place. It was a *taqiyya* and initiated for a strategic purposes in order to establish the Islamic community. When the community was established it was not tolerance but military campaigns that decided the destiny of Islam. See "There is no compulsion in Religion (Quran 2,256): Freedom of Religious Belief in the Qur'an," *The Bulletin of Henry Martyn Institute of Islamic Studies* 11 (JulyDec., 1992): 19-32. In response to Rispler-Chaim, I argue that the mere existence of such a sacred injunction is sufficient to show the intention of the Quran. If Risper-Chaim really wants to bring out the actual position of Islam with regard religious tolerance, he must compare it with historical Christianity and Judaism. No Muslim, however, claims that Islam can satisfy the requirements of the liberal values of the secular culture. But, its own history

injuctions which have provided a rationale for the religious tolerance that has characterised Islamic history. As Bernard Lewis points out, religious persecution of the members of other faiths was almost absent; Jews and Christians under Muslim rule were not subject to exile, apostasy or death that were the choices offered to Muslims and Jews in reconquered Spain. And also, Christians and Jews were not subject to any major territorial and occupational restrictions, such as was the common lot of Jews in premodern Europe.9

It would, however, be wrong to say that Muslims consider Judaism and Christianity being as authentic as Islam in leading to the truth. Islam considers itself superior to other religions when it presents truth. But what makes Islam different from other religions is that it tolerates the existence of other religions *while it is in power*. As a result of such a principle, although Islam had ruled for some thousand years over Christians and Jews, it did not encourage a systematic 'islamization' of the adherents of these faiths.10 Like any other religion Islam aims to propagate its beliefs. But what makes it different from other religions is that it did not establish an organisation or institution for its propagation. In its history, Islam did not have missionary societies or any missionary institution. The work of *da'wa* is always left to an individual effort.11 The Gülen movement in contemporary Islam, is an interesting case that would give us a clue as to which direction interreligious relations between Muslims and the adherents of other faiths can go in Turkey.

THE GROUND OF NEW THEOLOGICAL LANGUAGE: ISLAMIC INTER-FAITH DIALOGUE

Opposing most of the reactionary Muslim intellectuals and group leaders who adopt either reactionary or apologetic language, Gülen uses more open and tolerant discourse. I see such attitude as actualisation of Islamic potential. While some other Islamists and even fundamentalists are expressing hatred and intolerance towards those who do not think and

---

proves that Islamic power has tolerated the existence of other religions within its own realm.

9 Bernard Lewis, *The Jews of Islam* (Princeton: Princeton University Press, 1984), p. 8.

10 In *The Preaching of Islam: A History of Propagation of the Muslim Faith* (Lahore: Sh. Muhammad Ashraf, 1961) T. W. Arnold presents a historical account of the spread of Islam and concludes that Islam has expanded through persuasion and preaching rather than force and compulsion.

11 For instance, the Quran lays down the principles of propagating Islam: "Invite to the way of your Lord with wisdom and beautiful preaching; argue with them in ways that are best and most gracious: for your Lord knows best, who have strayed from His Path, and who received guidance (16:125)."

behave like them, Gülen is speaking of tolerance, forgiveness, love and peace. As John O. Voll rightly states that he is neither "fundamentalist" nor "secularist" and his ideas provides a vision that transcends modernity.12

The first principle he proposes in the context of interfaith dialogue, is that of tolerance and forgiveness. He derives this principle from the Quran by quoting these verses: "And the servants of (God) the All-Merciful are those who move on the earth in humility, and when the ignorant address them, they say: 'Peace' (25-63); Those who witness no falsehood, and, if they pass by futility, pass by it with honourable avoidance (25:72); And when they hear vain talk, they turn away wherefrom and say: "To us our deeds, and to you yours" (28:55). For him, one who feels responsible for spreading the truth of Islam, whom he calls the hero of love, ought to possess the character of gentleness and tolerance. In such behaviours, the hero of love must be as generous as Moses and Aaron who were commanded to behave tolerantly and to speak softly to the Pharaoh.13

The second principle is "meeting in common word". He takes this concept from this Quranic verse: "O people of the Book! Come to common terms as between us and you: that we worship none but God; that we associate no partners with Him; that we take not some from among ourselves Lords other than God" (3:64). From this standpoint he further develops and speaks of "the necessity of increasing common interests we share with the people with whom we are in dialogue".14 If these people are Jews and Christians, common interests and common word should be the meeting point. According to Gülen, the common word between Muslims and "the people of the book" is belief in God. Since the above-mentioned verse did not put the prophethood of Muhammad as a condition of coming terms, he appears to be ready to talk theologically to Christian and Jews without putting the prophethood of Muhammad forward. This, I believe, can be considered as a new step forward in interfaith dialogue. What about the sharp criticism of the Quran towards Jews and Christians? He answers this by suggesting "the verses condemning and rebuking the Jews and Christians are either about some particular Jews and Christians who lived in the time of the Prophet Muhammad or their own Prophets, such as Moses and Jesus, or those who deserved such condemnation because of their wrong beliefs or practices."15 He even broadens the boundaries of the ground of interfaith dialogue in order to embrace not only Jews and Christians but also all the good people of other faiths. He states:

---

12 John O. Voll, "Fethullah Gülen, Transcending Modernity in the New Islamic Discourse," *Turksih Islam and the Secular State; The Gülen Movement*, ed. M. Hakan Yavuz and John L. Esposito (Syracuse: Syracuse University, Press, 2003), p. 245.

13 Fethullah Gülen, *Love and the Essence of Being Human* (Istanbul: Jounalists and Writers Foundation Publications, 2004), p. 135.

14 Ibid., p. 169.

15 Fethullah Gülen, *Love and the Essence of Being Human*, p. 209.

Today there is needed for people who are virtuous, self-possessed, cautious, sincere and pure in heart, who do not steal or think too much of themselves, and who prefer others' well-being to theirs, and have no worldly expectations. If humankind can find people with these characteristics, it means a much better feature for the world is imminent.16

The third principle is that religions should not be taken as the instrument of the "clash of civilizations". Instead they ought to be utilised as the means for peace and tolerance in the world. As Voll indicates many social theories that have predicted the end of religion have failed. Secularisation is losing ground and desecularisation has become an important phenomena.17 In this process, religion is gaining an opportunity to play a significant role in shaping social movements in different countries. Since Gülen addresses and also offers the solution to the moral and social problems that were caused by globalisation, his ideas and his community have become an instrument of resacralization process in the Islamic community. Gülen argues that the world of today is in deep environmental, educational and philosophical crises. Now "in a world that is rapidly becoming smaller and in an era when time and space are shrinking" he argues "there is a need for a new way of thinking, a new approach to sciences, a new life philosophy, and new educational institutions." 18 He suggests that Huntington's claim about the "clash of civilizations" is a strategic move that aims to politically regulate the world rather than a sensible prediction of the future of the world. Instead he wants to talk about "the meeting of civilizations". He insists that religions especially Islam, are not and cannot be the source of conflict and war, but are instead the foundation of peace and unity. He argues:

In truth, no divine religion was ever based on conflict, whether it be the religions represented by Moses and Jesus, or the religion represented by Muhammad, upon them be peace. On the contrary, these religions, especially Islam, are strictly against disorder, treachery, conflict and oppression. Islam means peace, security and well being. Thus, in a religion based on peace, security and world harmony, war and conflict are malfunctioning things. The exceptional case is self-defence like when the body tries to get rid of germs that have attacked it, and this can be done only according to certain principles. Islam has always breathed peace and goodness. 19

SCIENCE AND RELIGION

In general one can speak of three different approaches towards Modernity in general, and modern science in particular in Islamic world.

---

16 Fethullah Gülen, *Love and the Essence of Being Human, p.* 170. 17 Voll, "Transcending Modernity", p. 242.

18 Fethullah Gülen, *Love and the Essence of Being Human,* p. 20. 19 Ibid. P. 202.

One is the fundamentalist attitude. Some of them aim to neglect or deny modernity and science totally like the Taliban. They live in this world, but their mentality has been shaped in the past. They are not able to meet the social problems of modernity and science by depending upon Islam and Islam's intellectual history. The second group one may call secularists. They do not consider Islam seriously as a world view. Modernity and modern science are totally welcomed at the expanse of the Islamic intellectual tradition. For them, there is of course conflict between science and religion. In this scientific age, religion can be functional as faith not as a total world view that characterises and gives meaning not only to nature but also to the history of humankind.

The third approach may be called synthesis between modernity and Islam, science and religion. Gülen is in this camp. He believes that in Islamic Universities, in the madrasas there was lack of interests in the experimental sciences. This was a mistake. That is why Islamic countries fell behind the developed Western countries. According to him, we need to make up foe this neglect since tomorrow's world will be built on knowledge and everything will take its strength and power from knowledge. 20 According to Gülen, although science is important, it is not sufficient for building a happy new world. There is urgent need for a new approach to the sciences and a new life of philosophy. He states:

Previous generations witnessed a bitter struggle that should never have taken place: science versus religion. This conflict gives rise to atheism and materialism, which influenced Christianity more than other religions. Science cannot contradict religion, for its purpose is to understand nature and humanity, which are each components of the manifestations of God's Attributes of Will and Power. Religion has its source in the Divine Attribute of Speech, which was manifested in the course of human history as Divine Scriptures, such as the Quran, the Gospels, the Torah, and others that have been revealed to just prophets since Adam. Thanks to the efforts of both Christian and Muslim theologians and scientists, it seem that the religionscience conflict that has lasted for a few centuries will come to an end, or at least its absurdity will finally be acknowledged.21

According to Gülen, modern science is lacking spiritual guidance. That is why we are witnessing so great social and environmental problems in our century. It is Islamic morality and spirituality that can be a guide for science. The Islamic intellectual tradition and Islam as living tradition possesses such merit. He is quite optimistic with regard to future of humanity:

Our old world will experience an amazing "springtime" before its demise. This springtime will see the gap between rich and poor narrow; the world's riches will be distributed more justly, according to work, capital and

---

20 M. Fethullah Gülen, *Toward Global Civilization of Love and Tolerance* (New Jersey: The Light, 2006), p. 255.

21 Fethullah Gülen, *Love and the Essence of Being Human,* p. 231.

needs; there will be no discrimination based on race, colour, language and world view; basic human rights and freedoms will be protected...

In this new spring time, when scientific and technological progress has been taken into consideration, people will understand that the current level of science and technology resembles the stage of life when an infant is learning how to crawl. Humanity will organize trips into space as if they were really travelling to another country.

But this new spring time will rise on the foundation of love, compassion, mercy, dialogue, acceptance of others, mutual respect, justice, and rights. In such a world, goodness and kindness, righteousness and virtue will form the basic essence of the world.

In conclusion, traditional Islamic theological language with regard to the adherents of other faiths, especially to Jews and Christians, carries the tone of language that belonged to the religiously divided world of the past. In traditionally constructed societies, polemical and reactionary languages were used in order to define, describe, determine and even condemn the "other". To communicate or to understand the other was not the issue of that time. Now we are living in a different time and in a different space. We, Muslims cannot carry on using the language that was originated for defining and determining, and not for communicating or understanding. In the modern milieu, in global world of today, we need a new theological language appropriate to our modern conditions. Fethullah Gülen as an Islamic scholar, a Sufi and an activist, has paved the ground for a new theological language. Tolerance, love, compassion and forgiveness constitute the content of this new discourse. But, most important of all, is the existence of a community that is ready to hear and do what he has suggested to them. They are the people who are able to actualise what has been offered to them. This is something significant.

CHAPTER XXX

THE POSSIBILITY, MEANING AND IMPORTANCE OF COMPARISON BETWEEN ISLAMIC AND WESTERN PHILOSOPHIES

WHAT IS CONTEMPORARY ISLAMIC PHILOSOPHY?

In contemporary Muslim territories we can find a great diversity of attitudes towards Philosophy. Hence, before dealing with the particular situation of Contemporary Islamic Philosophy, we would like to enumerate a few trends in the context of which the special identity of contemporary philosophical activity can be recognized. We shall then try to explain the main characteristics of Islamic philosophy as it is practiced in Iran. In the first place, however, we must deal with the fact that the different approaches to Philosophy in the Islamic world have essentially to do with different interpretations of the relation itself between Islam and Philosophy.1 Among these interpretations we find the following:2

1. The rejection of philosophy and of any rational approach to religious teachings with the emphasis placed on the ordinary meanings of Quran and hadith (Salafi approach).

2. The Ghazzalian approach, i.e., the one that we might call the philosophical rejection of philosophy. This is a common view in Malaysia and Indonesia, but with important similarities to the tafkik (separation) movement in Iran.

3. The mystical approach in Turkey3 and countries of North Africa like Morocco and Tunisia.

4. The revival of the Islamic philosophical heritage as it was instituted during the period from the 9th to the 13th centuries. Thinkers interested in this revival are more commentators than philosophers in their

---

1 Hassan Hanafi in a chapter in his book *Islam in the Modern World: Religion, Ideology and Development* (Cairo: Anglo-Egyptian Bookshop, 1995) classified some of these attitudes in chapter IV, pp. 457-561. I think he has introduced some of these trends but neglected some others that I try to mention them

2 Ayatollahy Hamidreza, "Philosophy in Contemporary Iran," *Revista Portuguesa de Filosofia,* vol. 62, No. 2-4, 2006.

3 You can find this approach in Shukran Vahide, *Islam in Modern Turkey: An Intellectual Biography of Bediuzzaman Said Nursi* (Albany: State University of NewYork, 2005).

own right. This position is particularly strong in schools and departments of Islamic philosophy in the Arabian countries that reject the *Salafi* approach.

5. The westernized contemporary approach to philosophy in Islamic countries and other parts of the world. Among the representatives of this approach we find thinkers like Muhammad Arkun, Hassan Hanafi, Nasr Hamed Abu Zaid, Ali Mazroui, Abdolkarim Soroush. They all have in common a rather secular approach based on different Western concepts of philosophy.

6. The more ideological approach represented by thinkers that attempt to find solutions for the practical problems affecting the Muslim world based on the premise that the best way of proceeding is to promote the return to the traditional doctrines of Islam.

7. The approach of traditionalist thinkers like René Guénon, Frithjof Schuon, and Nasr.

8. The approach of the Sadraian transcendental philosophy (philosophy of Mulla Sadra) in Iran, as well as in Pakistan and India.

THE BACKGROUND OF CONTEMPORARY ISLAMIC PHILOSOPHY

In the past, the interest of the Western world in learning about Islamic Philosophy was mainly centered on the question regarding the active influence of Muslim thinkers upon the historical formation of Christian scholasticism in the Middle Ages. For example, it is clear that in order to study the philosophical contribution of thinkers like Thomas Aquinas and Duns Scotus in their correct historical perspective we must also become acquainted with the thought of at least Avicenna (980-1037) and Averroes (1126-1198). Any adequate history of medieval Western philosophy should include in consequence an important chapter on the history of Islamic philosophy4.

This distance between the western intellectuals and Islamic Philosophy may have to do with the rather common view in the West that Islamic Philosophy came to an end with the death of Averroes (1126-1198) and/or ceased to exist when Ghazzali (1058-1111) produced his major attack against philosophical thinking in his influential book *Tahafut al-Falasifat*. But in reality what came to an end was nothing more than what shall be considered the first phase in the development of the whole history of Islamic Philosophy. It is true that with the death of Averroes, Islamic Philosophy ceased to be alive in the West, but this does not mean that it ceased to be alive in the East. It is also true that the Islamic philosophy did not develop in all Muslim countries after Ghazzali and Averroes particularly among Sunni Muslims, so that in the Arabian countries there was no longer a large interest in developing philosophy. The fact that the Sunni Muslims

4 Mehdi Mohaghegh and Tsihiko Izutsu, *The Metaphysics of Sabzavari* (Tehran: University of Teheran Press, 1977), p. 3.

were the majority in terms of population and the Arabian countries were the ones with closer ties to the West explains why the generalized assumption grew in the West that there was no longer Philosophy in the Muslim countries. Moreover, this assumption became necessarily an obstacle for the deepening of any relations between Islamic and Western Philosophy.

We must also add that even "histories" of Islamic philosophy written not as a chapter in the history of Western philosophy but independently and for its own sake were largely shaped by the idea that the golden age of Islamic Philosophy is to be found in the period of three centuries extending from Farabi to Averroes, and that after Averroes, in the ages subsequent to the Mongol invasion, and with the exception of a few isolated prominent figures (like Ibn Khaldun, for example), the Muslim world did not produce, when it comes to Philosophy, anything more than commentaries and commentaries of commentaries in a long and tedious series of lifeless and mechanical repetitions, without any spark of real creativity and originality.

That this is not a true picture of the historical facts has amply been made clear by the remarkable work done by scholars like Henri Corbin and Seyyed Hossein Nasr concerning the intellectual activity of the Safavid Dynasty. At any rate, it is only very recently that Orientalists have begun to realize that philosophical thinking in Islamic context did not irretrievably fall into decadence and fossilization after the Mongol invasion, as was commonly believed.

Indeed, we think that the kind of philosophy that deserves to be regarded as typically and characteristically Islamic developed much more after Averroes death than before it. We are talking about the typically Islamic philosophy that arose and matured in the periods subsequent to the Mongol invasion and found the culmination of its vigorous creativity in the Safavid period in Iran. This peculiar type of Islamic philosophy, which grew up in Iran among the Shiites, has come to be known as *hikmat* or "wisdom". We can trace the origin of the *hikmat* back to the very beginning of the above-mentioned second phase of the history of philosophy in Islam.

Hikmat is structurally a peculiar combination of rational thinking and Gnostic intuition, or, we might say, rationalist philosophy and mystical experience. It is a special type of ontological philosophy based on existential intuition of Reality, a result of the philosophizing applied on the Gnostic ideas and visions attained through intellectual contemplation. Historically speaking, this tendency toward the spiritualization of Philosophy finds its origin in the metaphysical visions of Ibn 'Arabi and Suhrawardi. In making this observation, however, we must not loose sight of the fact that *hikmat* is also endowed with a solid and strictly logical structure and as such it goes beyond Ibn 'Arabi and Suhrawardi and back to Avicenna and the first stage of development in the history of Islamic Philosophy.

Hikmat, having as it does these two distinctive aspects, must be approached from two different angles, if we are to analyze properly its formative process: (1) as a purely intellectual activity, and (2) as something based on trans-intellectual, gnostic experience - *dhawq* "tasting" as the mystics like to call it - of the ultimate Reality.

The most famous and important philosophers of the second phase of Islamic philosophy is Mulla Sadra (1572-1640). He had many innovative ideas in the realm of Philosophy (especially ontology) and became one of the brightest stars in the sky of Islamic philosophy. As a matter of fact, his novel ideas mark a turning point in Islamic Philosophy so that the philosophers that came after him were significantly affected by his views.

The appearance of an intellectual figure like Sadr al-Din Shirazi during the Safavid period is a clear indication of the presence in his own time of a strong intellectual tradition whose deepest currents he was able to so brilliantly bring to the surface. Mulla Sadra is a metaphysician and sage of outstanding stature who cannot be taken in isolation and separated from the tradition that produced him.

Of note, however, is the revival of Islamic intellectual life in the eastern lands of Islam, especially in Persia. During the twelfth and thirteenth centuries, this was made possible by the establishment of new intellectual schools by Suhrawardi and Ibn Arabi, followed by the resurrection of Ibn Sina's teachings during the middle decades of the thirteenth century by Khwajah Nasir al-Din Tusi. The background of Mulla Sadra must be sought in these schools as well as in the Sunni and shi'ite schools of *kalam* as they developed from the thirteenth to the sixteenth centuries.5

The four classical schools of the post-Mongol period, namely, the Peripatetic *(mashshai)*, the Illuminationist *(ishraqi)*, the Gnostic *('irfani)* and the Theological *(kalam)*, with all the inner variations contained in each of them, developed extensively during the four centuries preceding Mulla Sadra and also approached each other, preparing the ground for the major synthesis brought about by Mulla Sadra. Therefore, in order to understand the background of Mulla Sadra, it is necessary to delve into the development of each one of these schools as well as into the interactions that occurred between them during this very rich and at the same time most neglected period of Islamic intellectual life, from the thirteenth through the sixteenth centuries.6

THE CHARACTERISTICS OF SADRAEAN PHILOSOPHY

The Sadraen Philosophy can be characterized by the recognition of the following aspects:

1. Intrinsic compatibility between Religion and Philosophy;

---

5 Seyyed Hossein Nasr, *Sadraddin Shirazi and His Transendantal Theosophy* (Teheran: Institute for Cultural and Humanistic Studies, 1997), p. 16.

6 See Seyyed Muhammad Khamenei, ed. *Development of Wisdom in Iran and in the World* (Tehran: SIPRIn Publication, 2000), pp. 191-203.

2. Necessity of a serious rational study of the religious doctrines to the point of bringing together the views of Reason and the views proper to Religion ;7

3. Need for a combination of the four traditional schools present in the Islamic world, namely mysticism, peripatetic philosophy, illuminationist philosophy and *Kalam*;

4. Importance of studying Western approaches to Philosophy as well as other sources of human thought;

5. Need to proceed to a comparative study of the different philosophical views in order to explain the strengths and the weaknesses of transcendental philosophy;

6. Evolving character of Islamic Philosophy as a whole; 7. Philosophical primacy of ontology over epistemology and of reason over experience;8

8. Influence of theoretical philosophy on other dimensions of human thought and activity, namely politics, economy, education, aesthetics, ethics, etc.;

9. Importance of the attention to Quran and of the *hadith* and prayers - as an important source of knowledge - for a philosophy that tries to argue her own views based on reason alone and not on revelation;9

10. Importance of the dialogue among philosophers from different perspectives in order to achieve better ideas of how to promote the future of the human family.

The difficulties of having a comparative philosophy. Although we confront a lot of topics that have been studied in different philosophical schools and have been discussed by various philosophers and it seems that those are different answers to the same questions, there are some difficulties in accounting for similarities between them. Therefore comparative philosophy has been streanuous and far reaching, some of theses difficulties are as follows:

The historical background and geographic situation of philosophical problems and solutions make difficult the mutual understanding of two different philosophical schools belonging to the two paradigms in question. At first glance, we encounter one topic that is translated in two cultures and it seems that they are the same; but the deep meaning of that topic is connected to those cultural backgrounds that varied notably one from

---

7 For the position of reason in Shi'a and Mulla Sadra see Shomali, Mohammad, *Shi'I Islam: Origins, Faith and Practices* (London: ICAS Press), pp. 134-142.

8 See for example Muhammad Kamal, *Mulla Sadra's Transcendent Philosophy* (Burlington: Asgate Publishing Company, 2006), pp. 42-64.

9 Seyyed Muhammad Khamenei, *Mulla Sadra's Transcendent Philosophy* (Tehran: SIPRIn Publication 2004), pp. 39-43.

another.10 The hermeneutic situation of a word or a text is an obstacle for understanding them in another culture. Therefore there are some suspicions that we can understand similarities between two words in two cultures. Thus, some philosophical views from the perspective of another philosophical paradigm can not be sound.

The epistemological approach of modern philosophy and its subjective view based on a kind of humanism bring a sphere that is different from another intellectual and ontological attitude. It is difficult to criticize another philosophical tradition from Western-modern point of view.

It is also difficult to understand from a non-western philosophical perspective a Western view without having necessary knowledge from Western culture. In my view, the Christian background of Western philosophy (for both theistic and atheistic philosophies) is one of the most important paradigms of modern philosophy. It is confused in the translation of the important idea of Nietzsche that "God is dead" by nonwestern philosophies. A correct understanding og "God is dead" is not possible without understanding the Christian doctrine of God incarnated in Christianity. Without understanding the importance of history in Christian doctrine it is difficult to understand the various philosophies of history in many Western philosophical approaches.

It is also difficult to understand contemporary Islamic philosophies from the empirist or pragmatistic approach to philosophy that is the dominant philosophical method in Western philosophy. The rational attitude of Islamic philosophy differs from that in Western philosophy.

The orientalists in Western countries are guilty in this confusion. For them, the oriental culture must be understood carefully but from a Western point of view and must be judged based on Western values. But some useful attempts have a realistic awareness of this gap and the solution for building some bridges between all cultures. In a globalised world philosophy needs more mutual understanding than philosophical theories.

THE POSSIBILITY OF COMPARATIVE PHILOSOPHY

However, this does not mean that it is not possible to have comparative philosophy. If it were so, there would not be any meaning for dialogue and negotiation. All philosophical attempts for understanding other thoughts all over the world and in all periods of time in history (or the historical study of philosophical schools) presupposes the possibility of understanding others even in some main part of their thoughts. Although it

10 See Hamidreza Ayatollahy, "Hermeneutical Considerations in Translation of Philosophical and Religious Texts", *Translation Studies,* vol. 4, No. 15, 2006.

is possible to understand others, there are many considerations in translation of one thought in a culture to another culture.11

These considerations are the most important factors for comparative philosophy as a difficult but possible study that requires a long process to bring the other thought nearer.

The method of comparison. I believe that, for a best comparative study in philosophy, the comparison must pass through four stages of four hermeneutical rules in the view of Emilio Betti (1890-1968). Because of limitation in this paper, I point, only, to these four rules:12

1-The principle of hermeneutical autonomy of subjects 2-The principle of totality or the rule of coherence of meaning 3-The rule of actuality of understanding

4-The compatibility of meaning in understanding or the rule of hermeneutical correspondence of meaning.

THE ADVANTAGES OF ATTEMPTING A COMPARATIVE PHILOSOPHY

There are some factors that now make comparative study in Western and Islamic philosophies necessary. First, that the penetration of globalization in all dimensions of our life make it necessary to understand each other. The global awareness which conflicts local thoughts and the necessity of interaction between cultures requires a kind of mutual understanding. Cultural representations point to a deep variety due to the different foundations of those thoughts. Philosophy as analyzing the basic foundation of all cultural representations has a very important role in any interaction between cultures. This is what necessitates comparative philosophy.

Second, we can know ourselves not from an inner insight but from contrast with others. In otherness we understand the boundaries of self. A joke can make this truth clearer. A child showed his father a quite white paper and said to him "Father, look at my painting, is it nice!" The father replied "There is nothing in your paper!" to which the child explained "It is a white bear in the snowy surface of north pole, which is pursuing a white rabbit!"

---

11 See Hamidreza Ayatollahy, "Existence in Existentialism and Sadraean Principality of Existence, A Comparison", *Pajooheshname Ulome Ensani* (*Research Journal of Human Sciences),* (Tehran: University of Shahid Beheshti), vol. 51, No. 3, 2006.

12 Emilio Betti, *Allgemeine Auslegungslehre als Methodik der Geisteswissenschaften*, transl. in Joseph Bleicher (1980), *Contemporary Hermeneutics* (Routledge and Kegan Paul, 1962), pp. 57-85.

This is a joke but if it was correct without the boundaries of bear and rabbit noone could find anything and the more the contrast the more the intelligibility.

Every thought needs others to clarify itself. We can understand ourselves more and more with more understanding of the others. In comparative philosophy we can even know selfness and otherness.

THE NEED TODAY FOR A COMPARATIVE WESTERN AND CONTEMPORARY ISLAMIC PHILOSOPHY

The philosophy of Mulla Sadra, must be considered as one of the most important contributions of contemporary Islamic Philosophy specially in Iran. This philosophy has been continued and matured by scholars like Sabzavari and Tabatabaii and Motahhari. In fact, due mainly to its compatibility with the Islamic tradition a very honorable place within the context of Shiite Islamic thought was granted to this kind of philosophizing, so much so that it became part of the official learning and teaching in religious seminaries (*hozeh elmiyyeh*). Understanding and confronting every kind of rational and philosophical thinking has been a major duty of Islamic scholars in Shiite countries like Iran. Islamic philosophy has been a strong foundation of Iranian culture13 and due to the Iranian Islamic philosophical background that the people of Iran were preserved from Marxism and atheistic positivism.

Philosophical research in Iran is not focused only on Islamic philosophy. For more than 50 years, there has been an ongoing acquaintance of the Iranian culture with Western schools of thought, studied side by side. The number of works of the Western philosophical tradition translated into Persian is already quite significant. While Islamic philosophy represents the major interest of this domain in Iran, the comparative study of philosophy has become a major topic for academic dissertations, lectures, books and conferences. In Iran, most scholars believe that Islamic Philosophy has the power to seriously contribute to the solution of many contemporary problems.

SOME TOPICS IN COMPARATIVE PHILOSOPHY

There have been many topics for comparison between Western and contemporary Islamic philosophy with related comparative studies.14 These

---

13 Hamidreza Ayatollahy, "Interaction of Islamic and Western Philosophies," *Ishraq (Illumination)*, Islamic Philosophy Yearbook. In Russian. No.1, (Moscow, 2010)

14 Many papers in comparative philosophy can be found in Volume 3 and Volume 4 of series of books published from the papers presented at the World Congress on Mulla Sadra (Tehran, 1999) entitled: *Mulla Sadra and Comparative Studies* (Tehran: SIPRIn Publication)

topics can be classified in three types. First is comparison between philosophical views of a philosopher as a whole with another one. Second, it is also possible to compare one particularly philosophical issue in Islamic and western philosophies as a whole.15 Third, we can compare treatments of one philosophical issue or problem in the thoughts of two or more philosophers.

Some sample topics in each of these three kinds, with a good capacity for comparative studies:

1. Comparison between philosophical view of a philosopher as a whole with another one: For example Avicenna and Descartes; Avicenna and Kant; Mulla Sadra and Hegel; Mulla Sadra and Kant; Mulla Sadra and Heidegger; Tabatabaii and Whitehead; Motahhari and Hume.
2. Comparison between one particularly philosophical issue in Islamic and western philosophies as a whole. Topics could be as follows: Metaphysics, Being, Substance, Essence, Motion,16 Causation,17 Space and Time, Necessity and Contingency, Epistemology18, Philosophy of Religion, Ethics and Moral Philosophy, Aesthetics, Political Philosophy, Philosophy of Language, and Cosmology.

3. Comparison between treatments of one philosophical issue or problem in the thoughts of two or more philosophers: Existence in Existentialism of Heidegger and Sadraean Principality of Existence. 19 A Comparison between Kant's Theory of Analyticity and Mulla Sadra's. A Comparison between Ibn Sina and Aquinas on the Essence/Existence Distinction. Essence: Sadra and Husserl. Truth of Time in Mulla Sadra and Henry Bergson.20 An Analysis of Cosmological Argument Compared with

---

15 See for example: *Mulla Sadra's School & Western Philosopies*, edited by Seyyed Muhammad Khamenei (Tehran: SIPRIn Publication, 2005).

16 See Mahdi Dehbashi, *Transubstantial Motion and Natural World* (London: ICAS Press, 2010).

17 See for example the book: Seyed G. Safavi, ed., *Mulla Sadra & Comparative Philosophy on Causation* (London: Salman-Azadeh Publication, 2003).

18 See for example Misbah Yazd and Muhammad Taqi, *Philosophical Instructions: An Introduction to Contemporary Islamic Philosophy* (Binghamton: Binghamton University Press, Part II, 1999).

19 Hamidreza Ayatollahy, "Existence in Existentialism and Sadraean Principality of Existence, A Comparison", *Pajooheshname Ulome Ensani* (*Research Journal of Human Sciences*), University of Shahid Beheshti, Tehran, vol. 51, No. 3, 2006.

20 Ali Fathi and Hamidreza Ayatollahy, "Time in Mulla Sadra and Bergson" *Marefat-i Falasafi* (*Philosophical Inquiry* (Vol. 7, No. 2, 2010). A paper written with Dr. Ali Fathi.

Necessity-Contingency Argument in Islamic Philosophy. 21 A Comparison between Motahhari's Philosophical Analysis of Ethics with the Husserlian Phenomenological Method.22 The concept and status of virtue in Farabi and Aquinas. Natural Law theory of ethics in Aquinas and Mo`atazelah. A comparative study on the concept of secondary intelligible of Mulla Sadra and Kant's categories. The Subjectivity of the Subject: A Sadraean Answer to Heidegger's Question.23 Mental Causation: A Sadraean Solution. Possible Worlds: Islamic Philosophy and Western Modern Philosophy Comprised.

CONCLUSION

We suggest, therefore, that Philosophy is crucial for the furthering of any kind of positive dialogue between Iranian culture and the culture of other peoples and nations. In other words, we are convinced that Philosophy must play a very important role in furthering international peaceful relations. Many historical background factors constitute serious obstacles for the achievement of peaceful relations between countries. Moreover, the flood of false news and deficient political analysis, together with all the possible difficulties attached to the differences in the corresponding system of values, are abundant cause for conflict and misunderstandings. Accordingly, we advocate the recognition of the extraordinary role of reason and of rational thinking in order that differences and misunderstandings may not remain serious obstacles to peace and the mutual understanding of different cultures and civilizations.

---

21 Hamidreza Ayatollahy, "An Analysis of Cosmological Argument Compared with Necessity-Contingency Argument in Islamic Philosophy", *Qabasat,* vol. 11, No. 3, (Tehran, 2006)

22 Hamidreza Ayatollahy, "A Comparison between Motahhari's Philosophical Analysis of Ethics with the Husserlian Phenomenological Method," *Maqalat wa Barrasiha* (Faculty of Theology and Islamic Studies, University of Tehran, No. 74, 2004).

23 See the book: Mahmoud Khatami, *From a Sadraean Point of View: Toward an Ontetic Elimination of the Subjectivistic Self* (London: SalmanAzadeh Publication, 2004)

INDEX

Y

Z

Today there is urgent need to attend to the nature and dignity of the person, to the quality of human life, to the purpose and goal of the physical transformation of our environment, and to the relation of all this to the development of social and political life. This, in turn, requires philosophic clarification of the base upon which freedom is exercised, that is, of the values which provide stability and guidance to one's decisions.

Such studies must be able to reach deeply into one's culture and that of other parts of the world as mutually reinforcing and enriching in order to uncover the roots of the dignity of persons and of their societies. They must be able to identify the conceptual forms in terms of which modern industrial and technological developments are structured and how these impact upon human self-understanding. Above all, they must be able to bring these elements together in the creative understanding essential for setting our goals and determining our modes of interaction. In the present complex global circumstances this is a condition for growing together with trust and justice, honest dedication and mutual concern.

PROJECTS

A set of related research efforts is currently in process: 1. *Cultural Heritage and Contemporary Change: Philosophical Foundations for Social Life.* Focused, mutually coordinated research teams in university centers prepare volumes as part of an integrated philosophic search for self-understanding differentiated by culture and civilization. These evolve more adequate understandings of the person in society and look to the cultural heritage of each for the resources to respond to the challenges of its own specific contemporary transformation.

2. *Seminars on Culture and Contemporary Issues.* This series of 10 week crosscultural and interdisciplinary seminars is coordinated by the RVP in Washington.

3. *Joint-Colloquia* with Institutes of Philosophy of the National Academies of Science, university philosophy departments, and societies. Underway since 1976 in Eastern Europe and, since 1987, in China, these concern the person in contemporary society.

4. *Foundations of Moral Education and Character Development.* A study in values and education which unites philosophers, psychologists, social scientists and scholars in education in the elaboration of ways of enriching the moral content of education and character development. This work has been underway since 1980.

The personnel for these projects consists of established scholars willing to contribute their time and research as part of their professional commitment to life in contemporary society. For resources to implement this work the Council, as 501 C3 a non-profit organization incorporated in the District of Colombia, looks to various private foundations, public programs and enterprises.

PUBLICATIONS ON CULTURAL HERITAGE AND CONTEMPORARY CHANGE

Series I. Culture and Values
Series II. African Philosophical Studies Series IIA.
Islamic Philosophical Studies Series III. Asian
Philosophical Studies
Series IV. Western European Philosophical Studies Series IVA. Central and Eastern
European Philosophical Studies Series V. Latin American Philosophical Studies

Series VI. Foundations of Moral Education Series VII.
Seminars: Culture and Values Series VIII. Christian
Philosophical Studies

CULTURAL HERITAGE AND CONTEMPORARY CHANGE Series I. Culture

and Values

I.1 *Research on Culture and Values: Intersection of Universities, Churches and Nations.* George F. McLean, ed. ISBN 0819173533 (paper); 081917352-5 (cloth).

I.2 *The Knowledge of Values: A Methodological Introduction to the Study of Values;* A. Lopez Quintas, ed. ISBN 081917419x (paper); 0819174181 (cloth).

I.3 *Reading Philosophy for the XXIst Century*. George F. McLean, ed. ISBN 0819174157 (paper); 0819174149 (cloth).

I.4 *Relations between Cultures*. John A. Kromkowski, ed. ISBN 1565180089 (paper); 1565180097 (cloth).

I.5 *Urbanization and Values*. John A. Kromkowski, ed. ISBN 1565180100 (paper); 1565180119 (cloth).

I.6 *The Place of the Person in Social Life*. Paul Peachey and John A. Krom kowski, eds. ISBN 1565180127 (paper); 156518013-5 (cloth). I.7 *Abrahamic Faiths, Ethnicity and Ethnic Conflicts*. Paul Peachey, George F. McLean and John A. Kromkowski, eds. ISBN 1565181042 (paper).

I.8 *Ancient Western Philosophy: The Hellenic Emergence*. George F. McLean and Patrick J. Aspell, eds. ISBN 156518100X (paper). I.9 *Medieval Western Philosophy: The European Emergence*. Patrick J. Aspell, ed. ISBN 1565180941 (paper).

I.10 *The Ethical Implications of Unity and the Divine in Nicholas of Cusa*. David L. De Leonardis. ISBN 1565181123 (paper).

I.11 *Ethics at the Crossroads: 1.Normative Ethics and Objective Reason*. George F. McLean, ed. ISBN 1565180224 (paper).

I.12 *Ethics at the Crossroads: 2. Personalist Ethics and Human Subjectivity*. George F. McLean, ed. ISBN 1565180240 (paper). I.13 *The Emancipative Theory of Jürgen Habermas and Metaphysics*. Robert Badillo. ISBN 1565180429 (paper); 1565180437 (cloth). I.14 *The Deficient Cause of Moral Evil According to Thomas Aquinas*. Edward Cook. ISBN 1565180704 (paper).

I.15 *Human Love: Its Meaning and Scope, a Phenomenology of Gift and Encounter*. Alfonso Lopez Quintas. ISBN 1565180747 (paper). I.16 *Civil Society and Social Reconstruction*. George F. McLean, ed. ISBN 1565180860 (paper).

I.17 *Ways to God, Personal and Social at the Turn of Millennia: The Iqbal Lecture, Lahore*. George F. McLean. ISBN 1565181239 (paper). I.18 *The Role of the Sublime in Kant's Moral Metaphysics*. John R. Goodreau. ISBN 1565181247 (paper).

I.19 *Philosophical Challenges and Opportunities of Globalization*. Oliva Blanchette, Tomonobu Imamichi and George F. McLean, eds. ISBN 1565181298 (paper).

I.20 *Faith, Reason and Philosophy: Lectures at The al-Azhar, Qom, Tehran, Lahore and Beijing; Appendix: The Encyclical Letter: Fides et Ratio*. George F. McLean. ISBN 156518130 (paper).

I.21 *Religion and the Relation between Civilizations: Lectures on Cooperation between Islamic and Christian Cultures in a Global Horizon*. George F. McLean. ISBN 1565181522 (paper).

I.22 *Freedom, Cultural Traditions and Progress: Philosophy in Civil Society and Nation Building, Tashkent Lectures, 1999*. George F. McLean. ISBN 1565181514 (paper).

I.23 *Ecology of Knowledge*. Jerzy A. Wojciechowski. ISBN 1565181581 (paper).

I.24 *God and the Challenge of Evil: A Critical Examination of Some Serious Objections to the Good and Omnipotent God.* John L. Yardan. ISBN 1565181603 (paper).

I.25 *Reason, Rationality and Reasonableness, Vietnamese Philosophical Studies, I.* Tran Van Doan. ISBN 1565181662 (paper).

I.26 *The Culture of Citizenship: Inventing Postmodern Civic Culture.* Thomas Bridges. ISBN 1565181689 (paper).

I.27 *The Historicity of Understanding and the Problem of Relativism in Gadamer's Philosophical Hermeneutics.* Osman Bilen. ISBN 1565181670 (paper).

I.28 *Speaking of God.* Carlo Huber. ISBN 1565181697 (paper).

I.29 *Persons, Peoples and Cultures in a Global Age: Metaphysical Bases for Peace between Civilizations.* George F. McLean. ISBN 1565181875 (paper).

I.30 *Hermeneutics, Tradition and Contemporary Change: Lectures in Chennai/Madras, India.* George F. McLean. ISBN 1565181883 (paper).

I.31 *Husserl and Stein.* Richard Feist and William Sweet, eds. ISBN 1565181948 (paper).

I.32 *Paul Hanly Furfey's Quest for a Good Society.* Bronislaw Misztal, Francesco Villa, and Eric Sean Williams, eds. ISBN 1565182278 (paper).

I.33 *Three Theories of Society.* Paul Hanly Furfey. ISBN 9781565182288 (paper).

I.34 *Building Peace in Civil Society: An Autobiographical Report from a Believers' Church.* Paul Peachey. ISBN 9781565182325 (paper).

I.35 *Karol Wojtyla's Philosophical Legacy.* Agnes B. Curry, Nancy Mardas and George F. McLean, eds. ISBN 9781565182479 (paper).

I.36 *Kantian Form and Phenomenological Force: Kant's Imperatives and the Directives of Contemporary Phenomenology.* Randolph C. Wheeler. ISBN 9781565182547 (paper).

I.37 *Beyond Modernity: The Recovery of Person and Community in Global Times: Lectures in China and Vietnam.* George F. McLean. ISBN 9781565182578 (paper)

I. 38 *Religion and Culture.* George F. McLean. ISBN 9781565182561 (paper).

I.39 *The Dialogue of Cultural Traditions: Global Perspective.* William Sweet, George F. McLean, Tomonobu Imamichi, Safak Ural, O. Faruk Akyol, eds. ISBN 9781565182585 (paper).

I.40 *Unity and Harmony, Love and Compassion in Global Times.* George F. McLean. ISBN 9781565182592 (paper).

I.41 *Intercultural Dialogue and Human Rights. Luigi Bonanate, Roberto Papini* and *William Sweet*, eds. ISBN 9781565182714 (paper).

I.42 *Philosophy Emerging from Culture.* William Sweet, George F. McLean, Oliva Blanchette, Wonbin Park, eds. ISBN 9781565182851 (paper).

I.43 *Whence Intelligibility?* Louis Perron, ed. ISBN 9781565182905 (paper).

Series II. African Philosophical Studies

II.1 *Person and Community: Ghanaian Philosophical Studies: I.* Kwasi Wiredu and Kwame Gyekye, eds. ISBN 1565180046 (paper); 1565180054 (cloth).

II.2 *The Foundations of Social Life: Ugandan Philosophical Studies: I.* A.T. Dalfovo, ed. ISBN 1565180062 (paper); 156518007-0 (cloth). II.3 *Identity and Change in Nigeria: Nigerian Philosophical Studies, I.* Theophilus Okere, ed. ISBN 1565180682 (paper).

II.4 *Social Reconstruction in Africa: Ugandan Philosophical studies, II.* E. Wamala, A.R. Byaruhanga, A.T. Dalfovo, J.K. Kigongo, S.A. Mwanahewa and G. Tusabe, eds. ISBN 1565181182 (paper).

II.5 *Ghana: Changing Values/Changing Technologies: Ghanaian Philosophical Studies, II.* Helen Lauer, ed. ISBN 1565181441 (paper).

II.6 *Sameness and Difference: Problems and Potentials in South African Civil Society: South African Philosophical Studies, I.* James R.Cochrane and Bastienne Klein, eds. ISBN 1565181557 (paper).

II.7 *Protest and Engagement: Philosophy after Apartheid at an Historically Black South African University: South African Philosophical Studies, II.* Patrick Giddy, ed. ISBN 1565181638 (paper).

II.8 *Ethics, Human Rights and Development in Africa: Ugandan Philosophical Studies, III.* A.T. Dalfovo, J.K. Kigongo, J. Kisekka, G. Tusabe, E. Wamala, R. Munyonyo, A.B. Rukooko, A.B.T. Byaruhanga-akiiki, and M. Mawa, eds. ISBN 1565181727 (paper).

II.9 *Beyond Cultures: Perceiving a Common Humanity: Ghanaian Philosophical Studies, III.* Kwame Gyekye. ISBN 156518193X (paper).

II.10 *Social and Religious Concerns of East African: A Wajibu Anthology: Kenyan Philosophical Studies, I.* Gerald J. Wanjohi and G. Wakuraya Wanjohi, eds. ISBN 1565182219 (paper).

II.11 *The Idea of an African University: The Nigerian Experience: Nigerian Philosophical Studies, II.* Joseph Kenny, ed. ISBN 9781565182301 (paper).

II.12 *The Struggles after the Struggle: Zimbabwean Philosophical Study, I.* David Kaulemu, ed. ISBN 9781565182318 (paper).

II.13 *Indigenous and Modern Environmental Ethics: A Study of the Indigenous Oromo Environmental Ethic and Modern Issues of Environment and Development: Ethiopian Philosophical Studies, I.* Workineh Kelbessa. ISBN 9781565182530 (paper).

II.14 *African Philosophy and the Future of Africa: South African Philosophical Studies, III.* Gerard Walmsley, ed. ISMB 9781565182707 (paper).

II.15 *Philosophy in Ethiopia: African Philosophy Today, I: Ethiopian Philosophical Studies, II.* Bekele Gutema and Charles C. Verharen, eds. ISBN 9781565182790 (paper).

II.16 *The Idea of a Nigerian University: A Revisited: Nigerian Philosophical Studies, III.* Olatunji Oyeshile and Joseph Kenny, eds. ISBN 9781565182776 (paper).

Series IIA. Islamic Philosophical Studies

IIA.1 *Islam and the Political Order.* Muhammad Saïd al-Ashmawy. ISBN ISBN 156518047X (paper); 156518046-1 (cloth).

IIA.2 *Al-Ghazali Deliverance from Error and Mystical Union with the Almighty: Al-munqidh Min al-Dadāl.* Critical Arabic edition and English translation by Muhammad Abulaylah and Nurshif AbdulRahim Rifat; Introduction and notes by George F. McLean. ISBN 1565181530 (Arabic-English edition, paper), ISBN 1565180828 (Arabic edition, paper), ISBN 156518081X (English edition, paper) IIA.3 *Philosophy in Pakistan.* Naeem Ahmad, ed. ISBN 1565181085 (paper).

IIA.4 *The Authenticity of the Text in Hermeneutics.* Seyed Musa Dibadj. ISBN 1565181174 (paper).

IIA.5 *Interpretation and the Problem of the Intention of the Author: H.-G. Gadamer vs E.D. Hirsch.* Burhanettin Tatar. ISBN 156518121 (paper).

IIA.6 *Ways to God, Personal and Social at the Turn of Millennia: The Iqbal Lectures, Lahore.* George F. McLean. ISBN 1565181239 (paper). IIA.7 *Faith, Reason and Philosophy: Lectures at Al-Azhar University, Qom, Tehran, Lahore and Beijing; Appendix: The Encyclical Letter: Fides et Ratio.* George F. McLean. ISBN 1565181301 (paper).

IIA.8 *Islamic and Christian Cultures: Conflict or Dialogue: Bulgarian Philosophical Studies, III.* Plament Makariev, ed. ISBN 156518162X (paper).

IIA.9 *Values of Islamic Culture and the Experience of History, Russian Philosophical Studies, I.* Nur Kirabaev, Yuriy Pochta, eds. ISBN 1565181336 (paper).

IIA.10 *Christian-Islamic Preambles of Faith.* Joseph Kenny. ISBN 1565181387 (paper).

IIA.11 *The Historicity of Understanding and the Problem of Relativism in Gadamer's Philosophical Hermeneutics.* Osman Bilen. ISBN 1565181670 (paper).

IIA.12 *Religion and the Relation between Civilizations: Lectures on Cooperation between Islamic and Christian Cultures in a Global Horizon.* George F. McLean. ISBN 1565181522 (paper).

IIA.13 *Modern Western Christian Theological Understandings of Muslims since the Second Vatican Council.* Mahmut Aydin. ISBN 1565181719 (paper).

IIA.14 *Philosophy of the Muslim World; Authors and Principal Themes.* Joseph Kenny. ISBN 1565181794 (paper).

IIA.15 *Islam and Its Quest for Peace: Jihad, Justice and Education.* Mustafa Köylü. ISBN 1565181808 (paper).

IIA.16 *Islamic Thought on the Existence of God: Contributions and Contrasts with Contemporary Western Philosophy of Religion.* Cafer S. Yaran. ISBN 1565181921 (paper).

IIA.17 *Hermeneutics, Faith, and Relations between Cultures: Lectures in Qom, Iran.* George F. McLean. ISBN 1565181913 (paper).

IIA.18 *Change and Essence: Dialectical Relations between Change and Continuity in the Turkish Intellectual Tradition.* Sinasi Gunduz and Cafer S. Yaran, eds. ISBN 1565182227 (paper).

IIA. 19 *Understanding Other Religions: Al-Biruni and Gadamer's "Fusion of Horizons".* Kemal Ataman. ISBN 9781565182523 (paper).

Series III. Asian Philosophical Studies

III.1 *Man and Nature: Chinese Philosophical Studies, I.* Tang Yi-jie and Li Zhen, eds. ISBN 0819174130 (paper); 0819174122 (cloth).

III.2 *Chinese Foundations for Moral Education and Character Development: Chinese Philosophical Studies, II.* Tran van Doan, ed. ISBN 1565180321 (paper); 156518033X (cloth).

III.3 *Confucianism, Buddhism, Taoism, Christianity and Chinese Culture: Chinese Philosophical Studies, III.* Tang Yijie. ISBN 1565180348 (paper); 156518035-6 (cloth).

III.4 *Morality, Metaphysics and Chinese Culture (Metaphysics, Culture and Morality, I).* Vincent Shen and Tran van Doan, eds. ISBN 1565180275 (paper); 156518026-7 (cloth).

III.5 *Tradition, Harmony and Transcendence.* George F. McLean. ISBN 1565180313 (paper); 156518030-5 (cloth).

III.6 *Psychology, Phenomenology and Chinese Philosophy: Chinese Philosophical Studies, VI.* Vincent Shen, Richard Knowles and Tran Van Doan, eds. ISBN 1565180453 (paper); 1565180445 (cloth).

III.7 *Values in Philippine Culture and Education: Philippine Philosophical Studies, I.* Manuel B. Dy, Jr., ed. ISBN 1565180412 (paper); 156518040-2 (cloth).

III.7A *The Human Person and Society: Chinese Philosophical Studies, VIIA.* Zhu Dasheng, Jin Xiping and George F. McLean, eds. ISBN 1565180887.

III.8 *The Filipino Mind: Philippine Philosophical Studies II.* Leonardo N. Mercado. ISBN 156518064X (paper); 156518063-1 (cloth).

III.9 *Philosophy of Science and Education: Chinese Philosophical Studies IX*. Vincent Shen and Tran Van Doan, eds. ISBN 1565180763 (paper); 156518075-5 (cloth).

III.10 *Chinese Cultural Traditions and Modernization: Chinese Philosophical Studies, X*. Wang Miaoyang, Yu Xuanmeng and George F. McLean, eds. ISBN 1565180682 (paper).

III.11 *The Humanization of Technology and Chinese Culture: Chinese Philosophical Studies XI*. Tomonobu Imamichi, Wang Miaoyang and Liu Fangtong, eds. ISBN 1565181166 (paper).

III.12 *Beyond Modernization: Chinese Roots of Global Awareness: Chinese Philosophical Studies, XII*. Wang Miaoyang, Yu Xuanmeng and George F. McLean, eds. ISBN 1565180909 (paper).

III.13 *Philosophy and Modernization in China: Chinese Philosophical Studies XIII*. Liu Fangtong, Huang Songjie and George F. McLean, eds. ISBN 1565180666 (paper).

III.14 *Economic Ethics and Chinese Culture: Chinese Philosophical Studies, XIV*. Yu Xuanmeng, Lu Xiaohe, Liu Fangtong, Zhang Rulun and Georges Enderle, eds. ISBN 1565180925 (paper).

III.15 *Civil Society in a Chinese Context: Chinese Philosophical Studies XV*. Wang Miaoyang, Yu Xuanmeng and Manuel B. Dy, eds. ISBN 1565180844 (paper).

III.16 *The Bases of Values in a Time of Change: Chinese and Western: Chinese Philosophical Studies, XVI*. Kirti Bunchua, Liu Fangtong, Yu Xuanmeng, Yu Wujin, eds. ISBN l56518114X (paper).

III.17 *Dialogue between Christian Philosophy and Chinese Culture: Philosophical Perspectives for the Third Millennium: Chinese Philosophical Studies, XVII*. Paschal Ting, Marian Kao and Bernard Li, eds. ISBN 1565181735 (paper).

III.18 *The Poverty of Ideological Education: Chinese Philosophical Studies, XVIII*. Tran Van Doan. ISBN 1565181646 (paper). III.19 *God and the Discovery of Man: Classical and Contemporary Approaches: Lectures in Wuhan, China*. George F. McLean. ISBN 1565181891 (paper).

III.20 *Cultural Impact on International Relations: Chinese Philosophical Studies, XX*. Yu Xintian, ed. ISBN 156518176X (paper).

III.21 *Cultural Factors in International Relations: Chinese Philosophical Studies, XXI*. Yu Xintian, ed. ISBN 1565182049 (paper).

III.22 *Wisdom in China and the West: Chinese Philosophical Studies, XXII*. Vincent Shen and Willard Oxtoby. ISBN 1565182057 (paper) III.23 *China's Contemporary Philosophical Journey: Western Philosophy and Marxism: Chinese Philosophical Studies, XXIII*. Liu Fangtong. ISBN 1565182065 (paper).

III.24 *Shanghai: Its Urbanization and Culture: Chinese Philosophical Studies, XXIV*. Yu Xuanmeng and He Xirong, eds. ISBN 1565182073 (paper).

III.25 *Dialogue of Philosophies, Religions and Civilizations in the Era of Globalization: Chinese Philosophical Studies, XXV.* Zhao Dunhua, ed. ISBN 9781565182431 (paper).

III.26 *Rethinking Marx: Chinese Philosophical Studies, XXVI.* Zou Shipeng and Yang Xuegong, eds. ISBN 9781565182448 (paper).

III.27 *Confucian Ethics in Retrospect and Prospect: Chinese Philosophical Studies XXVII.* Vincent Shen and Kwong-loi Shun, eds. ISBN 9781565182455 (paper).

III.28 *Cultural Tradition and Social Progress, Chinese Philosophical Studies, XXVIII.* He Xirong, Yu Xuanmeng, Yu Xintian, Yu Wujing, Yang Junyi, eds. ISBN 9781565182660 (paper).

III.29 *Spiritual Foundations and Chinese Culture: A Philosophical Approach: Chinese Philosophical Studies, XXIX.* Anthony J. Carroll and Katia Lenehan, eds. ISBN 9781565182974 (paper)

III.30 *Diversity in Unity: Harmony in a Global Age: Chinese Philosophical Studies, XXX.* He Xirong and Yu Xuanmeng, eds. ISBN 978156518… (paper).

IIIB.1 *Authentic Human Destiny: The Paths of Shankara and Heidegger: Indian Philosophical Studies, I.* Vensus A. George. ISBN 1565181190 (paper).

IIIB.2 *The Experience of Being as Goal of Human Existence: The Heideggerian Approach: Indian Philosophical Studies, II.* Vensus A. George. ISBN 156518145X (paper).

IIIB.3 *Religious Dialogue as Hermeneutics: Bede Griffiths's Advaitic Approach: Indian Philosophical Studies, III.* Kuruvilla Pandikattu. ISBN 1565181395 (paper).

IIIB.4 *Self-Realization [Brahmaanubhava]: The Advaitic Perspective of Shankara: Indian Philosophical Studies, IV.* Vensus A. George. ISBN 1565181549 (paper).

IIIB.5 *Gandhi: The Meaning of Mahatma for the Millennium: Indian Philosophical Studies, V.* Kuruvilla Pandikattu, ed. ISBN 1565181565 (paper).

IIIB.6 *Civil Society in Indian Cultures: Indian Philosophical Studies, VI.* Asha Mukherjee, Sabujkali Sen (Mitra) and K. Bagchi, eds. ISBN 1565181573 (paper).

IIIB.7 *Hermeneutics, Tradition and Contemporary Change: Lectures in Chennai/Madras, India.* George F. McLean. ISBN 1565181883 (paper).

IIIB.8 *Plenitude and Participation: The Life of God in Man: Lectures in Chennai/Madras, India.* George F. McLean. ISBN 1565181999 (paper).

IIIB.9 *Sufism and Bhakti, a Comparative Study: Indian Philosophical Studies, VII.* Md. Sirajul Islam. ISBN 1565181980 (paper). IIIB.10 *Reasons for Hope: Its Nature, Role and Future: Indian Philosophical Studies, VIII.* Kuruvilla Pandikattu, ed. ISBN 156518 2162 (paper).

IIIB.11 *Lifeworlds and Ethics: Studies in Several Keys: Indian Philosophical Studies, IX.* Margaret Chatterjee. ISBN 9781565182332 (paper).

IIIB.12 *Paths to the Divine: Ancient and Indian: Indian Philosophical Studies, X.* Vensus A. George. ISBN 9781565182486. (paper). IIB.13 *Faith, Reason, Science: Philosophical Reflections with Special Reference to Fides et Ratio: Indian Philosophical Studies, XIII.* Varghese Manimala, ed. IBSN 9781565182554 (paper).

IIIB.14 *Identity, Creativity and Modernization: Perspectives on Indian Cultural Tradition: Indian Philosophical Studies, XIV.* Sebastian Velassery and Vensus A. George, eds. ISBN 9781565182783 (paper).

IIIB.15 *Elusive Transcendence: An Exploration of the Human Condition Based on Paul Ricoeur: Indian Philosophical Studies, XV.* Kuruvilla Pandikattu. ISBN 9781565182950 (paper).

IIIC.1 *Spiritual Values and Social Progress: Uzbekistan Philosophical Studies, I.* Said Shermukhamedov and Victoriya Levinskaya, eds. ISBN 1565181433 (paper).

IIIC.2 *Kazakhstan: Cultural Inheritance and Social Transformation: Kazakh Philosophical Studies, I.* Abdumalik Nysanbayev. ISBN 1565182022 (paper).

IIIC.3 *Social Memory and Contemporaneity: Kyrgyz Philosophical Studies, I.* Gulnara A. Bakieva. ISBN 9781565182349 (paper).

IIID.1 *Reason, Rationality and Reasonableness: Vietnamese Philosophical Studies, I.* Tran Van Doan. ISBN 1565181662 (paper).

IIID.2 *Hermeneutics for a Global Age: Lectures in Shanghai and Hanoi.* George F. McLean. ISBN 1565181905 (paper).

IIID.3 *Cultural Traditions and Contemporary Challenges in Southeast Asia.* Warayuth Sriwarakuel, Manuel B. Dy, J. Haryatmoko, Nguyen Trong Chuan, and Chhay Yiheang, eds. ISBN 1565182138 (paper).

IIID.4 *Filipino Cultural Traits: Claro R. Ceniza Lectures.* Rolando M. Gripaldo, ed. ISBN 1565182251 (paper).

IIID.5 *The History of Buddhism in Vietnam.* Chief editor: Nguyen Tai Thu; Authors: Dinh Minh Chi, Ly Kim Hoa, Ha thuc Minh, Ha Van Tan, Nguyen Tai Thu. ISBN 1565180984 (paper).

IIID.6 *Relations between Religions and Cultures in Southeast Asia.* Gadis Arivia and Donny Gahral Adian, eds. ISBN 9781565182509 (paper).

Series IV. Western European Philosophical Studies

IV.1 *Italy in Transition: The Long Road from the First to the Second Republic: The Edmund D. Pellegrino Lectures.* Paolo Janni, ed. ISBN 1565181204 (paper).

IV.2 *Italy and the European Monetary Union: The Edmund D. Pellegrino Lectures.* Paolo Janni, ed. ISBN 156518128X (paper).

IV.3 *Italy at the Millennium: Economy, Politics, Literature and Journalism: The Edmund D. Pellegrino Lectures*. Paolo Janni, ed. ISBN 1565181581 (paper).

IV.4 *Speaking of God*. Carlo Huber. ISBN 1565181697 (paper). IV.5 *The Essence of Italian Culture and the Challenge of a Global Age*.
Paulo Janni and George F. McLean, eds. ISBB 1565181778 (paper). IV.6 *Italic Identity in Pluralistic Contexts: Toward the Development of Intercultural Competencies*. Piero Bassetti and Paolo Janni, eds. ISBN 1565181441 (paper).
I.7 *Phenomenon of Affectivity: Phenomenological-Anthropological Perspectives*. Ghislaine Florival. ISBN 9781565182899 (paper).

Series IVA. Central and Eastern European Philosophical Studies

IVA.1 *The Philosophy of Person: Solidarity and Cultural Creativity: Polish Philosophical Studies, I.* A. Tischner, J.M. Zycinski, eds. ISBN 1565180496 (paper); 156518048-8 (cloth).
IVA.2 *Public and Private Social Inventions in Modern Societies: Polish Philosophical Studies, II.* L. Dyczewski, P. Peachey, J.A. Kromkowski, eds. ISBN. 1565180518 (paper); 156518050X (cloth).
IVA.3 *Traditions and Present Problems of Czech Political Culture: Czechoslovak Philosophical Studies, I.* M. Bednár and M. Vejraka, eds. ISBN 1565180577 (paper); 156518056-9 (cloth).
IVA.4 *Czech Philosophy in the XXth Century: Czech Philosophical Studies, II.* Lubomír Nový and Jirí Gabriel, eds. ISBN 1565180291 (paper); 156518028-3 (cloth).
IVA.5 *Language, Values and the Slovak Nation: Slovak Philosophical Studies, I.* Tibor Pichler and Jana Gašparí-ková, eds. ISBN 1565180372 (paper); 156518036-4 (cloth).
IVA.6 *Morality and Public Life in a Time of Change: Bulgarian Philosoph ical Studies, I.* V. Prodanov and A. Davidov, eds. ISBN 1565180550 (paper); 1565180542 (cloth).
IVA.7 *Knowledge and Morality: Georgian Philosophical Studies, 1.* N.V. Chavchavadze, G. Nodia and P. Peachey, eds. ISBN 1565180534 (paper); 1565180526 (cloth).
IVA.8 *Cultural Heritage and Social Change: Lithuanian Philosophical Studies, I.* Bronius Kuzmickas and Aleksandr Dobrynin, eds. ISBN 1565180399 (paper); 1565180380 (cloth).
IVA.9 *National, Cultural and Ethnic Identities: Harmony beyond Conflict: Czech Philosophical Studies, IV.* Jaroslav Hroch, David Hollan, George F. McLean, eds. ISBN 1565181131 (paper).
IVA.10 *Models of Identities in Postcommunist Societies: Yugoslav Philosophical Studies, I.* Zagorka Golubovic and George F. McLean, eds. ISBN 1565181211 (paper).

IVA.11 *Interests and Values: The Spirit of Venture in a Time of Change: Slovak Philosophical Studies, II.* Tibor Pichler and Jana Gasparikova, eds. ISBN 1565181255 (paper).

IVA.12 *Creating Democratic Societies: Values and Norms: Bulgarian Philosophical Studies, II.* Plamen Makariev, Andrew M. Blasko and Asen Davidov, eds. ISBN 156518131X (paper).

IVA.13 *Values of Islamic Culture and the Experience of History: Russian Philosophical Studies, I.* Nur Kirabaev and Yuriy Pochta, eds. ISBN 1565181336 (paper).

IVA.14 *Values and Education in Romania Today: Romanian Philosophical Studies, I.* Marin Calin and Magdalena Dumitrana, eds. ISBN 1565181344 (paper).

IVA.15 *Between Words and Reality, Studies on the Politics of Recognition and the Changes of Regime in Contemporary Romania: Romanian Philosophical Studies, II.* Victor Neumann. ISBN 1565181611 (paper).

IVA.16 *Culture and Freedom: Romanian Philosophical Studies, III.* Marin Aiftinca, ed. ISBN 1565181360 (paper).

IVA.17 *Lithuanian Philosophy: Persons and Ideas: Lithuanian Philosophical Studies, II.* Jurate Baranova, ed. ISBN 1565181379 (paper).

IVA.18 *Human Dignity: Values and Justice: Czech Philosophical Studies, III.* Miloslav Bednar, ed. ISBN 1565181409 (paper).

IVA.19 *Values in the Polish Cultural Tradition: Polish Philosophical Studies, III.* Leon Dyczewski, ed. ISBN 1565181425 (paper). IVA.20 *Liberalization and Transformation of Morality in Post-communist Countries: Polish Philosophical Studies, IV.* Tadeusz Buksinski. ISBN 1565181786 (paper).

IVA.21 *Islamic and Christian Cultures: Conflict or Dialogue: Bulgarian Philosophical Studies, III.* Plament Makariev, ed. ISBN 156518162X (paper).

IVA.22 *Moral, Legal and Political Values in Romanian Culture: Romanian Philosophical Studies, IV.* Mihaela Czobor-Lupp and J. Stefan Lupp, eds. ISBN 1565181700 (paper).

IVA.23 *Social Philosophy: Paradigm of Contemporary Thinking: Lithuanian Philosophical Studies, III.* Jurate Morkuniene. ISBN 1565182030 (paper).

IVA.24 *Romania: Cultural Identity and Education for Civil Society: Romanian Philosophical Studies, V.* Magdalena Dumitrana, ed. ISBN 156518209X (paper).

IVA.25 *Polish Axiology: the 20th Century and Beyond: Polish Philosophical Studies, V.* Stanislaw Jedynak, ed. ISBN 1565181417 (paper).

IVA.26 *Contemporary Philosophical Discourse in Lithuania: Lithuanian Philosophical Studies, IV.* Jurate Baranova, ed. ISBN 156518-2154 (paper).

IVA.27 *Eastern Europe and the Challenges of Globalization: Polish Philosophical Studies, VI.* Tadeusz Buksinski and Dariusz Dobrzanski, ed. ISBN 1565182189 (paper).

IVA.28 *Church, State, and Society in Eastern Europe: Hungarian Philosophical Studies, I.* Miklós Tomka. ISBN 156518226X (paper). IVA.29 *Politics, Ethics, and the Challenges to Democracy in 'New Independent States': Georgian Philosophical Studies, II.* Tinatin Bochorishvili, William Sweet, Daniel Ahern, eds. ISBN 9781565182240 (paper).

IVA.30 *Comparative Ethics in a Global Age: Russian Philosophical Studies II.* Marietta T. Stepanyants, eds. ISBN 9781565182356 (paper).

IVA.31 *Identity and Values of Lithuanians: Lithuanian Philosophical Studies, V.* Aida Savicka, eds. ISBN 9781565182367 (paper). IVA.32 *The Challenge of Our Hope: Christian Faith in Dialogue: Polish Philosophical Studies, VII.* Waclaw Hryniewicz. ISBN 9781565182370 (paper).

IVA.33 *Diversity and Dialogue: Culture and Values in the Age of Globalization.* Andrew Blasko and Plamen Makariev, eds. ISBN 9781565182387 (paper).

IVA. 34 *Civil Society, Pluralism and Universalism: Polish Philosophical Studies, VIII.* Eugeniusz Gorski. ISBN 9781565182417 (paper). IVA.35 *Romanian Philosophical Culture, Globalization, and Education: Romanian Philosophical Studies VI.* Stefan Popenici and Alin Tat and, eds. ISBN 9781565182424 (paper).

IVA.36 *Political Transformation and Changing Identities in Central and Eastern Europe: Lithuanian Philosophical Studies, VI.* Andrew Blasko and Diana Janušauskienė, eds. ISBN 9781565182462 (paper). IVA.37 *Truth and Morality: The Role of Truth in Public Life: Romanian Philosophical Studies, VII.* Wilhelm Dancă, ed. ISBN 9781565182493 (paper).

IVA.38 *Globalization and Culture: Outlines of Contemporary Social Cognition: Lithuanian Philosophical Studies, VII.* Jurate Morkuniene, ed. ISBN 9781565182516 (paper).

IVA.39 *Knowledge and Belief in the Dialogue of Cultures, Russian Philosophical Studies, III.* Marietta Stepanyants, ed. ISBN 9781565182622 (paper).

IVA.40 *God and the Post-Modern Thought: Philosophical Issues in the Contemporary Critique of Modernity, Polish Philosophical Studies, IX.* Józef Życiński. ISBN 9781565182677 (paper).

IVA.41 *Dialogue among Civilizations, Russian Philosophical Studies, IV.* Nur Kirabaev and Yuriy Pochta, eds. ISBN 9781565182653 (paper). IVA.42 *The Idea of Solidarity: Philosophical and Social Contexts, Polish Philosophical Studies, X.* Dariusz Dobrzanski, ed. ISBN 9781565182961 (paper).

IVA.43 *God's Spirit in the World: Ecumenical and Cultural Essays, Polish Philosophical Studies, XI.* Waclaw Hryniewicz. ISBN 9781565182738 (paper).

IVA.44 *Philosophical Theology and the Christian Traditions: Russian and Western Perspectives, Russian Philosophical Studies, V.* David Bradshaw, ed. ISBN 9781565182752 (paper).

IVA.45 *Ethics and the Challenge of Secularism: Russian Philosophical Studies, VI.* David Bradshaw, ed. ISBN 9781565182806 (paper).

IVA.46 *Philosophy and Spirituality across Cultures and Civilizations: Russian Philosophical Studies, VII.* Nur Kirabaev, Yuriy Pochta and Ruzana Pskhu, eds. ISBN 9781565182820 (paper).

IVA.47 *Values of the Human Person Contemporary Challenges: Romanian Philosophical Studies, VIII.* Mihaela Pop, ed. ISBN 9781565182844 (paper).

IVA.48 *Faith and Secularization: A Romanian Narrative: Romanian Philosophical Studies, IX.* Wilhelm Dancă, ed. ISBN 9781565182929 (paper).

IVA.49 *The Spirit: The Cry of the World: Polish Philosophical Studies, XII.* Waclaw Hryniewicz. ISBN 9781565182943 (paper).

IVA.50 *Philosophy and Science in Cultures of East and West: Russian Philosophical Studies, VIII.* Marietta T. Stepanyants, ed. ISBN 9781565182967 (paper).

Series V. Latin American Philosophical Studies

V.1 *The Social Context and Values: Perspectives of the Americas.* O. Pegoraro, ed. ISBN 081917355X (paper); 0819173541 (cloth).

V.2 *Culture, Human Rights and Peace in Central America.* Raul Molina and Timothy Ready, eds. ISBN 0819173576 (paper); 0819173568 (cloth).

V.3 *El Cristianismo Aymara: Inculturacion o Culturizacion?* Luis Jolicoeur. ISBN 1565181042 (paper).

V.4 *Love as the Foundation of Moral Education and Character Development.* Luis Ugalde, Nicolas Barros and George F. McLean, eds. ISBN 1565180801 (paper).

V.5 *Human Rights, Solidarity and Subsidiarity: Essays towards a Social Ontology.* Carlos E.A. Maldonado. ISBN 1565181107 (paper).

V.6 *A New World: A Perspective from Ibero America.* H. Daniel Dei, ed. ISBN 9781565182639 (paper).

Series VI. Foundations of Moral Education

VI.1 *Philosophical Foundations for Moral Education and Character Devel opment: Act and Agent.* G. McLean and F. Ellrod, eds. ISBN 156518001-1 (paper); ISBN 1565180003 (cloth).

VI.2 *Psychological Foundations for Moral Education and Character Development: An Integrated Theory of Moral Development.* R. Knowles, ed. ISBN 156518002X (paper); 156518003-8 (cloth).

VI.3 *Character Development in Schools and Beyond.* Kevin Ryan and Thomas Lickona, eds. ISBN 1565180593 (paper); 156518058-5 (cloth).

VI.4 *The Social Context and Values: Perspectives of the Americas.* O. Pegoraro, ed. ISBN 081917355X (paper); 0819173541 (cloth). VI.5 *Chinese Foundations for Moral Education and Character Develop ment.* Tran van Doan, ed. ISBN 1565180321 (paper); 156518033 (cloth).

VI.6 *Love as the Foundation of Moral Education and Character Development.* Luis Ugalde, Nicolas Barros and George F. McLean, eds. ISBN 1565180801 (paper).

Series VII. Seminars on Culture and Values

VII.1 *The Social Context and Values: Perspectives of the Americas.* O. Pegoraro, ed. ISBN 081917355X (paper); 0819173541 (cloth). VII.2 *Culture, Human Rights and Peace in Central America.* Raul Molina and Timothy Ready, eds. ISBN 0819173576 (paper); 0819173568 (cloth).

VII.3 *Relations between Cultures.* John A. Kromkowski, ed. ISBN 1565180089 (paper); 1565180097 (cloth).

VII.4 *Moral Imagination and Character Development: Volume I, The Imagination.* George F. McLean and John A. Kromkowski, eds. ISBN 1565181743 (paper).

VII.5 *Moral Imagination and Character Development: Volume II, Moral Imagination in Personal Formation and Character Development.* George F. McLean and Richard Knowles, eds. ISBN 1565181816 (paper).

VII.6 *Moral Imagination and Character Development: Volume III, Imagination in Religion and Social Life.* George F. McLean and John K. White, eds. ISBN 1565181824 (paper).

VII.7 *Hermeneutics and Inculturation.* George F. McLean, Antonio Gallo, Robert Magliola, eds. ISBN 1565181840 (paper).

VII.8 *Culture, Evangelization, and Dialogue.* Antonio Gallo and Robert Magliola, eds. ISBN 1565181832 (paper).

VII.9 *The Place of the Person in Social Life.* Paul Peachey and John A. Kromkowski, eds. ISBN 1565180127 (paper); 156518013-5 (cloth). VII.10 *Urbanization and Values.* John A. Kromkowski, ed. ISBN 1565180100 (paper); 1565180119 (cloth).

VII.11 *Freedom and Choice in a Democracy, Volume I: Meanings of Freedom.* Robert Magliola and John Farrelly, eds. ISBN 1565181867 (paper).

VII.12 *Freedom and Choice in a Democracy, Volume II: The Difficult Passage to Freedom*. Robert Magliola and Richard Khuri, eds. ISBN 1565181859 (paper).

VII 13 *Cultural Identity, Pluralism and Globalization* (2 volumes). John P. Hogan, ed. ISBN 1565182170 (paper).

VII.14 *Democracy: In the Throes of Liberalism and Totalitarianism.* George F. McLean, Robert Magliola, William Fox, eds. ISBN 1565181956 (paper).

VII.15 *Democracy and Values in Global Times: With Nigeria as a Case Study*. George F. McLean, Robert Magliola, Joseph Abah, eds. ISBN 1565181956 (paper).

VII.16 *Civil Society and Social Reconstruction*. George F. McLean, ed. ISBN 1565180860 (paper).

VII.17 *Civil Society: Who Belongs?* William A.Barbieri, Robert Magliola, Rosemary Winslow, eds. ISBN 1565181972 (paper).

VII.18 *The Humanization of Social Life: Theory and Challenges.* Christopher Wheatley, Robert P. Badillo, Rose B. Calabretta, Robert Magliola, eds. ISBN 1565182006 (paper).

VII.19 *The Humanization of Social Life: Cultural Resources and Historical Responses*. Ronald S. Calinger, Robert P. Badillo, Rose B. Calabretta, Robert Magliola, eds. ISBN 1565182006 (paper).

VII.20 *Religious Inspiration for Public Life: Religion in Public Life, Volume I.* George F. McLean, John A. Kromkowski and Robert Magliola, eds. ISBN 1565182103 (paper).

VII.21 *Religion and Political Structures from Fundamentalism to Public Service: Religion in Public Life, Volume II.* John T. Ford, Robert A. Destro and Charles R. Dechert, eds. ISBN 1565182111 (paper).

VII.22 *Civil Society as Democratic Practice*. Antonio F. Perez, Semou Pathé Gueye, Yang Fenggang, eds. ISBN 1565182146 (paper). VII.23 *Ecumenism and Nostra Aetate in the 21st Century*. George F. McLean and John P. Hogan, eds. ISBN 1565182197 (paper). VII.24 *Multiple Paths to God: Nostra Aetate: 40 years Later*. John P. Hogan, George F. McLean & John A. Kromkowski, eds. ISBN 1565182200 (paper).

VII.25 *Globalization and Identity*. Andrew Blasko, Taras Dobko, Pham Van Duc and George Pattery, eds. ISBN 1565182200 (paper). VII.26 *Communication across Cultures: The Hermeneutics of Cultures and Religions in a Global Age*. Chibueze C. Udeani, Veerachart Nimanong, Zou Shipeng, Mustafa Malik, eds. ISBN: 9781565182400 (paper).

VII.27 *Symbols, Cultures and Identities in a Time of Global Interaction.* Paata Chkheidze, Hoang Thi Tho and Yaroslav Pasko, eds. ISBN 9781565182608 (paper).

VII. 28 *Restorying the 'Polis':Civil Society as Narrative Reconstruction.* Yuriy Pochta, Rosemary Winslow, eds. ISNB 978156518 (paper).

VII.29 *History and Cultural Identity: Retrieving the Past, Shaping the Future*. John P. Hogan, ed. ISBN 9781565182684 (paper). VII.30 *Human Nature: Stable and/or Changing?* John P. Hogan, ed. ISBN 9781565182431 (paper).
VII.31 *Reasoning in Faith: Cultural Foundations for Civil Society and Globalization*. Octave Kamwiziku Wozol, Sebastian Velassery and Jurate Baranova, eds. ISBN 9781565182868 (paper).
VII.32 *Building Community in a Mobile/Global Age: Migration and Hospitality*. John P. Hogan, Vensus A. George and Corazon T. Toralba, eds. ISBN 9781565182875 (paper).

Series VIII. Christian Philosophical Studies

VIII.1 *Church and People: Disjunctions in a Secular Age, Christian Philosophical Studies, I*. Charles Taylor, José Casanova and George F. McLean, eds. ISBN9781565182745 (paper).
VIII.2 *God's Spirit in the World: Ecumenical and Cultural Essays, Christian Philosophical Studies, II*. Waclaw Hryniewicz. ISBN 9781565182738 (paper).
VIII.3 *Philosophical Theology and the Christian Traditions: Russian and Western Perspectives, Christian Philosophical Studies, III*. David Bradshaw, ed. ISBN 9781565182752 (paper).
VIII.4 *Ethics and the Challenge of Secularism: Christian Philosophical Studies, IV*. David Bradshaw, ed. ISBN 9781565182806 (paper). VIII.5 *Freedom for Faith: Theological Hermeneutics of Discovery based on George F. McLean's Philosophy of Culture: Christian Philosophical Studies, V*. John M. Staak. ISBN 9781565182837 (paper).
VIII.6 *Humanity on the Threshold: Religious Perspective on Transhumanism: Christian Philosophical Studies, VI*. John C. Haughey and Ilia Delio, eds. ISBN 9781565182882 (paper).
VIII.7 *Faith and Secularization: A Romanian Narrative: Christian Philosophical Studies, VII*. Wilhelm Dancă, ed. ISBN 9781565182929 (paper).
VIII.8 *Towards a Kenotic Vision of Authority in the Catholic Church: Christian Philosophical Studies, VIII*. Anthony J. Carroll, Marthe Kerkwijk, Michael Kirwan and James Sweeney, eds. ISBN 9781565182936 (paper).

VIII.9 *The Spirit: The Cry of the World: Christian Philosophical Studies, IX*. Waclaw Hryniewicz. ISBN 9781565182943 (paper).

The International Society for Metaphysics

ISM.1 *Person and Nature*. George F. McLean and Hugo Meynell, eds. ISBN 0819170267 (paper); 0819170259 (cloth).
ISM.2 *Person and Society*. George F. McLean and Hugo Meynell, eds. ISBN 0819169250 (paper); 0819169242 (cloth).

ISM.3 *Person and God.* George F. McLean and Hugo Meynell, eds. ISBN 0819169382 (paper); 0819169374 (cloth).

ISM.4 *The Nature of Metaphysical Knowledge*. George F. McLean and Hugo Meynell, eds. ISBN 0819169277 (paper); 0819169269 (cloth). ISM.5

Philosophhical Challenges and Opportunities of Globalization. Oliva Blanchette, Tomonobu Imamichi and George F. McLean, eds. ISBN 1565181298 (paper).

ISM.6 *The Dialogue of Cultural Traditions: Global Perspective*. William Sweet, George F. McLean, Tomonobu Imamichi, Safak Ural, O. Faruk Akyol, eds. ISBN 9781565182585 (paper).

ISM. 7 *Philosophy Emerging from Culture.* William Sweet, George F. McLean, Oliva Blanchette, Wonbin Park, eds. ISBN 9781565182851 (paper).

The series is published by: The Council for Research in Values and Philosophy, Gibbons Hall B-20, 620 Michigan Avenue, NE, Washington, D.C. 20064; Telephone and Fax: 202/319-6089; e-mail: cua-rvp@cua.edu; website: http://www.crvp.org. All titles are available in paper except as noted.

The series is distributed by: The Council for Research on Values and Philosophy - OST, 285 Oblate Drive, San Antonio, T.X., 78216; Telephone: (210)341-1366 x205; Email: mmartin@ost.edu.